D0073060

WITHDRAWN

Critical Essays on
Denise Levertov

811
L577zw

Critical Essays on Denise Levertov

Linda Wagner-Martin

G. K. Hall & Co. • Boston, Massachusetts

Copyright 1991 by Linda Wagner-Martin
All rights reserved.

First published 1990.
10 9 8 7 6 5 4 3 2 1

Library of Congress Cataloging-in-Publication Data

Critical essays on Denise Levertov / [edited by] Linda Wagner-Martin.
    p.   cm. — (Critical essays on American literature)
  Includes bibliographical references and index.
  ISBN 0-8161-8899-8
  1. Levertov, Denise, 1923– —Criticism and interpretation.
I. Wagner-Martin, Linda. II. Series.
PS3562.E8876Z6 1990
811'.52—dc20   90-38061
                                       CIP

The paper used in this publication meets the minimum requirements
of American National Standard for Information Sciences—Permanence
of Paper for Printed Library Materials, ANSI Z39.48-1984. ∞™

Printed and bound in the United States of America

CRITICAL ESSAYS ON AMERICAN LITERATURE

This series seeks to anthologize the most important criticism on a wide variety of topics and writers in American literature. Our readers will find in various volumes not only a generous selection of reprinted articles and reviews but original essays, bibliographies, manuscript sections, and other materials brought to public attention for the first time. This volume, *Critical Essays on Denise Levertov*, is the most comprehensive collection of essays ever published on one of the most important contemporary writers in the United States. It contains both a sizable gathering of early reviews and a broad selection of more modern scholarship. Among the authors of reprinted articles and reviews are Diane Wakoski, Joan Dargan, William Aiken, Deborah Pope, Kerry Driscoll, and Rudolph L. Nelson. In addition to a substantial introduction by Linda Wagner-Martin, there are two original essays commissioned specifically for publication in this volume, new studies by Jerome Mazzaro and Linda Wagner-Martin. We are confident that this book will make a permanent and significant contribution to the study of American literature.

JAMES NAGEL, GENERAL EDITOR

Northeastern University

1-23-91 InLS 45.68 GAffebll'91

ALLEGHENY COLLEGE LIBRARY

90-5051

*For Cheryl, Karen, Sheryl, Marcie,
Wendy, Sarah, Sally, Maria, Adele, Kelli,
Marilyn, Diane, Pat, Hilary, and Ann*

CONTENTS

CHRONOLOGY OF BOOKS

INTRODUCTION

Levertov as Poet

> The borderline—that's where, if one knew how one would establish residence. That watershed, that spine, that looking-glass . . . its own world . . .[1]

As Denise Levertov writes in her 1988 poem, "The Life of Art," the motive for any artist or writer is to create a new world, some "borderland," some place part fantasy, part truer-than-fact, where the life of the imagination supersedes commonplace activity. Whatever her other characteristics, Levertov has throughout her already long career impressed her readers and listeners with her complete dedication to poetry.

In August 1954, Levertov wrote to a friend that being able to work in one's poetry was the only important consideration of a chosen life; a few years later she warned a young woman poet, who was eager to meet her, that poetry took precedence during her day as mother, wife, homemaker—as well as poet.[2] Through the forty-five years of Levertov's career as a published poet (her first book appeared in England in 1946), this insistence on the primacy of her profession—being a poet—has marked her life and has undoubtedly led to the clear position of respect she holds within contemporary poetry circles.

In addition to her sixteen volumes of poetry, Levertov has published two collections of her essays on poetry, *The Poet in the World* (1973) and *Light Up the Cave* (1981). These essays have fostered wide understanding of the craft of modernist poetry, both within the world of poetry and without; many of Levertov's essays (some of which appeared originally in *The Nation* during the years she was poetry editor for that magazine), such as her comments on the work of H. D., have become classics. Truly seminal in her insistence on the seriousness of both poetry and its craft, Levertov has dominated that world of poetry born of the precepts of Ezra Pound and William Carlos Williams. Her extensive correspondence with Williams, Robert Creeley, James Dickey, Richard Deutsch, Robert Duncan, Donald Finkle, Robert Sward, and other poets, housed at Washington University in

1

St. Louis and elsewhere, shows the fervor of her belief in the practice of poetry and the dedication she has shown in writing about that practice. It is clear that the most important part of Denise Levertov's days, the heart of her time and her life, has been devoted to poetry and its philosophy.

That was her intention. In the preface to *Collected Earlier Poems, 1940–1960* (1979), Levertov recounts that she began writing at five and published her first poem in her late teens. As a young poet in England, Levertov had sent work to—and been encouraged by—T. S. Eliot, Herbert Read, Charles Wrey Gardiner, and other established writers.[3] *The Double Image,* her first collection, appeared in England in 1946, when she was twenty-three; several years later Kenneth Rexroth included her work in his collection *New British Poets.* By that time, 1949, Levertov had moved to the United States with her American husband, Mitchell Goodman, also an aspiring writer. Living alternately in New York and Mexico, Levertov and Goodman made use of friendships with Robert Creeley, Robert Duncan, Paul Blackburn, and later, Williams, and found the poetry of truly American voices. Though she had been born in England and had spent her first twenty-five years there, Levertov insisted that she had become an American poet, and her writing has been considered American throughout her career.

Levertov's first American collection was *Here and Now*, published in 1957 by Lawrence Ferlinghetti's City Lights Books in San Francisco. The same collection had been considered for inclusion in two series of poetry volumes planned by both Robert Creeley and Weldon Kees. As a newly arrived Americanist, Levertov's work was published in the best little magazines; other poets admired her accomplishments. Even before her first American book was published, she was in demand by other writers for appearances in little magazines and for readings. Levertov's second book, *Overland to the Islands,* was published by Jonathan Williams in 1958 in the North Carolina Jargon Books series. With her third, *With Eyes at the Back of Our Heads* (1960), Levertov found James Laughlin, the publisher whose New Directions Press became her permanent house. In the fall of 1989, New Directions published Levertov's sixteenth collection, *A Door in the Hive.*

For all Levertov's ostensible success, however, there has been a comparative scarcity of critical comment about her poetry. No other living women poet has held so secure a place in the list of established poets for so long: for forty years Levertov's poems have been included in nearly all anthologies of contemporary poetry—besides her own sixteen collections of poetry and the two volumes of essays. She is acknowledged to be one of the premier women poets of modern-day America, but there is less interest in her writing than might be expected from such prominence.

Levertov's critical reputation is an enigma. When she first appeared in the United States, critics linked her with either the Black Mountain poets (led by Charles Olson and Robert Creeley, whose work was frequently published in *Black Mountain Review*) or the Beats. Both designations were wrong: Levertov's only connection with Black Mountain College was her friendship with Creeley, and she was never in sympathy with the largely anarchic and drug-identified principles of the Beat writers. In the 1950s and 1960s, however, critics organized writers into schools and groups and found validity for their work in those classifications. It was logical that Levertov would be assimilated into categories that people found vital and new. Kenneth Rexroth, however, bluntly clarified the issue in 1965: "The universal respect in which she is held by Academics, Beats and Black Mountains has led her to be identified with one or the other by careless critics and anthologists. She is in fact classically independent."[4]

It is difficult to remember, here at the edge of the 1990s, that the concept of free verse, vers libre, was then still being questioned, if not directly attacked. William Carlos Williams wrote to Levertov in November 1953, for example, "You know what an advantage the poets who follow academic patterns possess, even such relatively acceptable poets as Richard Wilbur, with their regularly arranged lines, their rhymes and stanzaic forms. Do not underestimate it. The world they represent is not your world but it is a world that occupies the driver's seat."[5] Several of Levertov's best early essays ("Some Notes on Organic Form," "A Further Definition," and "Line-Breaks, Stanza-Spaces, and the Inner Voice") spoke to the issue of content and tone creating appropriate form, and she was often quoted in 1960s battles over poetic form and design.[6]

There was also an interest in including women writers in established poetic camps, even though no conscious "affirmative-action" movement existed—and most women poets tried to avoid being considered "women" writers. In the late 1950s and early 1960s, a largely undefined response to the genuinely androgynous voices and themes of some of the modernist poets—chiefly those just being discovered by the academy, such as Williams, H. D., and Hart Crane—led to the discovery of Levertov, Barbara Howes, Carolyn Kizer, Joanne Whalen, Carol Berge, Diane Wakoski, Joanne Kiger, Rochelle Owens, Adrienne Rich, Mona Van Dyne, Muriel Rukeyser, Sylvia Plath, Maxine Kumin and Anne Sexton.[7]

Yet Levertov remained strangely isolated in these poetry circles. She insisted that she did not want to be valued because she was a woman (not an unusual stance for women writers during these years), and that she partook of whatever traditions, themes, and language developments were useful to her work. She also insisted that she was not aligned with the Beat culture, seeing clearly the long-term problems with Ginsberg's emotion-inspired line. It was difficult to place Levertov; though she was an intimate friend of both Robert Duncan and Robert Creeley, she did not reside entirely within their camps, and for a short time, she served as James Dickey's literary executor.[8]

Levertov's isolation was increased by her very visible and purposeful involvement in anti-Vietnam activities during the 1960s and 1970s. With Levertov—whose poetry had been so convincingly meditative, untouched by any but the lyric impulse—the inclusion of "political" poetry in her oeuvre was threatening to her reputation. Critics had so thoroughly accepted Levertov's customary poetic practices that such a change—even transformation, in some readers' eyes—baffled them. As a result of this critical bewilderment (and the intransigent antipolitical stance of many literary observers), Levertov's collections since the late 1960s, beginning with *The Sorrow Dance* in 1967, polarized the world of poetry. Reviews of *The Sorrow Dance*, *Relearning the Alphabet* (1970), *To Stay Alive* (1971), and *Footprints* (1972) in particular showed the critical confusion: reviewers either denounced the political content or tepidly praised only the poems that perpetuated Levertov's earlier successes in the meditative lyric. She could not win. She was either doing the same old thing, writing the highly imaged, Wordsworthian moment or scene, or treading where serious poets had no need to be, in the realm of active political rhetoric.[9]

For many critics, everything *new* about Levertov's poetry after her fifth or sixth book was objectionable. Sane assessments such as Todd Gitlin's were rare:

> That Levertov has become a political activist doesn't seem to have damaged her gift of rhythm or her skill of fusing form and content, image and motion. My hunch is that the complete poet goes inward and outward at once, and finds the two meeting in a tension which, fully apprehended, makes a new creative energy.[10]

And although Levertov spoke eloquently about politics being a part of one's personal voice, about conviction having a part in all poetry—indeed, undergirding all poetry[11]—she was caught in the academic distinction between "good" poetry and "political" poetry, a distinction that permeates all literature, all art. The isolationism of "good" and "safe" art has yet to be called into question.

Levertov's fall from the favor that surrounded her earlier work blotted a critical reputation that had been moving surely toward its zenith. The earliest reviews of her poetry were uniformly good, and the attention she received was substantial. Levertov was clearly a poet's poet, and in poetry that is a good position to hold. The reviewers of Levertov's work are a who's who of American poetry—Kenneth Rexroth, David Ignatow, Victor Contoski, Eve Triem, James Wright, Jean Garrigue, Hayden Carruth, Daniel Berrigan, Diane Wakoski, George Bowering, Herbert Read, Josephine Jacobsen, Sandra Gilbert, Rachel Blau DuPlessis, Bonnie Costello, Kathleen Spivack, Robert Creeley. As David Ignatow pointed out in his 1975 *New York Times* review, "By nearly unanimous agreement Levertov was well on her way to becoming one of our leading poets. The onset of the Vietnam War began the decline of her reputation, coinciding with the reemergence of the genteel tradition of polite and ultra sophisticated writing, a fantastic paradox in the face of the disaster of the war."[12] The length of Levertov's publishing career and the diversity of critical opinion about her work make the history of her life as a poet both interesting and instructive.

Kenneth Rexroth's 1957 *Poetry* review of *Here and Now* was more an essay on Levertov's work through the previous dozen years than it was a book review. Rexroth claimed great distinction for the young British poet, setting her apart from the young American Beats (as being "more civilized" and knowing more than Ginsberg, Corman, Olson, Orlovitz, and Creeley)— as well as apart from her British peers. He admired her romantic traits, though he saw that she had evolved past them; he admired even more her fresh, and perfect, poetic idioms and rhythms.[13] Other reviewers were also pleased with some parts of Levertov's work: her prosody was varied and interesting, though enough like that of Ignatow and Williams to seem familiar. Her content was recognizable—the meditative poet's voice was built upon a kind of still-life image base. And her purpose was ultimately moral: Levertov wanted her readers to think about the important issues, about humane behavior, about nature, about religion. (Because Levertov followed Williams's maxim "No ideas but in things" so convincingly, her more abstract themes were less obvious than such themes were in poems by Richard Eberhart or William Meredith. Reviewers did not comment on this aspect of Levertov's writing until after *O Taste and See*, her 1964 collection. As long as she was even faintly identified with the Beat writers, no one entertained any notions of meditation or spirituality about her work.)

During the first three or four years of U.S. publication of her poem collections, Levertov was praised by James Wright, Gilbert Sorrentino, Ray Smith, Louis Simpson, Eve Triem, Stanley Kunitz, Thomas Parkinson, Hayden Carruth, Paul Goodman, Thom Gunn, and Paul Lauter, among others.[14] Her work was criticized by Robert Mazzocci and Jean Garrigue as being "too personal," but as Robert Creeley had pointed out, most poetry *is* personal because "one begins with oneself perhaps, and to that entity one joins one other; and from that it may well be that a third is conceived. And so on— because this is what the world is all about."[15] Another early criticism was of Levertov's style: John Napier and William Corrington used the adjectives "dead" and "dull," and John Simon, writing in the influential *Hudson Review*, included Levertov in a harsh critique of William Carlos Williams's work.[16] The general tenor of response, however, was excellent. Geoffrey Hartman, in *Kenyon Review*, praised her ability to create poems that were art, a "proper fixative, giving life firmness and dreams life," as in "To the Snake." X. J. Kennedy thought her technical abilities were superior, and M. L. Rosenthal, in one of the earliest American reviews, championed both her vision and her skill. He repeated his comments in his influential 1960 book, *The Modern Poets.*[17]

With the publication of Levertov's *O Taste and See* in 1964, following as it did the important 1961 *The Jacob's Ladder*, her interest in the meditative, the spiritual, and the mystical—though always grounded firmly in the tangible objects and experiences of daily life—grew clearer. Criticism accordingly reflected these thematic changes (if changes they were), which could not be overlooked. Frederick Eckman spoke of Levertov's "humanitas," based in her understanding of the need for personal responsibility; Louis Martz stressed her "elegaic" and contemplative tone and related her work to that of Wordsworth (though he noted occasional instrusions of the "beatnik" in it); Emmett Jarrett was interested in her poems that conveyed mystical insights through dreams. Godfrey John, writing in the *Christian Science Monitor*, compared Levertov to Tagore in her sensitivity to daily life and her application of the concrete to the spiritual. Although George Bowering stressed Levertov's sensuality (coupling her mystical insight with her feminism), an emphasis on gender or the sexual was not common during the 1960s, despite the attention paid to homosexual writing. Because Bowering's review appeared in *Tish*, a little poetry magazine published by young Canadian poets, it could be less conventional than the mainstream reviewing sources would have required. In Levertov's case, making the connection between the feminine and the mystical was long overdue.[18]

In Stephen Stepanchev's *American Poetry Since 1945*, Levertov received adequate attention, but the best assessment of her work to date, Ralph J. Mills, Jr.'s *TriQuarterly* essay, "Denise Levertov: Poetry of the Immediate" (also published as a chapter in his 1965 *Contemporary American Poetry*), gave readers ample reason to consider Levertov an established poet. Mills placed Levertov in the appropriate poetic context, but he also showed how she had deviated from the Pound-H. D.-Williams line by convincing her reader of the immediacy of her vision: "Her poetry is frequently a tour through the familiar and the mundane until their unfamiliarity and otherworldliness suddenly strike us. . . . Thus she engages very naturally in a persistent investigation of the events of her own life—inner and outer—in the language of her own time and place."[19] Mills's emphasis on Levertov's willingness to involve the "inner" as well as the "outer" was valuable and provided an enlarged context for reading her later 1960s work, which was about to startle the literary world.

The critical reception to Levertov's more political poetry began quietly enough. *The Sorrow Dance*, published in 1967, was a blend of her new, explicitly political interest with the personal and immediate work that readers were familiar with—though the overwhelming sorrow was caused by public events, not private ones. By the time Levertov's next three collections were published—*Relearning the Alphabet* (1970), *To Stay Alive* (1971), and *Footprints* (1972)—both the national political temper and her own role as an anti–Vietnam War activist were fully developed, and much of the reaction to her poetry was based on political sentiment rather than poetic standards. (Partly as a result of the critical attacks on these collections, she published her first collection of essays in 1973. The text of *The Poet in the World*, as well as the subtext, was precisely what the title indicates—the influence of all human concerns on the poetry-making process.)

In this group of poetry collections, *The Sorrow Dance* serves as introduction, alerting the reader to the need for jeremiad, for lament. With *Relearning the Alphabet,* Levertov attacks complacent use of language—which, in itself, is blameless—and demands that speakers, like writers, relearn what language can mean. The title of the 1971 collection, *To Stay Alive,* promises to shake the soporific effect that reading poetry has on some readers and makes understanding daily experience into a battleground of life and death. *Footprints* marks the path the initiated reader must take to both understand the times and survive them. The reader of these four collections has no doubt that Levertov is intensely serious about her political message, which, to her, is no different from—albeit even more important than—the themes of her previous poems.

At first, critics were not sure how they were supposed to respond to these poems; their tactic with *The Sorrow Dance* was to connect it with Levertov's earlier work and to mention only briefly that the book also contained political poems (almost as an aside). William H. Pritchard avoided dealing with the import of the poems and discussed the way Levertov achieves an "on-going suppleness" in her lines; he described her tone in *The Sorrow Dance* as "serious—often to the point of grimness (the poems on Vietnam are the most obvious case in point)—yet musical too, on the move in various and interesting ways." For Kathleen Spivack, the collection was another of Levertov's great books, for the usual reasons of thematic and stylistic artistry, and she mentioned what she called the "Vietnam poems" in one last, short paragraph: "It is the disparity between the delicacy of Levertov's lines and the brute horror with which she—and we—must deal that is most poignant. Her poems are a record of outrage. And indeed, it is not only as poems that they should be read, but as testimony."[20] Much like Pritchard's aside about "the poems on Vietnam," Spivack meant this coda as praise, of course, but in dodging a treatment of the "Vietnam poems" as *poems*—calling them "testimony"—she showed her own uneasiness.

That stance was common among reviewers. Ralph J. Mills, Jr., by the time of his 1973 review of *Footprints,* tried ameliorization. He described Levertov's "urgency of political commitment" in *Relearning the Alphabet* and *To Stay Alive* as a past concern. He then explained that her political activity "has not fundamentally damaged her poetry—though some may think so—by engaging it with public themes," and called for the recognition that Levertov's poetry should not be compartmentalized, "with one place for a more rhetorical kind of writing, *engagé,* and another given to the sacred speech of the true imagination." For Richard Pevear, however, *Footprints* showed "a certain presumptuousness" because Levertov's "political poems are not eloquent rhetoric, and not acute analysis, they are simply statements of her own convictions. Some of the poems in this book, like the 'New Year's Garland' for her students, are so strictly personal that you wonder why she thought anyone else should read them." Pevear's chief worries were not about Levertov's politics so much as her old-fashioned romanticism, but that concern was never widespread during the 1970s. Most critics fell out over the issue of whether or not Levertov's (or anyone's) political poems *were* poems. Marjorie G. Perloff concluded that much of the political writing was "bad confessional verse. Her anti–Vietnam War poems, written in casual diary form, sound rather like a versified *New York Review of Books*—the same righteous indignation, the same uncompromising moral zeal and self-important tone." Perloff, who thoroughly understood and appreciated what good confessional poems could be, was put off by Levertov's "facile polemics" and "careless rhythms" in *To Stay Alive*.[21] Perloff's was a common opinion of Levertov's "political" poems; it surfaced again and again during the later 1970s and the 1980s, occasioned in part by the publication in 1981 of Carolyn Forché's *The Country Between Us* (see Joan Dargan's essay in this collection). Essays about this critical problem, and this kind of poem, comprise nearly one-third of the essays section here because the controversy did not die with the end of action in Vietnam.

As Harry Marten pointed out in his 1979 review of Levertov's *Life in the Forest*, "Artistic longevity is always risky."[22] For whatever reasons, a writer's final reputation might be at great variance with his or her actual work, its value as art, and its eventual place in the literary paradigm. During the past fifteen years—the culmination and aftermath of Vietnam—reviews of Levertov's poetry and essay collections have all made mention of the role of "politics" in her poetry. Even the most positive reviews have been somewhat defensive not only about what might be seen as a period of time in Levertov's artistic career but about the pervasiveness of a combative theme, the ostensibly political subject matter that has—for this poet—become the norm. Levertov has spoken eloquently to this in her two collections of essays, as if defying critics to ignore the issue, and Hayden Carruth's review of *The Poet in the World* explicitly outlines the battle plan. In his thoroughly positive review of both the essay collection and Levertov's poetry oeuvre, Carruth quotes from various negative reviews of the "political" poetry collections. He then states that "none of the critics has taken the trouble to define the poem ['Staying Alive'] in the poet's terms." Carruth's strategy is to provide both definition and context so that the reader's concept of *poem* changes. His explanation that "much of 'Staying Alive' is what I call low-keyed lyric invocation of narrative; not narrative verse as such," is convincing, as is his modest claim, "I don't say the poem succeeds in every line. That would have been a miracle." Carruth's full strategy here requires length, time, and effort; but it is worth doing. (The essay appears in this collection.)[23]

With *The Freeing of the Dust* (1975) and, particularly, *Life in the Forest* (1978), Levertov moved to what most critics saw as surer ground. The latter volume was genuinely well received, and Harry Marten among others considered it a landmark collection. Marten declares Levertov's poems to be "exquisitely crafted lyrics" that, "in their reverence for language and life," continuously bring the reader into the full province of poetry. Marten does not approach the issue of politics directly but provides a scaffolding of acceptance that will allow so-called political poetry. N. E. Condini, writing in *National Review*, also gives the book high praise, saying that it "reads in fact like a Zen meditation on our place in the world." Condini's belief that "Levertov's political commitment is subdued here" might be one reason he finds the book important, but he does not stint his enthusiasm: "What glows amber-like throughout the book is the concern of the poet for the brutality she sees about her. . . . Without our response to layers of human spirituality, the earth—our existence itself—is cruel and meaningless."[24]

Bonnie Costello's *Parnassus* essay helps to explain why Levertov's 1978 collection has become central in many of the recent essays about her poetry as a whole. In creating a single manuscript from a loose assortment of moods and memories, Levertov has implemented her poetic rationale—"that the parts of a life have a necessary and tolerable coherence." Costello notes that readers need that sense of coherence, the belief in the possibility of order, particularly in troubled times. *Life in the Forest* seems to provide that order, and it does so by creating myth and ritual that readers recognize. Foreshadowing Rachel Blau DuPlessis's essay in *Shakespeare's Sisters*, Dianne F. Sadoff's essay (included here), and Estella Lauter's later book, *Women as Mythmakers: Poetry and Visual Art by Twentieth-Century Women* (both 1984), Costello describes the kinds of myth Levertov both draws from and creates, and also explains her impatience with some of Levertov's work:

> Denise Levertov has tried to show us a full and balanced life such as we all wish for, but as with most of us, her private and her public selves have never really agreed. And while she judiciously measures out her attentions to these quarrelsome, demanding siblings, we still feel that her most natural affection is for the elder, private self, relations with the other always seeming a bit strained, a bit superficial. We want from poetry a sign that our complex lives are manageable, but the symmetries of Levertov's world seem posed and inauthentic.

One of Costello's most severe criticisms is that while Levertov pretends to want a dialogue with her readers and the world, she is really creating monologues—emotionally based poems dependent on the single persona. And when she does write these "dialogues of one," they are "far from intimate. The emotions are narrated ('my throat clenches when I weep and can't make tears'), the truths sermonized ('perhaps we humans / have wanted God most as witness / to acts of choice / made without him'), the metaphors exhausted. . . ."[25]

Criticism of Levertov's work during the 1980s has been both uneven and unpredictable. It goes without saying that times have changed, that what the poetry world of the 1950s and 1960s would have been enthusiastic about no longer satisfies the various splinter groups of contemporary readers. Readers can no longer be identified as "political" or "apolitical," and outright military action is hardly the only battlefield. All life has become politicized, and the dissension that greeted antiwar poetry fifteen years ago now marks any literary discussion. How much is too much consciousness (or, unconsciousness)? How much is too much feminism (or "womanism," in Alice Walker's term)? How much is too much contrivance (the formal qualities of art)? How much can any written text do to or for the reader, given the feeling that no text exists in and by itself? All of these warring concerns—and others—are visible in reviews of Levertov's 1980s poem collections— *Candles in Babylon* (1982), *Oblique Prayers* (1984), *Breathing the Water* (1987), and *A Door in the Hive* (1989)—and in *Light Up the Cave* (1981), her second collection of essays.

Sandra M. Gilbert's work on Levertov during the 1980s is representative—as well as exemplary. In her 1977 *Contemporary Literature* essay, Gilbert places Levertov in the context of other American women poets, all suffering from various anxieties of authorship. Levertov's poems prove that she has been no more immune to the sense of inequity that plagued Plath and Sexton than were Rich or Wakoski; many of her poetic strategies allow for self-definition, so that she can create "recurrent self-defining statements— hypotheses, really." Because women poets cannot maintain the irony that would give them the distance to function fully as artists, they do differ from male poets, even from those who seem to write the same kinds of poetry— Lowell, Snodgrass, Berryman. Gilbert concludes that "the self-defining confessional genre, with its persistent assertions of identity and its emphasis on a central mythology of the self, may be (at least for our own time) a distinctively female poetic mode." What is important about this essay is that it links Levertov with women poets she herself might not claim association with, based on intrinsic evidence from her poetry.

In her *Parnassus* review, Gilbert stresses Levertov's reliance on the notion of the "split-self" (see Deborah Pope's study of that metaphor in this collection), but in Gilbert's view, such a self is hardly positive. The need to "twin" (what Gilbert calls the "strategy of doubling") carries risks. It can easily move the person to madness rather than to sanity. Gilbert admires Levertov's assuming the role of aggressive lover, writing "love" poems that focus on male beauty; but she is less sanguine about the results of Levertov's political work—again, Gilbert feels that Levertov cannot maintain the ironic distance to express real savagery or bitterness. In both politics and love, because Levertov writes necessarily as a woman while writing the kinds of poems male poets produce, she sometimes fails.[26]

One of the clearest areas for criticism in the 1990s is a reassessment of Levertov as a woman poet. Cursorily surveyed earlier by critics such as Ronald Wallace and Richard Gustafson, this approach to Levertov's work cries out for the attention of critics such as Nelly Furman, Mary Jacobus, Margaret Homans, and Susan Van Dyne, even though important work is already being done by Alicia Ostriker, Suzanne Juhasz, Sandra Gilbert and Susan Gubar, and Rachel Blau DuPlessis. Reviews by Margaret Randall and

Diane Wakoski of *Breathing the Water* and several of the essays included here supply excellent starting points.[27]

Another area explored by many of the reviews of Levertov's last three collections is Levertov's use of the spiritual, the overtly and uncompromisingly religious—in imagery as well as in content. Joyce Beck sees that much of Levertov's poetry is built around "religious meditative elements," and that that impulse has several sources in both her personal life and her literary background. Beck points out that Levertov acknowledges two muses for her poetry: "rational discrimination, the Apollonian guide who directs her in craftsmanship or in deliberate imaginative creation; and meditation, the Beatific 'breath' or Spirit who reveals to her the invisible substances of organic forms, or the Archetypes that arise from very deep associations." For Beck, Levertov's "joy," usually born of "cosmic connection," parallels Julia Kristeva's "jouissance." Holiness is the same as wholeness, and men as well as women need to learn to experience all kinds of growth and expansion. This approach is being used by Joan Hallisey, and much of Harry Marten's *Understanding Denise Levertov* also deals with her spirituality and its presence in both her later poems and her earlier ones.[28]

With the publication of *A Door in the Hive*, Levertov's sixteenth collection of poems, in the autumn of 1989, readers can assess for themselves what new directions Levertov's work has taken and what embroideries she has made on the already familiar patterns. Nevertheless, readers can be assured that Denise Levertov will have attempted further self-definition and further explorations into the nature of knowledge, humanity, and the mysteries of faith. The province of her poetry—and her life—has never been cautious or narrow.

LINDA WAGNER-MARTIN

University of North Carolina, Chapel Hill

Notes

1. Denise Levertov, "The Life of Art," *American Poetry Review* (March–April 1988), 24.

2. Denise Levertov, correspondence, 19 August 1954, and 1 May 1961 letters, held by the Washington University poetry archive, St. Louis, Missouri. Levertov's correspondence bears the unmistakable stamp of her high seriousness about both life and art and would bear a study in its own right.

3. Denise Levertov, "Author's Note," *Collected Earlier Poems, 1940–1960* (New York: New Directions, 1979), vii–x; and "Denise Levertov Writes," *The Bloodaxe Book of Contemporary Women Poets: Eleven British Writers*, ed. Jeni Couzyn (Newcastle-upon-Tyne, England: Bloodaxe Press, 1985), 75–79. See also Linda W. Wagner, *Denise Levertov* (Boston: Twayne, 1967); Linda Welshimer Wagner, "Introduction," *Denise Levertov: In Her Own Province* (New York: New Directions, 1979), ix–ixv; Suzanne Juhasz, *Naked and Fiery Forms: Modern Ameri-*

can Poetry by Women: A New Tradition (New York: Harper & Row, 1976); and Harry Marten, *Understanding Denise Levertov* (Columbia: University of South Carolina Press, 1988).

4. The wide influence of Donald M. Allen's *The New American Poetry, 1945–1960* (New York: Grove Press, 1960) and related volumes was hard to circumvent, although Rexroth's comment had appeared in *Saturday Review* in 1965 and again in *With Eye and Ear* (New York: Herder and Herder-Seabury Press, 1970), 69–77. Paul Breslin speaks to the difficulty of categorizing Levertov's work in his *The Psycho-Political Muse: American Poetry Since the Fifties* (Chicago: University of Chicago Press, 1987), 199–205; see also Frederick Eckman, *Cobras and Cockle Shells: Modes in Recent Poetry* (Flushing, N.Y.: Sparrow Press, 1958); Glauco Cambon, *The Inclusive Flame: Studies in American Poetry* (Bloomington: Indiana University Press, 1963); Roy Harvey Pearce, *The Continuity of American Poetry* (Princeton, N.J.: Princeton University Press, 1963); and M. L. Rosenthal, *The New Poets: American and British Poetry Since World War II* (New York: Oxford University Press, 1967), for a sense of early groupings of Levertov and her peers. See also James E. B. Breslin, *From Modern to Contemporary: American Poetry 1945–1965* (Chicago: University of Chicago Press, 1984), 143–75; Charles Altieri, *Enlarging the Temple: New Directions in American Poetry during the 1960s* (Lewiston, Penn.: Bucknell University Press, 1979); Lynn Keller, *Re-making It New: Contemporary American Poetry and the Modernist Tradition* (Cambridge: Cambridge University Press, 1987); and Richard Jackson, *The Dismantling of Time in Contemporary Poetry* (Tuscaloosa: University of Alabama Press, 1988), for more recent thinking about categories. The definitive study of the North Carolina aesthetic efforts is Martin Duberman, *Black Mountain: An Exploration in Community* (Garden City, N.Y.: Doubleday, 1973). For a full assessment of Levertov's critical position, see Liana Sakelliou-Schultz, *Denise Levertov: An Annotated Primary and Secondary Bibliography* (New York: Garland, 1988).

5. William Carlos Williams to Denise Levertov, 22 November 1953, in *Stony Brook* 1, no. 2 (Fall 1968), 163.

6. Denise Levertov, "Some Notes on Organic Form," "A Further Definition," and "Line-Breaks, Stanza-Spaces, and the Inner Voice," in *The Poet in the World* (New York: New Directions, 1973), 7–24. See also Levertov's essays, "Horses with Wings," in *What Is a Poet?* ed. Hank Lazer (Tuscaloosa: University of Alabama Press, 1987); "The Ideas of the Things," in *Ezra Pound and William Carlos Williams: The University of Pennsylvania Conference Papers*, ed. Daniel Hoffman (Philadelphia: University of Pennsylvania Press, 1983), 131–42; and "A Poet's View," *Religion and Intellectual Life* 1 (Summer 1984), 46–53.

7. Author's notes, University of British Columbia Poetry Conference, July 1963. Entire sessions by Levertov, Creeley, Olson, Ginsberg, and Duncan were devoted to reading poems by William Carlos Williams and Hart Crane, and Duncan repeatedly brought the work of H. D. into discussions. He was at that time writing the essays that contained his important statement on H. D.'s place in American poetics. Williams had written to Levertov about the gender issue, lamenting "the poet that is not in essence a woman as well as a man" (*Stony Brook* 1, no. 2 [Fall 1968], 166).

8. Author's correspondence with Levertov during 1977–78 while planning the New Directions volume, *Denise Levertov: In Her Own Province*. She is particularly upset with Rexroth's reference to her as a "poet of domesticity" and also counters his tracing certain poetic influences in her poems by stating that she went "directly" from being a British romantic to being influenced by Williams. Levertov's correspondence with James Dickey, Washington University poetry archive, particularly 3 May 1965 letter to Dickey; see also Levertov's "Serving an Art," in "Sexual Poetics: Notes on Genre and Gender in Poetry by Women," *American Poetry: A Triquarterly* 1 (1984), 74–75, and her earlier comments in "Poems by Women," *Trellis* (Spring 1975), 57–60.

9. More than fifteen years of commentary about Levertov's poetry is concerned with this problem. See the essays included in this collection, as well as John Felstiner, "Poetry and Political Experience: Denise Levertov," *Coming to Light: American Women Poets in the Twenti-*

eth Century, eds. Diane Wood Middlebrook and Marilyn Yalom (Ann Arbor: University of Michigan Press, 1985), 138–44; Cary Nelson, *The Incarnate Word* (Urbana: University of Illinois Press, 1973), and *Our Last First Poets: Vision and History in Contemporary American Poetry* (Urbana: University of Illinois Press, 1981); Colman McCarthy, *Inner Companions* (Washington, D.C.: Acropolis Books, 1975); James F. Mersmann, *Out of the Vietnam Vortex* (Lawrence: University of Kansas Press, 1974); Paul A. Lacey, *The Inner War: Forms and Themes in Recent American Poetry* (Philadelphia: Fortress Press, 1973).

10. Todd Gitlin, "The Return of Political Poetry," *Commonweal* (23 July 1971), 375–80.

11. Levertov herself has spoken and written frequently about the problem, as in the title essay from *The Poet in the World*.

> The obligation of the writer is: *to take personal and active responsibility for his words, whatever they are, and to acknowledge their potential influence on the lives of others*. . . . People are always asking me how I can reconcile poetry and political action. . . . Because I am a poet, I know, and those other poets who do likewise know, that we must fulfill the poet's total involvement in life. . . . The poet does not *use* poetry, but is at the service of poetry. To *use* it is to *misuse* it. A poet driven to speak to himself, to maintain a dialogue with himself, concerning politics, can expect to write as well upon that theme as upon any other. (114–15).

In the same collection, Levertov reprints "Statement for a Television Program" (never broadcast), which says in part: "One of the obligations of the writer . . . is to say or sing *all* that he or she can, to deal with as much of the world as becomes possible to him or her in language. I and most of my fellow American poets nowadays find ourselves inevitably—of necessity—writing more and more poems of grief, of rage, concerning the despoilment of the earth and of all life upon it, of the systematic destruction of all that we feel passionate love for, both by the greed of industry and by the mass murder we call war" (123). Many of Levertov's poems echo these convictions.

12. David Ignatow, *"The Freeing of the Dust,"* *New York Times Book Review* (30 November 1975), 54–55.

13. Kenneth Rexroth, "The Poetry of Denise Levertov," *Poetry* 91 (November 1957), 120–23. The most recent study of Levertov as a romantic poet is Inger Christensen's *The Shadow of the Dome: Organicism and Romantic Poetry* (Bergen, Norway: Studia Anglistica Norvegica, 1985), 93–116.

14. James Wright, "Gravity and Incantation," *Minnesota Review* 2 (Spring 1962), 424–26; Gilbert Sorrentino, "Measure of Maturity," *The Nation* 194 (10 March 1962), 220–21; Ray Smith, *"With Eyes at the Back of Our Heads," Library Journal* 85 (1 March 1960), 964; Louis Simpson, "A Garland for the Muse," *Hudson Review* (Summer 1960), 289–90; Eve Triem, "Three Poets," *Poetry* 96 (August 1960), 316–17; Stanley Kunitz, "Process and Thing: A Year of Poetry," *Harper's* (September 1960), 102ff.; Thomas Parkinson, *"With Eyes at the Back of Our Heads," San Francisco Chronicle* (28 February 1960), 22; Hayden Carruth, "Four New Books," *Poetry* 93 (November 1958), 109–10; Paul Goodman, "The International Word," *The Nation* 194 (21 April 1962), 3357–60; Thom Gunn, "Things, Voices, Minds," *Yale Review* 52 (Autumn 1962), 129–30; Paul Lauter, "Poetry Demanding and Detached," *New Leader* (15 May 1961), 22–23.

15. Robert Mazzocci, "Three Poets," *New York Review of Books* 3 (31 December 1964), 19; Jean Garrigue, *"With Eyes at the Back of Our Heads," Chelsea* 7 (May 1960), 110–12; Robert Creeley, *"Here and Now," New Mexico Quarterly* 27 (Spring 1957), 125–27.

16. John Napier, "A Brace of Beatniks," *Voices*, no. 174 (January–April 1961), 48–49; William Corrington, "Incontestably Dull," *Midwest*, nos. 5–6 (Spring 1963), 14–16; John Simon, "More Brass Than Enduring," *Hudson Review* (Autumn 1962), 455.

17. Geoffrey Hartman, "Les Belles Dames Sans Merci," *Kenyon Review* (Autumn 1960), 691–92; X. J. Kennedy, "Fresh Patterns of Near Rhymes," *New York Times Book Review* (29

April 1962), 29–30; M. L. Rosenthal, "In Exquisite Chaos," *The Nation* 187 (1 November 1958), 324–27, and *The Modern Poets: A Critical Introduction* (New York: Oxford University Press, 1960).

18. Frederick Eckman, "Total Individual Responsibility," *Midwest*, nos. 5–6 (Spring 1963), 16–19; Louis L. Martz, "Recent Poetry: The Elegaic Mode," *Yale Review* 54 (December 1965), 287–89; Emmett Jarrett, "Always in the Garden," *Secant* 2 (September 1965), 8–10; Godfrey John, "*O Taste and See*," *Christian Science Monitor* (30 July 1964), 5; George Bowering, "Blaser and Levertov," *Tish* (July 1965), 5–6.

19. Stephen Stepanchev, *American Poetry Since 1945* (New York: Harper & Row, 1965); Ralph J. Mills, Jr., "Denise Levertov: Poetry of the Immediate," *TriQuarterly* 4 (Winter 1962), 31–37, reprinted in *Contemporary American Poetry* (New York: Random House, 1965), 176–96.

20. William H. Pritchard, "*The Sorrow Dance*," *Hudson Review* (Summer 1967), 310–11; Kathleen Spivack, "Words and Silences," *Poetry* 112 no. 2 (May 1968), 123–25.

21. Ralph J. Mills, Jr., "*Footprints*," *Parnassus* (Spring–Summer 1973), 219–21; Richard Pevear, "*Footprints*," *Hudson Review* 26 (Spring 1973), 200–201; Majorie G. Perloff, "Poetry Chronicle, 1970–71," *Contemporary Literature* 14 (Winter 1973), 97–131. See also Peter Middleton, "Revelation and Revolution in the Poetry of Denise Levertov" (1974; London: Binnacle Press, 1981 reprint).

22. Harry Marten, "*Life in the Forest*," *New England Review and Bread Loaf Quarterly* 2 (Autumn 1979), 162.

23. Hayden Carruth, "Levertov," *Hudson Review* 27, no. 3 (Autumn 1974), 475–80.

24. Marten, "*Life in the Forest*," 162; N. E. Condini, "Embracing Old Gods," *National Review* 32 (21 March 1980), 360–61.

25. Bonnie Costello, "Flooded with Otherness," *Parnassus* 8, no. 1 (1979–80), 198–212; see also Rachel Blau DuPlessis, "The Critique of Consciousness and Myth in Levertov, Rich, and Rukeyser," in *Shakespeare's Sisters*, eds. Sandra M. Gilbert and Susan Gubar (Bloomington: Indiana University Press, 1984), and as Chapter 8 in DuPlessis, *Writing Beyond the Ending; Narrative Strategies of Twentieth-Century Women Writers* (Bloomington: Indiana University Press, 1985), 123–41; Estella Lauter, *Women as Mythmakers: Poetry and Visual Art by Twentieth-Century Women* (Bloomington: Indiana University Press, 1984).

26. Sandra M. Gilbert, " 'My Name Is Darkness': The Poetry of Self-Definition," *Contemporary Literature* 18 (1977), 4433–57; "Revolutionary Love: Denise Levertov and the Poetics of Politics," *Parnassus* 12 (1985), 335–51; and introductory essay to Gilbert and Gubar, *Shakespeare's Sisters*.

27. Ronald Wallace, "Alone with Poems," *Colorado Quarterly* 23 (1975), 341–52; Richard Gustafson, "Time Is a Waiting Woman: New Poetic Icons," *Midwest Quarterly* 16 (1975), 318. Consider, for example, such works as Nelly Furman, "The Politics of Language: Beyond the Gender Principle?" in *Making a Difference: Feminist Literary Criticism*, eds. Gayle Greene and Coppelia Kahn (New York: Methuen, 1985), 59–79; Mary Jacobus, introduction to *Women Writing*, ed. Mary Jacobus (New York: Barnes & Noble, 1979); Margaret Homans, *Women Writers and Poetic Identity: Dorothy Wordsworth, Emily Bronte, and Emily Dickinson* (Princeton, N.J.: Princeton University Press, 1980); Alicia Ostriker, *Stealing the Language: The Emergence of Women's Poetry in America* (Boston: Beacon Press, 1986).

28. Joyce Lorraine Beck, "Denise Levertov's Poetics and Oblique Prayers," *Religion and Literature* 18 no. 1 (Spring 1986), 45–61; see also Ronald Younkins, "Denise Levertov and the Hasidic Tradition," *Descant* 19 (1974), 40–48; Rudolph L. Nelson, "Edge of the Transcendent: The Poetry of Levertov and Duncan," *Southwest Review* 54, no. 2 (1969), 188–202; Joan F. Hallisey, "Invocations of Humanity: Denise Levertov's Poetry of Emotion and Belief," *Sojourners: An Independent Christian Monthly* (February 1986), 32–36; Harry Marten, *Understanding Denise Levertov*.

REVIEWS

ALLEGHENY COLLEGE LIBRARY

The Poetry of Denise Levertov   Kenneth Rexroth*

In my opinion Denise Levertov is incomparably the best poet of what is getting to be known as the new avant-garde. This may sound to some, committed to the gospel of the professor poets—the first commandment of whose decalogue of reaction is: the Age of Experiment Is Over—like saying that she is the leading Eskimo equestrienne. What I mean is that she is very much better than her associates, Charles Olson, Robert Creeley, Allen Ginsberg, Cid Corman, Chris Bjerknes, Gil Orlovitz and others who published in *Origin* and the *Black Mountain Review.* I don't believe these are bad poets— in fact I think they are the best of their generation and the only hope for American poetry. It is just that Denise Levertov has several things they haven't got, at least yet. In the first place, she is more civilized. One thing she has they lack conspicuously is what Ezra Pound calls culture—and which he is himself utterly without. She is securely humane in a way very few people are any more. This is not because she is English, of Welsh and Jewish parentage, although the fact that her father was a learned rabbi, the leading authority on *Kabballah,* who became an Anglo-Catholic priest, may have helped. She seems to have grown up in a household full of mildly bohemian scholarship, free-wheeling learning of the type Theodore Gaster made well known in his reminiscences of his own father (Rabbi Gaster and Paul Levertov were friends). Certainly this is a humanism older than the Renaissance, so well founded that it penetrates every bit of life. This is far from the humanism of Sigismonde Malatesta or even Henry Luce—it is more like Lao Tse. If it is really absorbed and manifest in an individual it becomes that rare thing, wisdom. I don't need to labor the point that there exist practically no wise poets nowadays and few for the last two hundred years.

This means that Denise Levertov knows more than her colleagues, far more than most; is far sounder than Olson, whose learning suffers from the same sort of Frobenius–Lost Atlantis provincial oddity as Pound's. Many of them know practically nothing, not even French and algebra. Because it is humane, her knowledge is the result of doing what came naturally. She has an almost perfect ear. Reading her, especially hearing her read aloud, you feel she must have literally absorbed the rhythms of great poetry with her

*From *Poetry* 91 (November 1957), 120–23. Copyright 1957 by the Modern Poetry Association. Reprinted by permission of *Poetry* and Bradford Morrow, for the Kenneth Rexroth Trust.

mother's milk. It is all so natural and so utterly removed from English 7649328 A, Forms and Techniques of English Verse (4 credits).

Nothing shows this better than the actual evolution of idiom and tone. During the years of World War II Denise Levertov came up as one of the best and one of the most individual of the young English Neo-Romantics. Comfort, Woodcock, Gascoyne, Gardiner, Tambimuttu, Read, the whole "leadership" of that "movement" were quick to recognize her as something very special indeed. She was naturally "romantic." She didn't have to believe in it or belong to it as a movement. She was built that way. I said of her then that "in poets like Denise Levertov this tendency (a sort of autumnal evening Weinerwald melancholy) reaches its height in slow, pulsating rhythms, romantic melancholy and indefinable nostalgia. Once these qualities would have been considered blemishes. Today they are outstanding virtues. For the first time, *schwarmerei* enters English verse." The only thing wrong with this statement in those days was that there weren't any "poets like Denise Levertov"; she was unique. And none followed her. The next crop, represented by Heath-Stubbs, seem like muggy little Brocklins cut out of cardboard in comparison. It was as though for a moment in the October moonlight a girl's voice sang faintly across the Danube, "Knowest thou a land where the pomegranate blooms. . . ." And then she gave it all up. "Hospital nurse, land-girl, charwoman, children's nurse, companion to an alcoholic . . . ," hitch-hiking over France the year after the War ended, she married a GI and came to the States. "She'll probably end up a professor's wife," said a friend in London in 1949, "pushing a pram in a supermarket." But Denise turned out to be made of tougher stuff, and besides, the GI was on the side of the angels. At first she fell under the influence of the Southern Colonels and the Country Gentlemen, but it didn't last long. We were all horrified. "So-and-so is a lot like our Empson," said she to me. Said I to her, " 'ceptin' that he never seen a book until he went to school and his folks still got cotton seeds in they hair. And besides, you are a leader of the very generation of revolt against the impostures of Empson, Richards, Eliot, and their sycophants." She allowed as how that was true. But nobody "influenced" her to turn away, pretty quick, from the smoking dogs and bicycling seals of the American academicians . . . it was her own good sense, the good sense of bona fide tradition, and an infallible ear. W. H. Auden spent years in America and never learned to use a single phrase of American slang without sounding like a British music-hall Yank comic and his verse remained as British, as specifically "school," as Matthew Arnold. In no time at all Denise came to talk like a mildly internationalized young woman living in New York but alive to all the life of speech in the country.

Her verse changed abruptly. It would be easy to say that it came under the influence of William Carlos Williams. It would be more true to say that it moved into the mainstream of twentieth-century verse. She writes like Williams, a little, but she also writes "like" Salmon, or Reverdy, or Char—or Machado—or Louis Zukofsky, or Parker Tyler, or Patchen, or the early Lowenfels, or me. After all, as Shakespeare said, we are all civilized men. I think she is a better poet than Salmon, as Williams is a better poet than Reverdy. If all her work of the past ten years were collected, I think she would show as the equal of Char and the better of all but a handful of American poets born in this century. (Certainly better than any French postwar poet—than Frenand or Cadon, or Becker, or Fallain, or Rousselot.) Her only rival amongst younger women in England is a lady someone once said wrote like an exquisitely well-bred lady's-maid, and who hasn't been up to her early snuff in many years. The only trouble with *Here and Now* is that it is much too small a collection, and it is a collection of her easiest verse. The fact that she has had to wait so long for publication and now is able to publish so little is a shame to American publishers who, year after year, put out the most meretricious, pompous, academic nonsense which gets meretricious, pompous, academic reviews in the literary quarterlies—and wins countless millions in Fellowships, Scholarships, Consultantships, Visiting Poetships. The official position is that people like Denise Levertov do not exist. Officialdom to the contrary, they very much do, and they will outexist the jerrybuilt reputations of the *Vaticide Review* by many, many long years. Nothing could be harder, more irreducible, than these poems. Like the eggs and birds of Brancusi, they are bezoars shaped and polished in the vitals of a powerful creative sensibility. No seminar will break their creative wholeness, their presentational immediacy. No snobbery will dissolve their intense personal integrity. However irrefrangible as objects of art, it is *that*, their personalism, that makes them such perfect poetic utterances. Denise may not ever have pushed a pram in a Cambridge, Mass. supermarket, but these are woman poems, wife poems, mother poems, differing only in quality of sensibility from thousands of other expressions of universal experience. Experience is not dodged, the sensibility is not defrauded, with any ambiguity, of seven types or seventy. One meets the other head on, without compromise. This, I was taught in school, many years ago, in a better day, is what makes great poetry great. And the rhythms. The *schwarmerei* and lassitude are gone. Their place has been taken by a kind of animal grace of the word, a pulse like the footfalls of a cat or the wing-beats of a gull. It is the intense aliveness of an alert domestic love—the wedding of form and content in poems which themselves celebrate a kind of perpetual wedding of two persons always realized as two responsible sensibilities. What more do you want of poetry? You can't ask much more. Certainly you seldom get a tenth as much.

[Review of *Overland to the Islands*]   Hayden Carruth*

Denise Levertov offers us something quite different, a free and supple poetry, personal, unaffected, mature. She is a wise and gifted poet. Last year, when she published a small pamphlet called *Here and Now*, Kenneth Rexroth praised her work highly and claimed her as a natural leader for his avant-garde, the coterie he has mustered to wage battle against the academic and metaphysical elements in American verse. Whatever Miss Levertov's personal affiliations may be, I think this was a disservice to her. She is not an experimentalist, she does not write in a context of revolt. True, her verse is unmetered; but this is 1958, the controversy Mr. Rexroth insists on pursuing today died painlessly some decades ago. Miss Levertov is not a leader. Instead she takes a small but clearly defined place among the minor, feminine poets, mostly American, who have done such good work in this century, and once we have understood what she is trying to do, we can see that her work is very much worth our attention.

In her theme, too, Miss Levertov offers us nothing particularly experimental. Her doctrine is the primacy of things, her approach the way of invocation. This is the kind of reism we have heard of before from Dr. Williams and the Objectivists. In fact it would be easy to put Miss Levertov down as a follower of Dr. Williams and let it go at that. This, I think, would be an error. I wish I knew enough of recent French poetry to speak authoritatively about the affinity I think I see between Miss Levertov's work and what little French verse has reached me. I can only apologize for my ignorance. But isn't there something of Char and Ponge and a few of the younger French poets in this virtually nuptial transcendence sought in the unities of objectification? At any rate, the free but purposeful directness of her writing and her care for the values of language bring Miss Levertov, I believe, much closer to the French than to the San Francisco school. Her superiority to most of the other young poets who are loosely classifiable in Mr. Rexroth's avant-garde is evident especially in the great skill with which she manages rhythmic pause and stress, and I should say that she pays as close attention to the small—and of course the large—motions of her verse as any poet writing in the classical tradition. Indeed, it would be a mistake to call her a romantic. Her work is a late aspect of the pre-classical pastoral, if we can imagine such a thing in English; it is writing that is skillful, unlabored, close to nature, seemingly indifferent to the codifications and orthodoxies yet to come.

Miss Levertov's new book, *Overland to the Islands*, contains a number of fine things. Some of them are "The Instant," "Action," "The Absence," "A Supermarket in Guadalajara, Mexico." At the same time I feel bound, in this brief tribute, to say that none of these new poems impresses me quite as much as the poem called "Beyond the End" from her previous collection.

*Reprinted by permission of the author from *Poetry* 93 (November 1958), 109–10. © Hayden Carruth 1958.

[Review of *With Eyes at the Back of Our Heads*]

Eve Triem*

In San Francisco I heard Denise Levertov read her poems. A girl, poignantly lovely. The poem on the page is faithful to her voice. Anyone who assumes that he can read this poetry while running is self-deceived. She thinks with authority; from the buttons and bus-tickets of existence, she contrives significance; her eternities have timeliness. Like Perry she is unconcerned with "newsprint facts," it is her excellence that she is intensely aware she is a "displaced" person—such perception Buddha had in his palace, the Christ in his fastings. Duncan said of her: "the care of the word . . . a guardian of inner orders." Rexroth wrote that she is superior to her former colleagues of the *Black Mountain Review*, "is securely civilized." Have her roots been fed by W. C. Williams or René Char? We might include the *Jataka Tales* or the *Lyra Graeca!* She uses devices, original or in new and disturbing ways. Warning: if you are sensitive only to traditional meanings, you will certainly miss the ideas that Denise Levertov fires at you. They will go by so fast you will not even know they were there. Examine "The Artist": "The artist: disciple, abundant, multiple, restless. / The true artist: capable, practicing, skillful; / maintains dialogue with his heart, meets things with his mind." There you have a paradigm presentation with the energy of talent— used in dynamic clusters (as in "The Gypsy's Window" in *Here and Now*), the power of the Cluster—like the primitive concept of God as a cluster of spirits. Each word adds a hot spark of *new* meaning. The reader has received an idea in the round—if he can receive. The "fact" is a physical energy, and in this open form poetry is observed with acuity. In "The Artist," the true artist uses words with the craftsman-control of the Toltec, the carrion artist is dealt with briefly, brusquely, contrast creating depth. An exalted pleasure in sensory experience ("The Departure," "The Great Dahlia," "February Evening in New York") brings into relief the frequent, sorrow-gripped moments. Even when she looks with hostile stare, life is continually celebrated. And consider "Takeoff." Undecorated insights. You are on your own; you read at your peril to seize her realities: "The mountains, through the shadowy / flickering of the propellers, steady, / melancholy, relaxed, indifferent, a world / lost to our farewells." Again, the power of the cluster, largely by the use of four adjectives which some frozen minds may still condemn as empathy. She is concerned with *impact*, produced by combining the simplest, uncannily chosen materials. In many poems, as in the title poem, she sees the world she lives in, not as projected by the status-seekers, but as it is. She does not like what she sees. In this book, the subtlest indictments abound of the feud in man's nature that commits him to inflict pain for pain's sake. Like most of us, she dwells on alien shores, but *she* is aware of it.

*Reprinted with permission from *Poetry* 97 (August 1960), 316–17. © 1960 by the Modern Poetry Association.

In conclusion, a quick look at the rest of the work. The prose-piece recalls Isak Dinesen, but it is her own fable. Her paraphrase of Gautier's "L'Art" is superb:

> The best work is made
> from hard, strong materials,
>   obstinately precise—
> the line of the poem, onyx, steel.
> . . . .
> Sculptor, don't bother with modeling
> pliant clay; don't let
>   a touch of your thumb
> set your vision while it's still vague.

"A Ring of Changes," a showcase of her choices, is a mature successor to the sharp, admirable love songs of *Here and Now.* Difficult to say whether it or "With Eyes at the Back of Our Heads" is the poem central to the book.

Describe the world as a mirage of multiplicities, chaos. Like Rilke—and the Psalmist—Denise Levertov so disposes her "objects" that chaos is disciplined to *order in transition.*

[Review of *With Eyes at the Back of Our Heads*]

Jean Garrigue*

Denise Levertov is concerned with making a certain kind of poem and achieving a certain kind of aesthetic effect by means of it. So far as I see it, it is a kind of askance impressionism, proceeding by indirections indirectly and by allusion, pitched in a low key, the approach quasi-conversational, informal, deliberately casual, rather intimate—a low key, yet by means and manner of juxtaposition striving to move into the high key of perception, "the quick of mystery" as she says, into that surprise that gets the poem off the ground into the shimmer and tremor of Possibles.

One especially sees this manner at work in certain poems, such as "A Straw Swan," "The Room," "The Vigil," "Girlhood of Jane Harrison," "Relative Figures Reappear" where the particulars are given a kind of abstract notation and where the large interest is simply in setting up relations between them or in giving proportions to those relations of a highly subtle and elusive kind. Attendant upon all this is her great interest in the look of things. She has a cultivated "painterly" eye and likes to isolate the looked-at thing in all of its detail, the looked-at thing as more or less the thing in itself, not involved in a conceptual order. So the lustre of surfaces and the glister of appearances is given much heed, and so is her concern to say the poem with as little stiffening

*Reprinted with permission from *Chelsea* 7 (May 1960), 110–12.

of rhetoric as is possible. In "A Ring of Changes" she glides from point to point as in a dream. Many of her poems seem to begin from the middle of reverie and end there, in a suspension of meanings. She is all for the undertone and the overtone and for that mystique of the arrangement of things whereby mysterious doors open briefly onto a view of other dimensions.

The only trouble is the doors don't stay open long enough or you don't know how or why they open. There is too much withheld. We are asked to move in a landscape of secrets but we're not quite allowed to share the secret. There is too much fragmentation, almost too much intentional disorganization, the opposing of jagged edges. I, for one, welcome the hard definiteness of "The Goddess":

> She in whose lipservice
> I passed my time,
> whose name I knew, but not her face,
> came upon me where I lay in Lie Castle!

That "Lie Castle" is original, moral, imaginative, a vigorous conception that keeps the poem firmly in rein, closing:

> [she] without whom nothing
> flowers, fruits, sleeps in season,
> without whom nothing
> speaks in its own tongue, but returns
> lie for lie!

Levertov would appear to have learned much from W. C. Williams but the wonder of Williams is that all that life going on and after gets subsumed somehow in the barbed vitality and cultivated roughness of the instant he chooses to let fly forth his hot arrows on. The "aesthetic" is fully trained upon existence; it serves as a transparent frame for its sources. What Williams didn't want of a contrapuntal organization and a formal subduing proceeded also out of innovation. He was inventing and he was the only bronco out there in the original wild American field of weeds and cinders. His radical strength and rootedness, his capacity to get and keep the poem in a uniqueness of reality belongs to him and is perhaps a secret that can't be passed on. If he was of the tribe that wanted to purify language this does not mean that his tribe has founded a school where all the lovely technics can be learned. For what technic does not go hand in hand with substance? Levertov's eye and flexible rhythms need to sharpen themselves on denser bodies of substance.

Gravity and Incantation   James Wright*

Gangs of versifiers in America have oft made night hideous with a miraculous variety of blats, gunks, and skreeks. Among them were the professionally "female" poets once wickedly labeled the "oh God the pain girls." Today, of course, we have several poetic schools of our own, and in their way they are probably even worse. But at least the caterwaulresses are gone. They are old, unhappy, far-off things, and battles long ago.

We have our own howls to inspire mad dreams of having an eardrum perforated for reasons of health. But the howls are not those of women. On the contrary, many women are writing fine poetry. Perhaps Nature herself has sent them to rescue us from a poetry that has become so bad as to be almost hair-raising.

I wish to discuss new books by two noble women [Isabella Gardner and Levertov] who are also two of the best living poets in America. They differ from each other; but their differences define their identities. By nature they resist absorption into any school. And, in being themselves, they touch certain beauties which are essential to poetry itself, whether written by man, woman, or child.

Miss Levertov has published several books during the past few years. Born in England, she first wrote with startling skill in traditional iambic style. After moving to the United States, of which she is now a citizen, she began to write poems in a measure which is sometimes called (mistakenly, I believe, as does Miss Levertov herself) "free verse." I have neither the space nor the full understanding required to discuss her prosody, but it should be discussed, for it is one of the most rewarding features of her moving poetry. Perhaps Miss Levertov herself will eventually write on the subject in relation to her own work. I hope she does. I have the impression that she is often misread and misinterpreted. I once read, in a foolish review, that Miss Levertov was simply writing imitations of W. C. Williams, whose style itself, compact of originality and even eccentricity, could not be imitated. Elsewhere, I have seen Miss Levertov associated, almost identified, with the Beats. (It is as though one had described Horace as one of the hangers-on of Byron during the later, riper part of his career.) Whether or not some person has approached her at a party to ask why she isn't Yeats, I do not know; but I would not be surprised; she apparently has had to put up with every other critical inanity imaginable, and she may as well finish the course. At any rate, she cannot be understood as a British poet who came to America and tried to assimilate the American language through the expedient of appropriating Dr. Williams's language bag and baggage. She has made her own discovery of America. The character of her poetry is remarkably American precisely *because* it is genuinely international. I have read that her father was a great

*Reprinted with permission from *Minnesota Review* 2 (Spring 1962), 424–26.

Jewish scholar and that she was educated at home. Her father must have been delighted; he must have felt like one of her readers; for her imagination is always religiously open, and it always responds to what touches it awake. It is a quick, luminous mind, protected by wisdom against falsity till its spirit is strong enough to do its own protecting. Her poetry caresses the English landscape, as in "A Map of the Western Part of the Country of Wessex" in her new book. It naturally embraces the local details of America, as in so many of her new and earlier poems. I begin to believe that her poetry is so beautifully able to acclimate itself to different nations (to their true places, not to their latest political lies) because her imagination was given its first shape and direction by a spirit of culture that traditionally has belonged to different nations. As far as I know, Miss Levertov's work has rarely been judged from this perspective—Kenneth Rexroth seems to have pointed it out only to be ignored by subsequent reviewers. In any case, the advantages offered this poet by her international heritage are displayed inescapably in her new book *The Jacob's Ladder.*

She has poems that lovingly touch the places of America, country and city alike, each with its continuous spirit and body. There are some poems— like the really splendid "In Memory of Boris Pasternak" and the difficult, harrowing sequence about the Eichmann trial—which explicitly confront international themes. But the international spirit blossoms most fully in the new poem entitled "A Solitude." Here the poet helps a blind man find his way through and out of a subway in New York City; and she allows the international inspiration to find its own fulfillment. For it touches the great theme: the particularly human. Her considerable talent blooms in this poem, which is, in Johnson's phrase, "a just representation of general na- ture." "A Solitude" is a special joy to those who have always felt the deep gravity which underlies Miss Levertov's work. "A Solitude" can stand up in the presence of Rilke's poems on the blind. Yes, I know what I am saying. And if it is justified, then it is easier to see why Miss Levertov's poems have been so maddeningly categorized by fools among fools. If Rilke, completely unknown in the United States, were to publish *Neue Gedichte* right now, it would probably be brushed off in an omnibus review. (Let's see, now . . . where did I leave that box of prefabricated phrases for omnibus reviews? . . . Ah, here it is: "Mr. Rilke should realize that, after all, Dr. Williams's notori- ous 'new territory' is really inseparable from his methods of arriving there, and it cannot be explored by the young. It is a pity that such a promising young writer should waste his energy by following roads already travelled by others. Besides, why isn't he Yeats?") Well, I am not called, much less chosen, to console Miss Levertov for the frustration of being misread by dead asses. Anyway, it just doesn't matter. "A Solitude" will outlive mis- readers, and categorizers, and her, and me, and perhaps that isn't enough. The poet must judge for herself. I will merely record my gratitude for the appearance of a noble poem—indeed, for a noble book.

Words and Silences   Kathleen Spivack*

In her newest book, *The Sorrow Dance*, Denise Levertov beautifully demonstrates the mastery over her medium—words and the silences between them—which she has been able to achieve. There is much to praise and much to quote here; for reasons of space I shall try to limit and to isolate.

First of all, the shape of her poems. This is hard to explain. She has an instinctive feeling for shaping a poem, letting out the lines easily. Her poems seem to flow effortlessly, nothing jars, you cannot imagine them contrived or rounded any other way. She knows the rhythm of the language, and when to end a line, when to end a stanza.

> Making it, making it
> in their chosen field. . . .

or, ending the poem "Bedtime":

> . . . we drowse as horses drowse afield,
> in accord; though the fall cold
>
> surrounds our warm bed, and though
> by day we are singular and often lonely.

There is an ease and rightness that is the fruit of discipline. Such craftsmanship is not as easy as it looks.

> A nervous smile as gaze meets
> gaze across
> deep
> river.
> What place
> for a smile here;
>   it edges away
> leaves us at each ravine's edge
> alone with our bodies. . . .

How does she know so well when to say and when to stop saying? It's a kind of tact unspoken in the placing of each word, each line and stanza.

Levertov has learned a great deal from Williams, and pays tribute in the poem "For Floss." But she has her own voice, and a European discipline underlying an American idiom and expansiveness.

Her Olga poems, written for her dead sister, are more complex and sometimes more turgid. They lack the clarity of the others, and are darkly unsettled and disturbing. One senses, in a dream way and long after putting down the poems, the restlessness of the sister, Olga, and her troubled relationship with family and world. The sister feels social injustice keenly, yet somehow this direct concern has become muffled, confused, and made more

*Reprinted with permission from *Poetry* 112, no. 2 (May 1968), 123–25.

painful by the slow paper piling up of her increasing isolation and illness. One does not catch the meaning of these poems by looking at them directly. They linger in the mind and the personae remain to haunt one.

> . . . Black one, black one,
> there was a white
> candle in your heart.

Finally, the Vietnam poems. It is the disparity between the delicacy of Miss Levertov's lines and the brute horror with which she—and we—must deal that is most poignant. Her poems are a record of outrage. And indeed, it is not only as poems that they should be read, but as testimony.

[Review of
Relearning the Alphabet]   Sister Bernetta Quinn, O.S.F.*

In her latest volume Miss Levertov inquires of the cold spring "what if my poem is deathsongs?" The singular *poem* suggests the elegy as unifying principle, like the city in Williams or the grass in Whitman, whereas the plural *deathsongs* defines her role as singer, a character developed in section four, where in a dramatic monologue a tree narrates the Orpheus myth. All human music has a dying fall, though few writers can so well analyze its poignancy as this Margaret who realizes full well she mourns first of all herself, experiencing death by imagination; then she grieves for the "burning babes" of Asia and the starved children of Africa; for young David, dead, and her friend Bill Rose, whose unanswered postcard haunts her; for the "wild dawns" of youth. An extract from her 1968–1969 notebook asks: "Is there anything / I write any more that is not / elegy?" Perhaps the answer is no. At any rate, one is grateful that with her beautiful honesty she looks squarely at the fact so many dare not face.

Gifted in seizing upon the unregarded image, Miss Levertov uses also the great traditional ones—for example, the moon. She identifies it with the ocean ("the great nowhere"); with mown grass; with a tiger that enters a bedroom to threaten lovers; with a coldness capable of burning the speaker to cinders.

Equally opposed to daytime reality is her symbolic employment of the dream. In "Riders at Dusk" she canters through a castled landscape, bewildered by the presence of a beloved but unknown companion: the situation is reminiscent of Emmaus. "The Rain" shows her trying "to remember old

*Reprinted with permission from *Poetry* 118 (May 1971), 97–98. © 1971 by the Modern Poetry Association.

dreams"; in the constant rain, life itself—voices, rooms, birds, hands—has become dream. "A Dark Summer Day" pleads for a jazz band to waken her with the news that life has been dreaming her. The entire book closes with her prayer to the *lares* of a house left to its profound dreams.

Related to the problem of reality vs. dream is that of identity. "Keeping Track" tells how she leaves her occupation of hulling strawberries or writing poems to check in a mirror as to whether or not she is still there. "Wind Song" reveals her search for a deeper self through a series of fiery metamorphoses. A related facet is the identity of others as treated in "Dialogue": the difficulty of "reaching" another and the importance of believing that persons are not objects but figures of more numinous being than sight perceives.

The title lyric, "Relearning the Alphabet," explores insights stemming from the twenty-six letters. If its lines resemble in their prosody the author of *Paterson* [William Carlos Williams], they do so without diminishing the force of Miss Levertov's own genius, almost blazing in its impact. It completes a collection rising from a season analogous to Keats's "golden year"— Keats, whose phrases weave in and out of these songs and whose "Ode to a Nightingale," as an autobiographical passage declares, is the only poem she ever memorized.

An enlargement of the spirit is effected by contact with Denise Levertov's dances, agonies, and playing on the ten-stringed lute. Like Orpheus, she uproots and then plants again in a new soil. No simplest sentence of daily life remains the same for this scholar, now that she has acquired a second alphabet, nor for those to whom she here teaches it. Prophet in the Flannery O'Connor sense, Miss Levertov has arrived at a vision counteracting the pain of mortality. She has discovered what Hopkins meant by "the dearest freshness deep down things."

[Review of *Relearning the Alphabet*]   Victor Contoski*

The best poetry of Denise Levertov makes itself felt first through sound. It seduces the ear. When a tree tells of Orpheus, the sound of music comes first. That is, the tree hears music before it knows *what* Orpheus is singing. Later the meaning comes almost automatically.

> Then as he sang
> it was no longer sounds only that made the music:
> he spoke, and as no tree listens I listened, and language
>   came into my roots
>   out of the earth,

*Reprinted with permission from *Sumac* (Spring 1971), 175–76.

> into my bark
>   out of the air,
>   into the pores of my greenest shoots
>   gently as dew
>   and there was no word he sang but I knew its meaning.

In "An Embroidery (II)" she lets us see how the poem comes to her, and we find that the title of a fairy tale contains the music (one almost wants to say "the meaning") of experience. "It was the name's music drew me first: 'Catherine and Her Destiny.' " Thus we are forced to think of the title as music before we even know what the story is about. And what subtle music! The *a, er,* and *in* sounds in *Catherine* are echoed in the next three words of the title: *and, her,* and *destiny.* The linking of girl and fate is done primarily through music. Our first responses are primitive, almost irrational, to such poetry. They are as basic as heartbeats. And look what she does with the *r* and *n* sounds in the next few lines.

> I knew there—glint from the fire
>   in a great hearth   awakening
>   the auburn light in her hair
>   and in the heaped-up treasure
>   weighed in the balance.

Have Pound, Sitwell, or H. D. ever put better music into poetry? And how appropriate to the sense of the poem! Catherine, it turns out is given a choice whether she prefers sorrow in youth and joy in age, or joy in youth and sorrow in age. The traditional tale has her choose sorrow in youth, but the poet asks, "What power would she have to welcome joy / when it came at last to her worn hands, / her body broken on Destiny's strange little wheel?" *Her* Catherine chooses joy in youth, which strengthens her for her years of pain. And we, in a sense, already know the decision of the poet's Catherine because of the joy we shared with her in the music at the beginning of the poem.

The book as a whole lacks the balance in Catherine's life. But if it has more sorrow, its joy is terribly intense—an earned joy. Yet even in ecstasy, sorrow is not far absent. The trees that dance to the music of Orpheus are also in agony. And look at these letters from her ABC poem, "Relearning the Alphabet."

> A
> Joy—a beginning. Anguish, ardor.
> To learn the ah! of knowing in unthinking
> joy: the belovéd stranger lives.
> Sweep up anguish as with a wing-tip,
> brushing the ashes back to the fire's core.

> D
> In the beginning was delight. A depth
> stirred as one stirs fire unthinking.
> Dark dark dark. And the blaze illumines
> dream.

The other roads of her life are shown in such poems as "Despair," "Tenebrae," "Biafra," and "A Marigold from North Vietnam." "Tenebrae" begins: "Heavy, heavy, heavy, hand and heart. / We are at war, / bitterly, bitterly at war." And in "The Heart" she begins: "At any moment the heart / breaks for nothing—." Yet in spite of mortality and disasters of history, it beats on. At times the central personality of the book becomes so overwhelmed with disasters that she cannot respond with the clear flashes of light, the intense moments of joy and agony that make the book great. In "From a Notebook: October '68–May '69" the poet is numbed by the events of our time and unfortunately numbs the reader too—not with the events but with the poetry.

> Their tears fall on sidewalk cement.
> The fence goes up, twice a man's height
> Everyone knows (yet no one yet
> believes it) what all shall know
> this day, and the days that follow:
> now, the clubs, the gas,
> bayonets, bullets. The War
> comes home to us. . . .

These lines (or notes, if you prefer) show little of Levertov's genius. Much as I share her sentiments, I cannot imagine this poetry being read with interest twenty years from now.

But much of the book is timeless. "The Broken Sandal," "The Cold Spring," "Despair," "The Heart," "Four Embroideries," "Wings of God," "Wanting the Moon," "Riders at Dusk"—these are works of lasting value. "Moon Tiger" is unforgettable for its lyrical compassion and tender humor. And "A Tree Telling of Orpheus" is, for my money, the finest of a fine lot. From *Relearning the Alphabet* it is easy to see why Denise Levertov is one of the poets of our time.

Levertov
Hayden Carruth*

What struck me first on reading *The Poet in the World*, which is a collection of Denise Levertov's prose writings about art, politics, and life in general—what struck me first, and what still strikes me in my reconsideration of the book as I prepare to write this review, though now in a stronger, richer way, is the force of the author's good sense and practical wisdom. To many readers this may seem surprising. Levertov's base, both philosophical and temperamental, is in Neoplatonism, as I think is well known; certainly it has been more than evident in her poetry for twenty years. But unlike many writers who share this broad neoplatonic provenance, she never, or hardly

*Reprinted with permission from *Hudson Review* 27, no. 3 (Autumn 1974), 475–80.

ever, steps outside her role as a working poet aware of the practical and moral relationships between herself and her poetic materials: her experience, her life, her humanity. She keeps her mind on the reality of imaginative process. She rarely veers into mystical utterance for its own sake.

Recently I was reading Gilbert Sorrentino's *Splendide-Hôtel*. It is a discussion, in the form of an extended personal essay on motifs from Rimbaud and Williams, of the role of the poet in history and civilization. Sorrentino is a fine writer. His book is thoughtful, lucid, wide-ranging, witty, in many ways a work of originality and imagination; I read it with pleasure. But I was aware all the time that his view of the poet—namely, as a person apart, somehow special and superior, exempt from practicality in his vocation, and better qualified than others to deal with the real world (in effect by creating his own super- or anti-reality)—is both antiquated and dangerous. It was dangerous when it was not antiquated, a century ago when it was the esthetic underground of the Victorian era, and it is equally dangerous, if not more, today. Many times, perhaps too many, I have argued this danger in the past, so I have no wish to revive the discussion here. And happily I need not, for Levertov has furnished the perfect answer to Sorrentino, and to a large extent from his own ground of feeling and ideas; I mean her essay entitled "The Poet in the World," the centerpiece of her book. It should be read by every poet in the country—in the world! Written from the working poet's point of view, out of Levertov's own active experience in the recent period of collaboration between poetry and politics, it has the immediacy and efficacy that my own more scholastic arguments, not to say tirades, doubtless lack.

Has Levertov solved the paradox of the poet as a specialist of sensibility in the practical human world? Not entirely. Her book contains many statements, and her poems many more, in which Sorrentino's view is at least implicit, and I suspect she could read *Splendide-Hôtel,* much of it anyway, without my degree of discomfort. Often she invokes The Poet in a role essentially vatic or ideally prophetic. Her affinity with Neoplatonism, from Plotinus to Swedenborg to Hopkins—a devious thread—is clear. My own base, which is not, whatever else it may be, Neoplatonism, makes me shy away from such statements. But always in her prose, and often in her poetry, there is this saving complementary strain, awareness of the poet as a craftsman engaged in a psychologically reasonable endeavor; ultimately her affinity is with makers more than seers, with Wordsworth and Rilke, Williams and Pound. The title of one of her essays gives it in a nutshell: "Line-Breaks, Stanza-Spaces, and the Inner Voice." Moreover, in her basic humaneness Levertov often realizes, reaches out to, and celebrates the poet in Everyman, at least *in posse*, thus incorporating a necessary disclaiming proviso among her attitudes. She does it best, I think, in the essay, cited above, that deals with sensibility as a moral and political instrument. The paradox remains, of course. It cannot be glossed over. Readers who are philosophically minded will be worried by it; some will be offended. But the point is that Levertov does not . . . well, I was going to say that she does not recognize it, but of course she does. Yet I think she does not *feel* it. She is not stopped by it, not boggled. She works through and beyond it, in her writing and in what we know of her life, conscious only of the wholeness of her vision. And she succeeds. She is practical.

This is the heart of the matter, I think. At any rate it is what I am interested in now: not the larger verities but her own work and the way her theoretical writing applies to her own work, particularly to her recent poetry. Undoubtedly her best known statement about poetry is the brief discussion of "organic form" that was originally published in *Poetry* in 1965, then reprinted a couple of times elsewhere before its appearance in her new book. It is a clear enough, and in some respects a conventional enough, statement; one hesitates to reduce it further than Levertov herself has already reduced it. But in essence it asserts that forms exist in reality as natural, or possibly more than natural, immanences, and that the poet perceives or intuits these forms through acts of meditation, which issue, once the perception has acquired a certain intensity, in the creation of verbal analogies; that is, poems. This is not simply the pathetic fallacy at work in a new way, because the analogy between poem and object is not superficial; there may be no resemblance whatever in exterior structures, textures, and styles. The resemblance is indwelling. Levertov refers to Hopkins and his invention of the word *inscape* to denote intrinsic, as distinct from apparent, form, and she extends this denotation to apply not only to objects and events but to all phenomena, including even the poet's thoughts, feelings, and dreams. She emphasizes the importance of the quality of meditation, speaking of it in basically religious language. Meditation is the genuine but selfless concentration of attention upon phenomena, the giving of oneself to phenomena, from which proceeds the recognition of inner form; it is, to use another of Hopkins' inventions, the disciplined or ascetic submission to "instress." And I must point out also, with equal emphasis, that although at times Levertov speaks of the poet as no more than an instrument of a larger "poetic power," and although more than once she implies that the poem as a verbal analogy may occur in part spontaneously in a sensibility which is thoroughly attuned to its object through a sufficient act of meditation, nevertheless she insists as well on the element of craft in the poetic process, the part played by verbal experiment and revision in bringing the poem into proper analogy to its phenomenal paradigm. The poem is a *made* object.

I don't say there aren't questions—risks, qualifications, paradoxes by the bucketful—and of course the entire complex is, as I have said, conventional, having appeared and reappeared at many times and in many places; yet Levertov's reformulation is very evidently her own, a personal vision, personal and practical; that is, *it comes from her practice.* One can't miss, either in her prose observations or in her poems, the way her understanding of what she is doing is instinctual at base, ingrained in her whole artistic personality.[1] Look at her poems up to about 1968. They are what we call "lyric poems," mostly rather short; they fall into conventional categories:

nature poems, erotic poems, poems on cultural and esthetic themes, and so on. Their style is remarkably consistent from first to last, changing only to improve, within its own limits, in matters of expressive flexibility, subtlety of cadence, integration of sonal and syntactic structures, and the like. But if the style is consistent the form is various, the *inner* form. From poem to poem each form is its own, each is the product of its own substance; not only that, each is the *inevitable* product—we sense it though we cannot demonstrate it—of its own substance. (She quotes Louis Sullivan approvingly: "Form follows function.") It has been customary to speak of the musicality of Levertov's poetry, and I have done so myself. But I think this is the wrong term. I doubt that she has been aware of music, e.g., as Pound was aware of it. But she has been deeply aware of formal consonance, of the harmony of inner form and vision; and certainly this, rather than the facility of artifice some critics have ascribed to her, is what lies at the root of her "musical" language.

Now we come to her recent work, particularly the long poem entitled "Staying Alive" (first published incompletely in her book *Relearning the Alphabet*, 1970, later in its completed state in *To Stay Alive*, 1971). It has been praised by some critics, but also dispraised by some—by a good many, in fact. I quote from the sheaf of reviews I have been at pains to collect. "Unfortunately the poems of *To Stay Alive* fail to connect. . . . Self-righteousness and sloganeering impair the language . . .; lofty moral injunctions . . . take the place of a larger vision," etc.; ". . . a moral builder, [not] art. . . . hardly the stuff of enduring poetry," etc.; ". . . discouraging to find Denise Levertov's poetry in this volume less fresh and less interesting than before and without a sense of new direction[!]," etc.; ". . . disappointing . . . exhaustion from too much struggle," etc.; ". . . depressing experience . . . self-indulgent spillings-out," etc.; ". . . poetic journalese . . . bad prose," etc. And a good deal more of the same.

But none of the critics has taken the trouble to define the poem in the poet's terms. It is, first, a sequence about the poet's life as a political activist from 1966 to 1970; second, an exploration of the sense and temper of those years generally; third, an attempt to locate and express the poet's own complex feelings, particularly with regard to questions of artistic responsibility; and fourth—and most important—a creation of poetic analogues to the inner form, the *inscape*, of that momentous "historical present." Remember the elements of poetic process as Levertov conceives them—perception, meditation, making—and then apply them to the *substance* of this long poem, those enormously intricate social, historical, esthetic, and moral *gestalten*. A whole nation, even the world, is involved here. No wonder the poem is multiform. It contains, what so annoys the critics, highly lyric passages next to passages of prose—letters and documents. But is it, after *Paterson*, necessary to defend this? The fact is, I think Levertov has used her prose bits better than Williams did, more prudently and economically; she has learned from *Paterson*. And aside from that, if one grants the need, in a long poem, for modulations of intensity, as everyone must and does, then why not grant the further modulation from verse into prose? It is perfectly feasible. Much of "Staying Alive" is what I call low-keyed lyric invocation of narrative; not narrative verse as such, not "thus spake mighty Agamemnon" or "the boy stood on the burning deck"; but instead—

> Brown gas-fog, white
> beneath the street lamps.
> Cut off on three sides, all space filled
> with our bodies.
>   Bodies that stumble
> in brown airlessness, whitened
> in light, a mildew glare,
>   that stumble
> hand in hand, blinded, retching.
> Wanting it, wanting
> to be here, the body believing it's
> dying in its nausea, my head
> clear in its despair, a kind of joy,
> knowing this is by no means death,
> is trivial, an incident, a
> fragile instant . . .

Brilliance is not wanted here, nor musicality (the superficial kind), but rather a strong supple verse, active and lucid; and this is exactly what we have. It changes; heightens and descends; turns soft or hard as the evolving analogy demands; it does the job. I repeat, the poem must be read whole. And readers who do this, as they easily can in one sitting, will see, I believe, or hear, precisely the consonance I spoke of in connection with Levertov's shorter lyrics, but now greatly enlarged and more varied: a just analogue for a complex phenomenon, unified in its whole effect, its vision, and its inner, "organic" form.

I don't say the poem succeeds in every line. That would have been a miracle. Sometimes the poet's perception or meditation apparently flagged; she tried to make up for it with acts of simple artistic will (as when she writes about her English friends whose lives "are not impaled on the spears of the cult of youth"). But such lapses are few. They do not disturb the unity of the poem.

As for the recurrent accusation of self-indulgence, who except the self can perceive, meditate, and create? Would the poem have been different if the poet had remained "anonymous" and "omniscient"? No, except for a possible loss of authenticity. Was De Tocqueville self-indulgent? Was Mrs. Trollope? Montaigne wrote: "I owe a complete portrait of myself to the public. The wisdom of my lesson is wholly in truth, in freedom, in reality"; and reality in this poem is in part the exemplary, very exemplary, responses of the poet to the perplexities of a time of rapid social disintegration. Clearly Montaigne was right for himself in his more moderate circumstances, and I think Levertov is equally right in the extremity of her (and our) circumstances. I also think that "Staying Alive" is one of the best products of the recent period of politically oriented vision among American poets.

Denise Levertov and I are good friends. Writing "Levertov" repeatedly where I would normally write "Denise" has seemed peculiar to me, even painful in a way. But I have done it and have reserved this acknowledgment until the end because I believe our friendship, which I suppose is rather well known, makes no difference and should make no difference to what I have written here. For that matter I am named in the preface of *To Stay Alive*, and I not only was shown the manuscript of *The Poet in the World* at an early stage of assemblage, I was later hired by its publisher to perform necessary copyediting before it was sent to the printer. So my bias is clear. If my view of Denise's work were antipathetic, obviously in the circumstances I would choose to say nothing about it. But the fact that my view is, on the contrary, sympathetic does not seem to me to detract from its usefulness. I have omitted many things about *The Poet in the World* that would have been said in the customary review. It is, for instance, a miscellaneous volume, springing from many miscellaneous occasions, and its tone ranges from spritely to gracious to, occasionally, pedantic. It contains a number of pieces about the poet's work as a teacher; it contains her beautiful impromptu obituary for William Carlos Williams, as well as reviews and appreciations of other writers. But chiefly the book is about poetry, its mystery and its craft, and about the relationship between poetry and life. It is an interesting and valuable book in general, and in particular it is an essential commentary on the poet's own poems and her methods of practice. It should be read by everyone who takes her poetry seriously.

Note

1. But this does not mean there were no antecedents. Who can disentangle the sources of instinct? I believe Levertov has mentioned somewhere an early admiration for Herbert Read, though his name does not appear in her book: Read, the poet and critic who stood so steadfastly against the Cambridge-dominated school of "objective method" in criticism and philosophy between the two wars. See his *Poetry and Experience*, 1967, esp. Ch. 3, "The Style of Criticism," where he quotes Goethe: "Whereas *simple imitation* flourishes under tranquil and satisfying conditions of existence, and whereas *mannerism* calls for a light touch and a fresh individuality, that which I call *style* rests on the deepest foundations of cognition, on the inner essence of things, in so far as this is given us to comprehend in visible and tangible forms." And notice how the meanings of "style" and "form" have been almost exactly reversed from their former meanings by the Black Mountain writers of the past twenty years, particularly Robert Duncan, whose idiosyncratic usage has influenced many others, including Levertov.

[Review of *The Freeing of the Dust*]   Linda Wagner*

Denise Levertov's poems have been an important part of the contemporary literary scene for twenty years. When the formalist 1950s relaxed to accept Allen Ginsberg's *Howl* and Robert Creeley's short-lined love poems, Levertov's work offered a kind of middle ground: poems in which rich sound patterns balanced "natural speech"; poems in which a humanistic credo—and the need to express it—overshadowed the mere presentation of an image. From the first, Levertov insisted that a poet had to use all available resources of language. She also declared firmly that every poet had a clear social responsibility.

In *The Freeing of the Dust*, Levertov's eleventh collection of poems, she continues to express these early convictions with even greater persuasiveness. Much of the rancor of her former social poetry has mellowed to an affirmation: bitterness has given way to the tranquillity of "A Place of Kindness" where

> . . . someone slow is moving,
> stumbling from door to chair
>
> to sit there patiently
> doing nothing but be,
> enjoying the quiet and warmth. . . .

"Imagination could put forth / gentle feelers there," the poet suggests, cognizant that the traditional role of the poet is to make, to shape. Even the ostensibly Vietnamese poems in this book emphasize reflective scenes (albeit at times ironically), as in the poem "In Thai Binh (Peace) Province," where Levertov's attention falls on "dark sails of the river boats, / warm slant of afternoon light / apricot on the brown, swift, wide river. . . . Peace within the / long war."

Such a change from relative stridency to careful repose suggests not that Levertov's political views have changed but rather that this collection of poems expresses the core of any writer's effectiveness: the humanity that forces one to take stands, the *angst* of seeing and living in a world that seldom meets ideal standards, but, too, the joy of glimpsing fulfillment at least occasionally. In "From a Plane," the opening poem of this book, Levertov speaks of "a reclamation of order" and "revisioning solace." And as other poems show, that journey to order and revisioning is the province of the poet.

The tone of many of the poems in *The Freeing of the Dust* is more quiet, more satisfied—not with the physical or social circumstances of life but with a human being's ability to cope with those circumstances. There is much

*Reprinted with permission of the author from *The Nation* 223 (14 August 1976), 121–23.

emphasis here on exploring the fullest ranges of consciousness and psyche, and I was reminded of her 1972 essay on Ezra Pound (from *The Poet in the World*) in which she praised his writing because "he stirs me into a sharper realization of my own sensibility. I learn to desire not to know what he knows but to know what I know: to emulate, not to imitate." Poems here echo with this completion of earlier promise, with the sense of Levertov as person knowing herself, being, and becoming, through both life and art. *The Freeing of the Dust* is an amazingly rich book, giving us the image of Levertov as fully realized poet, humanist, seer, and—not least—as woman. In the process of complete engagement, a poet who is also a woman must, finally, speak with a woman's voice: any denial of that primary identity would play havoc with the self-determination of the poem. There are perhaps too many women who use the crutch of sexual identity to make bad poems effective, but when Levertov creates the feminine identity, as in the evocative "Cancion," its use is powerful:

> When I am the sky
> a glittering bird
> slashes at me with the knives of song.
>
> When I am the sea
> fiery clouds plunge into my mirrors,
> fracture my smooth breath with crimson
>   sobbing.
>
> When I am the earth
> I feel my flesh of rock wearing down:
> pebbles, grit, finest dust, nothing.
>
> When I am a woman—O, when I am
> a woman,
> my wells of salt brim and brim,
> poems force the lock of my throat.

This short poem also suggests the stability of Levertov's performance as poet. She has long been admired for her use of richly sensual language and movement, regardless of a poem's subject matter. She often has written sensually about art, as she does here in "The Poem Rising by Its Own Weight"; and the long-lined rhythms of the poem that seemingly expresses a credo both personal and artistic, "Prayer for Revolutionary Love," are striking illustration of her verbal force.

This latter poem, one of the most effective in the book, emphasizes as well Levertov's almost mystical belief in "the unknown," the anima, the fruit of her ability to open self so that she might transcend self, through experience. Readers have often noticed Levertov's reliance on quasi-religious terms, and the definite spiritual feeling in some of her writing. This stance and vocabulary come to the surface again in these poems.

In many other ways, *The Freeing of the Dust* restates Levertov's strengths as poet. It also impresses with its versatility: there are seven groups of poems, ranging from the political poems to those about love and divorce; from masterful sequences to the single-image poems that reach further than any such poems have a right to. Not a collected or selected work, Levertov's eleventh book gives us the sense that the searching vicissitudes of American poetry during the past half-century have brought us to an art capable of expressing (and first recognizing) "despair" and "wildest joy":

> To make poems is to find
> an old chair in the gutter
> and bring it home
> into the upstairs cave;
> a stray horse from the pound,
> a stray boat on the weedy shore,
> phosphorescent.
>
> Then in the broken rocking chair
> take off—to reality!

[Review of *Life in the Forest*]   Harry Marten*

Artistic longevity is always risky. A poet who with the passing of years settles into a style becomes not a maker of poems but of artifacts. It is a pleasure to note, then, that with the publication of *Life in the Forest*, her twelfth book of verse, Denise Levertov continues to write exquisitely crafted lyrics. In their reverence for language and life, they make the reader continually aware that the poet's task is, as Levertov has said elsewhere, "to clarify . . . not answers but the existence and nature of questions."

Early linked by friendship to Robert Creeley and his *Black Mountain Review*, to Robert Duncan by shared imaginative resources, to Cid Corman, Charles Olson and Paul Blackburn by frequent publication in Corman's magazine *Origin*, to the Beats by various anthologists, and especially to William Carlos Williams, clearly a great source of nourishment for her as well as for most American writers of the last quarter century, Levertov nonetheless refuses category. She is like Wallace Stevens' "man of glass . . . the transparence of the place in which / He is," able to both reflect and reveal the truth in its inconsistencies.

The poet's "Introductory Note" to *Life in the Forest* explains at the outset a bit of the book's imaginative terrain. Having recently discovered in the stark simplicity of Cesare Pavese's poem-stories of the 1930s, *Lavorare*

*Reprinted with permission from *New England Review and Bread Loaf Quarterly* 2 (Autumn 1979), 162–64.

Stanca (Hard Labor), "a kind of ratification for a direction" her work "was already obscurely taking," Levertov notes an intention to "try to avoid over-use of the autobiographical, the dominant first-person singular of so much of the American poetry—good and bad—of recent years." Yet differences be-tween *Life in the Forest* and *Lavorare Stanca* reveal as much as sympathies. Not even in "Homage to Pavese," the first section of Levertov's book, does she insist upon what Pavese himself called the "*austerity* of style" or the "close, possessive, passionate adherence to the object" and the "surrendering to the plot" that impelled so many of his poems.

Levertov shares the honesty of Pavese's descriptions, the incisiveness and clarity with which he was able to sketch landscapes and the people who inhabit them—

> . . . There are places in the city
> where there are no streets, only alleys where the sun
>   doesn't reach
> and the wind never blows ("A Season," tr. W.
> Arrowsmith)

> . . . In the winter fog
> the man lives jailed between streets, drinking
> his cold water, biting his crust of bread. ("Simplicity,"
> tr. W. Arrowsmith)

Nonetheless she gives her attention not so much to the qualities of the object perceived, or alternatively to the interior of the perceiver's mindscape, as to the relationships between the world "out there" and its apprehension by a receptive sensibility. In the far ranging geographies of *Life in the Forest*, seer and things seen are mutually activating—whether we are in the rain and heat of Oaxaca where a seller of serapes makes his endless rounds, or amidst the assembled memories, possessions and sickroom detritus of an old woman dying too slowly, "at home, yet far away from home, / thousands of miles of earth and sea, and ninety years / from her roots."

The mysterious process of discovery in which interior and exterior meet and define one another is nowhere clearer than in the intense evocations of Levertov's mother-daughter poems:

> . . . Now mother is child . . . at the mercy
> of looming figures who have the power
> to move her, feed her, wash her, leave or stay
> at will. And the daughter feels, with horror,
> metamorphosed: *she's* such a looming figure—huge—a
>   tower
> of iron and ice—love
> shrunken in her to a cube of pain
> locked in her throat. ("A Daughter (I)")

And wherever we turn in this splendid collection we find "the seed of change . . . seeing not only *what is* but *what might be*"—in the designs of

"Blake's Baptismal Font," in the presence of "Chekhov on the West Heath," or when sharing the articulation of an extreme privacy in the entries of "Metamorphic Journal."

Levertov mixes long lines which propel poetic narratives ("Writing to Aaron," "The Cabdriver's Smile") and sharp images that crystallize moments of immediate experience ("A Visit," "The Blue Rim of Memory," "A Woman Pacing Her Room . . ."). She plays logical syntax against the brief hesitations in thought and feeling that, in large part, determine line breaks—

> . . . Among sharp stones, below,
> of the hospital patio,
>   an ugly litter of cigarette stubs
> thrown down by visitors leaning, anxious or bored,
> from other balconies. ("A Daughter (II)")

And the tensions of tone and meaning that result dislocate the reader, compelling him out of complacencies of observation and into active participation as he reads. Levertov's introductory remarks even invite one to take a hand in reassembling the shifting shapes that comprise the whole book— suggesting that in reading from section to section we perceive overlapping sections, kinship groups, internal associations from poem to poem.

Not all of the poems of *Life in the Forest* are fully created. The sequence of love poems, "Modulations for Solo Voice," is especially disappointing. The emotional declarations often seem strained, offering cliches which convince us simply that the experience is too self-serious and self-enclosed to make good poetry:

> I wanted to learn you by heart.
> There was only time
> for the opening measures. ("From Afar")

Still, the "Epilogue" to the series which Levertov calls from a "cheerful distance" "*Historia de un amor*" has an exactness of irony and a satisfying emotional resonance which goes a long way toward rescuing the whole, sending us back to reconsider even the weak poems of the sequence in light of such final insights as "I thought I had found a fire / but it was the play of light on bright stones."

If one believes with Octavio Paz, as I do, that "poetry is metamorphosis, change, an alchemical operation" and that "the poem is a work that is always unfinished, always ready to be completed and lived by a new reader," one can only be pleased to have Levertov's latest effort, whatever its lapses. More than thirty years after her first volume, she reminds the reader that her best poems fulfill as well as any poetry can her own stated goals for fine writing. *Life in the Forest* "sets in motion . . . elements in the reader that otherwise would be stagnant. And that movement . . . cannot be without importance if one conceives of the human being as one in which all the parts are so related that none completely fulfills its function unless all are active."

Flooded with Otherness

Bonnie Costello*

In recent volumes [*The Freeing of the Dust* (1975) and *Life in the Forest* (1978)], Denise Levertov has tried to show us a full and balanced life such as we all wish for, but as with most of us, her private and her public selves have never really agreed. And while she judiciously measures out her attentions to these quarrelsome, demanding siblings, we still feel that her most natural affection is for the elder, private self, relations with the other always seeming a bit strained, a bit superficial. We want from poetry a sign that our complex lives are manageable, but the symmetries of Levertov's world seem posed and inauthentic. Though she has proven many times over that she is capable of those "piercing glances into the life of things" which Marianne Moore looked for when she bought pictures, as Levertov has widened her lens, she has distorted too much that is real and recalcitrant.

In *The Freeing of the Dust* Levertov's quest for equilibrium has shaped the whole volume. Each of the nine sections is grouped according to related themes or perspectives, each unit and the whole rounded off in an arc of reassurance, with nature and solitude offsetting the vicissitudes of love and marriage, domestic life counterbalancing politics. It is easy enough to gain perspective from a distance; whether from an ivory tower or an aeroplane, "always air / looked down through, gives / a reclamation of order, re- / visioning solace." The book begins with the pilot's weather report. Of course life is down there glittering in the muck and the traffic jams, and we must descend "like coins of hail" to "the planet under the clouds." Yet the formulas of ideology, morality, even theology don't really accommodate the realities of fields and gardens, bedrooms and living rooms, welfare hotels and bombed villages. Though she admits at the end of the book that the "smoky map" is based on a bird's-eye view, her overconfidence in the telling of particular stories belies the humility of her conclusions.

Life in the Forest is a looser assortment of moods and memories to which Levertov has applied the same principle, that the parts of a life have a necessary and tolerable coherence. She has held this belief from the first, and has represented it beautifully in the small world of her early poetry as a thread, a dance, a ladder from earth to heaven; these delicate metaphors, however, are not sufficiently ballasted against the tempests of adult life— family deaths, divorce, national and international crimes. In search of a "continuum" she still listens for the "voice of scarabe, / dungroller / working survivor," but whereas he emerged naturally from the soil of *The Jacob's Ladder*, in *Life in the Forest* he is *a deus ex machina*. In troubled times we want something that is genuine, even if it is insufficient, mysterious, or bad news.

Myth and ritual are, of course, the natural devices of poets who believe (or want to believe) that life is not random or trivial. With her "voyages" and

*Reprinted, as excerpted, from *Parnassus* 8, no. 1 (1979–80), 198–212.

"journeys," her "vigils," "communions," "chants," and "psalms," Levertov
has ritualized the quotidian from sunup to sundown:

> leaving the store with groceries, bathed—
> all!—utterly
>
> > in this deepening, poised,
> > fading-to-ivory oxbowed river of
>
> light,
> one drop
> of crimson lake to a brimming
> floodwater chalice
> and we at the lees of it—("Chant: Sunset, Somerville, Late Fall '75")

We all know the holiness of a sunset can lift us into heaven from Somerville
as well as Katmandu. This lovely drift of words and sounds carries us willingly down a moat of doubtful metaphors. When Levertov fancies her lover
as Cupid, herself as Psyche, and the mailman as Mercury, the mythic note
demonstrates "the art of sinking in poetry." Why must every bus trip be a
"journey," every rambling friend a "wanderer?" Why, asking directions of a
blind man, must she imagine she is "consulting the oracle?"

Alone with the elements or the spirits, her public self silent, Levertov is
often charming and inventive, and we leave her a wide margin for fantasy.
"The Freeing of the Dust," for example, lets us taste and see the reconciliation of spirit and body.

> Unwrap the dust from its mummycloths.
> Let Ariel learn
> a blessing for Caliban
> and Caliban drink dew from the lotus
> open upon the waters.

Myth, however enigmatic, seems immanent here and in "Life in the Forest"
where Levertov writes her own rebellious story of how the poet got her
spots.

> > > How Eternity's
> > silver blade filed itself fine
> > on the whetstone of her life!
> > > How the deep velours
> > of the wings, the mystery of the feelers,
> > > drew amazed cries from her
> > when the butterfly came forth
> > and looked at her, looked at her, brilliantly gazing.
> > > It was a man, her own size,
> > and touched her everywhere.

We believe again in Adam and Eve when we can see their "four prehensile,
elegant, practical feet." Such representations, though they may be conspicu-

ously framed—as embroideries, emblems, etchings—draw us into their mythic space.

It is this way of thinking in myth, rather than transcribing conscious experience into myth, that characterizes the best poems of *With Eyes at the Back of Our Heads* (1960), in which Levertov, dissatisfied with the disembodied abstraction of her first book, *The Double Image* (1946), and the flat literalness of her second, *Here and Now* (1957), first tried to represent "the dynamic experiencing of archetypal characters and actions." These poems have an inherent concreteness and confident logic both crystal clear and impenetrable as crystal. As they journey through an inner geography ("mountain / green, mountain / cut of limestone, echoing / with hidden rivers, mountain / of short grass and subtle shadows") or draw the world into the cantilevered mirrors of the self, they have the rhythm of a heartbeat, a hypnotic pounding in our ears.

> The eye, luminous, grayblue,
> a moonstone,
> brimmed over with mercury tears
> that rolled and were lost in sunny dust.
> The world in the lustre of a
> black pupil moved its clouds
> and their shadows. Time
> had gathered itself and gone. The eye
> luminous, prince of solitude.

When Levertov makes myth serve humanity—that idol of prophets and politicians—it is sluggish in its duties. She is a dreamer at heart, and her best moments are stolen, solitary ones, glimpses of a landscape at 1:00 A.M. when "humanity" has long since gone to bed. Recently Levertov has used dream to diagram experience (the anguish of her mother's death, the uncertainty of a love affair); but if these are to be read as dreams at all we can be sure the superego has done a lot of work to get them into their present, analyzable shape, for again the language is more illuminating when it is aimed at the border between the human and the non-human, or into the caverns of the unconscious. In *The Double Image,* in fact, she is a little wary of dream, which does not so much clarify her relations with others as disrupt them, and draws her away from the security of familiar rooms . . .

. . . By the time she writes *With Eyes at the Back of Our Heads* her vision is completely adjusted to the dark, and her imagination naturalized into the element it fathoms, the "lagoon" where "the imagination swims, / shining dark-scaled fish, / swims and waits, flashes, waits and / wavers, shining of its own light." What she finds down there is always rich and strange. . . .

In *The Freeing of the Dust* and *Life in the Forest* Levertov has tried to renew her "romance" with "the dense, preoccupied, / skeptical green world, that does not know us." As in any romance, this involves a certain distortion, making the other an image of our moods and desires. Levertov has never had a mind of winter; nature always has a human voice, even when it behaves as a stranger, but when she adulterates her affair with nature, bringing in a third party, the effect is, as usual, a weakening of the bond. . . .

. . . "Organic form" is a kind of catch-all phrase and not very useful in discriminating artists, but Levertov's attraction to the idea is understandable when we examine her beginnings. What made her a poet is that she knew such forms were inadequate to her needs even before she knew how to correct them. It is "too easy," she tells herself in one early poem,

> to write of miracles, dreams where the famous give
> mysterious utterance to silent truth;
> to confuse snow with the stars,
> simulate a star's fantastic wisdom.

Since there are "no miracles but facts," she must learn to "write of the real image, real hands . . . the loaf on the bare table" in the language of men and women. To write of "here and now" (the title of her second volume) is a harsh sentence for a heart grown addicted to absences, to the "spindrift" of "ephemeral eternity." The cures poets administer to themselves are seldom mild, and Levertov's "cure of the ground," on the advice of Dr. Williams, required a temporary abjuration of the balmy vaguenesses and dreamy sonorities of *The Double Image.* This new spareness was not always austere, however. The highly circumscribed pictures in *Here and Now* occasionally have the emotional clarity and sparkle of the best in H. D.: "The water / flashes / each time you / make it leap— / arching its glittering back." . . .

There are poems in *The Jacob's Ladder* and *O Taste and See* where the miracle of fact is exquisitely revealed in the miracle of form. "Stonecarver's Poem," with the dazzle and compression of a diamond, can stand as an example of her best achievement.

> Hand of man
> hewed from
> the mottled rock
>
> almost touching
> as Adam the hand of God
>
> smallest inviolate
> stone violet.

There is nothing in the two latest volumes that equals this. Clearly Levertov was growing restless in such confined quarters, even if they do look out onto worlds. As she herself says, she felt "a recurring need . . . to vary a habitual lyric mode." So she opened up the line again, sometimes to the margin. The temporal forms of diary, dialogue, anecdote, and report disturbed the lyric poise; the discursive mode moved in with the reflective; the blunt assertion bullied the delicate gesture; and the sequestered world of private meditation was stormed by the cries of a wider world that demanded immediate response. . . .

We may agree, and yet disagree, with Auden that "poetry makes nothing happen." It can bring an intimacy to the news, can show us the human heart of cruelty, the human form of terror, as no cover of *Newsweek* can. And because poetry is not history it can sometimes save us from the tyranny of history. It is to Levertov's credit that she is willing to take on the challenges of political poetry. At every phase of her writing since *Relearning the Alphabet* she has tried to overcome "the distance" between "the evening's silent dream" and the nightmare printouts of war and poverty. In *The Freeing of the Dust* she has placed the political section between two that deal with private themes, in order to show how public issues interrupt our lives. In *Life in the Forest* the political poems appear in a section called "Continuum," suggesting a struggle beyond personal loss and joy. Identification is the greatest tool of persuasion: to enter the shattered domestic life of victims is to imagine ourselves as victims. *Relearning the Alphabet* was Levertov's most successful effort of identification, for it showed how history had turned the very tools of the poet—language and imagination—into cruel weapons of distortion. ("We had to destroy the village in order to save it.") As headlines invade the quiet rooms of lyric, as photos are "torn" from *"The Times"* and "news items" force themselves on our attention, we do sense the urgency. Nonetheless our imaginative sympathy is not won simply by thrusting data at us and shouting slogans, however effective such tactics may be in protest rallies. . . .

Levertov is really a romantic poet, giving what she gazes at "the recognition no look ever before granted it." This is much the same compliment Coleridge paid to Wordsworth, and it is how Levertov identifies her archetypal poet in the lyrical "Growth of a Poet." That the poem is paired with another more discursive and anecdotal, "Conversation in Moscow," which deals with the poet as social critic, suggests a continued division between her private and public selves. The two come together rhetorically in the "mineshaft of passion," but between the deep canyon of "duende" and the Black Sea of "human reality" lies a continent she is only beginning to cross. . . .

[Review of *Collected Earlier Poems* *1940–1960*]

Doris Earnshaw*

Denise Levertov was fitted by birth and political destiny to voice the terrors and pleasures of the twentieth century. Granddaughter on her father's side of a Russian Hasidic Jew and on her mother's of a Welsh mystic,

*Reprinted with permission from *World Literature Today* 55 (Winter 1981), 109–10.

she has published poetry since the 1940s that speaks of the great contemporary themes: Eros, solitude, community, war. In "Illustrious Ancestors" she describes these fathers, and then, "thinking some line still taut between me and them," gives her poetic credo:

> . . . I would like to make . . .
> poems direct as what the birds said
> hard as a floor, sound as a bench
> mysterious as the silence when the tailor
> would pause with his needle in the air.

How consistently she has constructed her poems of hard, solid and mysterious qualities can be seen in the new collection of early work. The 131 poems include the entire texts of her first New Directions volumes—*Here and Now* (1957), *Overland to the Islands* (1958) and *With Eyes at the Back of Our Heads* (1960)—twenty hitherto uncollected poems and eight selections from her first British volume, *The Double Image* (London, Cresset, 1946). An "Author's Note" tells of lost early poems and letters—particularly one long letter to her from T. S. Eliot which she hopes will surface—and of her debt to Kenneth Rexroth. She relates the story of her arrival via the back stairs at the Cresset Press, flushed with the achievement of landing a job as a nurse in a London hospital.

Perhaps because she was educated by private tutors in her English childhood, Levertov seems never to have had to shake loose from an academic style of extreme ellipsis and literary allusion, the self-conscious obscurity that the Provençal poets called "closed" (*trobar clus*). Other poets—Adrienne Rich, for example—move away from an early brilliant but rigid and pedantic voice to direct and personal speech. A reading of Levertov's early work shows her to be remarkably consistent in theme and form throughout her career. A recent verse mass (soon to be given a dramatic performance) takes up the threads of her first passion for physical beauty and emotional sincerity in human life. The tone is deeper and more tragic, naturally, as both private and public life move through these dreadful decades; yet even her first published poem, the haunting eight-line lyric "Listening to Distant Guns," sounds the message of her perceptions, senseless terror and sacred natural existence. As an "evacuated" English girl in the southern countryside, she could hear the booming of cannon across the Channel.

Many poems of these early volumes are set in Mexico; others have New York or suburban country as their locale. Levertov plays with dialects and language, though not often. Her favorite style is to use a narrative as slightly sketched background for the presentation of a state of mind. Feeling is brought to clear expression while story or dramatic element is a shadow. Always rooted in the presence of a tangible, visible reality, the poems caress objects with praise, "a cold primrose sting / of east wind," "a luxury of open red / paper roses." Word and object are handled with a peasant strength, direct and wise. Titles are short, only one or two words.

The influence of Rilke is here: "Burn, burn the day. The wind / is trying to enter and praise you." In an age of sarcasm, individual and mass alienation and "double-voiced" words, as Mikhail Bakhtin shows, when few famous poets in the West are being arrested for their political views, Levertov both writes and lives her belief in the poet as bringer of praise and hope. The publication of her early work reveals the good seed from which a rich harvest has come.

[Review of *Candles in Babylon*]   James Finn Cotter*

Denise Levertov is a poet whose public outspokenness has not harmed her reputation as a highly private poet. *Candles in Babylon . . .* displays the same technical expertise that marked her previous dozen books; there is little in the open form that she cannot manage: nostalgia, protest, satire or story. "The Great Wave" catches the excitement of swimming at the shore as a child, while "The Art of the Octopus" is a perfect description and allegory. Levertov admits that one piece, written for an antidraft rally, really is a speech rather than a poem. Unfortunately, too many others move in the same direction, where good causes bury good poetry. Even her "Mass for the Day of St. Thomas Didymus" strikes me as pulpit oratory sprinkled with omnipresent "we's"—a word that the poet should use more sparingly. Poetry should entice and not force us to acceptance.

[Review of *Light Up the Cave*]   Rochelle Ratner**

As in her previous prose collection, Levertov is still "The Poet in the World," intertwining memories of childhood, poetics, and political views—often in a single essay. One sees much maturation since the earlier book. Even if her poetic concepts were formulated in the 1950s, they are all the more crucial today when many poets write in open forms "without much sense of why they do so or of what those forms demand." On the political level, her deepened understanding is reflected in the brilliant exploration "On the Edge of Darkness: What Is Political Poetry?" If other pieces are too heavily didactic, particularly in the section titled "Political Commentary," one still appreciates them as part of Levertov's total outlook. A vital book.

*From *America* 148 (29 January 1983), 75–76. Reprinted with the permission of America Press, Inc., 106 West 56th Street, New York, NY 10019. © America Press 1983.
**Reprinted with permission from *Library Journal* 106 (1 September 1981), 1632.

[Review of *Light Up the Cave*]   Daniel Berrigan, S.J.*

The hallmark of Denise Levertov's prose is something so simple and elusive as clear-eyed common sense. In the nature of things, so esoteric a virtue has not been grandly rewarded. Common sense? Mainline writers, along with their multicorporate pushers, have stampeded toward the rainbow named Avarice; others have shown a sorrowful, even despairing obsession with the Confession That Bares All.

Levertov is aware of the implications here, destructive as they are of political understanding and writers' craft. And of life itself, as in writers who have constructed a game called despair; and played it, bullet to head.

She takes up such matters, despair, anomie, political indifference, matters which most writers today prefer to keep decently out of sight and mind. She analyzes despair and its practitioners, and those who justify it as a resource. And by a parallel right instinct, she avoids the rapacious rush to trivialize life, to bring it in line with a desperate and trivial culture.

She is that rara avis, a poet, a political writer, very much a woman. These are the poles of her art as of her existence. She stays close to essentials, and the resolve, in the best sense, has paid off. Her writing remains wonderfully contemporary, it walks with us, illumines the journey of conscience that began in civil rights days and continues on into the eighties and the antinuclear struggle.

She charts the essentials; how we grew, what mistakes we made, how we failed one another, what gains and losses percolated, boiled over. And perhaps, most important, how we've grown, and into what. ("We" being the phalanx of ages, backgrounds, hopes, tactics, that started marching in the fifties and continues till now.)

There is a measure of courage required to march and be arrested. And there is another sort of courage, intelligence, and discipline implied in setting down a record of the march, the arrests, the meaning of it all. Their tone, excitement, verve! In the lives of most who take part, there is no comparable taste of the lost American art known as community.

Her essays thus hearten young and old alike; they are a diary of our neglected soul. Norman Mailer did something like this in the sixties; but since those heady days and nights, he, like most such marchers and writers, has turned to other matters. (I remember half seriously writing Mailer in 1980, announcing that we of the Plowshares Eight were prepared to name him the chronicler of our crime and punishment. He responded by sending a [small] check to the defense committee. Otherwise, no taker.)

Levertov is still marching, still recording the march. There are dazzling skills here; they start in the feet, rhythmically implanted in mother earth, and make their way, mysterious, tingling, into hand, fingers, pen. It begins with courage, a continuity of courage, a cold stream in the temperate larger

*Reprinted with permission from *American Book Review* 5, no. 2 (January–February 1983), 14.

stream of soul. Robert Frost's contrary stream, headlong in the one direction when the rivers of a given time, and the voice of those rivers, would have us believe that "all is well."

"All is well" was the siren voice of the seventies. That the word was a lie, a blockage of soul, a numbing that threatened to turn us shortly dead—this seemed to penetrate almost no one. Many writers were ensconced on campuses where moral insolvency and bonhomie went hand in hand. A very few made it big, with what came to be known as "blockbusters." (The term, one recalls, referred to the largest of the prenuclear bombs of World War II.) Others joined the urban working class, one met them driving cabs or doing short-order cooking or cleaning or acting as security guards. A few came and went in academe, an adjunct job here and there, hewers of wood and drawers of water so to speak, untenured and unrehabilitated. They published where they could in little magazines and presses, counted themselves lucky to publish at all.

But at the same time, writers like Levertov kept to the themes, kept to the marches, kept being arrested. The big sleep was on, but some were awake through the seductive night. The questions kept them awake. Were humans, any humans, going to make it through the century? Would there be a next generation? Were we intent, as a people, on bringing down the world, and if so, by what authority, in whose name? Who was the enemy anyway? Why was all the mad intemperate talk (winnable nuclear war, limited nuclear war) coming from one side, ours; and all the talk of mitigation, dread, disarmament, coming from the "enemy"?

The questions, until recently, kept being ignored. So did the questioners, including the questioning writers like Levertov. I presume that this is her history, as it is of a few others. She tells of that comatose decade, the seventies, almost as though it hadn't existed. She marches, keeps something alive, is personally dispassionate. There was work to be done, that was all. It little mattered that the work was despised or ignored or neglected. It was simply there, as evil was, as the world was; as hope was. She is passionate only about the issues, life or death. In this she, so to speak, turns the cultural method on its head. That is to say, American writing in the seventies, both prose and poetry, was disproportionately passionate about the self, and correspondingly numb (passion not being in large supply) toward the public weal and woe. Thus was a natural balance thrown out of kilter.

In insisting on this balance, and thus restoring it, Levertov reminds me of Paul Goodman; in political sanity, in large scope and interest, in intellectual clarity—and especially in moral unabashedness. I think of her, as I recall him, unashamed to be old-fashioned and patriotic, calling the country to accounts, being (horrors!) "judgmental" toward morons and rogues in high places, linking her work to spirits like Thoreau, Emerson, Hawthorne, Melville, Mother Jones, John Brown, the Quaker chroniclers—and, in our lifetime, to the incomparable Martin Luther King and Dorothy Day. Moralists, poets, activists, pacifists, abolitionists, prolabor, propoor, prohuman, these formed her history, as ours, if we can but rise to it; living it, rising to it, testing its native decency against the manifest social indecency of war, piratical economics, hatred of the poor, racism, nouveau riche clowning, the mad mutual rhythms of waste and want.

I have not so much as mentioned the richness and scope of her literary criticism. *Multum in parvo;* the entire book is beyond praise. I think of how, in a sane time, such a book and those which preceded it, including poetry, short stories, literary essays, social criticism, would form a university course entitled something like: A Renaissance Woman of the Late Twentieth Century. But this is dreaming; it would mean crossing jealous frontiers, violating "expertise."

Meantime, for those who come on this book, there is much to ponder, much to learn. Since these essays were published, several of her themes have grown, imperceptibly and ominously, like stalactites aimed at the heart of things. The despair for instance, which she analyzes so acutely, a point of departure for a debased theory of "art at the extremes"—despair has spread, become the national mood, from sea to shining sea. Its articulations, symbols, justifications are all about, infect everything; grab and run economics, chic selfishness, parasitic evangelism. Not merely a few poets are cultivating it, but the public at large, its institutions, those who read, those who manage, the image makers. Fear at the heart; a heart of darkness, frivolity at the surface.

All this being our predicament, political responsibility, resistance, together with the recounting and pondering and exemplifying—these can no longer be viewed as a choice in a range of choices. Our options, as they say, are no longer large. The eye narrows (the choices narrow), when we look (when we refuse to look) into the medusa mirror—the Mark 12 A for example, a first-strike nuclear warhead, destroyed by eight of us in September 1980. Or when in nightmare, there slides toward us head-on the monstrous pirana, a nuclear submarine named Trident. Its prey we know. Knowing, we may choose to do nothing; which is to say, to go discreetly or wildly mad, letting fear possess us and frivolity rule our days.

Or we may, along with admirable spirits like Denise Levertov, be driven sane; by community, by conscience, by treading the human crucible.

[Review of *Oblique Prayers*]   George Economou*

Denise Levertov's sixteenth book of poetry, *Oblique Prayers*, offers her readers more of that which has captured their attention over the past three decades. The first of its four sections, "Decipherings," contains poems of

*Reprinted with permission from *World Literature Today* 59 (Summer 1985), 430.

personal reflection on such subjects as memories of topographies and lovers, a vision of departed friend and fellow poet James Wright as she rides a train through his native Ohio ("Jim / can't speak anymore, he's dead, / but I swear / he's here / making me look, he's here / angry and loving and full of *Sehnsucht*"), or a dream of a sweater, "knit by an oriole," that she finds in the woods and, upon waking, would give to James Laughlin.

"Prisoners," part two, treats historical and political themes in poems that are informed with Levertov's acute sensitivity to what keeps going wrong in the world. The third part presents fourteen poems by the contemporary French poet Jean Joubert in the original with facing translations by Levertov. Through her close and careful versions, the poet, who is preparing a book-length selection of Joubert's work, introduces him to an American readership. The last section, "Of God and the Gods," consisted of meditative lyrics that are more concerned with divine immanence than with transcendence, as the jacket copy proclaims. The lead poem in this part, "Of Rivers," illustrates this admirably and represents Levertov at her best—perceiving and pursuing rather than preaching.

> Rivers remember
> in the pulse of their springs,
> in curl and slide and onrush
> lakeward and seaward,
> a touch
> shuddering them forth,
> a voice
> intoning them into
> their ebbing and flood:
> fingertip, breath
> of god or goddess in whom
> their fealty rests
> rendered by being unceasingly
> the pilgrim conversation of waterflesh.
>
> That remembrance
> gives them their way
> to know, in unknowing flowing,
> the God of the gods, whom the gods
> themselves have not imagined.

It is remarkable that *Oblique Prayers*, like most of its predecessors, shows few signs of any changes or challenges to the pieties and poetics Levertov has embraced since her early career. Such steadfastness has attracted and kept an audience for Levertov, but it also produces a troubling predictability that can be countered only by a newly taken risk or direction.

[Review of *Breathing the Water*]   Margaret Randall*

Four strong poets.** Four poets who speak out of a breadth of female experience and vision. Each has a particular voice and uses it without looking back. Levertov and Piercy especially move through a broad range of concerns, listening to the inner sounding as well as to the larger, more political concerns. Yet perhaps the only particularity these poets share is that energy of naming that emerges from each one's commitment to a retrieval of memory; and, truly, few strong women poets today do not share this. . . .

Memory is retrieved in Denise Levertov's *Breathing the Water,* and there are moments of connection with Gallagher's voice; but Levertov is both stronger and wilder, more explosively contained and—when she lets go—more dazzling. Speaking, as well, of travelers and rivers, of the woman's life in its deepening reflection, she says: " 'You give me / my life,' she said to the just-written poems, / long-legged foals surprised to be standing . . . But the traveler's words / are leaven. They work in the poet. / The river swiftly / goes on braiding its heavy tresses, / brown and flashing, / as far as the eye can see." Levertov takes risks also in her line breaks and juxtaposition of language.

Particularly moving are a series of poems written to friends who have died young, or a sister who may be dead only in her relationship to what we understand as the world. I am referring to "In Memory: After a Friend's Sudden Death," "Missing Beatrice," and "To Olga." The reverent physicality of the first poem is as successful as any I have read. In "To Olga," as in so much of Levertov's work, the poem ends once, then again—and perhaps yet again. The poet takes another risk and wins. Death is her terrain, as well, in "During a Son's Dangerous Illness." The incomprehensible fact of a child dying before a parent becomes a brilliant metaphor for the unanswerable question: "Parent, child—death ignores / protocol, a sweep of its cape brushes / this one or that one at random / into the dust; it was / not even looking. / What becomes / of the past if the future / snaps off, brittle, / the present left as a jagged edge / opening on nothing?"

This poet has been around for a while; she has published seventeen fine books of poetry before this one. She consistently reveals a fierceness crafted to perfection yet clothed in a particular enigmatic intention understandably difficult to label or contain. Recently, one critic termed her "Christian" (with a capital C). I disagree. Perhaps the best disavowal comes from a poem in this new collection: "Much moves in and out of open windows / when our attention is somewhere else, / just as our souls move in and out of our bodies sometimes. / Everyone used to know this, / but for a hundred years or more / we've been losing our memories" ("Window-Blind").

*Reprinted with permission from *Belles Lettres* 4, no. 1 (Fall 1988), 8.
**Randall reviews current books by Tess Gallagher, Linda Pastan, and Marge Piercy, as well as Levertov.

In Levertov's coming to terms with memory, she is clear about how and why it is ripped from us. For me, her most memorable work combines her fine-tuned human sensibility with what some would call more political concerns, as in "Every Day" and "Carapace." And I would like to quote a third, "Poet Power," in full:

> Riding by taxi, Brooklyn to Queens,
> a grey spring day. The Hispanic driver,
> when I ask, "Es usted Mexicano?" tells me
> No, he's an exile from Uruguay. And I say,
> "The only other Uruguayan I've met
> was a writer—maybe
> you know his name?—
>   Mario Benedetti?"
>   And he takes both hands
> off the wheel and swings round,
> glittering with joy: "*Benedetti!*
> Mario Benedetti!!"
>   There are
> hallelujas in his voice—
> we execute a perfect
> figure 8 on the shining highway,
> and rise aloft, high above traffic, flying
> all the rest of the way in the blue sky, azul, azul!

"Making Peace" is another of these poems where the internal and not-so-external-as-we-might-hope planes merge and function as a whole. "Peace, not only / the absence of war" she demands, reminding the reader of her contention that peace is hard to imagine, so contextualized has it been in threats of war.

Song of Herself

Diane Wakoski*

Others will speak of her spirit's tendrils reaching
almost palpably into the world;

but I will remember her body's unexpected beauty
seen in the fragrant redwood sauna . . . (p. 23)

American poetry, like American culture, has manifested from the beginning an unlikely combination of the material and the spiritual. We are pragmatists, grounded in our physical world, but for some reason we do not accept this as a limitation. We continue to see the spiritual rising out of the

*Reprinted with the author's permission from *Women's Review of Books* 5 (February 1988), 7–8.

material, and our great poets like Whitman talk as if God were in all of us intermingled with the natural world:

> I have said that the soul is not more
>   than the body,
> And I have said that the body is not
>   more than the soul,
> And nothing, not God, is greater to one
>   than one's self is . . .

In his excellent book, *Kenneth Patchen and American Mysticism* (University of North Carolina Press, 1984), Ray Nelson traces the Whitman tradition and shows the mainstream poets of our culture reaching for a religious experience which is not doctrinally located, though the Quaker religion has in fact influenced more than its share of our writers. Levertov is no exception to this, and in her most recent collection of poems she can no longer conceal the fact that she is a religious poet, though like Whitman and Emerson she certainly has experienced no conversion or long-time adherence to a particular dogma or theology or even an organized religion.

Levertov's poetry, like most American mysticism, is grounded in Christianity, but like Whitman and other American mystics her discovery of God is the discovery of God in herself, and an attempt to understand how that self is a "natural" part of the world, intermingling with everything pantheistically, ecologically, socially, historically and, for Levertov, always lyrically. Perhaps her search has from the beginning looked like an aesthetic rather than religious quest, though from the beginning she has spoken of God and never seemed to be unwilling to label her own journey as spiritual. But until now her somewhat inconsistent politics, and a stance which certainly embraces no specific religious doctrine or set of religious observances, have confused the issue.

In *Breathing the Water* the linking of body and soul through God is made so clear that even the most obtuse reader can see it. In meditating on the religious mystic Lady Julian of Norwich, Levertov asks that we see the world as a hazlenut placed in the hand in order to understand the relationship between God and humanity:

> God for a moment in our history
> placed in that five-fingered
> human nest
> the macrocosmic egg, sublime paradox,
> brown hazelnut of All that Is—
> made, and belov'd, and preserved.
> As still, waking each day within
> our microcosm, we find it, and ourselves. (p. 78)

It hasn't always been so obvious what Levertov was up to, and some of the pleasures of this book come from seeing the focusing of a lifetime career of writing beautiful, lyric poems, interspersed with militant political ones.

What becomes apparent in *Breathing the Water* is that a distinct mystical religious vision has informed the poetry from the very beginning, and a struggle to understand God's meaning and intentions for the world.

Levertov's early poetry was a celebration, among other things, of the sexual, Dionysian creative powers of her feminine self and world. In one of my favorites of her lyrical invocations to the powers that be, "To the Snake," from *With Eyes at the Back of Our Heads* (1960), she hangs a snake around her neck and sings to it, telling it that while she reassured her "companions" that the snake was "harmless" in spite of its "cold pulsing throat" which "hissed" at her, she herself "had no certainty" but knew that she needed to hold it there. She releases the snake back to nature, where it "faded into the pattern / of grass and shadows," and concludes the poem "and I returned / smiling and haunted, to a dark morning." In this poem, as in Whitman's lines in *Song of Myself*, "I bequeath myself to the dirt to grow from the grasses I love, / If you want me again look for me under your bootsoles," Levertov longs to identify herself with the natural world, to mingle with it, even though she is not quite sure it will not harm her.

The second section of *Breathing the Water* opens with a poem called "Zeroing In." A man and a woman compare the dangers of life to walking in a landscape dotted with bogs. The man tells the story of a dog he had as a boy which had to be put down because it bit a child who touched an injured spot on its head; at the end of the poem the woman says

> "Yes, we learn that.
> It's not terror, it's pain we're talking about:
> those places in us, like your dog's bruised head,
> that are bruised forever, that time
> never assuages, never." (p. 19)

Life, the snake, in the earlier poem, is only potentially dangerous; in this last book, Levertov shows us how dangerous the natural forces are. Yet no knowledge keeps the speaker from touching the bruised spot, just as no warning keeps the young poet from putting the snake around her neck.

Levertov's single best collection of poems, *Life in the Forest* (1978), included a series of poems about the last year of her mother's life, which was lived in Mexico; that semitropical landscape becomes for Levertov an embodiment of the archetypal Garden. It is in this book that we first begin to see how seriously Levertov has pursued the myth of the Garden from her early sense of herself, like Eve, daring to mingle with it, embracing the snake as a necklace in spite of her friends' warnings. The constant temptations of life never deter her, though she always suspects their danger. In "Death in Mexico" her vision of what that danger is emerges. Describing the English-style country garden which her mother has created around her house in Mexico and cultivated carefully over the years, Levertov depicts its rapid crumbling and disintegration after only a few weeks of neglect during her mother's terminal illness. The landscape is returning to its natural jungle state, and in its ruins Levertov sees a primitive reality.

> Gardens vanish. She was an alien here,
> as I am.
>
> . . . .
>   Old gods
> took back their own.

This is what must be feared; that in death, in each personal death, civilization as we know it dies. Perhaps the "old gods" are the body, the physical world, always there and always with a primitive power and potentially dangerous capability. Like all mystics, Levertov believes in a God or the knowledge of a God within oneself which is beyond doctrine and organized religion. Sometimes this God takes the face of art or civilization or government or human will, but the marrying of those two elements, the body and the spirit, must be a marrying of the "old gods" and the personal God. "Life in the forest" will always be dangerous and primitive, but we cannot resist the beauty of the snake.

One of the loveliest poems in *Breathing the Water* is "The Well."

> At sixteen, I believed the moonlight
> could change me if it would.
>   I moved my head
> on the pillow, even moved my bed
> as the moon slowly
> crossed the open lattice.

In this poem, a kind of latter-day "Eve of St. Agnes," Levertov tells us how she religiously (my word; she uses "diligently") "moonbathed" as others sunbathe. On the dark nights she permitted herself to sleep deeply; it was the bathing in darkness, not the sleepless moonlit nights, which left her feeling refreshed "and if not beautiful / filled with some other power." That "power" by implication is the power of poetry, of creation, and comes neither out of sun nor moon nor any kind of light, but from darkness.

What is this "well"? Is it the unknowable? As a poet who writes often about light, Levertov offers us this puzzling image to work with. As a spiritual seeker, even at sixteen, "moonbathing" did not change her as she wished; but when she allowed herself back into the well of the unknown darkness, she was renewed. The "Old gods" which take over in so much of Levertov's vision, as she describes them in "Death in Mexico," are "obdurate, blind, all-seeing." They "admit / no regret" and "bitterness is irrelevant."

Perhaps one of the reasons no one has noticed that this clergyman's daughter has really been writing religious poetry all these years is that she has always spoken an orthodox Christianity of love while simultaneously offering this vision of the attractive yet terrible dark world of the "Old gods." Sometimes it is the real world of the "dark morning" Levertov has to return to after the light ecstasy of experiencing the snake, sometimes it is the unfathomable cruelty of war or disease; sometimes it is only sleep, and sometimes it is the stone stairway to the spiritual itself, the Jacob's Ladder. Her ambivalence tests the reader, must constantly puzzle the reader. Is this darkness the unknown? Or God? Or the opposite of God? Is moonbathing a failed spiritual exercise but still necessary? Is the "dark morning" beautiful, or only inevitable?

The vision of a marriage of body and spirit is what allows Levertov to move beyond her politics, her Christian morality and most of all her Romantic fear of the darkness. Levertov offers earth images, Dionysian images, of fertility coming from the buried seed, the physical not the spiritual. "In Memory: After a Friend's Sudden Death," quoted at the beginning of this essay, continues

> And I will speak
> not of her work, her words, her search
> for a new pathway, her need
>
> to heedfully walk and sing through dailiness
> noticing stones and flowers,
>
> but of the great encompassing *Aah!* she would utter,
> entering slowly, completely, into the welcoming whirlpool. (p. 23)

This is the whirlpool of the redwood sauna, but it is also the attraction of the snake, or the darkness at the bottom of a well, which allows renewing sleep.

Like Whitman, Levertov implies that "to die is different from what any one supposed, and luckier"; these scenes of darkness, as we fall from the Garden into the possibly dangerous world, are irresistible—like the snake, "glinting arrowy / gold scales," with "the weight of you on my shoulders, / and the whispering silver of your dryness / . . . close at my ears—" which will give her enough pleasure to face "the dark morning." And it is this interaction between the light (the world of breath) and the dark (the refreshment of nothingness, or the water at the bottom of the well) which makes Levertov's mystical vision a religious one. For her, God is the author of paradoxes.

Like Whitman, Levertov's religion is the religion of self, but a cosmic self whose God or approach to God comes through the marrying of body and spirit. It is the human hand that holds God's hazlenut and, as Lady Julian does, understands the immensity of God's love. Like Lady Julian, Levertov refuses to be confounded by war and the darkness of human misery; she tries, as in "The Well," to see it as a source of rest. Her struggle is Lady Julian's struggle, and Job's, to understand God in order to be able to accept contradiction.

In the title poem of *The Jacob's Ladder* (1961), Levertov wrote "The stairway is not / a thing of gleaming strands . . . It is of stone." In the poem, the angels are on the stone steps, brushing their wings against her. In the same collection there is an earlier poem, also called "The Well." In that poem, "the Muse" wades into dark water, and Levertov finds the word *water* spelled out on her left palm. The purpose of Levertov's long journey as a poet and a spiritual being has been to learn how to "breathe the water," the "water" written earlier on her palm, the water of life, of baptism; how to understand the darkness of the forest she must return to after sensing the beauty of the snake around her neck or bathing in moonlight. It is the fusion of these two that has always been the goal of Levertov's vision: to find a God in this intermingling of flesh and spirit, something, as she says in "Variation and Reflection on a Poem by Rilke," which will "let you flow back into all creation."

Essays

Inside and Outside in the Poetry of Denise Levertov

Diana Collecott*

I

"We awake in the same moment to ourselves and to things." This sentence from Jacques Maritain was chosen by the Objectivist poet George Oppen as an epigraph to his book *The Materials*.[1] Its presence there accents a paradox central to some of the most interesting American writing today. "Objectivism" is a term very loosely used at present, and I can think of no better way of giving it definition, than by recalling Louis Zukofsky's gloss on the word *Objective* in the special number of *Poetry Chicago* he edited in 1930. First he takes a definition from Optics; "An Objective—the lens bringing the rays from an object to a focus." Then he offers its "Use extended to poetry." "Desire for that which is objectively perfect."[2] The Objectivist movement initiated by Zukofsky in the thirties was a programmatic formulation of the poetic theory of Ezra Pound and the poetic practice of William Carlos Williams over the previous twenty years. In particular, it derived from Pound's effort, through the Imagist movement, to replace what he called "the obscure reveries / Of the inward gaze" with a poetry concentrated on outward things. Hardness, edge, were the qualities that recommended the work of H. D. and Marianne Moore to him; he praised in their poems "the arid clarity . . . of *le tempérament de l'Américaine*."[3]

Yet neither Pound nor Zukofsky was so ignorant as to emphasise the outward eye to the exclusion of what goes on inside the seeing mind. Indeed, Zukofsky claims that, among the Objectivists, "Writing occurs which is the detail, not the mirage, of seeing, of thinking with the things as they exist. . . . Shapes suggest themselves, and the mind senses and receives awareness" (*Prepositions,* 20). It is implied here that the eye is the focal point in a two-way process. This vivid commerce between inside and outside is a distinctive feature of the poets of the Black Mountain school, who have assimilated the discoveries of the Objectivists and their predecessors in the American *avant garde*. Consider Robert Creeley's

*Reprinted with permission from *Critical Quarterly* 22 (1980), 157–69.

> I keep to myself such
> measures as I care for,
> daily the rocks
> accumulate position[4]

Here, interpenetration between the inner world of the poet and the outer world of objects, establishes a mode of writing which Denise Levertov has made hers also.

II

Denise Levertov is an American by adoption. She was born near London, of Russian and Welsh parentage, in 1923. In 1948 she married the American writer Mitchell Goodman, and went to live in the United States. By then, she had already published a first book of verse in England; Kenneth Rexroth has described her, at her debut in the Britain of Dylan Thomas, as "the baby of the New Romanticism."[5] These early poems were accomplished precisely insofar as they were "obscure reveries / Of the inward gaze": weighted with symbolism, they have a dream-like immobility. One is reminded of Charles Olson's claim that Williams, following in the footsteps of Whitman, taught American poets to *walk*.[6] No "new measure" had reached British writers at that time. Hence Levertov recalls: "Marrying an American and coming to live here while still young was very stimulating to me as a writer, for it necessitated the finding of new rhythms in which to write, in accordance with new rhythms of life and speech."[7] After first finding affinities with academic writers such as Richard Wilbur, Levertov began the search for new rhythms in the milieu of the Black Mountain poets. With Rexroth's encouragement, she submitted herself to a fresh apprenticeship with the work of Williams; she wrote of this, around 1960: "I feel the stylistic influence of William Carlos Williams, while perhaps too evident in my work of a few years ago, was a very necessary and healthful one, without which I could not have developed from a British Romantic with almost Victorian background, to an American poet of any vitality" (*The New American Poetry*, 441). "Vitality" strikes a keynote here. It reminds us of Robert Duncan's contention that the essential difference between American and British poetry in our era is that the first is *active*, it moves. "In American poetry," he writes, "the striding syllables show an aesthetic based on energies."[8] For Denise Levertov, the main transmitter of this aesthetic was Charles Olson's essay "Projective Verse"—an essay, incidentally, which Williams thought so summative of his life's work, that he included it intact as a chapter of his *Autobiography*. The most influential formulation of this essay is not Olson's own, but a statement attributed to Edward Dahlberg: "one perception must immediately and directly lead to a further perception."[9] Thus, a couple of decades after Zukofsky's "Objective," the new school of poets insisted afresh on the *act* of perception, or rather on a series of acts which would shape the poem after their kind.

III

One poem of Levertov's which exemplifies these new influences, and her own discovery of "new rhythms," is the title piece of *Overland to the Islands,* the volume published by Jargon Books in 1958.

> Let's go—much as that dog goes,
> intently haphazard. The
> Mexican light on a day that
> —"smells like autumn in Connecticut"
> makes iris ripples on his
> black gleaming fur—and that too
> is as one would desire—a radiance
> consorting with the dance.
>   Under his feet
> rocks and mud, his imagination, sniffing,
> engaged in its perceptions—dancing
> edgeways, there's nothing
> the dog disdains on his way,
> nevertheless he
> keeps moving, changing
> pace and approach but
> not direction—"every step an arrival."[10]

This poem is "about" movement. It begins with the casual invitation "Let's go" and then introduces the dog, as an example of movement; thereafter, poet, poem and reader move with him, "intently haphazard"; one could almost say that the dog *is* the projective movement of the poem: his interest leads us from one perception to the next. Levertov has no inhibition about presenting the dog, "his imagination, sniffing, / engaged in its perceptions," as a model for the poet; but neither does she attempt to press this conclusion upon us. She does not stop to do this, as she too "keeps moving."

Anyone familiar with the poetry of Carlos Williams will feel at home here. In such poems as "Pastoral" or "The Poor" or "By the Road to the Contagious Hospital," Williams is equally undemanding in relation to his environment, equally unwilling to press a comparison; he is content to record, and move on. The very dog of Levertov's poem is known to us from the opening lines of *Paterson* Book I, where Williams declares his intent "To make a start, / out of particulars," and slyly presents himself as "Sniffing the trees, / just another dog / among a lot of dogs."[11] Even the mannerisms in Levertov's poem—the quotation in the fourth line, the parenthesis by which she succeeds in all but keeping herself out of the poem ("and that too / is as one would desire")—are redolent of the master.

In a comment on "Overland to the Islands" Levertov says: "The last phrase, 'every step an arrival,' is quoted from Rilke, and here, unconsciously, I was evidently trying to unify for myself my sense of the pilgrim way with my new American, objectivist-influenced, pragmatic, and sensuous longing for the Here and Now. . . ."[12] Later, Levertov identifies what she calls here "the pilgrim way" as "a personal fiction." It is certainly a *supreme* fiction, in Stevens' sense, since when she describes life as a pilgrimage, she is interested in the pursuit of a reality beyond that of the everyday, the "Here and Now." Yet Levertov's very sure-footedness in the *Here and Now* (the title incidentally, of her first American collection) makes her refuse to leave behind the contingent world in pursuit of a transcendent reality. Thus the common dog, with its iridescently "gleaming fur," can act as an avatar to her, but thus also, the "rocks and mud" beneath its feet are essential to its imaginative progress.

IV

Denise Levertov's belief that one's inner discoveries should move hand in hand with one's outward perceptions has been the main impulse of her experiments in writing and her discussions of poetics. "Some Notes on Organic Form," dated 1965, is one of her earliest published statements on a rethought Romanticism. In it, she emphasises the concept that "there *is* a form in all things (and in our experience) which the poet can discover and reveal" (*The Poet in the World,* 7).

This essentially Platonic version of the artist's task is perhaps the last thing that one would expect from a confessedly "American, objectivist-influenced, pragmatic" writer. It leads Levertov to revive Hopkins's terms *inscape* and *instress,* and to add: "In thinking of the process of poetry as I know it, I extend the use of these words, which he seems to have used mainly in reference to sensory phenomena, to include intellectual and emotional experience as well . . ." (*The Poet in the World,* 7). In another essay, she goes further than this, and argues that, just as "the *being* of things has inscape" so too does the poet's own being, and that the act of transmitting to others the inscape of things, is also the act of awakening one's own being (*The Poet in the World,* 17).

It is by such steps that we arrive at that flow between inside and outside that Williams characterized as "an interpenetration, both ways." In the opening of *Paterson* Book II, "Sunday in the Park," Williams presents such interpenetration in overtly sexual terms; "Dr. Paterson" is speaking:

Outside
          outside myself
                    there is a world,
he rumbled, subject to my incursions
—a world
          (to me) at rest,
                    which I approach
concretely—
          The scene's the Park
          upon the rock,

                    female to the city
            —upon whose body Paterson instructs his thoughts
            (concretely) (*Paterson*, 57)

Here Paterson's role in relation to the rest of the world is obviously masculine: the objective world is "subject" to him; some lines further on, he "starts,
possessive, through the trees"; yet within a page, he is describing himself as
not merely possessive but "passive-possessive," and he seems to present this
as a proper condition for the poet.

There are, in Levertov's writings, an almost equal number of descriptions of the poetic process as a passive and so-to-say "female" condition, as
there are equations for a more aggressive and "male" activity. She appears to
have taken to heart Williams's advice, in a letter he wrote her, that a poet
must be "in essence a woman as well as a man."[13] Indeed, she comments
from her own experience, with unusual honesty: "Perhaps I don't know
myself very well, for at times I see myself as having boundless energy and a
savage will, and at other times as someone easily tired and so impressionable
as to be, like Keats, weighed down almost unbearably, by the identities
around me . . ." (*The Poet in the World*, 216).

                                    V

This combination of receptivity and creative energy appears to be essential not only to Denise Levertov's identity as a poet, but also to her sense of
herself. In a comparatively recent poem, she records her delight at an interpretation of her name in its Hebrew meanings. D or Daleth means, "door";
hence we get:

        entrance, exit,
        way through of
        giving and receiving
        which are one[14]

"Giving and receiving" are capable of becoming "one" in an American poetic
which can incorporate somatic awareness—the body's sense of itself, as well
as of the objects around it—in the disposition of words on the page.

Levertov has clearly cultivated such awareness at a subtle level. She
speaks of *waiting* for the poem "in that intense passivity, that passive intensity, that passionate patience that Keats named Negative Capability" (*The
Poet in the World*, 29). Reading her poetry and prose we realize that she
writes best from that state of restful alertness in which, Wordsworth claimed,
"we see into the heart of things." Hence "vision," "inscape," "revelation" are
keywords in her criticism, and she frequently cites such writers as Coleridge, Emerson, Rilke, in trying to identify the special value of such insights
to poetic composition. One such passage, from Carlyle, is worth quoting, as
it seems to express her own experience: "A musical thought is one spoken by
a mind that has penetrated to the inmost heart of the thing; detected the

inmost mystery of it, namely the melody that lies hidden in it; the inward harmony of coherence which is its soul, whereby it exists, and has a right to be, here in this world" ("Prospectus," *Sartor Resartus;* cited in *The Poet in the World,* 17). "To write is to listen" says Levertov, an analogy with Picasso's "To draw is to shut your eyes and sing" (*The Poet in the World,* 229). Carlyle, Picasso, Levertov, all imply that the value they seek in art is *inside* as well as *outside,* that the song is "there" ready to be transcribed by him who hears it, that the composition exists already only to be seen by the artist.

VI

For Levertov, this knowledge does not undermine the outward senses, but substantiates them. Poetry requires, she says, the "utmost attentive-ness," and the eye has a crucial part to play in bringing her poems into being. In "Pleasures," for instance, seeing is a means of discovering the hidden properties of ordinary objects:

> I like to find
> what's not found
> at once, but lies
>
> within something of another nature,
> in repose, distinct.

The rest of the poem gives specific instances of this kind of discovery of the unknown within the known:

> Gull feathers of glass, hidden
>
> in white pulp: the bones of squid
> which I pull out and lay
> blade by blade on the draining board—
>
> > tapered as if for swiftness, to pierce
> > the heart, but fragile, substance
> > belying design.[15]

Such lines are themselves acts of attention: their breaks indicate her careful scrutiny ("lay / blade by blade"); they record her reading of nature's book. We are reminded irresistibly of Thoreau, one of the American authors to whom Levertov constantly returns, and of Emerson, whose "Ask the fact for the form" was almost a slogan to the writers of the Black Mountain school.

Creeley, in fact, coined the expression: "Form is never more than exten-sion of content." Levertov amends this to read: "Form is never more than a *revelation* of content" (*The Poet in the World,* 13). Thus the composition of the poem itself regarded as a vehicle for revelation; indeed, Levertov argues that the very spaces on the page help the mind to fresh insights into the nature of things.

VII

If poetry is to become a simple act of transcription from nature, the poet must abandon his traditional role of supremacy over things. These writers believe that meaning is pre-existent in things: it does not depend on structures of thought and feeling imposed by the poet. Thus simple contingency offers a means to transcend itself, and Levertov can write: "A poetry that merely describes, and that features the trivial egotism of the writer (an egotism that obstructs any profound self-explorations) is not liberated from contingency . . ." (*The Poet in the World*, 95). In castigating egotism here, Levertov echoes, perhaps, Olson's account of the modern poet's necessary relation to the world, for which he invents the term "Objectism." "Objectism [he writes in "Projective Verse"] is the getting rid of the lyrical interference of the individual as ego, of the "subject" and his soul, that peculiar presumption by which western man has interposed himself between what he is as a creature of nature . . . and those other creations of nature which we may, with no derogation, call objects" (*The Poetics of the New American Poetry*, 156). Olson's prime example of "Objectism" is W. C. Williams. Williams once described in a letter to Marianne Moore a youthful experience in which, he said, "everything became a unit and at the same time a part of myself." "As a reward for this anonymity," Williams concluded, "I feel as much a part of things as trees or stones."[16]

Joseph Hillis Miller is surely right to see this "anonymity," this abandonment of the separate ego, as an abandonment also of that separation between the inner world of the subject and the outer world of objects which is a debased inheritance from Romanticism. "In Williams's poetry [Miller writes] there is no description of private inner experience. There is also no description of objects which are external to the poet's mind. Nothing is external to his mind. His mind overlaps with things; things overlap with his mind."[17] Thus Williams may be placed at an extreme remove from the young T. S. Eliot who found in the philosophy of F. H. Bradley a congenial account of the prison of subjectivity: "My external sensations are no less private to myself than are my thoughts or my feelings. In either case my experience falls within my own circle, a circle closed on the outside; . . . In brief, regarded as an existence which appears in a soul, the whole world for each is peculiar and private to that soul."[18] This ontological distinction between Williams and Eliot informs the modes of their writing and the attitudes they have to their readers. Where Eliot claims the artist's prerogative to pre-select experience for the reader, Williams complains that "There is a constant barrier between the reader and his consciousness of immediate contact with the world."[19] He thus takes his stand with Whitman, who told his reader in "Song of Myself":

> You shall not look through my eyes either, nor take things from me,
> You shall listen to all sides and filter them for yourself . . .

For Levertov, as for Whitman and Williams, experience is a continuum. Geoffrey Thurley recognises this, when he says of her work: "In place of the refined poetess sitting isolated among the teacups, socially aligned with her visitors but privately alienated from them, we encounter . . . the poet-housewife/mother . . . whose living-space coincides with [her] aesthetic space. The old separation of the *avant garde*, in which the private world of poetic experience excluded the actual grubby world of social living, is replaced by a unified continuum."[20]

VIII

In Levertov, as in Williams, there is no blurring of the edge between self and objects, but it is not a cutting edge: she is as free as he is of the *angst* that has dogged Romantic writers up to our own day. Hence the attitude with which she approaches the world is essentially one of wonder, of delight. Her poems bear out Williams's dictum that "There is a long history in each one of us that comes as not only a reawakening but a repossession when confronted by this world."[21]

For Levertov, writing is a way of recording such acts of "reawakening," of "repossession"; it is radiant with *recognition:*

> That's it, [she exclaims in "Matins"]
> that's joy, it's always
> a recognition, the known
> appearing fully itself, and
> more itself than one knew (*The Jacob's Ladder*, 57)

The perpetual problem of a poetry of recognitions is that it may only rarely get beyond exclamation. This poem, for instance, is punctuated by ejaculations of "the authentic!" and simply offers us fragments of experience that have struck the poet as in some way "authentic." Such writing remains obstinately Imagist, and lays itself open to the criticism of an early American review of Imagism, that: "Poem after poem of this sort is full of the simple wonder of a child picking up pebbles on the beach. . . ."[22] However, if we can accept such naivete as, in itself, "authentic," then we can begin to appreciate that it does not simply negate all our previous expectations of poetry, but offers a distinctively new mode.

IX

In order to describe this mode, I find myself falling back on Roman Jakobson's well-known distinction between the metaphoric and metonymic poles of discourse.[23] You will recall that Jakobson associates metaphor, the assertion of similarity, with poetry, and with Romantic modes of experience. Metaphor and simile record the Romantic poet's efforts to identify *likeness* in the world about him, to impose his meanings on it, to span the felt distance between subject and object. Metonymy, on the other hand, rests on *contigu-*

ity; it is enough for things to be associated in space for them to be placed together in discourse. Thus Jakobson identifies metonymy as the pole towards which prose, and in particular the literature of Realism, tends.

We can see then that Henry James, who argues that "Life is all inclusion and confusion; art is all discrimination and selection," would be inclined to metaphor and symbolism, by Jakobson's definition; whereas Balzac, who expressed his intent to "set forth in order the facts," is metonymic or Realist—if we may assume that, for him, the order in which the facts naturally occur is a sufficient order. Williams must undoubtedly be categorised with Balzac, since he overtly refuses the egotist's or artist's privilege of discrimination, in favour of transcription. "What is there to select?" he asks, "It *is.* . . ."[24]

Williams explicitly rejected metaphor and simile early in his poetic career. Here is a significant passage from the Prologue to *Kora in Hell* (1917):

> Although it is a quality of the imagination that it seeks to *place together* those things which have a common relationship, yet the coining of similes is a pastime of a very low order. . . . Much more keen is that power which discovers in things those inimitable particles of dissimilarity to all other things which are the peculiar perfections of the thing in question. . . . This *loose linking* of one thing with another has the effects of a destructive power little to be guessed at. . . . All is confusion, yet it comes from a hidden desire for the dance. (*Imaginations,* 18–20; my emphases)

This is a charter for the metonymic writer. It lies behind all Williams's efforts to establish a new mode of writing, in the face of Eliot's tremendous success as a symbolist poet. Confronted by that success, he wrote in *Spring and All:* "how easy to slip / into the old mode, how hard to cling / to the advance" (*Imaginations,* 103). The "old mode" is the mode of symbolism, of metaphor; the "advance," as Williams saw it, was the move beyond Romantic dualism into the metonymic mode.

The alternative to metaphor, in Williams's view, was a stress on particulars—hence the well-known slogan "No ideas but in things"; and hence, too, the injunction of *Paterson* Book III:

> —of this, make it of *this,* this
> this, this, this, this. (*Paterson,* 168)

Multiplicity, the listing of things without violating their particular existence, becomes a deliberate strategy, and is responsible for the shape of Williams's poems on the page. "By the brokenness of his composition," he wrote, "the poet makes himself master of a certain weapon which he could possess himself of in no other way" (*Imaginations,* 16).

The first poem of *Spring and All* demonstrates this strategy in its local detail:

> All along the road the reddish
> purplish, forked, upstanding twiggy
> stuff of bushes and small trees . . .

It stops short of personification even though "sluggish / dazed spring approaches"; the poem continues:

> They enter the new world naked
> cold, uncertain of all
> save that they enter. (*Imaginations*, 95)

The reader may extrapolate from these lines a metaphor for the immigrant's
bleak prospect of America, or for the baby's arrival in the world, but he is not
entitled to do so by the mode of the poem.

This is a major difficulty for English students coming to Williams from a
training in reading Eliot's poetry or indeed any poetry in the European
metaphoric tradition—and in that we must include such writers as Wallace
Stevens and Robert Frost. Because Williams is a metonymic poet, his work
often seems, to the uninitiated, close to prose. His own development, indeed, involved a rejection of Keats's idiom in favour of the kind of Whitmanesque jottings that Allen Ginsberg has referred to as "prose-seeds."[25]
Metonymy was the natural medium in which he could set down the contigu-
ous patterns of his perceptions. Hence the necessity to his work, and to that
of the writers who followed him, of typographic freedom, of open form,
which allows the "prose-seeds" to establish their own growth.

X

This is the context of Levertov's belief that "Form is never more than a
revelation of content," and of her own poetic practice. In her writing, as in
Williams's, there is no *depth*, no measurable distance between what is said
and what is meant. In this, both differ from the most well-intentioned of the
Transcendentalists. Tony Tanner has pointed out the strain inherent in Thoreau's attempts to "move from the surface detail to the Universal benevolent
One which underlay it . . .," the evidence in his writing of "an effort of
penetration, a will to seduce the larger meaning out of the small particular."[26]

Levertov seems, like Williams, to have achieved a concatenation of the
"surface detail" with the "larger meaning." Her poetry may be said to be *all
surface*. I have attempted to show that this is not a matter of style alone, but
of the poet's state of awareness. Thus she writes:

> . . . life is in me, a love for
> what happens, for
> the surfaces that are their own
> interior life[27]

In passages such as this, it seems to me that Williams's phrase "passive-
possessive" gets its full complement of meaning. Love is a precondition of
Levertov's relaxed relationship with herself and with things. This persists in
The Sorrow Dance at the very threshold of her poems against the Vietnam

war. My last example, "Joy," is from this volume. It has an epigraph from Thoreau, which robustly insists:

> You must love the crust of the earth on
> which you dwell. You must be able to
> extract nutriment out of a sandheap.
> You must have so good an appetite as
> this, else you will live in vain.

> Joy, the "well . . . *joyfulness* of
> joy"—"many years
> I had not known it," the woman of eighty
> said, "only remembered, till now."

> Traherne
> in dark fields.
>   On Tremont Street,
> on the Common, a raw dusk, Emerson
> "glad to the brink of fear."
>   It is objective,

> stands founded, a roofed gateway;
> we cloud-wander

> away from it, stumble
> again towards it not seeing it,

> enter cast-down, discover ourselves
> "in joy" as "in love."[28]

In this poem, the very scraps of discourse are like the crusts from which Thoreau's nutriment must be extracted. Here the contiguity is not of things, but of "prose-seeds," disparate recognitions. The poet allows them to lie, like found-objects, on the page, and to offer a sense of revelation analogous to her own.

It is in this sense that the poem *moves:* that is, it moves *us,* just as the original experience moved the poet. It also moves, as "Overland to the Islands" moved, towards a final discovery. In Levertov's words "the metric movement, the measure, is the direct expression of the movement of perception" (*The Poet in the World,* 11). Here the measure enacts the meaning as "we / cloud-wander / away from it" and "stumble again towards it." The poem approaches its meaning in just such an oblique manner—via the words and experience of others, to a direct statement ("It is objective") which recalls the signal "It quickens" of Williams's "At the Ball Game." Like Williams, Levertov seems intent on using the brokenness of things as a vehicle for wholeness, and she does indeed offer an analogy for this wholeness, close to the centre of the poem: "stands founded, a roofed gateway." Again, I restrain myself from the term "metaphor," since it seems to me that the gateway is *there,* just as the experience is there, to be entered—an entry which is not simply into the full value of the world outside, but also the full value of the world within oneself. This is what the poem ultimately "discovers" to us:

> and we discover ourselves
> "in joy" as "in love."

Notes

1. George Oppen, *The Materials* (New York: New Directions, 1962).

2. Louis Zukofsky, "An Objective," *Prepositions* (London: Rapp & Carroll, 1967), 20.

3. Ezra Pound, "A List of Books" in *Ezra Pound: Selected Prose 1909–65,* ed. W. Cookson (London: Faber & Faber, 1973), 394.

4. Robert Creeley, *Poems 1950–65* (London: Calder & Boyars, 1966), 190.

5. Kenneth Rexroth, *Assays* (New York: New Directions, 1961), 189.

6. Charles Olson, "*Paterson* (Book Five)," *Evergreen Review* 2, no. 9 (Summer 1959), 220–21.

7. Denise Levertov, "Biographical Note" in *The New American Poetry,* ed. Donald M. Allen (New York: Grove Press, 1960), 441.

8. Robert Duncan, "Notes on Poetics Regarding Olson's *Maximus,*" *Black Mountain Review* (1956) in *The Poetics of the New American Poetry,* eds. Donald Allen and Warren Tallman (New York: Grove Press, 1973), 187–88.

9. Charles Olson, "Projective Verse," *The Poetics of the New American Poetry,* 149.

10. Denise Levertov, "Overland to the Islands," *The Jacob's Ladder* (New York: New Directions, 1961), 73.

11. William Carlos Williams, *Paterson* (New York: New Directions, 1963), n.p.

12. Denise Levertov, "The Sense of Pilgrimage," *The Poet in the World* (New York: New Directions, 1973), 69.

13. William Carlos Williams, letter of 23 August 1954, in "Letters to Denise Levertov," *Stonybrook* 1, no. 2 (1968), 163–64.

14. Denise Levertov, "To Kevin O'Leary, Wherever He Is," *Footprints* (New York: New Directions, 1972), 26.

15. Denise Levertov, *With Eyes at the Back of Our Heads* (New York: New Directions, 1960), 17–18.

16. William Carlos Williams, letter of May 1934, *The Selected Letters of William Carlos Williams,* ed. John Thirlwall (New York: McDowell, Obolensky, 1957), 147.

17. J. Hillis Miller, "Introduction," *William Carlos Williams: A Collection of Critical Essays* (Englewood Cliffs, N.J.: Prentice-Hall, 1966), 7.

18. F. H. Bradley, *Appearance and Reality,* cited in T. S. Eliot, "Notes on *The Waste Land*" in *The Collected Poems of T. S. Eliot 1909–35* (London: Faber & Faber, 1936), 84.

19. William Carlos Williams, *Spring and All* in *Imaginations,* ed. Webster Schott (New York: New Directions, 1970), 88.

20. Geoffrey Thurley, *The American Moment* (London: Edward Arnold, 1977), 119.

21. William Carlos Williams, *The Autobiography of William Carlos Williams* (New York: Random House, 1951), 19.

22. Lewis Worthington Smith, "The New Naivete," *Atlantic Monthly* (1916), cited by Glynn Hughes, *Imagism and the Imagists* (London: Oxford University Press, 1931), 67.

23. Roman Jakobson, *Fundamentals of Language* (The Hague: Mouton, rev. edn. 1975), 90–96.

24. William Carlos Williams, "Introduction" to Byron Vazakas, *Transfigured Night* (New York: Macmillan, 1946), xi.

25. Allen Ginsberg, "Notes for *Howl* and Other Poems," *The New American Poetry*, 414–15; see also *The Autobiography of William Carlos Williams*, 53.

26. Tony Tanner, "Pigment and Ether: A Comment on the American Mind," *BAAS Bulletin* 7 (1963), 40–45.

27. Denise Levertov, "Entr'acte," *To Stay Alive* (New York: New Directions, 1971), 66.

28. Denise Levertov, "Joy," *The Sorrow Dance* (New York: New Directions, 1967), 33.

Homespun and Crazy Feathers: The Split-Self in the Poems of Denise Levertov

Deborah Pope*

When I am the sky
a glittering bird
slashes at me with knives of song.

When I am the sea
fiery clouds plunge into my mirrors,
fracture my smooth breath with crimson sobbing.

When I am the earth
I feel my flesh of rock wearing down:
pebbles, grit, finest dust, nothing.

When I am a woman—O, when I am
a woman,
my wells of salt brim and brim,
poems force the lock of my throat. ("Cancion")

I

The term *split-self* was first given significance for women's poetry in Florence Howe's introduction to *No More Masks*.[1] It describes an opposition women feel between essential aspects of the self, between what is socially prescribed on the basis of gender and what is defined on the basis of self, between what a woman feels she should be and what she feels she is. Denise Levertov has written a substantial number of poems exploring this duality, the pain and frustration of which often belie the joyous poet, celebrating the

*Reprinted with permission of Louisiana State University Press from *A Separate Vision: Isolation in Contemporary Women's Poetry*, 85–115. © 1984 by Louisiana State University Press.

world and self, she is generally taken to be. Levertov particularly identifies the two selves with the domestic gender role and the artist. The former occupies a safe position, accepted and esteemed by society in general and males in particular, while her counterpart haunts the fringes of human intercourse, isolated from men and women alike, and repressed by the woman of whose psyche she is part.

The traditional female is associated with the enclosed world of the household, kitchen, and bedroom. In her guise as mother, wife, and helpmate, she exhibits a basic passivity and immobility that Levertov characteristically reinforces with images of sleeping. The artist, however, inhabits an unbounded world of independence, movement, and vitality; her freedom and power can be both stimulating and threatening. Her symbols are the moon, the forest, water, and places of mystery, imagination, and ritual. Unlike the relatively static domestic self, the artist initiates actions, undertakes journeys. Choices made by this self in favor of uncertainty, even pain, become artistic choices and entail the necessity of confronting unfamiliar experiences and environments, unlike those of security and ease in which the domestic self rests. Yet, the artist appears in clothes and circumstances that stamp her as an indifferent mother, a poor housekeeper, a woman whose disregard of social conventions keeps her an exotic, eccentric figure. These dichotomies are not unique, certainly, to Levertov, either in their particular traits or in the split-self strategy, but she is worthy of focus for the persistence of the theme in her work and for the paradigm she presents for examining both the repression and resolution possible through such poems.

It is important to distinguish the images of enclosure and passivity connected to the gender role from images of victimization. Levertov as an artist may struggle against the enervating or limiting influence of the gender role, but as a mother, wife, and woman in her society, she is also powerfully drawn to it. Significantly, she rarely portrays this self as a victim. To society and to herself, the figure, compounded of what Woolf called "the angel in the house" and what Tillie Olsen calls "the essential, maintenance-of-life angel," has the full weight of tradition and cultural approbation behind her. The "angel" in Levertov's poetry is not weak, bitter, or isolated, nor does Levertov caricature her in any way that would trivialize the tremendous pressure she exerts against the competing artist self. It is the latter who carries the burden of guilt, fear, and alienation for her rebellion. Clearly this split carries implications for male and female relationships in the poems, since it is the power of the masculine, patriarchal world that stands most firmly behind the persuasive cultural power of the gender roles enacted by the self. Frequently, poems in which Levertov writes of her isolation from a particular lover are at heart manifestations of the split-self. In these poems the man, who is the spokesman for the domestic self, implicitly exerts pressure on the woman to be passive and dependent and to fulfill her role, while the artist self struggles for validation and freedom.

Anais Nin wrote in her journals what is perhaps one of the most moving statements of the dilemma of conflicting selves in the woman writer, wherein her desire to be loved by men, to be accepted by culture as womanly, rises up to silence the power and voice of the artist.

> I did not want to rival man. . . . I must protect them [sic], not outshine them. . . . I did not want to steal man's creation, his thunder.
> Creation and femininity seemed incompatible. The *aggressive* act of creation.
> . . . To create seemed to me such an assertion of the strongest part of me that I would no longer be able to give all those I love the feeling of their being stronger, and they would love me less.
> An act of independence would be punished by desertion. I would be abandoned by all those I loved.
> Men fear women's strength. I have been deeply aware of men's weakness, the need to guard them from my strength.
> I have made myself less powerful, have concealed my powers.
> . . . I have concealed my abilities like an evil force that would overwhelm, hurt, or weaken others.
> I have crippled myself.
> Dreams of Chinese women with bound feet.
> I have bound myself spiritually.
> I have associated creation with ruthlessness, absence of scruples, indifference to consequences.
> . . . The creator's guilt in me has to do with my femininity, my subjection to man.
> Also with my maternal self in conflict with my creative self.
> . . . Guilt about exposing the father.
> Secrets
> Need of disguises.
> Fear of consequences.
> Great conflict here.[2]

The long, slow cadence of the beginning builds to a litany of confession, a lamentation of loss and mutilation of the self in its fundamental aspects, maternal and artistic, dutiful and powerful, communal and solitary. The terse, almost telegraphic language at the end comes like cries of grief. These griefs, the "great conflict" of which Nin so eloquently writes, flow through Levertov's poetry.

Denise Levertov was born October 24, 1923, in London, and spent her girlhood in suburban Ilford, Essex. It was a stimulating, intellectual household, her father being a respected Hasidic scholar and her mother strongly Welsh in background. Levertov and her elder sister, Olga, never attended public schools but were educated privately at home by their parents and tutors. For a time Levertov pursued serious work as a ballerina, and later she served as a nurse during World War II. Her first collection of poetry, *The Double Image*, was published in 1946 by the Cresset Press in London. In

1947, she married Mitchell Goodman, an American novelist. They lived in France, Mexico, and Maine, and eventually settled in New York City with their son, Nikolai, where they lived until their divorce in 1974.

From the beginning, Levertov's poetry demonstrates a continuity of theme and expression concerning central divisions in the self. Her work is a compelling account of the presence of the split, but also of manifold efforts to disguise it, minimize it, dissociate herself from its power. Even *The Double Image*, which most critics tend to pass over as too youthful and derivative to consider with Levertov's "real" work, has hints of this theme. Levertov, who confesses to having been embarrassed later by *The Double Image*, has developed a new appreciation of the ties between her first book and her maturer work, stating simply, "I have always—even in the muzzy adolescent vagueness of *The Double Image*—written out of my own experience as I grasped it, so that the field has grown larger as I walked through it, one might say, but yes, it is the same field."[3] The very title of the book points to an awareness of duplicity in vision, a duality in life and perception. The morbidity of the book issues partly from its backdrop of war, partly from its derivative romanticism, but there is a significant continuity in the poet's pessimistic rendering of lovers doomed to mutual isolation through the masks they assume or the blindness they exhibit in attempting to understand each other. This situation appears in such poems as "For B. M.," "Return," "Meditation and Voices," "Barricades," "The Dreamers," and "Two Voices." In "Two Voices," the result is a type of split-self poem. It could be read as a conventional dialogue poem between personifications of life and death or dynamic and static aspects of nature, or more interestingly, as a poem in which the woman speaker is trying to tell her lover what her inner self is truly like. Against his protestations, which emphasize her as the quiet, beautiful feminine ideal he beholds, she asserts the harsher reality of her turbulent artist self. The two voices represent the divergent views of her womanness.

> What can I give you? I am the unseizable
> indigo and wandering sea. I give
> no love but music, cold and terrible airs
> to darken on your heart as albatross
> obscures the gleaming water with a wing.
>
> *Be silent. You are beautiful; I hear*
> *only the summer whisper on the shore.*
>
> What can I give you? I am that great tree,
> the greem penumbra of forgotten dreams.
> I send a leaf to greet you, but no more;
> my branches rustle in the wind of death.
>
> *Be still; I hear no menace in the wind;*
> *the tree is mine, and grows about my heart.*

I am the wind. *I hold you.* I am gone,
shade of no substance. What is it you hold?

Shadow, I love you.

Free me. I am death.

Levertov's conception here of the artist self contains the imagery she will return to again and again—coldness, darkness, wings, violent movement, a strong connection with natural elements, a sense of freedom and escape. Yet, at the same time, the artist's power is unwomanly ("cold and terrible airs"), threatening both to men (an "albatross"; "I give no love") and even, it is implied, to herself ("I am death"). What the man reinforces and persists in seeing is the opposite of the artist—a static figure who is beautiful, "only the summer whisper on the shore," and without menace of any kind. To the man, this woman "is mine"; the woman responds, "Free me." Although the speaker claims great power and independence, she can only feel these compulsively, but not yet with joy. Because her qualities seem irreconcilable with the male's feminine ideal, she faces the isolation and torment of her gifts. Thus the stage is set for subsequent split-self poems wherein the choice is forged between being the artist or the loved one of others, between risky freedom and safe enclosure, wherein to be true to the self is to be dangerous to others.

Particularly through her early work—*The Double Image, Here and Now, Overland to the Islands,* and *With Eyes at the Back of Our Heads*—her fear and ambivalence toward the split predominate, coupled with attempts to deny it. In the middle period—from *The Jacob's Ladder* through *To Stay Alive*—Levertov begins to work toward achieving wholeness of purpose and identity in the split-self poems. At each stage appear poems of at least temporary resolution, where the split either balances tenuously or one self achieves ascendancy. It is this final sense of resolution that emerges in her more recent work, *The Freeing of the Dust* and *Life in the Forest.*[4] Having fully chosen the artist and worked through the guilt and anger of casting off the less authentic self, Levertov effectively moves beyond the need and urgency of split-self poems.

II

"The Dogwood" from *Overland to the Islands* is an excellent example of the early split-self poems wherein the speaker resists admitting the inner divisions and their implications.

The sink is full of dishes. Oh well.
Ten o'clock, there's no
hot water.

The kitchen floor is unswept, the broom
has been shedding straws. Oh well.

The cat is sleeping, Nikolai is sleeping,
Mitch is sleeping, early to bed,
aspirin for a cold. Oh well.

No school tomorrow, someone for lunch,
4 dollars left from the 10—how did that go?
Mostly on food. Oh well.

I could decide
to hear some chamber music
and today I saw—what?
Well, some huge soft deep
blackly gazing purple
and red (and pale)
anemones. Does that
take my mind off the dishes?
Adn dogwood besides.
Oh well, Early to bed, and I'll get up
early and put
a shine on everything and write
a letter to Duncan later that will shine too
with moonshine. Can I make it? Oh well.

The opening stanzas succinctly capture the woman's domestic ennui and
distraction. The only one awake in a house of sleepers, she is worrying
about running the household, meeting social commitments, and having her
son home from school. To each of these demands on her time, energy, and
management her response is the same "Oh well." In the pivotal fourth
stanza, her focus shifts for the first time from flat, laconic statements to
sensuous poetic language. The dogwood of the title aligns with the anemones outside the house in a visual, suggestive environment that handicaps
her attention to the more prosaic inside environment represented by the
house and family. Incipient tensions between them precipitate the need for
a decision either to continue her poetic musings about the beauty that she
willingly allows to distract her or to turn back to her duties inside—a
decision in favor of her art or the demands of her domestic role. Her
solution is unsatisfactory. She gets short-term relief by making no choice at
all; she merely decides to go to bed, early, temporarily silencing both
selves.

The speaker has evaded confronting the oppositions in her life, evaded
the nature of her boredom and inactivity, and unconvincingly postponed
matters until the next day, when she will try to placate the voices by shining
up both the furniture and her art. The final irony—besides the ludicrous
comparison of a superficial gloss of furniture polish with the work of the

imagination—lies in the fact that when at last she allows herself to indulge her poetic images and thoughts, it is in a letter to a male poet (the reference is to Robert Duncan). She will make an effort to impress him with her "shine" (as she tries to satisfy her husband by being a good housekeeper), instead of directing her energy and insights into creating her own poem. Her world in miniature in this poem is a constant, depleting effort to shine for a male domestic and literary world and to deflect her instincts to write a poetry of her own. The consequences of this deflection, as the poem demonstrates, are inner contradictions, distractions (note the chopped phrasings, the interruptions and questions), weariness, and, worst of all, silence. Hence her final question, "Can I make it?," resonates with the desperation of all she is struggling to do: to satisfy her social roles, to keep alive her imagination, to maintain contact with the artistic world, and lastly to survive at all, to "make it," with so many claims upon her. Her response is one final "Oh well," at once bitter, nonchalant, and still maddeningly evasive. This phrase, repeated some seven times in the relatively short poem, acquires a complexity by the end, forcing one's attention to the pun. Often in her work Levertov uses the image of the well, frequently with female connotations, to refer to sources of poetic inspiration. Thus, the colloquial phrase functions as an embedded apostrophe to her buried self and her poetic power, both in danger of disappearing under the multiple pressures of gender roles. "The Dogwood" is a deceptively simple imagistic and syntactic elucidation of Tillie Olsen's conviction that women, through traditional socialization, have been made "mediocre caretakers of their own talent: that is, writing not first. . . . It is distraction, not meditation, that becomes habitual; interruption, not continuity; spasmodic, not constant, toil. Work interrupted, deferred, postponed, makes blockage—at best lesser accomplishment. Unused capacities atrophy, cease to be."[5]

Another submerged split is apparent in the poem "The Absence," also in *Overland*. Here again the speaker, awake while her male partner sleeps, feels spiritually isolated, longing for something she cannot quite name.

> Here I lie asleep
> or maybe I'm awake yet—
>
> not alone—and yet
> it seems by moonlight
>
> I'm alone, hardly hearing
> a breath beside me. And those shadows
>
> on the wall indeed are
> not shadows but the
>
> featherweight dancing echoes
> of headlights sliding by.

Here I lie and wonder
what it is has left me, what element.
I can't remember my dreams
by morning.
        Maybe, as Frazer tells,

my soul flew out in that moment
of almost sleep. If it should go
back to the scenes and times
of its wars and losses

how would I ever lure it
back? It would
be looking for something, it would be
too concentrated to hear me.

O moon, watching everything,
delay it in the garden among the white flowers

until the cold air before sunrise
makes it glad to come back to me through the screens.

The speaker has a haunting sense of being literally and psychologically divided, missing some vital part of herself. She associates this absent element with her dreams and imagination, wondering if it may be her very soul that has left her for the more complex emotional landscape of the past. She seems to envy her soul its freedom and intensity (recall the distraction that plagued the speaker in "The Dogwood"), and fears her soul will not willingly return to the life she offers it. Although warm and safe, this world is also screened off and enclosed. The speaker hopes a delay among the garden and its white flowers will compel the soul's return, but this seems uncertain. Although dark and cold, the garden is also the only visually appealing place in the poem. As in "The Dogwood," the speaker outwardly dwells in ease and security (the peacefully sleeping households, the warm rooms, the shiny furniture), while an inner self exists in a landscape of mystery and threat (the anemones are dark, "blackly gazing," the dogwood has sacrificial connotations, the soul is out in the night chill). Levertov leaves little doubt, however, that the latter is the place where poems are found.

In her early collections, though, she remains unwilling to fully embrace the contradictions and difficulties of the divided self in her own person, preferring to submerge expressions of it or else to project it onto third persons, as in "The Earthwoman and the Waterwoman" (in *Here and Now*) and "Sunday Afternoon" (in *Overland*).

The Earthwoman and the Waterwoman

The earthwoman by her oven
    tends her cakes of good grain.

> The waterwoman's children
> are spindle thin.
> The earthwoman
> has oaktree arms. Her children
> full of blood and milk
> stamp through the woods shouting.
> The waterwoman
> sings gay songs in a sad voice
> with her moonshine children.
> When the earthwoman
> has had her fill of the good day
> she curls to sleep in her warm hut
> a dark fruitcake sleep
> but the waterwoman
> goes dancing in the misty lit-up town
> in dragon-fly dresses and blue shoes.

The split assumes definite shape and embodiment in these two—the angel-in-the-house, or earthwoman, and the exotic outsider, or waterwoman. The former is the admirable domestic, a good mother and cook, whose days are bounded by a "warm hut" and whose nights are given over to sleep. Her rootedness is symbolized by her "oaktree arms." Her opposite, the waterwoman, does not sleep, and dances through the town wearing dubious clothing. Her images are those of the (female) imagination—the moon and water. She is the singer, the poet, but she is also the outcast, since her behavior does not conform to the ideal of the domestic earthwoman. Levertov's attitude toward her is both envious and rejecting; the poet possesses freedom and vitality, but her children suffer and her voice is sad. The waterwoman's children are a likely reference to Levertov's poems, and the adjectives of insubstantiality ("thin," "moonshine") that describe them indicate her troubled sense of them. The paradox of "gay songs in a sad voice" is a reference to her inability to correlate experience with expression, the crisis of language caused by the split-self. In any case, Levertov still distances herself from the split by projecting it onto these folk forms and by using two women rather than a single woman divided against herself.

Another split-self poem, "Sunday Afternoon," draws on the contradictory socialization of young girls who are balanced at the point in adolescence when they straddle the freedom and movement of childhood and the curtailment and passivity of womanhood.

> After the First Communion
> and the banquet of mangoes and
> bridal cake, the young daughters
> of the coffee merchant lay down
> for a long siesta, and their white dresses
> lay beside them in quietness
> and white veils floated
> in their dreams as the flies buzzed.

> But as the afternoon
> burned to a close they rose
> and ran about the neighborhood
> among the half-built villas
> alive, alive, kicking a basketball, wearing
> other new dresses, of blood-red velvet.

The first part mingles marriage symbols with overtones of death, negatively prefiguring the passive feminine postures the girls inevitably must adopt, while the second half of the poem literally resurrects them ("they rose / . . . alive, alive") back into a world of colors, passion, and freedom that is associated with masculine activity (the basketball). The villas, "half-built," signal the enclosures already being erected to contain these girls who "rose," "ran," and kicked but whose future is to "lay," float, and dream.

Similar distinctions frame the poem "Something to Wear," from *Here and Now*, but carry more pointed implications for the women poet.

> To sit and sit like the cat
> and think my thoughts through—
> that might be a deep pleasure:
>
> to learn what news
> persistence might discover,
> and like a woman knitting
> make something from the
> skein unwinding, unwinding,
> something I could wear
>
> or something you could wear
> when at length I rose to meet you
> outside the quiet sitting-room
>
> (the room of thinking and knitting
> the room of cats and women)
> among the clamor of
>
> cars and people,
> the stars drumming and poems
> leaping from shattered windows.

The speaker defines two distinct feminine and masculine spheres. The former is quiet, still and passive, while the latter is full of activity, spectacle, exchange, and, significantly enough, poetry. She must rise from the feminine space (note the same verb used here as in "Sunday Afternoon" for passage between these worlds) to meet the man and write her poems. Even the thinking and persistence she envisions is only something that "might" occur in her room; it is a pleasure she has yet to "learn." But the world of poetry "shatters" the calm retreat of the speaker. It is not peaceful and repetitious like knitting, but various, clamorous, even violent—"stars drumming and poems / leaping from shattered windows."

A repeated problem in these poems and others through the early collections (for instance, "The Gypsy's Window," "Mrs. Cobweb," "Sharks") is that Levertov consistently locates poetry in realms that seem unavailable to her as a woman, realms she can only enter in disguise or by risking her status as a good, acceptable woman. The titles of both *Here and Now* and *Overland to the Islands* establish goals and means of poetic expression—full participation in the immediate world and in the quest—but the poems themselves tend to fall away from these ideals; Levertov cannot fully risk herself as a poet, since to do so is to risk also her society's concept of her as a woman. Thus, in *Here and Now*, the emphasis on an ethic of joyous immediacy falters in the split-self poems ("The Earthwoman and the Waterwoman," "Mrs. Cobweb," "The Gyspy's Window"), in poems in which the speaker cannot write what she wants ("The Rights") or in which she must repress her femininity to write ("Something to Wear"). Even in such love poems as "The Lovers," "Marriage," and "Marriage (II)," the woman does not experience the world firsthand in a participatory "here and now," but emerges mainly as a passive receiver of colors, images, and emotions brought to life for her by the intercession of a dominant male figure.

Similarly, in *Overland to the Islands*, the title poem sets out the motif of the eclectic journey as the proper undertaking of the artist. Yet, since the journey necessitates the very qualities that are attributes of the unacceptable self—movement, independence, and personal power—the poems tend to show the frustration and stagnation of the journey. It is no surprise, then, when Levertov writes of losing her direction, of being unable to communicate, in "The Dogwood" and "The Absence"; of activity that is merely frantic and purposeless, in "Merritt Parkway"; of being frightened off when she ventures into new regions, in "The Sharks"; and of crying out to the red flowers to rouse her anger and spirit when she is closed off by oppressive comfort and security, in "A Song." She remains essentially passive, hoping for some stronger force to rescue her. Because of pressure exerted by others and her own internalization of their values, she is unable to rebel successfully against the domestic self, and her poetry becomes an increasingly contradictory, problematic pursuit.

The result is a crisis of language: a poet who is dishonest to herself cannot be true to her art. "The Whirlwind," one of the final poems in *Overland*, explodes with the power of the struggle in the poet and forces the issue of the integrity of an art based on denial of half the artist's energy and instinct.

> The doors keep rattling—I
> stick poems between their teeth to
> stop them. The brown dust
> twirls up outside the window, off

the dead jicama field, scares the curtains,
spirals away to the dirty hollow
where the cesspools are, and the most ants,
and beyond—to the unfenced pasture land, where nothing
will get in its way for miles and it
can curtsey itself at last into
            some arroyo. The doors
keep rattling—I'm
shivering, desperate for a poem
to stuff into their maws that will
silence them. I know what they want:
they want
in all their wooden strength
to fly off on the whirlwind into
the great nothingness.

The doors represent her threshold into the outer world, in the true direction of her art and desires. The doors must fling open, just as the windows of "Something to Wear" must shatter and the screens in "The Absence" must be transited, in order that the enclosures and barriers to her authentic self may be removed. The doors are like giant mouths ("maws," "teeth") symbolizing repressed expression that threatens to burst forth. She wants to silence them with false poems but becomes desperate when she cannot write them quickly enough. The irony is that she is trying to use poems to disguise her experience (she knows what the doors want), which itself prevents the poems from coming. Poems open doors; they do not close them. The wind appears as a female power, possibly the muse, by the curious personification in line 10. The speaker is fighting her own power, turning one self (the silencing poems, the intact, safe enclosure) against the other self of open doors, mystery, and presumably a more complex reality and experience. However, an allegiance between the two becomes more terrifying the more she denies it, as shown in the image of the whirlwind and the projection onto it of her worst fears: isolation and nothingness.

The resolution of these early split-self poems is reached in the strong poem, "The Goddess," from *With Eyes at the Back of Our Heads* (published two years after *Overland to the Islands*), capping for the moment the intertwining crisis of language and self. Unable to take herself firmly enough in hand as a poet, unwilling to open the doors, so to speak, the artist self is literally and decisively thrown out of her safe, enclosed world by no less a figure than the Muse herself.

She in whose lipservice
I passed my time,
whose name I knew, but not her face,
came upon me where I lay in Lie Castle!

Flung me across the room, and
room after room (hitting the walls, re-
bounding—to the last
sticky wall—wrenching away from it
pulled hair out!)
till I lay
outside the outer walls!

There in the cold air
lying still where her hand had thrown me,
I tasted the mud that splattered my lips:
the seeds of a forest were in it,
asleep and growing! I tasted
her power!

The silence was answering my silence,
a forest was pushing itself
out of sleep between my submerged fingers.

I bit on a seed and it spoke on my tongue
of day that shone already among stars
in the water-mirror of low ground,

and a wind rising ruffled in the lights:
she passed near me returning from the encounter,
she who plucked me from the close rooms,

without whom nothing
flowers, fruits, sleeps in season,
without whom nothing
speaks in its own tongue, but returns
lie for lie!

This is an extraordinary denouement for a poet depleted by enclosures, domesticity, and dormant energies yet fearfully clinging to the security these offered. She has implicitly cried out for a revolutionizing force but has been afraid to act. The Muse must literally haul and maul her weak sister outside the walls of "Lie Castle," a poetry that has become false to her needs and experience. The poet, from her new position of freedom, can now admit the dishonesty and encoding of her art: "She in whose lipservice / I passed my times, / whose name I knew but not her face . . . without whom nothing / speaks in its own tongue, but returns / lie for lie!" Everything that has become associated with the domestic self—sleep, warmth, walls, tidiness, passivity—violently reverses as the speaker lies splattered with mud out in the cold. A forest rousing from hibernation between her fingers suggests the new growth and force of her writing to come, while power stirs in her mouth under the stern injunction to tell the truth of her experience. Recalling the dramatic circumstances surrounding the poem's creation, Levertov writes, " 'The Goddess' . . . is not based on a dream but on an actual waking vision. . . . The poem's energy arises from an experience of awakening to the truth and to the necessity for truthfulness—an experience sufficiently profound to produce the image of Truth as a Goddess and to produce that image spontaneously."[6]

III

"The Goddess" climaxes the sequence of split-self poems in Levertov's early work. In her next book, *The Jacob's Ladder* (1961), no split-self poems appear; however, her sixth book, *O Taste and See* (1964), picks up the theme again—in "In Mind" and "Melody Grundy," which recall figures like Mrs. Cobweb and the Waterwoman; in "Gone Away," a companion poem to "The Absence"; and in "Song for Ishtar," which, like "The Goddess," is another climatic resolution poem. Another poem in this volume, often anthologized, assumes the dynamics of the split-self without actually delineating the respective personae. "Hypocrite Women" acknowledges the disguises women adopt, the suppression they practice to preserve a patriarchal view of them that does not accurately reflect their lives and thoughts. Levertov has plainly acknowledged that while the poem "was written before the women's movement existed in present form, it's written in some recognition of how those stereotypes do in fact oppress one as a woman."[7] "Hypocrite Women" takes a harsher view of the gender role than most split-self poems, in which, however discomfiting this self might be, it is almost always treated with respect and sympathy. Instead, in "Hypocrite Women," Levertov comes down hard on the lies and misery perpetuated by women's continuing silence and self-trivialization. Again the split-self is connected to the crisis of women's language. Levertov emphasizes verbs of expression: "how seldom we speak"; "we are too much women to own to such unwomanliness"; "we say nothing of this later." Women are isolated from themselves, from each other, from men, and from language.

On the strength of this admission about women, which is also an admission about herself, Levertov follows "Hypocrite Women" with the poem "In Mind." This poem marks the first time she acknowledges the presence of the split in herself without efforts to submerge or deny it.

> There's in my mind a woman
> of innocence, unadorned but
>
> fair-featured, and smelling of
> apples or grass. She wears
>
> a utopian smock or shift, her hair
> is light-brown and smooth, and she

              is kind and very clean without
              ostentation—

                     but she has
              no imagination.

                     And there's a
              turbulent moon-ridden girl

              or old woman, or both,
              dressed in opals and rags, feathers

              and torn taffeta,
              who knows strange songs—

              but she is not kind.

In essence, the Earthwoman and Waterwoman have reappeared, with the important difference being the poet's personal avowal of the split. Still present is the ambivalence toward the artist, whose decisiveness, after "The Goddess," seems to have fallen into doubt again. The poet, retaining her stigmas of ostracism and bad temper, has improved little over her earlier delineations.

If "In Mind" seems a throwback to past struggles, at least "Song for Ishtar," the opening poem of the volume, throws its weight with full force on the side of the "moon-ridden girl."

              The moon is a sow
              and grunts in my throat
              Her great shining shines through me
              so the mud of my hollow gleams
              and breaks in silver bubbles

              She is a sow
              and I a pig and a poet

              When she opens her white
              lips to devour me I bite back
              and laughter rocks the moon

              In the black of desire
              we rock and grunt, grunt and
              shine

As in "The Goddess," the poet confronts her muse, though the poet has now increased in confidence and aggressiveness, as Levertov chooses the artist self without qualification, ambivalence, or guilt. The poem is a rich celebration of feminine power and creativity that embraces the crude and the spiritual, the physical and the psychic, both "pig" and "poet." Playing on the old folk belief of the moon's ability to impregnate women, the interaction of the poet with her muse uses language and motions of sexuality to achieve an epiphany of self-fertilization, whereby the poet creates out of her own self and power: "the mud of my hollow gleams / and breaks in silver bubbles." Levertov is not afraid to characterize the artist as exotic or coarse, or to overturn cultural signposts of feminine appeal by calling herself a pig. Indeed the overtones of the poem suggest a retreat not only from men's gender expectations but from men as sexual partners. The woman alone, or in partnership with her muse, is explosively sexual. The poet has reached a fullness of creative and natural independence in her raucous, shining identification with a female cosmos.

Just as "Song for Ishtar" opens the collection *O Taste and See*, a split-self poem, "The Wings," opens her next book, *The Sorrow Dance* (1967), and plays again on familiar patterns: oppositions of vulnerability and power, immobility and flight, female and male, death and birth. The central tension revolves around the unknown contents of a heavy black hump the speaker carries on her back.

> Something hangs in back of me,
> I can't see it, can't move it.
>
> I know it's black,
> a hump on my back.
>
> It's heavy. You
> can't see it.
>
> What's in it? Don't tell me
> *you* don't know. It's
>
> what you told me about—
> black
>
> inimical power, cold
> whirling out of it and
>
> around me and
> sweeping you flat.
>
> But what if,
> like a camel, it's
>
> pure energy I store,
> and carry humped and heavy?
>
> Not black, not
> that terror, stupidity

of cold rage; or black
only for being pent there?

What if released in air
it became a white

source of light, a fountain
of light? Could all that weight

be the power of flight?
Look inward: see me

with embryo wings, one
feathered in soot, the other

blazing ciliations of ember, pale
flare-pinions. Well—

could I go
on one wing,

the white one?

The initial descriptions emphasize the weight and mystery of the woman's encumbrance; the hump suggests something of both a witch's physical deformity and her magic sack. Its repellent aspects are stressed by the "you," who is probably male, in terms characteristic of male denigration of witches and powerful women: "Black inimical power," unwomanly coldness, and unnatural strength (power capable of sweeping the man flat). He resorts to other common terms of dismissing a woman's force as "stupidity," "terror," or "cold rage." His impulse is to fear and negate the hidden part of the speaker. The woman, however, looks for the other, more positive possibilities in herself, though her style of bemused interrogation makes this dissension from the man's opinion almost apologetic. She asks five questions about the nature of this appendage; under her effort to redefine it, the hump assumes connotations of a birth sack, "humped and heavy" containing "embryo wings." The heavy, old self might shed to reveal new movement and beauty, "the power of flight." The climax of the poem is the speaker's imperative to the man, "Look inward: see me." It is an injunction both to look deeply into himself to see the misconceived image of her he harbors there, and into her to recognize her heretofore disguised but authentic self. Still, the poem concludes unsatisfactorily in a way reminiscent of "The Dogwood." The series of questions, the parenthetical "Well," and the irresolution in the final lines leave the speaker wondering if she can make it on one white wing alone, since she feels compelled to reject the black one (colored with cultural fears and apprehensions). The questions, as well as the continuing split, protect the speaker and the man from the full assertion of her power, but they limit it, too.

The centerpiece of *The Sorrow Dance* is the long sequence, broken into six sections, titled the "Olga Poems." These present the painful process of Levertov's coming to terms with the death of her older sister in 1964. The sequence recounts the troubled relationship between the two sisters, from their great intimacy in childhood to the years of eventual alienation and distance. Olga, the older by nine years, was from the beginning a figure of power and authority in her younger sister's eyes. She taught her music, fantasy, ideas, and stories; her presence dominated their childhood world. Throughout her later life, however, Olga was on uneven terms with her family and only sister, largely as a result of her political fervor and willful temperament. In the "Olga Poems," Levertov speaks of her sister's "rage" and "dread," which apparently collapsed gradually into an embattled, paranoid personality that finally estranged her from everyone.

The "Olga Poems" function as memoriam, but they are also, perhaps unconsciously to the poet, a continued working out of the split-self duality in the persons of the two very distinct sisters, Denise and Olga Levertov. In this projection, Olga becomes the isolated artist self, and Denise becomes the well-behaved, traditionally feminine girl. The image patterns throughout the poem support this interpretation. Olga is described with the same adjectives and details that have become linked with the artist in previous split-self poems. The opening stanzas begin to distinguish the two sisters along the lines of the familiar division.

> By the gas-fire, kneeling
> to undress,
> scorching luxuriously, raking
> her nails over olive sides, the red
> waistband ring—
>
> (And the little sister
> beady-eyed in the bed—
> or drowsy, was I? My head
> a camera—)
>
> Sixteen. Her breasts
> round, round, and
> dark-nippled—

Olga, the exotic, sensual sister, luxuriates in the warmth and in her body, while the other sister watches in circumspect fascination from the bed. Olga is described as having dark physical coloring, another distinction between the selves, since frequently in Levertov's poems the traditional woman is fair, while the artist is dark or associated with vibrant colors. Another early difference between the sisters was their social conscience; Olga's empathy for human suffering left Levertov unmoved.

> . . . human shame swept you
> when you were nine and saw
> the Ley Street houses,
>
> grasping their meaning as *slum*.
> Where I, reaching that age,
> teased you, admiring
>
> architectural probity, circa
> eighteen-fifty, and noted
> pride in the whitened doorsteps.

Olga's imaginative and artistic pursuits seem foremost in Levertov's recollection of their childhood relationship. She puts words to music, sight-reads the Beethoven sonatas, composes verses, sings songs with her sister, and fantasizes adventures for the two of them during long walks and long days in the park. The only difficulty with seeing Olga in these poems as the artist self is Levertov's own attitude toward her sister: she seems to reject and dissociate herself from the very characteristics which distinguish Olga as an artist. The suspicion arises that Levertov is most uncomfortable with the unwomanly, unfeminine aspects of her sister. For instance, she is put off by Olga's high-pitched voice, her "nagging insistence," her "picking those endless arguments," her intellectualism (*"Everything flows* / she muttered into my childhood"). Above all, she is uncomfortable with her sister's intensity and assertiveness.

> The high pitch of
> nagging insistence, lines
> creased into raised brows—
>
> Ridden, ridden—
> the skin around the nails
> nibbled sore—
>
> You wanted
> to shout the world to its senses,
> did you?—to browbeat
>
> the poor into joy's
> socialist republic—
> What rage

Curiously, the details and terms she uses to convey her sister's personality are reminiscent of the negative sanctions used against the artist self elsewhere in Levertov's poems and traditionally used against women for being unfeminine and masculine.

> Black one, incubus—
>   she appeared
> riding anguish as Tartars ride mares

over the stubble of the bad years.

In one of the years
    when I didn't know if she were dead or alive
I saw her in dream

haggard and rouged
    lit by the flare
from an eel- or cockle-stand on a slum street—

was it a dream? I had lost

all sense, almost, of
    who she was, what—inside of her skin,
under the black hair
            dyed blonde—

it might feel like to be, in the wax and wane of the moon

By the end of the "Olga Poems," Levertov has not really expressed an understanding of, or admiration for, her sister. This occurs, however, with some conviction in two poems that appear later in *The Sorrow Dance* and in the facts of Levertov's life. One of the poems that serves as a sort of epilogue to the memoriam, "A Note to Olga (1966)," recounts Levertov's arrest during a demonstration against the Vietnam War. The conclusion approaches a point of emotional and psychological identity with her dead sister, as Levertov feels in herself the stirring power of an ardent political commitment. Almost unconsciously her life has begun to assume more affinity with Olga's.

Though I forget you
a red coal from your fire
burns in that box.

On the Times Square sidewalk
we shuffle along, cardboard signs
—Stop the War—
slung around our necks.
. . . .
—It seems
you that is lifted

limp and ardent
off the dark snow
and shoved in, and driven away.

Levertov came to see the epilogic nature of this poem after *The Sorrow Dance*. When the "Olga Poems" were reprinted in *To Stay Alive* (1971), her overtly political, antiwar book, "A Note to Olga" was placed immediately following the sequence.

The second poem, though, is a far more intriguing afterword, at once more subtle and comprehensive than "Note to Olga." The poem, "A Vision," describes an almost archetypal dream of two powerful angels stopped in mid-flight at the sight of each other. "These two"

> so far as angels may dispute, were poised
> on the brink of dispute, brink of
> fall from angelic stature,
> . . . .
> These two hovered dazed before one another,
> for one saw the seafeathered, peacock breakered
> crests of the other angel's magnificence,
> different from his own,
>
> and the other's eyes flickered with vision of
> flame petallings, cream-gold grainfeather glitterings,
> the wings of his fellow,

This poem is a symbolic enactment of the confrontation Levertov had desired with her sister, but missed. Levertov, whose element and colors are associated with water, is a blue-green angel, and Olga, whose element is fire and whose colors are red, brown, and gold, is a flame-colored angel. (Twice in the "Olga Poems," Levertov visualizes her sister by fires; she repeatedly associates her with the earth and its hues, and is fascinated by her eyes, which she describes as gold—"Your eyes were the brown gold of pebbles under water"; "gold brown eyes"; "gold gravel.") In "A Vision," at the mediating distance of the dream, the sisters come face to face with their mingled envy, anger, and love. Their hate can pull them down into eternal, mutually destructive divisiveness; their love can raise them to a new level of awareness of their beauty—a recognition between women, of women. At the climax of the dream, "the intelligence proper to great angels flew into their wings":

> So that each angel was iridescent with the strange newly-seen
> hues he watched; and their discovering pause
> and the speech their silent interchange of perfection was
>
> never became a shrinking to opposites,
>
> and they remained free in the heavenly chasm . . . .

IV

"Never became a shrinking to opposites"—this is precisely what the recurring split-self poems had threatened. Now, through the exhaustive emotional recapitulation of her sister's life and her own connections to that life, Levertov achieves an understanding and healing in "A Vision" that allows her finally to "remain free" of self-defeating reduction. Her new vision of wholeness, built on "newly seeing," preserves her from a fruitless polarization of emotions and capacities. "A Vision" significantly marks the end of the split-self as it has been worked out in its various manifestations. This form appears only twice after *The Sorrow Dance:* in "Embroidery (I)," from *Relearning the Alphabet* (1970), and "The Woman," from *The Freeing of the Dust* (1975). Moreover, in an interesting development, each time it occurs the pairs are sisters.

"Embroidery (I)," built on the folktale of the two sisters, Rose White and Rose Red, uses imagery familiar from earlier split-self poems. Rose Red, the domestic self, prepares dinner, tends the hearth, and waits for the bear's return, while Rose White, the artist, sits to one side, her grey eyes looking off into the forest, away from the warm room. Rose Red, true to her name, has an "ardent, joyful / compassionate heart," attuned to the needs of the male bear, while her sister is "pale, turning away when she hears / the bear's paw on the latch." It is not the bear, but the "scent of the forest" in his fur, the air of the outside world, that fascinates Rose White. Later, in their beds, Rose Red falls into the customary sleep of the domestic self, dreaming "she is combing the fur of her cubs / with a golden comb." But in the posture characteristic of the artist, Rose White lies awake. In these particulars, the poem is similar to other poems of its type, but it is more charming and fanciful. However, some remarkable distinctions become apparent on closer scrutiny. There is no perceivable tension between the Roses, nor does either hinder the other's pursuits. Rather than a split they appear as a unit, exemplified by the song they sing together.

> it is a cradle song, a loom song,
> a song about marriage, about
> a pilgrimage to the mountains
> long ago.

The song embraces "opposites"—motherhood (cradle) and artistry (loom), domesticity (marriage) and exploration (a pilgrimage to the mountains)—the directions hitherto presented as irreconcilable in Levertov's poetry. Moving further toward the new sense of resolution and inclusion, "Embroidery (I)" closes with the forecast of Rose White's marriage to the bear's brother "when the time is ripe." The selves coexist peacefully, singing together, and each shall marry in her own time; their unprecedented sisterhood betokens new strength and possibility.

Similarly in "The Woman," though the selves are one person, they are implicitly sisters, characterized more by the solidarity between them than by their differences.

> It is the one in homespun
> you hunger for
> when you are lonesome;
>
> the one in crazy feathers,
> dragging opal chains in dust
> wearies you

wearies herself perhaps
but has to drive on
clattering rattletrap into

fiery skies for trophies,
into the blue that is bluer
because of the lamps,

the silence keener because it is solitude
moving through multitude on the night streets.

But the one in homespun
whom you want is weary
too, wants to sit down

beside you neither silent
nor singing, in quietness. Alas,
they are not two but one,

pierce the flesh of one, the other
halfway across the world, will shriek,
her blood will run. Can you endure
life with two brides, bridegroom?

The selves seems nearly identical in their characteristics to the women in "In Mind" except for the extraordinary empathy that now binds them. If one is pierced, the other will bleed; they are "two brides," suggesting new life and new emotional fidelities, and both are "weary" of the old, divisive relationship. The women are aligned with themselves; it is the man who cannot or will not admit their essential oneness, but pursues a separation that is no longer tenable. Thus, the speaker's concluding question, and the question ending "Embroidery (I)," is addressed not to herself but to her male partner. Each poem finishes with uncertainty about the "bridegroom," the man who must, it is implied, accept himself in a new way, just as the woman has come to a new understanding of herself. The questions at the end of the split-self poems have spoken to doubts and paradoxes in the female speaker. Now the queries shift to problems outside the self, where the unnatural, inhibiting conceptions still remain.

After the "Olga Poems," Levertov achieves peace with her split-selves. Their antagonism with each other no longer energizes poems, but the divided perspectives they represented still operate in the world. Increasingly, the split is found between the woman and the masculine-defined world, whether represented by the barbarism of war and urban terror, or the individual lover who is the spokesman for patriarchal values that would limit the woman in ways she once limited herself. This theme is found in Levertov's poems from the beginning, but reaches explicitness in two poems in *O Taste and See*—"The Ache of Marriage" and "About Marriage." It is hinted at in a third poem,

"Losing Track." The isolation of the female speaker subjected to the gender expectations of the man underlies "The Cold Spring," "A Hunger," and "Adam's Complaint" in *Relearning the Alphabet*. The biographical denouement to this theme comes in the divorce poems of *The Freeing of the Dust*.

Recalling the concluding question of "The Wings"—"could I go / on one wing, / the white one?"—it is as if Levertov now realizes no flight is possible with only half her power. She must go on both wings, expending all her potential, black and white, just as she is both brides. Levertov was speaking about the dissociation of "humane responsibility" from "objective research" when she wrote the following passage, but it applies equally to the integrity of the self and the perversity of "shrinking to opposites": "Any human faculties and potentials that become divorced from the whole of which they are parts are . . . distorted. The compassionate imagination demands of us a wholeness and a constant interplay of functions. When we split ourselves up into opposing factions, fragments—intellect and emotions, body and spirit, private and public, etc.—we destroy ourselves."[8] From the early poems, in which she feared and repressed her oppositions, to the poems in which she was able to admit their centrality but remained ambivalent and threatened, Levertov finally moves from split-selves to healed selves through acceptance and integration. "A Woman Alone," from her excellent collection *Life in the Forest* (1978), is a poem made possible by the resolution of the split-selves. In it Levertov celebrates the various aspects of her womanness and power without the guilt or fear present in earlier works.

> a kind of sober euphoria makes her believe
> in her future as an old woman, a wanderer,
> seamed and brown,
>
> . . . .
> an old winedrinking woman, who knows
> the old roads, grass-grown, and laughs to herself . . .
> . . . .
> . . . she thinks maybe
> she could get to be tough and wise, some way,
> anyway. Now at least
> she is past the time of mourning,
> now she can say without shame or deceit,
> O blessed Solitude.

Whole, self-assured, she stakes out a direction in which women grow wise and independent, moving into age with joy and inner beauty, even though—perhaps even because—men no longer figure centrally in their lives. As a poem of freedom and of women alone, it is a validation poem that points to new myths. Traditionally, as one critic has pointed out,

> the wise old man tells what experience has taught him, now too late to
> enjoy, then too quick to savor in fullness. The wise old woman, on the

other hand, is generally wise by virtue of magic or herbal cookery. Her wisdom has been regarded as rather bogus or too supernatural to be dealt with. She has paid for it, like Cassandra, by her coupling with a god or devil. As she ages, like Snow White's step-mother, she approaches her mirror only in shadows; and if the mirror speaks back, she candies an apple with poison for the fair, young, and fertile.[9]

These myths of a "wise" woman regard her only in her relation to men—her magic or insight effected by the supernatural agency of men, or her actions prompted by fear of losing her sexual attractiveness, the only thing that makes her worthwhile. Levertov's speaker, though she remembers men with pleasure, is not dominated by efforts to please them; though she is surprised by age, she is graceful in handling it. Without apology, regret, or disguise, she is a woman who is aging and alone, but who is also strong, wise, and laughing to herself. Rather than "shrinking to opposites," she expresses a "sober euphoria" of integrated, realized life and selfhood, celebrating possibilities and "believ[ing] in her future as an old woman."

Notes

1. Florence Howe, "Introduction," *No More Masks: An Anthology of Poems by Women*, eds. Florence Howe and Ellen Bass (New York: W. W. Norton, 1973), 27–33.

2. Anais Nin, entry for January 1943 in *The Diaries of Anais Nin*, vol. 3, cited in *Woman as Writer*, eds. Jeanette Webber and Joan Grumman (Boston: Beacon, 1978), 36–37.

3. Ian Reid, "Everyman's Land: An Interview with Denise Levertov," *Southern Review* 8 (1972), 236.

4. Denise Levertov, *Here and Now* (San Francisco: City Lights Books, 1957); *Overland to the Islands* (Highlands, N.C.: Jargon, 1958); *With Eyes at the Back of Our Heads* (Norfolk, Conn.: New Directions, 1960); *The Jacob's Ladder* (New York: New Directions, 1961); *O Taste and See* (New York: New Directions, 1964); *The Sorrow Dance* (New York: New Directions, 1967); *Relearning the Alphabet* (New York: New Directions, 1970); *To Stay Alive* (New York: New Directions, 1971); *Footprints* (New York: New Directions, 1972); *The Freeing of the Dust* (New York: New Directions, 1955); *Life in the Forest* (New York: New Directions, 1978).

5. Tillie Olsen, "One Out of Twelve: Women Who Are Writers in This Century," *Working It Out*, eds. Sara Ruddick and Pamela Daniels (New York: Pantheon, 1977), 331, 334. See also, for a further testament to the conflicts of writer and housekeeper, such comments as Katherine Mansfield's in a letter to John Middleton Murry, in *Images of Women in Fiction*, ed. Susan Koppelman Cornillon (Bowling Green, Ohio: Popular Press, 1973), 108.

6. Denise Levertov, "The Sense of Pilgrimage," *The Poet in the World* (New York: New Directions, 1973), 72–73.

7. Levertov was responding to an interviewer's remark that "Hypocrite Women" would not satisfy militant feminists; for her full answer, see Anthony Piccione and William Heyen, "A Conversation with Denise Levertov," *Ironwood* 4 (1973), 23.

8. Denise Levertov, "On 'The Malice of Innocence': Poetry in the Classroom," *American Poetry Review* 1 (1972), 44.

9. Richard Gustafson, " 'Time Is a Waiting Woman': New Poetic Icons," *Midwest Quarterly* 16 (1975), 318.

Denise Levertov: Poetry of
the Immediate
Ralph J. Mills, Jr.*

American poetry at the present time sustains two extremes, with a wide range of practice in between in which the best—as well as the most truly advanced—writing is usually done. One extreme is represented by the academic poets. The term does not necessarily apply to all poets who happen to teach in universities for their living, but denotes those writers whose materials are often selected from the history of literature and culture, and whose methods are dictated by the critical theories of what poetry ought to be. At the opposite extreme, the Hip writers mistake the exhibition of hysteria and the release of invective, unhindered by the requirements of craft, for poetry. Whitman and Rimbaud, the "true gods" the Hip writers claim for their masters, had both the genius and the strength to navigate the rapids of emotion and vision in which these self-styled successors capsize and drown.

At the same moment—around 1957—that such figures as Ginsberg and Kerouac began to make news, a number of other, previously little-known poets also published their own books and caused a less sensational but more worthy stir. Some of them may even have been loosely associated in the minds of their audience with the Hip writers next to whom they were occasionally printed; but there is little resemblance except in their mutual rejection of the ruling literary and critical modes. And these poets differ greatly among one another as well. All of them, however—and I include here poets such as Robert Creeley, Paul Carroll, Frank O'Hara, John Ashbery, Barbara Guest, Gary Snyder, David Ignatow, Brother Antonius, Galway Kinnell, and John Logan, in addition to Denise Levertov—aim at an expression of the most personal kind of experience, an authentic statement about themselves, what they see and know, suffer and love; their responses to the things, relationships, and heightened instants of their lives. The tendencies of these poets lead them to the repudiation of Eliot's belief in an "objective correlative" that screens the author from his work and maintains the privacy of his life as an individual. The idea of masks that explains so much modern poetry of the post-Symbolist generation has no value for these younger poets, who really walk naked, as Yeats said poets should.

We have considered elsewhere how the poetry of Robert Lowell moves into this same area of highly personal or confessional, though he comes from a very different corner of the literary map than does Denise Levertov or Robert Creeley or David Ignatow. The latter have steeped themselves for a long time in that tradition of modern writing whose pioneers are William Carlos Williams, Ezra Pound, and H. D.

Among her fellow-poets in this tradition, Denise Levertov stands out as one whose art, fresh and compelling, convinces us of her genuine rapport

*Reprinted with permission from *Contemporary American Poetry* (New York: Random House, 1965), 176–96.

with the reality she presents at its core. Her poetry is frequently a tour through the familiar and the mundane until their unfamiliarity and other-worldliness suddenly strike us. Her imaginative gaze feasts on the small objects we usually treat as insignificant appendages to our lives, or pauses with affectionate interest on the seemingly trivial activities in which we spend so much of those lives. Thus she engages very naturally in a persistent investigation of the events of her own life—inner and outer—in the language of her own time and place, and completes that investigation in the forms emerging from what she discovers as it is translated into words. Miss Levertov shares the spirit of Martin Buber, for she always says "thou" to the persons, occasions, and objects she encounters; that is her imagination's essential humanizing gesture toward every aspect of existence.

As I have already indicated, Miss Levertov, along with a variety of other poets, departs sharply from the poetic and critical line passing down through Yeats, Eliot, Auden, and the critics who have developed aesthetic views from their initiative. In the introduction to his anthology *Contemporary American Poetry*, Donald Hall offers a good summary description of qualities empha-sized by the poets working in the opposing tradition, with its foundation in the example of William Carlos Williams. "This poetry," Hall tells us, "is no mere restriction of one's vocabulary. It wants to use the language with the intimacy acquired in unrehearsed unliterary speech. But it has other charac-teristics which are not linguistic. It is a poetry of experiences more than of ideas. The experience is presented often without comment, and the words of the description must supply the emotion which the experience generates, without generalization or summary."

In allying herself with this movement, Miss Levertov had to grapple with prevailing literary modes and, finally, to discard them. A struggle of this sort, the purpose of which is to open a way for poetic development, normally makes or breaks a writer—that is, if he or she dares to undertake it, as many do not—and it is a real sign of Miss Levertov's abilities that she has returned victorious. But the effort to win a voice of one's own amounts to nothing or becomes artificial unless it has been prompted by the conditions of human experience itself, by all that is cast into the poet's field of vision in the course of living. Poetry, if it will earn its name, must never begin with experience at second hand, but with a steady eye on what surrounds us everywhere. As the French philosopher Jacques Maritain says in his *Art and Scholasticism*, "Our art does not derive from itself alone what it imparts to things; it spreads over them a secret which it first discovered in them, in their invisible substance or in their endless exchanges and correspondences." Miss Levertov has learned this lesson well, and it is identical to the one her art teaches us. The conclusion of her "Note on the Work of the Imagination" (*New Directions* 17, edited by James Laughlin) adds to the quotation from Maritain a consider-ation of this spiritual faculty which makes the poetic object possible; she writes, "What joy to be reminded . . . that the Imagination does not arise from the environment but has the power to create it!"

Some poets make their published poems the battleground for style and individuality, and the reader can witness the spectacle, and its success or failure. In Denise Levertov there is an unseen conflict which occurred somewhere in the eleven-year span between her first book, *The Double Image* (1946), published in England before she came to the United States, and her next, *Here and Now* (1957), issued by Lawrence Ferlinghetti's City Lights Bookshop in San Francisco. Kenneth Rexroth, who anthologized her work some years ago in his *New British Poets*, placed her then as one of the most promising neo-romantics of the war period; but his later statements about her writing, collected in *Assays* (1961), indicated that he believes—as I do— that Levertov's full powers as a poet began to unleash themselves only after she had been in America awhile and, as Rexroth says, had come "to talk like a mildly internationalized young woman living in New York but alive to all the life of speech in the country."

The poems included in *The Double Image* give evidence of a true poetic gift in their author, though they are not marked with those characteristics of thought and rhythm and speech that would insure them as her handiwork, and hers alone. I don't mean that the poems are imitations; on the other hand, they seem to partake of a general mood in English poetry of the time, owing, no doubt, to the war. Here is world-weariness, disenchantment, a flirtatiousness with death and the twilight regions of the spirit. Somehow a vein of uncertainty runs through these pieces, as if the poet almost suspected herself in what she was doing. I am sure, however, that I could never gain such an impression if Miss Levertov had published only that single volume or if she had continued in her initial style. She served her poetic apprenticeship in works suffused with vague emotion, filled with whispers of mortality and unrest, the damp vegetation of England, and murmurs of perishable love. I will quote just a few lines from one of these early poems, "Five Aspects of Fear," before approaching her more central productions:

> In fear of floods long quenched, waves fallen,
> shattered mirrors darken with old cries;
> where no shot sounds the frightened birds go flying
> over heights of autumn soft as honey:
> each country left is full of our own ghosts
> in fear of floods quenched, waves fallen.
> Rags of childhood flutter in the woods
> and each deserted post has sentinels;
> bright eyes in wells watch for the sun's assassin:
> the regions bereft of our desires are haunted,
> rags of childhood flutter in the woods.

Something of the Georgians lingers on in this passage with its rural withdrawal from contemporary affairs, but the strongest and most obvious pull is toward Surrealism, which had crossed the channel in the 1930s and was still a strong influence during the war. Miss Levertov tries, by means of dreamlike associations and indefiniteness of imagery, to articulate as nearly as possible the purity of her emotions, unsoiled by the concrete of the particular. That vagueness is far removed from what we have come to know as the essential poet in her, the poet whose sleeves are rolled and who wrestles up to her elbows in the dust of a common world. In this poem the effects are atmospheric; the words, I believe, are supposed to bear a cumulative weight of feeling *apart* from any denotation. How different from the present Denise Levertov, who senses her materials as a Giacometti or a David Hare senses the materials of his sculpture. Her "Pleasures," as she calls them in the title of a later poem, are now quite altered:

> I like to find
> what's not found
> at once, but lies
>
> within something of another nature,
> in repose, distinct.
> Gull feathers of glass, hidden
>
> in white pulp: the bones of squid
> which I pull out and lay
> blade by blade on the draining board—
>
> > tapered as if for swiftness, to pierce
> > the heart, but fragile, substance
> > belying design. Or a fruit, *mamey,*
>
> cased in rough brown peel, the flesh
> rose-amber, and the seed:
> the seed a stone of wood, carved and
>
> polished, walnut-colored, formed
> like a brazilnut, but large,
> large enough to fill
> the hungry palm of a hand.

The reader will not be wrong, I think, if he or she sees in this poem, behind its fascination with the beauty of small objects and concealed things, an allegorical statement of the poet's own concern with material reality. In forcing tangible things to disclose their truths and felicities, she urges human reality to yield some of its secrets—and its covert analogies and predilections too.

The change that takes place between her first and second books—in a decade that saw Miss Levertov leave England, travel in Europe, meet the American novelist Mitchell Goodman, marry him, and settle in this country— is remarkable and must have demanded no less than a complete renovation of her poetic values. But this revolution of the heart, the head, the senses, how worthwhile it all was! She was compelled to start from scratch, and that meant for Miss Levertov a confrontation of the happenings of her life. What she so shrewdly observed was that the ordinary is extraordinarily unusual:

> What a sweet smell rises
>   when you lay the dust—
> bucket after bucket of water thrown
> on the yellow grass.
>   The water
>
> flashes
> each time you
> make it leap—
>   arching its glittering back.
> The sound of
>   more water
> pouring into the pail
> almost quenches my thirst.
> Surely when flowers
> grow here, they'll not
> smell sweeter than this
>   wet ground, suddenly black.

Of course, as Kenneth Rexroth further noted, Miss Levertov came under novel influences in America that were quite unlike any English ones. He names as a chief influence the poet we have already mentioned, the writer whose lessons she must have learned well, though without sacrificing her own intentions and capacities. That poet is the late William Carlos Williams. It is likely that she also learned from Rexroth's own poetry and from the Imagists; in her moving tribute to H. D. entitled "Summer 1961" she records some of her debts to Williams, Pound, and H. D.:

> They have told us
> the road leads to the sea,
> and given
>
> the language into our hands.

Perhaps if we look at a brief but fairly representative poem by Williams to remind ourselves of certain qualities in his work we will be able to determine, by comparison with Miss Levertov's "Laying the Dust" above, some of their similarities. Williams' poem is called "Between Walls":

> the back wings
> of the
>
> hospital where
> nothing
>
> will grow lie
> cinders

> in which shine
the broken

> pieces of a green
bottle.

Clearly, this poem has little relation to the kind of poetry in the ascendancy during the first half of the twentieth century; the poetry of the French Symbolists has had no bearing on what we read in these lines. Again, if we try to apply the sort of exegesis to Williams' poetry—or to Miss Levertov's, for that matter—that is used on Eliot's or Rilke's or Valery's, we shall miss the point and look foolish. Ingenious explication is beside the point here and will bury the meaning of both poems; we should do better to contemplate them as we would a painting. Williams' attraction to the *disjecta membra* of the physical world, particularly of the modern urban setting, sets a firm precedent for Miss Levertov's own poetic venture. We should not forget, either, Williams' insistence that the moral responsibility of the American poet lies in using his native tongue "to represent what his mind perceives directly about him," because this endeavor is, to a degree, Miss Levertov's. Yet there is also a gradual inward turning in her latest poetry and an increasing preoccupation with parable, dream, and interior illumination that are foreign to Williams' imagination.

Williams was for years a champion of younger writers in the United States and, further, was a stalwart foe of the post-Symbolist literature of Yeats and Eliot, as well as an opponent of what he thought was an outworn tradition of English verse forms and meters. It is hardly by accident, then, that young poets, in search of a way past the official poetic idiom, looked to Williams' writings and his viewpoint for guidance. The rejection of conventional for organic form; the repudiation of established metrical patterns in favor of what Williams called "the variable foot"; the return to the spoken language, the American spoken language—these are some of the most prominent results of the senior poet's influence. These younger poets likewise avoid in general the habit of making their work a repository of intellectual history, learning, and fragments of the European cultural heritage. I should like to call the poetry of Miss Levertov, and that of a number of her contemporaries, "poetry of the immediate."

My term requires some explanation. I do not mean by "the immediate" an art without craftsmanship, an art that fixes on the disorder of sheer impulse or emotional notation. Miss Levertov has never allowed her poetry to become even slightly vulnerable to that kind of charge—a glance at any one of her poems will prove it. Moreover, we need only cite the comment she supplies from Donald Allen's anthology *The New American Poetry 1945–1960*, where there is no mistaking her distaste for sloppy composition: "I long for poems," she writes, "of an inner harmony in utter contrast to the chaos in which they exist." Poetry must not be a shapeless replica of external things but an organically formed transfiguration of them in which the transfiguration, rather than poetic convention, dictates the form. What I call "the immediate," then, signifies the complex relationships existing between the poet and the elements that are close at hand in her personal experience. The things, the happenings, the thoughts and dreams that are subjective events in themselves—everything that falls within the circumference of the poet's life as an individual—become the matter of poetry. The author's private circumstance is explored, its potentialities drawn out; but however far her speculations lead her, Miss Levertov never oversteps that circumference. Instead, she creates from within herrself an attitude with which to face her environment, as in her poem "Something to Wear":

> To sit and sit like the cat
> and think my thoughts through—
> that might be a deep pleasure:
>
> To learn what news
> persistence might discover,
> and like a woman knitting
>
> make something from the
> skein unwinding, unwinding,
> something I could wear
>
> or something you could wear
> when at length I rose to meet you
> outside the quiet sitting-room
>
> (the room of thinking and knitting
> the room of cats and women)
> among the clamor of
>
> cars and people,
> the stars drumming and poems
> leaping from shattered windows.

This poem grows around the mind's self-reflective activity. While poems about poetry, the act of composition, or the mind contemplating its own powers and processes are common in the literary history of the past 170 years—Mallarmé and Wallace Stevens, for example, expended much of their artistic energy on these themes—Denise Levertov treats such matters in a more personal, autobiographical way than most previous poets have done. Mallarmé, in his famous sonnet, "La vierge, le vivace et le bel aujourd'hui," depicts the poet's failure of imagination through the remote but lovely symbolic image of a swan trapped in ice and earthbound:

> Un cygne d'autrefois se souvient que c'est lui
> Magnifique mais qui sans espoir se délivre
> Pour n'avoir pas chanté le région où vivre
> Quand du stérile hiver a resplendi l'ennui.

(A swan of former times remembers it is he
Magnificent but who without hope gives himself up
For not having sung of the region where he should
     have been
When the boredom of sterile winter was resplendent.)
(Translation by Wallace Fowlie, from *Mallarmé*, 1953)

But however acutely the poet has felt the anguish of impotence in his art, he has removed those feelings from the sphere of his own life and incorporated them into the symbolic universe of his poetry. Stevens is less divided; indeed, his notebooks indicate that he wished to have his theory of the imagination become a cosmic view that could be shared by all men. Nonetheless, Stevens' poetry is generally impersonal and almost totally divorced from the important details of his existence as a man. Miss Levertov does not recognize such separations and refuses to hide her life from her imagination. Yet she may have learned from Stevens—as well as from her own thoughts or from other poets' work—that poetry can be involved in the mind's activity as an individual goes about his daily business of registering and interpreting and responding to surrounding reality. The poem "Something to Wear" describes in part the preparations the mind or self makes to encounter this reality ("the clamor of / cars and people . . . ") and to elicit from it the substance of art and beauty ("the stars drumming and poems / leaping from shattered windows"). The contemplating self of the poem's beginning does not keep to solitude but, as in "Matins," vii, goes out to meet the world and come upon the stuff of poetry there:

    Marvelous Truth, confront us
    at every turn,
    in every guise, iron ball,
    egg, dark horse, shadow,
    cloud
    of breath on the air,

    dwell
    in our crowded hearts
    our steaming bathrooms, kitchens full of
    things to be done, the
    ordinary streets.

    Thrust close your smile
    that we know you, terrible joy.

Thus for Denise Levertov, as for certain other poets, it is proper, even imperative, for the literary enterprise to concentrate on assigning judgment and value, on finding the marvelous, within the particular range of personal observation and knowledge. If such writing is criticized for a lack of ambitious scope, one might reply that it compensates by a penetrating and scrupulous honesty, by a fundamental human resonance that is anything but restricted, and by a fidelity to the experience of contemporary life. Younger writers today, of almost every allegiance or group, have withdrawn their efforts from the elaboration of symbolic systems and mythologies; the *Cantos, The Waste Land, The Duino Elegies,* although they are still widely admired, apparently are looked upon as distant accomplishments. Now poets believe they must use art to define the space they inhabit as persons—if I may be permitted the figure—the space in which they exist, choose and assert value, love and hate and die. And so for Miss Levertov the poem is an instrument of personal measure, of tests and balances, estimating and preserving the valuable in the teeth of a public actuality that day by day magnifies its impersonality, falsity, and unreality. A poem such as "The Instant" rises out of personal experience and the depth of genuine emotion and significance attached to it by the author. As Miss Levertov's own testament the poem cannot be refuted or denied, for it stands well inside the space her poetic imagination circumscribes about her life as she lives it. Here is the complete poem, taken from her third book *Overland to the Islands* (1958); to cut it would be to destroy the form of an experience as she has realized it:

> "We'll go out before breakfast, and get
> some mushrooms," says my mother.
>
> Early, early: the sun
> risen, but hidden in mist
>
> the square house left behind
> sleeping, filled with sleepers;
>
> up the dewy hill, quietly with baskets.
>
> Mushrooms firm, cold:
>   tussocks of dark grass, gleam of webs,
> turf soft and cropped. Quiet and early. And no valley
>
> no hills: clouds about our knees, tendrils
> of cloud in our hair. Wet scrags
> of wool caught in barbed wire, gorse
> looming, without scent.
>   Then ah! suddenly
> the lifting of it, the mist rolls
>   quickly away, and far, far—
>
> "Look!" she grips me. "It is
>   Eryri!
>   It's Snowdon, fifty
> miles away!"—the voice
> a wave rising to Eryri,
> falling.
>   Snowdon, home
> of eagles, resting-place of
> Merlin, core of Wales.

                              Light
          graces the mountainhead
          for a lifetime's look, before the mist
              draws in again.

   This poem is both an abbreviated narrative, dramatic in character (in this it resembles many poems by Robert Creeley, Paul Carroll, and others), and a spiritual adventure of a nearly ineffable sort. Within the tradition of post-Symbolist literature such a private illumination as the poet has here would be objectified into the order of a larger metaphorical universe—which is not to say that its value would be sacrificed, but that the value would be transmuted. But in the present poem the experience remains unchanged, is viewed in its own terms. Miss Levertov molds the event into art without abandoning the quality of direct utterance or leaving the domain of her life. The instant to which the poem's title refers is the moment of enlightenment that occurs when mist and clouds part to expose the far-off mountain peak shining in the early light of day and richly endowed with legendary meaning. Still, the poem retains its status as a poem of fact, so to speak, emerging from ordinary circumstances and immediate life, and returning there. We are acquainted with this kind of illumination in Blake or Rilke, though for them it confirms the basis of a whole mythological scheme: the world of things ablaze with the eternal Being they mirror. But to find any metaphysical revelation in Miss Levertov's art we must enter the precincts of the poet's own existence, for she justifies her art through that existence, as well as her existence through her artistic perception.
   Miss Levertov's primary intention as a poet has not been the statement of visionary experiences but rather the dogged probing of all the routine business of life in search of what she calls "the authentic" in its rhythms and its details. Her marriage may be a subject for investigation:

                    I want to speak to you.
                    To whom else should I speak?
                    It is you who make
                    a world to speak of.
                    In your warmth the
                    fruits ripen—all the
                    apples and pears that grow
                    on the south wall of my
                    head. If you listen
                    it rains for them, then
                    they drink. If you
                    speak in response
                    the seeds
                    jump into the ground.
                    Speak or be silent; your silence
                    will speak to me. ("The Marriage, II")

or the city's winter streets and the snatches of conversation overheard there:

As the stores close, a winter light
  opens air to iris blue,
  glint of frost through the smoke,
  grains of mica, salt of the sidewalk.
As the buildings closed, released autonomous
  feet pattern the streets
  in hurry and stroll; balloon heads
  drift and dive above them; the bodies
  aren't really there.
As the lights brighten, as the sky darkens,
  a woman with crooked heels says to another woman
  while they step along at a fair pace,
  "You know, I'm telling you, what I love best
  is life. I love life! Even if I ever get
  to be old and wheezy—or limp! You know?
  Limping along?—I'd still . . ." Out of hearing.
To the multiple disordered tones
  of gears changing, a dance
  to the compass points, out, four-way river.
  Prospect of sky
  wedged into avenues, left at the end of streets,
  west sky, east sky: more life tonight! A range
  of open time at winter's outskirts. ("February Evening in New York")

This delighted involvement with what most of us continually neglect as trivia or noise, and the ability to carry out, as Marianne Moore and William Carlos Williams do, poetic conquests in the category of the prosaic, are so natural to Miss Levertov's temperament that she seems scarcely to think of them. She is totally alive to each fluctuation, each breath and vibration of the atmosphere through which she moves with watchful ease. Poetry speaks to her with the innocent tongues of children:

Martha, 5, scrawling a drawing, murmurs
"These are two angels. There are two bombs. They
are in the sunshine. Magic
is dropping from the angels' wings."
Nik, at 4, called
    over the stubble field, "Look
the flowers are dancing underneath the
tree, and the tree
    is looking down with all its apple-eyes."
Without hesitation or debate, words
used and at once forgotten. ("The Lesson")

Even though I find it hard to picture Miss Levertov as an aesthetic theorist musing abstractly upon the rightful function of poetry in a hyper-industrialized society, I am sure that in practice poetry is for her an integral part of the acts, thoughts, and gestures of living. In many of her poems we cross into a world very like our own, with the same ornaments and refuse, commonplaces and strokes of grace, but it is also a world made splendid and different by this poet's wise and clear apprehension of it, her abundant imagination. Poems do more than leap from windows; they appear in the humblest, most mundane things, such as this image, seized from a minute's glance out of the poet's kitchen window over the city at sunset:

> On the kitchen wall a flash
> of shadow:
> > swift pilgrimage
> of pigeons, a spiral
> celebration of air, of sky-deserts.
> And on tenement windows
> a blaze
> > of lustered watermelon:
> stain of the sun
> westering somewhere back of Hoboken.
> > ("The World Outside, I")

The quotidian reality we ignore or try to escape, Denise Levertov revels in, carves and hammers into lyric poems of precise beauty. As celebrations and rituals lifted from the midst of contemporary life in its actual concreteness, her poems are unsurpassed; they open to us aspects of object and situation that but for them we should never have known. And that is no mean achievement for any poet, though it is not the only one Miss Levertov can boast. Another side of her work has slowly asserted itself in two later books, *With Eyes at the Back of Our Heads* (1960) and *The Jacob's Ladder* (1961). I have already alluded to this visionary disposition in discussing "The Instant," but the subsequent pieces rely much more on dream, mystical imagery, and meditation than they do on external conditions that are suddenly transfigured. Some of these poems reflect on the sources of art and imagination and are developments in the line of "Something to Wear," though they find their materials in a deeper layer of consciousness. "The Goddess," "The Well," and "The Illustration," from *The Jacob's Ladder*, are excellent representatives of this category. Other poems press forward on a spiritual journey whose purpose is to uncover the nature of self and its destiny. Miss Levertov's father was a Russian Jew who later became an Anglican clergyman; something of this combination, plus her reading in Biblical, Hasidic, and other mystical writings, undoubtedly has had a decisive influence on these poems.

An example of her meditational poetry is the title poem "With Eyes at the Back of Our Heads"; here Miss Levertov brings to focus two planes of reality that seem to be distant but somehow border one another. The problem is how to get from the first into the second, and the poet addresses herself to it:

With eyes at the back of our heads
we see a mountain
not obstructed with woods but laced
here and there with feathery groves.

The doors before us in a facade
that perhaps has no house in back of it
are too narrow, and one is set high
with no doorsill. The architect sees

the imperfect proposition and
turns eagerly to the knitter.
Set it to rights!
The knitter begins to knit.

For we want
to enter the house, if there is a house,
to pass through the doors at least
into whatever lies beyond them,

we want to enter the arms
of the knitted garment. As one
is re-formed, so the other,
in proportion.

When the doors widen
when the sleeves admit us
the way to the mountain will clear,
the mountain we see with
eyes at the back of our heads, mountain
green, mountain
cut of limestone, echoing
with hidden rivers, mountain
of short grass and subtle shadows.

Miss Levertov gives us here a parable of the inner life, a metaphorical presentation of spiritual pilgrimage in the individual. The heart of the poem appears paradoxical because the mountain, which is an image of paradisical proportions, a depiction of the Great Good Place, is seen only within, by intuition (the "eyes at the back of our heads"), while the obstacles to be overcome and those to which we have to accommodate ourselves lie before us. Yet, as in Heraclitus and Eliot's *Four Quartets*, the way forward and the way back are one and the same. Thus movement ahead, with the alterations of the self it requires, will be completed in a reconciliation of the inner image of a desired goal with a personal condition of life. Perhaps what we are being told is, "The Kingdom of God is within you." In this, as in her other remarkable poems, Miss Levertov subtly points the way to see with our whole sight.

To Celebrate: A Reading of
Denise Levertov
Thomas A. Duddy*

In "A Note on the Work of the Imagination" Denise Levertov describes how a dream once helped to re-inforce her faith in the power of the imagination to re-create "reality":

> I had been dreaming of a large house, set in a flat landscape, . . . At a certain point I half awoke, and when I returned to the dream I was conscious that I was dreaming. . . . What gripped me was the knowledge that I was dreaming, and vividly. A black, white and gray tiled pavement I crossed—how "real" it felt under my feet! . . . At length I came into a small bedroom fitted with a washbasin and mirror and the idea came to me of looking in the mirror as a test of how far in fidelity the dream would go; but I was afraid. I was afraid the mirror would show me a blank, or a strange face—I was afraid of the fright that would give me. However, I dared: and approached the mirror. It was rather high on the wall, and not tilted, so that what first appeared, as I slowly drew near, was the top of my head. But yes, surely something was wrong—a misty whiteness glimmered there!
>
> I crept nearer still, and standing straight, almost on tiptoe, now saw my whole face, my usual face-in-the-glass—pale, the dark eyes somewhat anxious, but in no way changed, or lacking or causing me fear. What then was the radiant glimmer that had startled me just before?
>
> Why!—in the dark, somewhat fluffy hair was a network of little dew or mist diamonds, like spiders' webs on a fall morning! The creative unconscious— the imagination—had *provided,* instead of a fright, this exquisitely realistic detail. For hadn't I been walking in the misty fields in the dewfall hour? Just so, then, would my damp hair look. I awoke in delight, reminded forcibly of just what it is we love in the greatest writers . . . *that following through,* that *permeation* of detail—relevant, illuminating detail—which marks the total imagination, distinct from intellect, at work.[1]

As a statement on the poetic imagination, this prose passage has a vividness of psychology that is unique among the poetics of any writer I know. It is remarkable prose from a very remarkable poet. I quote it at length, of course, not as primary material, but as the illuminating key to what I find central in Miss Levertov's poetry. In its concern with the imagination's relation to actuality, the passage focuses on a recurrent source of tension in her work: the effort to create a circumstance in poetry that will celebrate reality while remaining faithful to its facts. The test at the mirror is thus Miss Levertov's dream-allegory of the poet's two-fold obligation. First he must portray with verisimilitude the facts of his world (the "usual face-in-the-glass"); second he must discover that unexpected, illuminating detail (the

*Reprinted with permission from *Criticism* 10, no. 2 (1968), 138–52.

"misty whiteness" in the dreamer's hair) which makes it possible for celebration to take place. I should make it clear now that by "celebration" I am not referring only to the kind of spontaneous delight in nature's regeneration that we get in a poem like "The Cuckoo Song." It is, more often, not so much a joy in the things of the earth as it is a moment of awareness in which the poet's identity is discovered in the things of the earth, both in time and in space. As a pervasive theme in her poems, this quest for an authentic mode of celebration illustrates a body of poetry ambitiously confronting its primary intentions. In intention, as well as in achievement, Denise Levertov seems to me to be a major poet.

In the dream passage the triumph of the imagination (and art) over reality is accomplished with relative ease: the dreamer, to a certain extent, wills it so. In the poems, however, the conflict is not so easily resolved. In "The Goddess" especially, which in 1966 Miss Levertov significantly called her favourite poem, Truth's victory is achieved with all the violence we expect from a battle scene in *Beowulf.* The speaker of the poem (the poet as Platonic falsifier) is visited by the Goddess, a kind of Muse of Poetic Truth, and consequently thrown out of her home, Lie Castle. The Goddess:

> Flung me across the room, and
> room after room (hitting the walls, re-
> bounding—to the last
> sticky wall—wrenching away from it
> pulled hair out!)
> till I lay
> outside the outer walls!²

Outside the castle the speaker feels a new awareness, a sense of the vitality and language of the earth. In the mud into which she has been hurled she discovers the concealed forests sleeping within seeds. As in the dream passage the speaker is brought to a consciousness of the authentic by an illuminating fact, a permeating detail which allows the earth to speak for itself ("I bit on a seed and it spoke on my tongue") and which is the stuff of poetic truth. Both the dream passage and "The Goddess," then, though "The Goddess" is more nightmarish than dream-like, are allegories of revelation and poetic faith. In justifying her selection of "The Goddess" as her favourite composition, Miss Levertov wrote:

> I have chosen it because it is one that recalls to me one of those confrontations with Truth that every person, every soul, must somehow experience if he or she is to live, to grow; and especially one who is a poet—for poets have a genius for lying and an adoration for the truth, and it may be that the driving impulse of every poet is to maintain the dynamic interplay of these two passions.³

There may be some hyperbole here, I am not sure, but what this explanation unquestionably reveals is a poetics of morals, though not, of course, in the facile nineteenth century sense. Shelley's notion of the poet as spokesman of

Truth is given a shifted emphasis in Miss Levertov's image of the poet as one who resists falsehood, especially of the potential "lie" in every poem.

Despite the affirmative resolution of "The Goddess," most renderings of the conflict between the fictive and the authentic come to no such transcendent conclusions. More representative are those poems which end on a note of self-conscious frustration. Such poems usually illustrate the speaker's fear that to say anything at all is to say more or less than the truth, a fear, as it were, that the dream-mirror will reflect only distortions. Often this hesitation to speak is a result of the poet's essential distrust of language, an attitude expressed in "The Third Dimension" from *Here and Now:*

> a simple honesty is
>
> nothing but a lie.
> . . . .
> but love
> cracked me open
>
> and I'm
> alive to
>
> tell the tale—but not
> honestly:
>
> the words
> change it.[4]

This reluctance to commit oneself to the act of language is, appropriately enough, an attitude assumed most of all in the early love poems. In "The Marriage, II," also from *Here and Now,* the speaker ends: "Speak or be silent: Your silence / will speak to me." Unable to articulate anything more meaningful than silence (a recurrent word in Denise Levertov's early poetry), speech remains ineffectual redundancy. This hesitating voice is not, of course, unique with Miss Levertov; we find it in no less a poet than Milton. And for both poets, John Milton and Denise Levertov, this reluctance implies a level of celebration that is frustratingly beyond the poets' powers to achieve. With Milton this reluctance takes the form of a self-conscious statement of inadequacy as spokesman for the Puritan ideal. With Miss Levertov it is more generally a fear that language is not an accurate metaphor for existential awareness. But though language may misrepresent the celebrant's gifts:

> I want to give you
> something I've made
>
> some words on a page—as if
> to say "Here are some blue beads"

> or, "Here's a bright red leaf I found on
> the sidewalk"
>
> . . . .
> But it's difficult, . . .

yet the need to celebrate urges us on (cf. "Lycidas") to the next poem:

> If
>
> I ever write
> a poem of a certain temper
>
> (wilful, tender, evasive,
> sad & rakish)
>
> I'll give it to you. ("The Rights," *Here and Now,* p. 9)

Beyond the inherent lie in words, "truth" and "revelation" are also frustrated by the equivocal nature of reality itself. The attempt to celebrate thus becomes a contest between the poet's "adoration for the truth," manifest in his discovery of the illuminating fact, and his fear that the particular engagement with reality that that fact represents is half-truth or, worse, complete distortion. Given an ambiguous, deceptive, almost impregnable condition of reality, how then does the poet proceed? What if there *is* no fact which, in its truth, celebrates? Terror, after all, may be a more accurate response to reality, and it has its own facts. A poem which dramatizes the poet's precarious faith in her perception is "At the Edge," from *With Eyes at the Back of Our Heads.* Here celebration is reduced to an assumed condition, a hypothetical truth which is juxtaposed to another, more frightening possibility. In its shift in tone, it is "The Goddess" in reverse:

> How much I should like to begin
> a poem with And—presupposing
> the hardest said—
> the moss cleared off the stone,
> the letters plain.
> How the round moon
> would shine into all the corners
> of such a poem and show
> the words! Moths and dazzled
> awakened birds
> would freeze in its light!
> The lines would be
> an outbreak of bells
> and I swinging on the rope!
>
> Yet, not desiring apocrypha
> but true revelation,

what use to pretend the stone discovered,
anything visible?
That poem indeed
may not be carved there, may lie
—the quick of mystery—
in animal eyes gazing
from the thicket,
a creature of unknown size,
fierce, terrified, having teeth or
no defense, but whom
no And may approach suddenly. (*With Eyes* . . . , p. 49)

The first stanza is fanciful, gently ironic, and infinitely cheerful. The hypothetical discovery of illuminating fact, "the moss cleared off the stone," produces a poet-celebrant of extraordinary vitality, and the stanza progresses from the initial statement of pre-supposition to the final exuberant exclamation of church bells ringing. But the church bells don't quite ring true, and the childlike quality of this metaphor is just fanciful enough to remind us that it is, after all, only a condition of wish-fulfillment and not "true revelation." To this loud "yes" of the opening stanza, the second one replies with a regretful "no." From bell-ringing naivete the poem's tone suddenly shifts to doubt and fear, those things which experience teaches us. In its movement from innocence to experience, the poem's structure suggests the initial stages of Blake's five-stage journey of the soul. And much more obviously Blakean is the "fact" which illuminates Miss Levertov's alternative truth: the ominous "creature of unknown size" waiting at the edge of the jungle. While more forbidding, this "truth" is yet no more the point of the poem than was that in the first stanza. Truths cancel each other out, as it were, and the reader is left at the end of the poem with unresolved tension. "At the Edge," in its portrayal of the celebrant as escapist, reveals more than any other of Denise Levertov's poems does a refusal to furnish easy solutions to difficult poetic problems. Celebration is thus made to seem a remote possibility not only because "the words change it," but also because reality does not so easily give up its truths.

In what circumstances, then, can celebration take place? In the two pieces that I have discussed as examples of celebration, "A Note on the Work of the Imagination" and "The Goddess," it occurs, significantly, in non-"realistic" situations. "The Goddess" affirms, but in the other-worldly circumstance of allegory. In "A Note on the Work of the Imagination" celebration is twice-removed: it occurs within the general context of the dream-state, and more particularly as a moment of recognition in the looking-glass. What this non-realistic, sometimes surrealistic, circumstance suggests (and it exists in many poems) is the essentially medieval notion that ultimate truth is accessible only in dreams. And Miss Levertov tells us as much in "Matins," a poem from *The Jacob's Ladder:*

> The authentic! Shadows of it
> sweep past in dreams,
>
> . . . .
>
> as we think an undercurrent
> of dream runs through us
> faster than thought
> towards recognition.[5]

This passage, and the whole of "Matins," speaks directly to the mode of thought necessary to apprehend truth. It does not mean, of course, that the celebrant be in an actual state of sleep. For celebration of the authentic can take place, as "Matins" shows us, in so literal a circumstance as "rising from the toilet seat." What is meant by "dream," then, is not the medieval concept, but a condition which seems to combine both the natures of Joycean epiphany and Blakean mysticism. Like the epiphany, celebration occurs at random moments of ordinary experience when one is "off-guard." Recognition is surprise, a moment in which the earth, unsolicited, is allowed to speak for itself: "I bit on a seed and it spoke on my tongue," as Miss Levertov writes in "The Goddess." Thus a poem like "At the Edge" falls short of celebration, not only because of equivocal reality, but also because of its voice, which is too hyper-actively seeking what only the passive but sensitive mind can hope to achieve. The extent to which Denise Levertov's "celebration" resembles Blake's mysticism is more difficult to discuss. In Blake's vision of "a world in a grain of sand," we have a transcendent, neo-Platonic grasp of "reality." Like Blake, Miss Levertov also sees *more* than the grain of sand, but the direction of her awareness is not beyond, but *within* the grain of sand. Hers is not so much a transcendental reality as it is an *immanent* one. "No ideas but in things," said Dr. Williams. Thus the discovery of the authentic, while threatening to become mysticism, constantly falls back upon and within the facts of ordinary existence. Celebration then becomes the recognition of a more "real" reality. While brushing her hair in rhythmic strokes, the speaker of "Matins" breaks the handle of her hairbrush:

> That's it,
> that's joy, it's always
> a recognition, the known
> appearing fully itself, and
> more itself than one knew.

Through a series of such epiphanies, "Matins" moves to its concluding, more general recognition, in which the speaker urges Truth to "Thrust close your smile / that we know you, terrible joy." Like Sisyphus, whose existential awareness combines recognition of the absurd and joy *in* that recognition, the speaker of "Matins" celebrates an ambivalent situation in perception.

While "Matins" exemplifies recognition as a typical instance of Denise Levertov's thematic pre-occupations, the poem shows, too, that recognition is often the strategy of her work as well as its subject. In "Some Notes on

Organic Form" the poet defines organic poetry in part as "a *method of apperception*, i. e., of recognizing what we perceive . . . a sequence or constellation of perceptions of sufficient interest, felt by the poet intensely enough to demand of him their equivalence in words."[6] Through this method of apperception the poet is then *"brought to speech."* "Matins" perfectly reveals this method of apperception at work. The accumulated moments of awareness, from the first epiphany to the concluding recognition of ambivalent Truth, are precisely that re-enactment in language of the process by which the poet is brought to speak. The poem thus demonstrates the primary concept of organic poetry: that form must follow function.

As statements of apperception, many poems are specifically a working out of the relationship between the past and the present and between the remote and the immediate. A pre-occupation with the past has always been, of course, a typical stance of the Romantic poet, but it is seldom that Denise Levertov allows the poem to become merely a Wordsworthian celebration of lost innocence or former glory. "In Abeyance," from *O Taste and See,* approaches this Wordsworthian sense of the past in its nostalgia for the lost ritual of Homeric Greece, but the tone is so severely under-stated that it never really becomes melancholy. Even when the poem is substantively concerned with the non-present, the speaker's (and the reader's) attention is usually directed to the present. "To the Reader," the introductory poem from *The Jacob's Ladder,* demonstrates this immediacy:

> As you read, a white bear leisurely
> pees, dyeing the snow
> saffron,
>
> and as you read, many gods
> lie among lianas: eyes of obsidian
> are watching the generations of leaves,
>
> and as you read
> the sea is turning its dark pages,
> turning
> its dark pages.

On one level, the poem may serve as a reminder of the great continuum of space and time, and the images pull the reader away, as it were, from his specific situation *as* reader. On a more significant level, however, "To the Reader" insists upon a greater awareness of the present, the immediate situation. The reader is thrust back to his immediate circumstance not only by the refrain "as you read," but also because the awareness that the poem invites the reader to engage is an immediate, present action of thought, possible only here and now.

In most poems which celebrate the awareness of juxtaposed past-present realities, the present is emphasized by a vivid rendering of the immediate poetic drama, both in voice and image. "The Garden Wall," which exemplifies almost everything I have said about Denise Levertov so far, also reveals this immediacy. The poem begins with a voice firmly grounded in the homely familiarity of the poem's circumstance:

> Bricks of the wall,
> so much older than the house—
> taken I think from a farm pulled down
> when the street was built—[7]

In measuring one fact of his reality (the age of the bricks) in terms of other facts, the speaker here displays a voice as ordinary as that of any vague musing. There is reminiscence here, but not revelation. Then follows a detailed description of the wall in its setting;

> Modestly, though laid with panels and parapets,
> a wall behind the flowers—
> roses and hollyhocks, the silver
> pods of lupine, sweet-tasting
> phlox, gray
> lavender—

Keatsian in its sensuousness, this passage paints a "realistic," yet meaningful, picture of the wall in perspective. The flowers, the conventional details of *new* life and proof of the natural cycle, splash color onto the poet's canvas and easily upstage the old wall, which acts as scenic background and "foil" to the flowers. In voice and in image the poem is thus far stock Romanticism. But uniquely Denise Levertov is the rest of the poem, where the "illuminating fact" allows the metaphysic of the poem to enter. The speaker of the poem waters the flower bed and undeliberately allows spray from the garden hose to wash away from the wall "pocks and warts" of dirt. Thus baptized, the wall-within-the-wall rivals the flowers in brilliance of color:

> a hazy red, a
> grain gold, a mauve
> of small shadows, sprung
> from the quiet dry brown—

In recognizing the correspondence between the wall and the flowers, the speaker further acknowledges the great continuum, that "all ages are contemporaneous." The poem ends in revelation:

> archetype
> of the world always a step
> beyond the world, that can't
> be looked for, only
> as the eye wanders,
> found.

For a number of reasons, I am tempted to call "The Garden Wall" Denise Levertov's most representative poem. As organic poetry it is exemplary: the psychic growth of the speaker, as a mode of apperception, is itself the logic or form of the poem. The drama of the poem is properly ordinary in the sense that watering the garden is quotidian action. The discovery of the colorful wall, moreover, demonstrates Miss Levertov's joy in the unfolding of inner realities. This sense of discovery is most explicitly expressed in "Pleasures": "I like to find / what's not found / at once, but lies / within something of another nature" (*With Eyes . . .* , p. 17). Typical also in "The Garden Wall" is its revelation, which synthesizes the randomly experienced surprise of epiphany and the more profound insight of the Platonic cast of mind. And finally "The Garden Wall" is representative of that greater sense of the present, the immediate moment, which revelation inspires. As the ligature between old and new, and as the archetype which obliterates the tyranny of measurable time, the "narrow bricks of another century" dramatize existential consciousness. Awareness is, and is the object of, celebration.

This sense of present awareness is a constant pre-occupation especially of *O Taste and See,* and as the volume's title suggests, it is a condition of the *body*'s awakening as well as the mind's. In this sense celebration combines awareness of the body and nature's readiness with the deeper understanding of the archetypes. In "The Disclosure" physical awakening is embodied in the literal circumstance of birth, of the opening cocoon. What emerges is not the fanciful butterfly nor the Gothic moth of "indecipherable / gold": instead out pushes "some primal-shaped, plain-winged, day-flying thing." The whole point of the poem is the disclosure and the celebration of all that is miraculously ordinary. Not old, but "primal," the "thing" is thus archetypally a reminder of time's continuum and an emblem of ordinary man in his present circumstances, as opposed to the gorgeous butterfly and moth, symbols of a romanticized past. More clearly an example of awareness as the awakening of body and mind is "The Coming Fall," which shows how the awareness of passing time affects nature and man. The poem opens with a description of the eastern sky trying to hold back the night. The east is "flinging / nets of cloud / to hold the rose light a moment longer." The east, with despair and a sense of loss, resists the inevitable passage of time, not knowing that we cannot make our sun stand still. Contrasted to this Epicurean regret for the dying of the light is the Peripatetic attitude of the ant which abides the present by prudently arranging for the coming darkness. The passage is one of Denise Levertov's great details:

> The ants
> on their acropolis
> prepare for the night. (*O Taste and See*, p. 38)

While not necessarily referring to the specific hill on which the Parthenon sits, "acropolis" cannot easily avoid that association. In thus providing a creature so far down on the great chain as the ant with a habitat so exalted as the acropolis, the poet produces a detail of surprising magnitude and, in context, a chilling sense of foreboding. Following this is a more or less

Keatsian description of the coming fall (cf. "To Autumn"), which is in turn followed by a shadowy picture of "human figures" silhouetted against the dying sun. It is with the human consciousness of time's passage that the last, the climactic section of the poem is concerned. Unlike the backward looking eastern sky or the forward looking ant, the poet responds with a more intense appreciation of the present:

>A sense of the present
>rises out of earth and grass,
>enters the feet, ascends
>
>into the genitals, constricting
>the breast, lightening
>the head—a wisdom,
>
>a shiver, a delight
>that what is passing
>is here, as if
>a snake went by, green in the
>gray leaves.

The ascendant motion of the "sense of the present" parallels the psychic process of revelation. The ascendance "into the genitals" is, of course, a sexual awakening—a spontaneous delight in the body's ripeness, and more generally a joy in the life of sensation. The further movement upwards to the heart and ultimately to the head initiates the second awakening—revelation or existential understanding. The movement Denise Levertov gives to the "sense of the present" is thus a kinetic metaphor for the causal relationship implied in her Biblical allusion: "O taste [be responsive to sensation] and see [then understand]." This dual process (a favourite borrowing from Locke and Hartley's sensationalism of most of the English Romantics) is brilliantly synthesized at the end of the poem in the snake simile. Traditionally an emblem of divine wisdom, the snake is coloured green, equally traditional in its association with physical regeneration. (As in "The Garden Wall," the poet uses colour functionally as "illuminating fact"). The "green snake," while thus synthesizing *and* enlivening a conventional symbolism, crystallizes the poet's sense of awareness as a physical and a cerebral engagement with the present. Like "The Garden Wall," "The Coming Fall" underlines central preoccupations of the whole of *O Taste and See.*

In discussing near the beginning of this essay those forces antagonistic to celebration, I spoke of "At the Edge" as an example of those poems in which celebration is frustrated by interior (distrust of language) and exterior (ambiguous reality) powers. The *dramatization* of that failure was the speaker's inability to clear the moss off the stone, to view the illuminating fact. The happy resolution to this "problem poem" was "The Garden Wall," where the bricks of the wall, equal in substance to the stone, *are* discovered in the properly random experience of the properly passive speaker.

Yet in some poems where celebration is indeed achieved, the very difficulty and precariousness of that achievement is suggested in the *kind* of fact discovered. Lacking the solidity and endurance of the undiscovered stone or the discovered bricks, some illuminating facts are conspicuously fragile and delicate. The victory of the dreamer's creative imagination in "A Note on the Work of the Imagination," for example, depends upon "a network of little dew or mist diamonds," a circumstance as ephemeral as the dream-state itself. Similar "nets" appear throughout the poems. "Nets of cloud" vainly postpone darkness in "The Coming Fall." A mysterious "net of threads / finer than cobweb and as / elastic" draws the speaker of "The Thread" irresistibly to a "stirring of wonder" (*The Jacob's Ladder*, p. 48). Similarly, hair, as in "A Note on the Work of the Imagination," appears as significant detail in "Luxury" (*The Jacob's Ladder*, p. 52) and in "A Psalm Praising the Hair of Man's Body" (*O Taste and See*, p. 82). Perhaps the most original expression of the delicate, the slender illuminating fact is in "The Crack," where a metaphor of spring enters the house through a crack in the wintry window pane;

> While snow fell carelessly
> . . . .
> a spring night entered
> my mind through the tight-closed window,
> wearing
>
> a loose Russian shirt of
> light silk.
>   For this, then,
> that slanting
> line was left, that crack, the pane
> never replaced. (*O Taste and See*, p. 28)

In the very best sense of the word, "The Crack" seems to be one of Denise Levertov's most charming poems. "The loose Russian shirt of light silk" is a wonderfully sensuous metaphor for a spring night, and the crack in the pane seems a properly delicate entrance for a metaphor so fanciful. Despite the slender, almost infinitesimal opportunity the crack provides, awareness does indeed creep through, and easily, with no sense of conflict. We are thus reminded of the struggle to celebrate only slightly, in the "fact" of the cracked pane, if not in its function in context. The improbability that aware-ness will be achieved juxtaposed to the ease with which it *is* achieved pro-duces an irony more fanciful, I think, than imaginative. In a poem called "Art," from *With Eyes at the Back of Our Heads*, Miss Levertov advises the practising artist to work with "hard, strong materials" and to forego "easy rhythms" and "pliant clay." "The Crack," though a good poem, is atypically not cast in those harder materials. The typical poem in which the process of celebration is acted out is a virile confrontation, and it is made of unyielding stone. "The Jacob's Ladder," one of Denise Levertov's most brilliant achievements, is precisely this kind of poem. I quote it in its entirety at the end of this essay.

In having chosen to limit my discussion of Denise Levertov to those poems which *enact* apperception (both of the imagination and of existential consciousness), I have necessarily avoided speaking of those poems, many of which are my favourites, in which celebration is an accomplished fact. "Luxury," for example, is an exuberantly girlish celebration of the speaker's sexuality. "A Psalm Praising the Hair of Man's Body" is another feminine celebration, though the voice is here that of a primal earth-mother. But the tone of exaltation in these poems is static, and my subject has been celebration as a dynamic force. Like the English Romantics, especially like Keats, Wordsworth, and Blake, Denise Levertov places great faith in the power of the poetic imagination to unlock realities. Accordingly, the urge to celebrate is the attempt of the imagination (the eyes at the back of our heads) to ascend (the Jacob's ladder) to a recognition (tasting and seeing) of the present (here and now). The effort to celebrate is not easy. The poem ascends and the ascent is hard:

> The stairway is not
> a thing of gleaming strands
> a radiant evanescence
> for angels' feet that only glance in their tread, and need not
> touch the stone.
>
> It is of stone.
> A rosy stone that takes
> a glowing tone of softness
> only because behind it the sky is a doubtful, a doubting
> night gray.
>
> A stairway of sharp
> angles, solidly built.
> One sees that the angels must spring
> down from one step to the next, giving a little
> lift of the wings:
>
> and a man climbing
> must scrape his knees, and bring
> the grip of his hands into play. The cut stone
>
> consoles his groping feet. Wings brush past him.
> The poem ascends.

Notes

1. Denise Levertov, "A Note on the Work of the Imagination," *New Directions 17* (1961), 48–49.

2. Denise Levertov, *With Eyes at the Back of Our Heads* (New York: New Directions, 1960), 43; hereafter cited in text.

3. Denise Levertov, "The Goddess" in *Poet's Choice*, eds. Paul Engle and Joseph Langland (New York: Dell, 1962), 210–12.

4. Denise Levertov, *Here and Now* (San Francisco: City Lights, 1957), 25–26.

5. Denise Levertov, *The Jacob's Ladder* (New York: New Directions, 1961), 57–58.

6. Denise Levertov, "Some Notes on Organic Form," *Poetry* 106 (September 1965), 240.

7. Denise Levertov, *O Taste and See* (New York: New Directions, 1964), 60.

From Reverence to Attention:
The Poetry of Denise Levertov   Julian Gitzen*

Denise Levertov's name has long been associated with those of Charles Olson, Robert Duncan, and Robert Creeley. Despite the ample justification for placing her in this company, and despite the similarities, for instance, between "projective verse" as defined by Olson and "organic form" as defined by Levertov, there is a danger that exclusive comparison of her writing with that of the Black Mountain or Projectivist poets may obscure the uniqueness of her own poetic theory and practice. A separate study of her work must recognize her strong affinities with Keats and Stevens, as well as with Pound, Williams, and Olson. In fact, as a theoretician she aligns herself primarily with Keats and to a lesser degree with Hopkins, although she is certainly indebted to Williams and Olson for their defense of fluid form and "irregular / measure."

Before examining her poetry, it may be useful to review her poetic theory, which is essentially psychological. That is, she emphasizes the mental condition of the poet rather than the qualities of the finished poem. The state of mind which she regards as most conducive to successful writing resembles Negative Capability as described by Keats: "It struck me what quality went to form a Man of Achievement, especially in Literature, and which Shakespeare possessed so enormously—I mean *Negative Capability*, that is, when a man is capable of being in uncertainties, mysteries, doubts, without any irritable searching after fact and reason."[1] Levertov speaks admiringly of "that intense passivity, that passive intensity, that passionate patience which Keats named Negative Capability and which I believe to be a vital condition for the emergence of a true poem."[2] Singling out for approval a related Keatsian pronouncement that "The Genius of Poetry must work out its own salvation in a man: It cannot be matured by law and precept, but by sensation & watchfulness in itself,"[3] she asserts that a poet who would write well must bring to his subject the "ecstatic *attention*, the *intensity*, that would penetrate to its reality" (*PW*, p. 97). A poet whose attention to his

*Reprinted with permission from *Midwest Quarterly* 16 (1975), 328–41.

subject is sufficiently keen will not need to search for appropriate words, for those words will suggest themselves to him. The writer's success will depend upon his "attention, and on the degree to which he is able to translate into words, that which he experiences; or rather, on how well he can listen for the words that are its incarnation, its *taking on the flesh*. . . . Yes, there *is* something of labor in the creative process: but it consists in that *focusing of attention upon what is given*, and not in the 'struggle for expression' " (*PW*, p. 223).

While Levertov's conception of the poet as an intense Keatsian observer shapes the core of her theory of "organic form," she also makes use of Hopkins's term "inscape" in extended form. Beginning with Hopkins's definition of "inscape" as an object's "intrinsic form," she argues that "intellectual and emotional experience" as well as objects or living beings may possess "inscape," and that the poet conscious of such form may seek to reproduce it by analogy in a shaped poem. The author seeking to recreate a given inscape must "contemplate" it with Keatsian watchfulness. If his attention remains steady, the first words of the poem eventually will come to him. They may be, of course, mere "forerunners," unsuitable for the final draft, but serving to provoke in turn "the words which are the actual beginning of the poem." The poet's mental energy must not slacken, however, until he has completed a poem the form of which reflects to his satisfaction the form of its subject: "It is faithful attention to the experience from the first moment of crystallization that allows those first or those forerunning words to rise to the surface: and with that same fidelity of attention the poet, from that moment of being let in to the possibility of the poem, must follow through, letting the experience lead him through the world of the poem, its unique inscape revealing itself as he goes" (*PW*, p. 9).

Although her major essay, "Some Notes on Organic Form," makes only passing mention of imagination, it is obvious from other critical remarks that Levertov, like Keats, regards imagination as an indispensable poetic faculty. Like Stevens, however, she conceives of imagination as being more closely akin to understanding than to fancy or fantasy, and she probably would agree with Stevens's conclusion that imagination seldom fruitfully transcends reality, but performs a vital service in illuminating or modifying the real. For example, she assumes that imagination is responsible for Keatsian empathy, as illustrated in his famous remark, "If a Sparrow come before my Window I take part in its existence and pick about the Gravel."[4] Levertov contends: "No recognition of others is possible without the imagination. The imagination of what it is to *be* those other forms of life . . . is the only way to recognition" (*PW*, p. 53). The imagination, then, as Levertov conceives of it, is the power of mentally recreating reality. In "A Note on the Work of the Imagination" she recalls one of her dreams, the graphic intensity of which she attributes to her imagination. For instance, her image in a mirror included "a network of little dew or mist diamonds" sprinkled in her hair. Wondering at the power of imagination to introduce "this exquisitely realistic detail" appropriate to a dream in which she had "been walking in the misty fields in the dewfall hour," she concludes, "I awoke in delight, reminded forcibly of just what it is we love in the greatest writers . . . that *following through*, that *permeation of detail . . .* which marks the total imagination, distinct from intellect, at work. . . . Mere Reason can place two eyes and a nose where we suppose them to be. But it was Imagination put seed pearls of summer fog in Tess Durbeyfield's hair . . . and it was the same holy, independent faculty that sprinkled my hair with winter-evening diamonds" (*PW*, p. 204). Furthermore, while attention or understanding may merely record or classify current experiences, imagination can mentally create phenomena belonging to the author's past or which are not a part of his own experience. It is thus distinguished as a creative faculty which reproduces or reshapes reality. It should be added, however, that in her poems, as distinct from her criticism, Levertov's imagination does occasionally operate freely in the realm of vision or dream, bringing into tangible form spiritual figures such as angels ("A Vision") or the Muse ("The Goddess"), or taking a purely fantastic turn, as in "The Departure."

In the poems, imagination is normally associated with the moon, and poems like "Song for Ishtar" underline its central importance in the creative process. Indeed, "At the Edge" makes creativity almost synonymous with imagination:

> How much I should like to begin
> a poem with And—presupposing
> the hardest said—
> the moss cleared off the stone,
> the letters plain.
> How the round moon
> would shine into all the corners
> of such a poem and show
> the words!

Although the moon is cold, it suits Levertov's purposes to envision it as burning with a "cold fire," since, as we will see, she associates fire with energy, and she regards the mental energy of imagination as the "source / of mind's fire." Thus, it is the "cold fire" of the moon (imagination) which activates "a woman [who] has that cold fire in her / called poet" ("The Elves"). This fire engenders art, but it can be cruelly tyrannical and implacable in its manipulation of reality, a point central to "In Mind," a poem in which Levertov envisions her mind as inhabited by two women. One is innocent and "unadorned but / fair featured," but she lacks imagination. The second is a "turbulent moon-ridden girl," who "knows strange songs— / but she is not kind." The awesomeness of imaginative power is further underlined in "Moon Tiger," the very title of which is indicative. For the artist, however, the exercise of imagination is compulsive, and his vision is altered as a result. Another of Levertov's favorite Keatsian remarks is, "The Imagination may be

one continuing on at the expense of another, and some detours are inevitable. "A Defeat in the Green Mountains" describes how a woman "drawn by the river sound" brings two "unwilling" children with her to the verge of a river. They stop at the bank, confronted by "a movement crossing / their halted movement." Since the river is too powerful and deep for them to cross, the woman trudges back with the children to the

> main road—defeated,
> to ponder the narrow
> depth of the river,
> its absorbed movement past her.

Movement is change, and change can be painful, but with admirable consistency the poet welcomes and celebrates change, despite its attendant inconvenience or pain. "A Sequence" draws an analogy between a skyline being altered by the construction of a large building and changes occurring in the lives and personalities of a married couple. Although the rising building alters the view, the change is enriching:

> . . . "The skyline's changing,
> the window's allowance of sky is
> smaller
>   but more
> intensely designed, sprinkled
> with human gestures."

Similarly, changes in personality or temperament may contribute to human welfare, a point dramatized by the "angel of happiness" who appears to the couple and sets fire to "the paraphernalia / of unseen change." Despite eyes smarting from the smoke, the pair "laugh and warm" themselves.

It is characteristic that in this instance fire is the agent of consuming change. Following literary tradition, Levertov consistently employs fire-imagery as an emblem of energy-discharge. For instance, she represents sexual excitement as fire or flame, as in "Eros at Temple Stream":

> our hands were
> flames
> stealing upon quickened flesh until
> no part of us but was
> sleek and
> on fire

Intense energy or vitality in any form, however, is likely to be represented by fire. In "Obsessions" the poet and her husband have returned to the city after spending some time in the country. She questions whether they were compelled to return because only the city could offer them that suitably energetic atmosphere in which "the most life [is] burned," but rejects the idea that cities have a "monopoly / of intense life." She knows that the sun burned with the same brilliance in the country, and that their emotions were equally powerful in that rural setting "where the city's ashes that we brought with us / flew into the intense sky still burning."

Energy in nearly all forms is attractive to Levertov, but nowhere more so than when manifested in art. One is reminded of Olson's definition: "A poem is energy transferred from where the poet got it . . . by way of the poem itself to . . . the reader. . . . Then the poem itself must, at all points, be a high energy-discharge." Levertov would certainly agree that the language and thought of a poem should radiate energy. Appropriately enough, she is interested in music and dance, both of which employ considerable energy to produce effects of harmony and grace. Since she equates energy with movement, she envisions music as a form of movement, as in "Six Variations":

> Two flutes! How close
> to each other they move
> in mazing figures,
> never touching, never
> breaking the measure,
> as gnats dance in
> summer haze all afternoon. . . .

Conversely, movement itself may attain for her a harmony reminiscent of music, as in the "melody moving downstream" of a "string of barges / moving with / the river." The music of the barges' movement is

> sung if it is sung
> quietly
>
> within the scored
> crashing and the
> almost inaudible hum impinging
> upon the river's
> seawardness

Music has a further appeal to Levertov, since, like Stevens, she believes poetry and music to be closely related (*cf. PW*, p. 24). An art form even more closely suited to her temperament and outlook, however, is the dance. An experienced ballet dancer, she recalls in "Dance Memories" how

> the joy of leaping, of moving by
> leaps and bounds, of gliding
> to leap, and gliding
> to leap becomes, while it lasts,
> heart pounding, breath hurting,
> the deepest, the only joy.

Energy disciplined to graceful expression arouses a coveted joy in the artist and, presumably, brings satisfaction to his audience.

Levertov approves of the remark by the German sculptor and playwright Ernst Barlach, "Every art needs two—one who makes it, and one who needs it." Accordingly, the artist has an obligation to his audience as well as to himself. Levertov's concern for the needs of her readers is further illuminated by her admiration for Ibsen's statement, "The task of the poet is to make clear to himself, and thereby to others, the temporal and eternal questions." Ibsen's words were the inspiration for "Three Meditations," in which the poet describes herself as "I multitude, I tyrant, / I angel, I you, you / world." Commenting about this poem, she refers to the poet as a "microcosm" reflecting the "tyrannies, injustices, hopes and mercies" of the larger world, and, alluding to Ibsen's dictum, she concludes, "What the poet is called on to clarify is not answers but the existence and nature of questions; and his likelihood of so clarifying them for others is made possible only through the dialogue within himself" (*PW*, p. 45). Levertov thus joins a growing number of leading American poets, including Lowell, Roethke, Plath, Snyder, and Bly, who have turned to autobiographical verse on the initial premise that the thoughts, feelings, and activities of the poet are representative of (and therefore of interest to) other men.

Levertov's autobiographical poems reflect a personality dominated by intense feeling. Characteristically, she has written numerous love poems, such as "The Wife," "The Ache of Marriage," "Love Song," "About Marriage" "Our Bodies," "Losing Track," and "Bedtime." Although joy is the emotion she cherishes, other poems are devoted to "Terror," "Despair," grief or sorrow ("Lamentation," "To Speak") and agony ("As It Happens"). Among the most powerful emotions in her verse are those aroused by her reaction to U.S. intervention in Vietnam. Although horror at the spilling of innocent blood is not unusual, her own revulsion is intensified by an empathetic tendency to recreate in herself the fear and anguish of the Vietnamese. Her identification with the Vietnamese is recorded explicitly in "Glimpses of Vietnamese Life," a journal of her visit to Hanoi in 1972. Her anger at the failure of others to share her reaction explodes when she is subjected to the expression of well meaning but misplaced sympathies directed toward herself and her husband (a codefendant in the Spock trial). She is gripped by

> a cramp of fury at the mild
> saddened people whose hearts ache
> not for the crimes of war,
> . . . but for us. ("Prologue: An Interim")

In anguish she cries, "There comes a time when only anger / is love" ("I Thirst"). She later admits, however, that anger of such intensity survives in her only momentarily: "I wrote it, but know such love / only in flashes" ("Report").

Eventually, Levertov's joy-seeking temperament prompts her toward the losing of anger in an effort to create conditions more conducive to joy:

> Joy—a beginning. Anguish, ardor.
> To relearn the ah! of knowing in unthinking
> joy: the belovéd stranger lives.
> Sweep up anguish as with a wing-tip,
> brushing the ashes back to the fire's core.
>   ("Relearning the Alphabet, 'A' ")

The mention of fire here is a reminder that the poet believes joy results only from willing expenditure of energy. She turns her own abundant energy toward social improvement, not hesitating to take a militant part in efforts at reform, as in her frontline support of the People's Park at Berkeley. Hers is an admittedly idealistic vision, but it nourishes such unimpeachable sentiments as longings for true common brotherhood, a lessening of private greed, and an end to the abuse of power. Her efforts at political and social reform are entirely consistent with her personality and outlook, for her practice of counting the misfortunes and wrongs of others as her own intensifies her social consciousness, while her belief that vitality is synonymous with change encourages her to assume that social or political change is likely to be beneficial. Her thought and feeling thus combined to produce during the stress of the later Sixties numerous poems of social criticism, having a more evident didactic strain than her earlier work. In these poems, however, Levertov's interests remain unchanged. In *The Poet in the World* (pp. 54–55) she declares, "All the thinking I do about poetry leads me back, always, to Reverence for Life as the ground for poetic activity; because it seems the ground for Attention. . . . Attention is the exercise of Reverence for the 'other forms of life that want to live.' The progression seems clear to me: from Reverence for Life to Attention to Life, from Attention to Life to a highly developed Seeing and Hearing, from Seeing and Hearing . . . to the Discovery and Revelation of Form, from Form to Song." Social concern combines with reverence for life and with Levertov's characteristic balance between the imaginative (represented by the moon) and the real in the recent "3 a.m., September 1, 1969":

> Warm wind, the leaves
> rustling without dryness
> hills dissolved into silver.
>
> It could be any age,
> four hundred years ago or a time
> of post-revolutionary peace,
> the rivers clean again, birth rate and crops
> somehow in balance . . .
>
> In heavy dew
> under the moon the blond grasses
> lean in swathes on the field slope. Fervently
> the crickets practice their religion of ecstasy.

Notes

1. John Keats to George and Tom Keats, December 21, 1817.

2. Denise Levertov, *The Poet in the World* (New York: New Directions, 1973), 97; here-after cited in the text as *PW*.

3. John Keats to James Augustus Hessey, October 9, 1818.

4. John Keats to Benjamin Bailey, November 22, 1817.

5. Ibid.

Denise Levertov, Robert Duncan, and Allen Ginsberg: Modes of the Self in Projective Poetry

William Aiken*

One of the interesting puzzles for any observer of developments in projective verse over the years is the continued close relationship and poetic trade-off between Denise Levertov and Robert Duncan, two poets so op-posed in their methods and effects as to defy even the unpredictability of poetic friendships and influence. Of the respect and sympathy between the two, however, there can be no question. As early as 1959 Levertov spoke of Duncan as one of the two "chief poets among [her] contemporaries" (*The New American Poetry*, p. 412). Somewhat later, in an interesting essay on projectivism, "Some Notes on Organic Form," Levertov cites Duncan more than once as being important to her in clarifying ideas about organic poetry. In addition there is the dedication of her long poem "Relearning the Alpha-bet" ("For R., who read me"), the Duncan epigraph in her long "Eichmann" poem, and the frequent mention of Duncan in her 1971 collection *To Stay Alive*. Duncan, in return, has defended Levertov at some length against a critic's charge of sentimentality (*The Truth and Life of Myth*, pp. 33–36), and has replied to her poem "Claritas" (on the careful refining and crafting neces-sary in poetry) with his own poem "Answering" ("The song is a work of the natural will"). In addition, it would appear that both the title poem of Dun-can's 1968 collection *Bending the Bow* ("I would play Orpheus for you again") and many other poems in that volume are written with Levertov directly in mind as potential reader.

Yet the work of these two poets is different in appearance, technique, content and aim. Levertov's poems are characteristically short and self-contained; Duncan's are long and require of the reader considerable knowl-edge of his other poems. With Levertov you always know at the outset what the subject is (her titles telling you so); with Duncan you almost never know. Levertov frequently describes natural phenomena; Duncan almost never

*Reprinted with permission from *Modern Poetry Studies* 10 (1981), 200–32.

does. Duncan's diction is primarily connotative, Levertov's denotative. Duncan is full of puns, alliteration and assonance—sound building on sound. Levertov is almost without puns, and alliteration and assonance are rare, used primarily when a poem is designed to chart sounds which have actually been heard (as with the songs of chickadee, sparrow, and wood-dove). For Duncan the sound tends to lead the meaning on, which accords with Charles Olson's recommendations in "Projective Verse." For Levertov the meaning, the perception, leads the sound on. Duncan has said that poetry was a means whereby he could discover himself. Levertov has said poetry is a means to communicate a discovery already made in order "that they who cannot see may see" (*The New American Poetry,* p. 412). With Duncan, in poem after poem, there is a kind of risky, unforeseen unfolding of the inner man, tending toward public confession. With Levertov, at least until about 1965, there has been a characteristic reluctance to unfold herself in the way Duncan does. Duncan more than once has quoted a passage from Olson emphasizing the insularity of the poet: "The poet cannot afford to traffic in any other sign than his one, his self, the man or woman that he is. There are only his own composed forms, and each one the issue of the time of the moment of his creation, not any ultimate except what he in his heat and that instant in its solidity yield."[1] When Levertov quotes Olson there is a final emphasis on something other than insularity: "The only object is a man, carved out of himself, so wrought he fills his given space, makes traceries sufficient to others' needs (here is social action, for the poet, anyway, his politics, his news)" ("Three Meditations," *The Jacob's Ladder*). It would seem, in fact, that the work of Duncan and Levertov represent polar possibilities in organic poetry and present a contrast so great as to suggest a third possibility—the eventual poetic synthesis of their different orientations in an organic work of lasting power.

It is generally agreed, I think, that the patient and exact delineation of external forms, based on an unharried fidelity to visual, auditory, and kinetic observation, is one of the distinguishing qualities of Levertov's best work. To this it might be added that the forms she chooses to imitate are frequently at a considerable remove from her own private concerns and uncertainties, or, to put it another way, are self-contained, and thus do not upset, through their importunacy, her own focused powers of concentration. What Levertov says of the autobiographical heroine of her story "Say the Word" can well apply to herself as poet: "She felt herself nourished by the sense of distance" (*O Taste and See,* p. 41). This need for distance helps to explain why Levertov writes so many memorable poems about dogs, blind men, drowsing men, cats, birds, old men, and vegetative nature generally (trees, tulips, roses, etc.). Many of the objects Levertov chooses to describe can be watched without their watching back. They are, like the lost soul she describes in "The Absence," "too concentrated to hear me" (*The Jacob's Ladder*). Because they are self-contained, they allow for a quietness of observation which somehow tends to raise trivial things above the commonplace, as again is suggested in

"Say the Word." This same quality of distancing is noticeable in her poems about places. Levertov has written a number of good poems about Mexico, and England (after ten years' absence) and Europe (after twenty years' absence), but very few striking poems about the United States itself, probably because its presence is too oppressive and upsetting. As a tourist she is permitted to observe without the necessity of personal involvement, an involvement which would have the effect of modifying the self-contained ambience she wishes to record. Even in her love poems a certain distance is maintained: there is a frequent use of shadow and outline, the effect of silhouette, a personal disengagement, a reflectiveness, as for example, in "Losing Track" (*O Taste and See*) which begins:

> Long after you have swung back
> away from me
> I think you are still with me.

The poem, which describes the speaker as a pier, touched by a boat that the tide brings in and swings away, ends:

> I know I'm
> alone again long since,
>
> . . . .
> a light growth of green dreams drying.

The same tendency to objectify or distance the personal is reflected in an earlier poem, "The Wife" (*With Eyes at the Back of Our Heads*), where one tends to marvel not at the tone or the quality of the feeling, but at the image and its striking development:

> A frog under you,
> knees drawn up
> ready to leap out of time.

Such observations are not meant in derogation of Levertov, but serve simply to point up what she herself has recognized as having been, until about 1965, the distinctive quality in her work. There is a peacefulness, a poise, a tempered joy, a clarity of vision, a certain imperturbability in her best poems much like the imperturbability of the forms she imitates. And there is a concurrent lack of self-indulgence and maundering, a capacity to hold herself lightly, which allows her to celebrate those external forms and yet to maintain their mystery. As she says in "Illustrious Ancestors": "I would like to make / . . . / poems direct as what the birds said, hard as a floor, sound as a bench, / mysterious as the silence when the tailor / would pause with his needle in the air" (*The Jacob's Ladder*).

Since 1965, however, Levertov has admitted to a decline in poetic inspiration, a lessening in her ability to observe clearly, and thus even to enjoy external forms. In "Advent 1966," for instance, she speaks of "my strong sight, / my clear caressive sight, my poet's sight I was given / that it might stir me to song" as being "blurred" because of the Vietnam War (*Relearning the Alphabet*). Just as her sight is "blurred" there is a "buzzing" in her ears, and her poise and imperturbability are upset. In the opening poem of this volume, "The Broken Sandal," she wonders where she can walk "unless hurting," and where she can stand "if I'm / to stand still now," the implication being that she can neither move nor stand still without personal hurt, which results in the loss of inner peace and poetic concentration. In "Not Yet" she says, "And if the well goes dry— / and it has: / and if the body-count goes up— / and it does" there is "nothing to do but take / crumbs that fall from the chickadee's table / —or starve." This is her excuse for "grudgingly" smiling at the sounds of chickadees and crickets, sound which would have been perfectly sufficient for her poetry in earlier days. In "Life at War" (*To Stay Alive*, reprinted from *The Sorrow Dance*), Levertov writes, "Nothing we do has the quickness, the sureness, / The deep intelligence living at peace would have"; and the uncertainty, the sheer struggle to survive as person and poet is evident throughout much of the volume. Only towards the end of *To Stay Alive* (in a poem recounting a recent visit to England) does Levertov speak again of "a love for /what happens, for / the surfaces that are their own / interior life."

Unlike most projectivists Levertov has not been interested in word-play and puns. It is the play of images that seems to excite her. One thinks of phrases typical of Levertov as having a minimal (or very subtle) aural binding power: a dog sniffing along "intently haphazard," an old woman "dressed in opals and rags," "honey and fog, the nose / confused," cats "stretching in the doorways, / sure of everything," petals falling "with that sound one / listens for." And actually when we come to such a description as that of the old man in "Shalom"—"Starladen Babylon / buzzes in his blood"—or the phrase "moss / by matchlight" in "Into the Interior," we are a little surprised. This is not to say that Levertov is insensitive to sounds—quite the contrary. Her work more than that of any other projectivist reflects Pound's definition of prosody as "the total articulation of the sound of the poem"; but the insistent aural binding quality common to so many projectivists is characteristically subordinated in Levertov's work to some other consideration deriving from the thing observed: the sound does not lead the meaning on; rather the feeling or observation leads on the sound. This is true, I believe, even of such a striking line as "red roses, contralto, roses," where the smooth, deep richness Levertov perfectly captures for the mind turns out to be a trifle difficult to pronounce, and of the line "a light growth of green dreams drying" where, though the meditative sound quality of the line is superb, difficulties of actual voicing once again occur.

Because of these qualities which one comes to expect in Levertov's work, much of the poetry she has published since 1965, and especially in the volumes *Relearning the Alphabet* and *To Stay Alive*, are apt to strike one as radical departures from a kind of poetry which she seemed to have made uniquely her own. In fact, there seems to be operating a kind of reversal of poetic direction and effect which can be associated with projectivists more generally, wherein the more a poet strives for "inter-personal communication" the more inaccessible that poet becomes. In an attempt to make her poems more immediate and responsive to political realities and to put herself on record as a casualty of the Vietnam War, by way of presenting the particulars of her own troubled life, and of the troubled lives of those around her, Levertov has managed temporarily to sacrifice those qualities of containment, calm observation, and imperturbability which have made her past poems unique. As the content of her poems has become more personal the poetry itself has become less distinctive. In addition, poems which before had been self-contained, now become dependent for their effect on other poems, as in so much of Robert Duncan's work. For the first time the struggle *towards* poetic vision is itself articulated. And in an attempt to restructure her work more meaningfully, as she herself explains, she has reprinted in *To Stay Alive* many poems which had earlier appeared in *Relearning the Alphabet* and *The Sorrow Dance*.

One cannot blame Levertov for this. Surrounded by suicides, her husband threatened with jail, her "revolutionary" sister dead, Levertov's artistic concentration had been, for the moment, destroyed. The titles of the books themselves are suggestive of radical acts carried out simply to insure poetic and personal survival. Yet however understandable the personal reasons for Levertov's publishing her poems during this period may be, it must be recognized that the poems themselves are a running contradiction of precepts she had earlier set down regarding poetic content, form, and intention. As to the personal element in poetry, Levertov had written in 1959 for Donald Allen's *New American Poetry:* "I believe poets are instruments on which the power of poetry plays" (p. 411). The use of the word *instruments,* along with the whole drift of the sentence structure, suggests a passivity and impersonality at odds with her later practice. As to political content and intention, Levertov had said: "I do not believe that a violent imitation of the horrors of our times is the concern of poetry. Horrors are taken for granted. Disorder is ordinary. . . . I long for poems of an inner harmony in utter contrast to the chaos in which they exist. Insofar as poetry has a social function it is to awaken sleepers by other means than shock" (p. 412). In contrast to this statement, many of the poems in *Relearning the Alphabet* and *To Stay Alive* deal directly with military horror and political, social, and psychological disorder. Respecting organic form as it unfolds naturally from clear and calm observation, Levertov had said in her poem "Art" (*With Eyes at the Back of Our Heads*): "Sculptor / . . . / don't let / a touch of your thumb / set your vision while it's still vague." In contrast to this, many of the poems in the volumes in question were written and published, as Levertov herself admits, while the vision behind them was still vague.

It is, of course, perfectly reasonable for a poet to change her views about poetry and for the character of her poetry to change as a result. In fact, W. H. Auden has argued that such change is one of the distinctive qualities of a strong poet. I do not think, however, that Levertov's views have changed in any essential way from what they were in 1959, and the evidence for such an opinion is contained in her 1972 volume, *Footprints.*

There is, to be sure, an expansion of content in *Footprints,* and also an extension of control. There are more portraits of persons in this volume, for instance, than in any of her previous books including those on Vietnam, and the portraits themselves are less impersonal than in earlier work. There is less distance, less "levitation"; the people walk on the ground. There is, for example, the portrait of one of her students:

> Hey Ernie, here you come suavely
> round the corner in your
> broken-windowed bus
> and brake elegantly and swing
> open the door so I can get in and ride on, sitting
> on crumpled poems among guitars and
> percussion sets.
> What can I say, Ernie?—
> Younger than my son, you are
> nevertheless my old friend
>
> whom I trust.

To my mind, the friendly openness of this poem, along with its casual tone, is a distinct gain for Levertov, possibly attributable to her involvement with young people during the period of war protests. On the basis of such a poem one might even tentatively agree with Levertov's observation later in this same volume: "I found eyesight wasn't so utterly / my way of being / as I'd supposed" (p. 55).

On the other hand, eyesight is still very much Levertov's way of being, as she makes clear in "Memories of John Keats," which tends to be a restatement of her earlier poetic priorities:

> *Watchfulness and sensation* as John Keats
> said to me
> for it was to me
> he said it
>   (and to you)
> . . . .
> *watchfulness was his word*
> *sensation*
>   *and watchfulness in itself*
> *the Genius*
> *of Poetry must work out*
> *its own salvation in a man* (p. 45)

There is also in this volume the return of the dog (in "The Roamer"), as he "flumps down" after his journey from "South Boston or the Reservoir." "Where have I been / without the world?" Levertov asks. "Why am I glad /

he wolfs his food and gathers / strength for the next journey?" In reading these lines it is hard not to think of Levertov's earlier poem, "The Dog of Art":

> . . . the Dog
> of Art turns to the world
> the quietness of his eyes.

In *Footprints* there is also a resumption of interest in the self-contained, as reflected in the poem "A Defeat in the Green Mountains," in which a mother with her young children is prevented from reaching some open fields by a "baffling scratchy thicket" and returns to her point of departure,

> defeated
> to ponder the narrow
> depth of the river,
> its absorbed movement past her. (p. 2)

And there is in *Footprints* a return of joy in observed things along with the mastery of image one had come to associate with Levertov.

> Nothing I see
> fails to give pleasure,
>
> no thirst for righteousness
> dries my throat, I am silent
> and happy, and troubled only
> by my own happiness. Looking,
>
> looking and naming, I wish the train now
> would halt for me at a station in the fields
> . . . .
>   In the deep aftermath
> of its faded rhythm, I could become
>
> a carved stone
> set in the gates of the earthly paradise,
>
> an angler's fly
> lost in the sedge to watch the centuries.
> ("By Rail through the Earthly
>   Paradise, Perhaps Bedfordshire")

Finally, the last poem in *Footprints*, "Knowing the Way," indicates that Levertov has lost none of her ability to imitate the external forms of nature. Though perhaps slight in content, it is a good demonstration of Levertov's ability to articulate the sounds of a poem in accordance with what is perceived. Deriving from the perception of the wood-dove's sound—low in the throat, deliberate, tentative—along with the perception of its bold take-off and vivid flight, the poem demonstrates firm control of syllable and pace, the general movement of the vowels being from low or middle frequency to high frequency and the movement of the lines from deliberation and care to speed and release.

> The wood dove utters
> slowly
> > those words he has
> to utter,
> and softly.
> > But takes flight
> boldly,
> and flies fast.

Giving such details their full weight, it would seem that *Relearning the Alphabet* and *To Stay Alive* represent a deflection from Levertov's natural development as a poet. Such a deflection was caused, I believe, by Levertov's close relationship with Robert Duncan, who has been a continuing advocate of the personal, the inchoate, and the flawed in poetry for many years. Duncan has said, for example:

> In my work I evolve the form of a poem by an insistent attention to what happens in inattentions, a care for inaccuracies; for I strive in the poem not to make some imitation of a model experience but to go deeper and deeper into the experience of the process of the poem itself. . . . Often I must force myself to remain responsible to the error that sticks in pride's craw; not to erase it, but to bring it forward, to work with it, even if this flaw mar a hoped-for success. . . . The work of art is itself the field we would render the truth of. Focusing in on the process itself as the field of the poem, the marring discord must enter the composition." (*The Truth and Life of Myth*, pp. 46 and 64).

In contrast to Levertov, who may be provisionally described as an "organic imagist," Robert Duncan is best understood as an allegorist. The story Duncan tells is his own story—his quest for identity, both personal and poetic—and the symbols he uses are *aural* symbols. Whereas with symbolists generally the image normally precedes the meaning (e.g., Moby Dick is first a white whale before he is anything else), with an allegorist such as Duncan meaning habitually precedes image (e.g., the mouth is a conduit to the heart and a means to the expression of love before it is anything else). Inward constructions and consistencies are always more important to Duncan than the physical constructions of the outside world. A second characteristic of Duncan's poetry is that images tend to form clusters of meaning not according to similarities in their visual appearance, or in what they are in themselves, but according to similarities in the sounds of the words which refer to those images. To the usual symbolist there may be a connection between a pool, a woman's eye, the sun, a planetary hemisphere, a geometric form, because of the circular or spherical appearance of each. Or with Snyder, for example, there may be a connection betwen dandelion fluff, a burr, the roots of a shrub, a man's hair, a thicket, because they are all natural, stringy, perishable growths. There is little in the sound of these words which would bring them together. With Duncan, however, sounds are all important, especially if poetry, as in his case, is to tell a personal story or to present a single man as a trope for all existence—man as myth.

The source of the idea of man as myth in projective poetry directly prepares for Duncan's very personal use of sound. Originally Charles Olson had called attention to Jane Harrison's discussion of the meaning of myth as not just a "purely fictitious narrative" but as a correlative to the action of ritual:

> "A *mythos* to the Greek was primarily just a thing spoken, uttered by the *mouth*. . . . Possibly the first *muthos* was simply the interjectional utterance *mu*, but it is easy to see how rapid the development would be from interjection to narrative. Each step in the ritual action is shadowed as it were by a fresh interjection . . . till the whole combines into a consecutive thing."[2]

Robert Duncan cites this same passage from Harrison as an epigraph for his prose volume *The Truth and Life of Myth*. Duncan adds, however, a definition from the Liddell and Scott Greek-English Lexicon: "μύδω (A) To make the sound μὺμῦ or μυμῦ, to murmur with closed lips, to mutter, moan . . . (B) to drink with closed lips, to suck in. . . ." In the opening paragraph of *The Truth and Life of Myth*, subtitled "An Essay in Essential Autobiography," Duncan writes: "The myth-teller beside himself with the excitement of the dancers sucks in the inspiring breath and moans, muttering against his willful lips; for this is not a story of what he thinks or wishes life to be, it is the story that *comes to him* and forces his telling."

What comes to Duncan as poet and myth-teller are sounds in certain repetitive patterns (assonance, consonance, alliteration) which have a binding symbolic force for the poet out of all proportion to their force for the general reader. Words occur in his own work less personal and to address himself, on occasion, to the realities of the outside world. This is particularly evident towards the end of *Bending the Bow*, where Duncan begins to speak of the Vietnam War. Yet, just as with Levertov, this new mode is not really congenial to him, which can be seen from the fact that when Duncan temporarily abandons his usual procedure of inward concentration on his own sufferings to focus on the sufferings of others, he is still so committed to his own problems that the suffering particulars of others dissolve before he has a chance to transcend them.

The effects and some of the implications of this trade-off between Levertov and Duncan become a subject for further examination.

Since Denise Levertov, in her long "notebook" poem, "To Stay Alive," and Robert Duncan, in "Passages 26" and "-27" (*Bending the Bow*) and also

Allen Ginsberg, in "Wichita Vortex Sutra" (*Planet News*), have all written about the Vietnam War with a number of the same emphases—the political and military misuse of language, the physical and mental suffering of civilians and soldiers, both in America and Asia, the cooperation of commercial interests in the war venture, and the need to transcend or transform such evils— it is of interest to see how these three temperamentally dissimilar organic/ projective poets treat essentially the same subject. Such a study may help to distinguish between two different tendencies in organic poetry—the visual, phenomenal, and outward (Levertov), and the aural, personal, and inward (Duncan)—as they come to terms with the same subject. Comparison of the two will suggest the further possiblity of their conflation in the work of Ginsberg, whose poems sometimes strike out as a blending of the visual and the visionary, the aural and the oracular.

Because of the length of Levertov's "To Stay Alive" (over sixty pages) it is difficult to suggest anything here but the bare lineaments of its general pattern, but that should be enough to indicate its relationship to Ginsberg's and Duncan's poems on the same subject. The poem is composed of four major "Parts," preceded by a "Prologue" and punctuated by three "Entr'actes." In the Prologue, as in the beginning of Ginsberg's and Duncan's poems, there is a concern for language, as Levertov quotes some children she overheard playing a little game in a laundromat.

> "When I say,
> *Do you want some gum? say yes.*"
> "Yes . . ." "Wait!—Now:
> Do you want some gum?"
> "Yes!" "Well yes means no,
> so you can't have any."

A few lines later Levertov quotes a United States major:

> "It became necessary
> to destroy the town to save it."

In between and following these quotes Levertov apostrophizes language:

> O language, virtue
> of man, touchstone
> worn down by what
> gross fiction . . .
>
> O language, mother of thought,
> are you rejecting us as we reject you?

But Levertov does not, for the moment, pursue this theme of langauge. She shifts away to dwell on eighteen-year-old de Courcy Squire, jailed for sitting down in front of a police wagon, and now in the sixty-fifth day of a hunger strike. She also thinks of the upcoming trial of her husband, indicted for antiwar activities, the self-immolation of Norman Morrison and Alice Hertz, and the jailed Dennis Riordan and Bob Gilliam, whose words, finally, were "good, / language draws breath again in their *yes* and *no.*" Interspersed among her reports of young war resisters are reminiscences of her own gentle childhood, and contempt for "the sympathy of mild good folk" who exude "a kind of latex from their leaves."

In Part I the major theme of "To Stay Alive" is stated—whether to choose "Revolution or Death." It should be emphasized, however, that this is not merely a political choice but a personal one. Quite literally, as this Part and, indeed, the rest of the poem show, Levertov is struggling to survive. First she thinks of Keats's "Nightingale" ode and a death which is not "obscene." She is drawn to that possibility. Then she thinks of "Lorie's" fight for life ("If she can live I can live"). Then she recalls her own recklessness in running into traffic to flag a cab ("Is that how death is, / that poor, that trivial?"). Finally she thinks of the suicide of Bill Rose, whose postcard had lain unread on her windowsill for six months. By the time she read it he had killed himself. Throughout this Part there is the grief of goldengrove "unleaving all around [her]; I live / in goldengrove." The final lines of Part I echo the opening lines: "Life that / wants to live. / (Unlived life / of which one can die)," lines which again recur at the very end of the entire poem.

The Ent'racte between Parts I and II recreates the marking of time in winter: "It becomes / November without one's knowing it," "flies dream in dying," there is a "terror / as of eclipse. / The whites graying." Levertov feels "luxury" in the knowledge of her bad memory.

Part II begins in despair ("Can't go further, / If there's to be a / second part, it's not / a going beyond, I'm / still here"), followed by a meditation on the meaning of revolution, which "now roars, a toneless constant." The meditation leads to the proposition, "THERE IS ONLY AS MUCH PEACE AS THERE ARE PEACEFUL PEOPLE," which then is followed by a scene of peace—Levertov and her students clearing refuse from People's Park in Berkeley: "O happiness / in the sun! Is it / that simple, then, / to live?" But the next day the police come and fence off the park, and Levertov lists nine practical things people can do to safe-guard future protests against such actions, one of which is flying kites to scare off helicopters. Part II ends with a metaphoric rendering of the revolution itself: a tree rising from the flood, a hand lifted out of the flood, a sea full of swimmers.

The long Entr'acte between Parts II and III shifts the meaning of revolution from "peacefulness" to violent protest, and begins and ends with descriptions of demonstrations in which Levertov herself participates. First, at the Justice Department the poet recognizes her "hunger" for "anguish": "Wanting it . . . wanting it real." Six months later, at another demonstration, she mocks Judy Collins singing about "L-O-O-O-V-E": "Judy, understand: / there comes a time when only anger / is love." In between these descriptions are quotations from Gandhi ("cultivate / the art of killing and being killed"), poems about the devil, who "swarms into 'emptiness' " like "flies buzzing" in a jar, and guilty recollections of feeling human ("the way a cloud's a cloud") or experiencing happiness at Casa Felice on Cape Cod ("I drop / plumb into peace for a day").

Despite the revolutionary fervour apparent in this second Entr'acte, which one somehow expects to be amplified, in Part III there is a shift of scene from "Amerika" to England and Europe, which Levertov is visiting after a long absence. In Trieste she wonders if she's a "cop-out" or merely "on holiday." She remembers the ambivalence of having wanted "oblivion" in Boston, but never for very long, because "some hunger for revelation" would keep her up half the night. In Rijeka she notices "the easy-going goodness of people" in the company of five Sudanese, to one of whom she gives her Panther button. In London she admires the gentleness of the people:

> it's in the way
> three young workmen in the Tube
> smiled to each other
> admiring their day-off purchases,
> new shirts—
>
> it's in the play-talk
> of children, without irony:
> not *cool*, not
>   joshing each other,
>
> and in the way
> men and women of any age maintain
> some expectation of love,
>
> (not pickups, but love) and so
> remain beautiful.

Because of such scenes, she says: "Now I can barely remember what it is / to want oblivion."

On an Adriatic island she argues the relative merits of revolution and "peace without hope," sadly commenting, "I have / not hope for it, / only a longing. . . . " Finally she recalls a friend's terrifying dream—trapped in a tunnel, "great dogs blocking / each end of it"—for which the remedy was found to be to "sit down / in the middle of the tunnel / quietly." "The dogs / will not go away," her friend says; "They must be transformed." It is with this emphasis that Part III ends: Levertov is advised to "TRANSFORM / the dogs" with her "firey stillness": "Get down into your well, / it's your well / go deep into it / into your own depth as into a poem."

The Entr'acte which follows Part III suggests a possible solution for Levertov's continuing personal and poetic dilemma. In "Let Us Sing unto the Lord a new Song" Levertov speaks of the two pulses of revolution and poetry which she had noticed in a young friend of hers. Revolution she describes as "heart's fire," poetry as "heart's river": "when their rhythms / mesh / . . . / the singing begins."

Thus in Part IV Levertov returns to America, despite the fact that England had "turned out to be home," determined to remember the advice of her friend Bet, which she repeats: "It's your own well. / Go down / into its depth." She experiences happiness again in dancing with a happy person: "The reason for happiness is, / happiness exists." She experiences joy in viewing Zen paintings in the Boston Museum. She remembers the communal happiness in cleaning up the People's Park. And she remembers Albert Camus: " 'I discovered inside myself, even in the very midst of winter, an invincible summer.' "

Still, she is plagued by the suffering of her friends: "Judy had killed herself a full two weeks / before my hours of dancing began." Grandin had also killed himself. "Judy ignored the world outside herself, / Grandin was flooded by it." The Hopkins poem she had alluded to earlier returns: " 'Sorrow's springs are the same.' " She is "still in the grim / middle of the tunnel," "striving mainly / to get down into [her] well in hope." Repeating her earlier choice, "Yes, I want / revolution, not death," she rejects the suicide Mayakofsky's argument that "life must be started quite anew" before the "singing can start up." Mayakofsky didn't understand that "Only conjunctions / of song's / raging magic / with patient courage / will make / a new life." In other words, the revolutionary rage must occur in poetry, written with patient courage, for a new life to begin. Accordingly, she rejects her earlier argument, "There comes / a time / when only anger / is love," saying "I can't sustain for a day / that anger." The anger will occur in the poetry, and while she waits to "recharge [her] batteries" she will "hold fast" to two things: her earlier idea that "When the pulse rhythms / of revolution and poetry / mesh, / then the singing begins"; and her "love / of those who dare, who do dare / to struggle, dare to reject / unlived life, disdain / to die of *that*."

With this emphasis "To Stay Alive" ends. There has been no transformation of personal suffering nor any transcendence of the particulars of military and social injustice, no matter how earnestly such transformation and transcendence have been sought. There has been no "raging magic," only the promise of it, and no "new life," only the longing for it. Because of Levertov's uncompromising commitment to particulars she is utterly unable to "transform the dogs." It need hardly be said that these are not the quiet-eyed dogs of art that "bring back the world," but the raging "dogs of war." In this poem, in fact, Levertov appears to have entirely forgotten about the quiet dogs which have been so serviceable to her in the past. On the other hand, in writing this poem Levertov seems actually to have been able *to stay alive*. She has worked out an alternative to both suicide and "unlived life of which one can die." She has pursued a process of self-examination in which her basic identity is brought into question and then reaffirmed. In this sense "To Stay Alive" is very much like the "preparations" of Robert Duncan, poetry seen as a means by which one's inner nature can unfold.

If Levertov in "To Stay Alive" is like Duncan in making her poetry more expressive of personal suffering, Duncan, in "Passages 26" and "-27" is like

Levertov in making his poetry more responsive to the particulars of the outside world. "Passages 26," entitled "The Soldiers," begins with a quotation from the media which emphasizes the indiscriminate slaughter occurring in Vietnam: " 'No-man's land in which everything moving / —from Saigon's viewpoint—was 'hostile'." Duncan then speaks of the soldiers engaged in that slaughter in a strangely mingled tone of pity and contempt, immediately comparing them with poets: "They've to take their souls in the war / as the followers of Orpheus take soul in the poem / the wood to take fire from that dirty flame! / in the slaughter of man's hope / distil the divine potion, forbidden hallucinogen / that stirs sight of the hidden / order of orders!" Duncan then speaks of the mystery of creation (*"Dieu, dont l'oeuvre va plus loin que notre rêve"*), its darkness the poet, "Dr Dee" (for *Duncan*) "pretend [s] a convocation of powers" of the universe, as though a man held the moon, a thin wafer, "under his tongue":

> (under the cloak of his poem   *he* retires
>   invisible
>   so that it seems no man   but a world speaks
> for my thoughts are servants of the stars, and my words
>   (all parentheses opening into
> come from a mouth that is the Universe   *la bouche d'ombre*
>   (The poet-magician Dr Dee in his black mirror
>   calls forth his spirits from their obscurity).

The result of the magic act is as follows:

> For now in my mind all the young men of my time
> have withdrawn allegiance from *this world*, from public things.
>
> and as their studies in irreality deepen,
>   industries, businesses, universities, armies
>   shudder and cease.

The explanation for this effect is that:

> we have but to imagine
>   ourselves the Lover
>   and the Beloved appears
>   . . . .
> they draw from the War Itself withdrawing
>   this breath between them.
>
> In this rite the Great Magician stirs in His dream,
> and the magician dreaming   murmurs to his beloved:
>   *thou art so near to me*
>   *thou art a phantom that the heart*
>   *would see—*
> and now the great river of their feeling grows so wide
>   its shores grow distant and unreal.

So Duncan's poem on the Vietnam War ends, a poem which has included some interesting things: the idea of the poet-magician's "rite," in which he first invokes "his spirits," then shuts from his mind "this world," then receives in his dark mouth (*"la bouche d'ombre"*) the "moon" of reflected light, which is "held under his tongue" so that there is a communion between Chaos and God, the Lover and the Beloved, the Poet and the Muse, a communion first imaged as "breath" and finally as a "great river of feeling." One sees easily enough what Duncan is doing, and even hears the anagramatic pun on "draw"—"War"—"withdraw," but the poem as a whole has the remoteness of pantomime. Somehow the transformation or transcendence which occurs here is not a deeply felt personal act, as it is in Ginsberg's "Wichita," but simply pretense. Just as the soldiers are not real in "Passages 26," but rather constructions of the mind, so here in "Passages 27" the attempt to withdraw from those soldiers and the actuality of war is similarly unreal: not even the poet as magician believes it. Constantly undercutting the theme of the poem (that the poet can magically create his own world of first things, his beloved, his meadow) are phrases like: "in which I pretend," "so that it seems," "for now in my mind," "we have but to imagine," "a phantom that the heart would see"—so that in the end little magic, and certainly no mystical rite, has been accomplished. What kind of magic can occur in a poem where the focus is all on the magician and there are no props to manage, nothing to make disappear? Or, if this is some kind of auto-exorcism, what kind of exorcism can be accomplished when the actuality of the evil to be exorcised is itself in question?

The failure of the Vietnam poems by Levertov and Duncan shed considerable light on a difficulty in projective poetic theory as first promulgated by Charles Olson. This theory holds that the sounds of a poet and his own experiences are sufficient to organize a poem and create meaningful "interpersonal communication" with the reader. For Olson as for most of his followers form is simply an extension of content and content is always and only the poet's own experience. How then, one is stirred to ask, does a projective poet write a political poem, if such a poem is to be understood as an expression, not of the experience of a single poet-person, but of the experience of the polis? It would seem that the difficulty can only be mediated if the poet succeeds in transcending the personal and somehow embodying the experience of the polis as a whole in his work. But again it is evident that this can only be done if the poet can forget himself long enough to make the experience of the polis his *own* experience. It is not enough for a poet to imagine himself a symbol of the polis (as perhaps Duncan does), for the concerns of the people must emotionally become his own concerns. At the same time, however, the poet cannot be *overcome* by the experiences of others (as Levertov is) so that artistic integrity itself and the organizing powers associated with it are bitterly undone or at least effectually weakened. It is just here, I think, that the spontaneous synthetic power of a poet like Allen Ginsberg becomes important if projective poetics is to have more than just a fanciful appeal.

If Denise Levertov's "To Stay Alive" is so weighted down with poignant particulars that no effort at transformation can be successful, and Robert Duncan, in "Passages 26" and "27," is so removed from particulars that any assertion of their transformation strikes one as hollow, Allen Ginsberg, in "Wichita Vortex Sutra," seems to have managed both the articulation of particulars and their imaginative transcendence. It appears that Ginsberg's powerful emotional response to the inhumanity that war represents, as it is reflected early in the poem, allows him finally to negate that war, to eliminate it entirely from his system of recognitions. No poem that I have seen dealing with the Vietnam period in American life is so packed with angry details at the beginning—the minutiae of newspapers, radio reports, advertising slogans, all of which tend to falsify reality—and so blithe and ethereal at the end. The personal and poetic transformations Ginsberg works in "Wichita," from almost total submersion in and obsession with political and military detail and dishonesty to final disbelief and liberation from such detail, is most unusual. . . .

Notes

1. The passage from Charles Olson's "Against Wisdom as Such" (*Human Universe and Other Essays*, 69) appears in Duncan's "Nel Mezzo Del Cammin Di Nostra Vita," *Roots and Branches*, 22–23, and in "Reflections," *Bending the Bow*, 38–39.

2. Quoted in Charles Olson, *The Special View of History* (Berkeley, Calif.: Oyez Press, 1970), 21–23.

Works Cited

Donald M. Allen, ed., *The New American Poetry, 1945–1960* (New York, 1960).
Robert Duncan, *Bending the Bow* (New York: New Directions, 1968).
———, *Roots and Branches* (New York: Scribner's, 1964).
———, *The Truth and Life of Myth* (Fremont, Mich., 1968).
Ginsberg, Allen, *Planet News* (San Francisco, 1968).
Levertov, Denise, *Footprints* (New York, 1972).
———, *The Jacob's Ladder* (New York, 1961).
———, *O Taste and See* (New York, 1964).
———, *Relearning the Alphabet* (New York, 1970).
———, "Some Notes on Organic Form," *Poetry* 106 (September 1965).
———, *The Sorrow Dance* (New York, 1967).
———, *To Stay Alive* (New York, 1971).
———, *With Eyes at the Back of Our Heads* (New York, 1960).

A Sense of Unremitting Emergency:
Politics in the Early Work of
Denise Levertov   Kerry Driscoll*

Over the past twenty-five years, Denise Levertov's poetry has evolved from a detached, meditatively lyric style, filled with richly detailed evocations of landscapes and moments of ecstatic vision, to one steadfastly grounded in the social and political exigencies of contemporary life: war, nuclear power, the arms race, and the flagrant, widespread abuse of human rights. Many readers and critics alike have reacted hostilely to this development,[1] decrying Levertov's activism as an unfortunate side tracing of her true talent and lamenting the privileging of didacticism over song in her later work.

To deny the validity of this controversial aspect of Levertov's writing— regardless of how strident, radical, or naively idealistic her political views might seem—is to misjudge grievously both the scope of her overall poetic achievement and the very integrity of her identity as an artist. The political poems she began writing in the early 1960s do not represent an abnegation or abandonment of the values articulated in her previous work; on the contrary, they attest to a deepening and intensification of those values through a sustained commitment to social action. The core of Levertov's vision is, and always has been, humanism; in this respect, the increasingly political nature of her writing from *The Jacob's Ladder* to the present marks the blossoming and maturation of an inherently empathic sensibility. To be a poet means, for her, to be utterly human, fully alive in one's mind and senses, keenly attuned to the diverse rhythms and mysteries of life. In her 1973 collection of essays, *The Poet in the World,* Levertov equates the two terms, stating: "When I say I speak as a poet, it is the same as to say I speak as a human being."[2] The primary task of the poet, in her estimation, is to "translate" this heightened awareness of life's plenitude into language, and in so doing, celebrate and conserve the profound "miracle of being" (114).

It is this same life-affirming stance which underlies, and to some extent, determines the character of Levertov's engagement with politics. For example, when asked in a 1968 interview whether her anti-war activities had produced an effect on her art, she responded:

> In some ways it's the other way around. I have found myself as a poet, long before this particular involvement, saying things in poems which I think have moral implications. I think that if one is an articulate person, who makes certain statements, one has an obligation as a human being to back them up with one's actions. So I feel that it is poetry that led me into political action and not political action which has caused me to write poems more overtly engaged than those I used to write. . . . There is no abrupt

*Reprinted with permission from *Centennial Review* 30 (Spring 1986), 292–303.

separation between so-called political poetry and so-called private poetry in an artist, who is in both cases writing out of his own inner life.[3]

Levertov indicates in this statement that her involvement with politics was the direct, natural outgrowth of a moral obligation she felt to stand by certain attitudes and values expressed in her poetry, a desire to reinforce the rhetoric of personal conviction with public action. Although she does not specify the exact nature of these convictions in the interview, this information can be readily gleaned from her work itself. The various definitions Levertov has offered of the term "politics" over the years are especially helpful in understanding the roots of her activism. In *Light Up the Cave*, for example, she declares that politics is the critical examination of "our immediate social environment whether favorable or unfavorable,"[4] while in the poem "The Phonecall," she describes it on a more personal level as "the word I use to mean / striving for justice and for / mercy."[5] Given the expansive parameters of these definitions, it is evident that Levertov regards politics as a phenomenon which no sensitive, thoughtful individual can avoid, particularly at this moment in history; *any* judgment or interpretation of the external world has potentially political implications. Politics is therefore an integral and inevitable facet of daily life, indeed, of consciousness itself; as such, Levertov insists, it is "no more alien to the medium [of poetry] than any other human concern" (*LC*, 128). The key phrase here is "human concern"— the poet's absolute, impassioned commitment to the affirmation of life also entails rigorously defending it against possible threat or destruction:

> The poet in our time . . . must live in the body as actively as he lives in his head; he must learn to extend himself into whatever actions he can perform, in order to be "part of the solution and not part of the problem"; he must do whatever he can see to do to bring down the World Federation of Death, Inc. If he does not struggle against war and oppression, he will negate whatever his words may say, and will soon have no world to say them in. (*PW*, 106)

In the starkest, most elemental terms, Levertov sees the poet engaged in a struggle of life against "Death, Incorporated," the huge, faceless aggregate comprised of governments, armies, multi-national corporations and other insentient forces. The issue of political involvement thus extends far beyond individual conscience to a broader, more fundamental concern, namely, the artist's role in and responsibility to society. The series of dichotomies around which Levertov's statement is structured—mind/body, thought/action, detachment/participation, oppression/freedom, problem/solution— all suggest that political activism is a moral imperative for the poet because it offers a means of safeguarding life. Word and world cannot be divorced from one another in the present day without disastrous consequences; in fact, some of Levertov's harshest invective is directed against the pervasiveness of public apathy which indirectly aids the progress of these destructive forces by posing no resistance to them. Poetry, she believes, can serve as a "revolu-

tionary stimulus, awaken[ing] us from our sloth" through the vivid recreation and experience of life's beauty. "We must not go down into the pit
we have dug ourselves by our inhumanity without some taste, however
bitter, of that abundance" (PW, 99). The poet's essential task then is to rescue
us from our own indifference and inhumanity by rekindling a sense of sympathy and reverence for our fellow creatures—to reestablish what Walt Whitman a century earlier called "the path between reality and the soul."

Although the Vietnam War was undeniably the major catalyst in politiciz-
ing Levertov's poetry, it was neither the source nor primary impetus in the
development of her political sensibility. Vietnam was an external factor
which, through its blatant violation of her personal value system, provided
an irresistible call to action. Levertov's political consciousness springs rather
from a convergence of inner and outer experience that can be traced back to
her earliest compositions. In the *Collected Earlier Poems, 1940–1960*, one
finds numerous intimations of her mature ideological stance, manifested
largely through a persistent preoccupation with the "interplay of psychic and
material life" (PW, 248). Poems like "Listening to Distant Guns" and "Christmas 1944" explore the uneasy balance between Levertov's private, inner life
and the vast historical forces (in this case, World War II) that impinge on it
from without. Though she herself is safe from the ravages of the war's destruction, it is nonetheless impossible for her to deny the ugly fact of its existence.
The war's dissonance, "its long sagas of sorrow,"[6] gnaw at her consciousness,
undermining the tranquility of her immediate surroundings and posing a
serious dilemma: how can these disparate worlds—private/public, inner/
outer—be reconciled and integrated?[7] In the poem, "Beyond the End," from
her 1957 collection *Here and Now*, Levertov speculates that this gulf can
only be bridged by a tremendous act of will—daring to accept and fully
inhabit the conditions of one's own existence:

>   not to
> "go on living" but to quicken, to activate: extend:
> . . . .
>   . . . Maybe it is
> response, the will to respond ("reason
> can give nothing at all/like
> the response of desire") maybe
> a gritting of the teeth, to go
> just that much further, beyond the end
> beyond whatever ends: to begin, to be, to defy. (CEP, 30)

In my estimation, however, it is not until the publication of *The Jacob's
Ladder* in 1961 that Levertov was able to actualize this "will to respond" and
successfully surmount the barriers separating self and world. Significantly,
this text also heralds the emergence of a distinctly political voice in her work.
The conjunction of these two developments is not all coincidental; in fact, as
the poem "Three Meditations" reveals, they are quite closely related. "Three
Meditations" is a landmark, not only in terms of *The Jacob's Ladder*, but

Levertov's poetry as a whole because it documents her pivotal realization that there is no sharp dividing line between the personal and political. As such, it embodies the essence—the unchanging core—of her political beliefs.

As its title suggests, the poem consists of three sections, each of which corresponds to a particular phase in Levertov's thinking about a single theme—that of the poet's role in society. The epigraphs that precede each meditation are taken from the work of three writers whom Levertov admires and has been influenced by: Charles Olson, Henrik Ibsen, and D. H. Lawrence. All three quotations pertain in some way to the poet's purpose or "function"; thus, they provide a scaffolding that assists Levertov in articulating her own views on the subject. Interestingly, the Olson quote which opens "Three Meditations" contains an oblique definition of the term "politics" and underscores the inherently political nature of the poet's task:

> the only object is
> a man, carved
> out of himself, so wrought he
> fills his given space, makes
> traceries sufficient to
> others' needs
>   (here is
> social action, for the poet,
> anyway, his
> politics, his
> news)[8]

These lines concern the evolution of the poet's selfhood, the process whereby he strives to achieve his maximum human potential and so "fill his given space." By extending his powers of reflection and intuition to the limit, the poet becomes an example to others: his life is a conscious work of art, carved and wrought into a distinctive design, which by virtue of its beauty and integrity, fulfills a basic social need. Olson's use of the word *traceries* is especially significant in this regard, since it most commonly refers to the intricately patterned Gothic frames of stained glass windows, and thus evokes both a source of illumination and moral inspiration; moreover, the verb *trace* itself suggests imitation and emulation. Levertov's meditation plays on these subliminal associations by describing the poet as a source of light, one whose dreams and unconscious thoughts are translated into "shining petals" which counter the dull glare of the world's "death mirrors." Levertov's words in Part One take the form of a direct address to the reader, enjoining him or her to experience and incorporate as much of the physical world as possible:

> Breathe deep of the
> freshly gray morning air, mild
>   spring of the day.
> Let the night's dream-planting
>   bear leaves

> and light up the death-mirrors with
> shining petals. . . .
> Live
> in thy fingertips and in thy
> hair's rising; hunger
> be thine, food
> be thine and what wine
> will not shrivel thee. (*JL*, 29)

The first meditation celebrates the primacy and vitality of the senses as well as the value of attuning oneself to natural cycles. A subtle cyclical movement is embedded into the lyric itself, which progresses from morning to evening and repeatedly alludes to the process of growth, blossoming, and decay. This experiential knowledge of the physical environment deepens man's awareness of his own creatureliness and thus enhances his reverence for all life. Yet, as Levertov reveals in Part Two of the poem, this benign, Emersonian immersion in nature does not suffice; the poet must do more in order to connect the internal and external realms.

The Ibsen quotation that introduces the second meditation reinforces Olson's statement about the poet as a model or exemplar for society at large: "The task of the poet is to make clear to himself, and thereby to others, the temporal and eternal questions" (*JL*, 30). This "task" is both introspective and open-ended: the poet's role is not to provide answers or pat solutions to the problem of being human, but rather to discover, formulate, and ultimately differentiate between the "temporal and eternal questions." This internalized process of clarification through self-knowledge turns outward and establishes a vital link with the human community through the act of writing. As Levertov states in her essay, "Origins of a Poem," "The act of realizing inner experience in material substance is in itself an action *towards others*, even when the conscious intention has not gone beyond the desire for self-expression" (*PW*, 49); thus, writing itself—committing one's thoughts to paper—takes on an inescapably political dimension.

In Part Two of the poem, Levertov's intention has clearly gone beyond the simple "desire for self-expression" to the exploration of a trait shared by all people, past and present. The idyllic natural setting of the first meditation abruptly yields to a dark, apocalyptic vision, a descent into the unchartered regions of the self. History and personal consciousness converge, as the sack of Rome by thronging hordes of barbarians melds into the metaphorical "darkness" that Levertov finds within her own heart. Through her deft use of imagery, the boundaries between the objective and subjective, the physical and spiritual, disappear:

> Barbarians
> throng the straight roads of
> my empire, converging
> on black Rome.

There is darkness in me.
Silver sunrays
sternly, in tenuous joy
cut through its folds:
mountains
arise from cloud. (*JL*, 30)

A harsh, discordant energy is unleashed in the poem through her interrogation of this ominous darkness:

Who was it yelled, cracking
the glass of delight?
Who sent the child
sobbing to bed, and woke it
later to comfort it?

The poet's response to these questions, "I, I, I, I," isolated as it is in a separate line and infused with a strong staccato rhythm by virtue of its punctuation, serves as a graphic visual representation of the antagonistic split Levertov perceives within her psyche. The ego is fractured, splintered into a multiplicity of conflicting emotions. In acknowledging that an innate capacity for anger, aggression, and violence coexists alongside her impulse to love, celebrate, and conserve, Levertov exposes the dualistic core of all humanity, the freakish trait that allows us to simultaneously be the inflicter of pain and punishment and the comforter who alleviates that pain:

I multitude, I tyrant,
I angel, I you, you
world, battlefield. (*JL*, 30)

In this sequence, Levertov succeeds in imaginatively bridging the gap between self and other, spirit and material substance, internal and external experience; she projects her identity progressively outward until she encompasses the entire world. These lines echo Whitman's famous statement, "I am large, I contain multitudes," in *Song of Myself*, but with one crucial difference: whereas Whitman identifies primarily with the downtrodden and oppressed (the hounded slave, the martyr, the wounded soldier), Levertov is able to place herself in the antithetical positions of oppressor and oppressed. Speaking of this section of the lyric in "Origins of a Poem," she asserts that one of the major values in following Ibsen's dictum and asking herself the "temporal and eternal questions" was

coming to realize how much the apparently external problems have their parallels within us. . . . Man has to recognize not only that he tends to project his personal problems on the external world but also that he is a microcosm within which indeed the same problems, the same tyrannies, injustices, hopes, and mercies act and react and demand resolution. (*PW*, 45)

Thus, in the process of coming to know and understand herself more intimately, the poet gains deeper insight into the complexities and contradictions of the phenomenal world.

The final epigraph, which is the most cryptic and obscure of the three, seems startlingly optimistic in the wake of the apocalyptic vision that precedes it. It begins, appropriately, with a question, and thereby relates back to Ibsen's statement in Part Two: "And virtue? Virtue lies in the heroic response to the creative wonder, the utmost response" (JL, 30). This question arises logically out of the implications of the second meditation, since if we as humans are capable of committing atrocities against one another, the existence of virtue in our lives becomes dubious and problematic. Through Lawrence's words, Levertov suggests that the poet must not be paralyzed by the knowledge of this destructive capacity within, but continue to sing about the "creative wonder"—the beauty and plenitude of earthly existence.

The third meditation returns to a tranquil natural setting like that of Part One, yet the poet now views the landscape from a much different perspective. Nature is no longer benign, but tainted and threatening; death, in the form of chemical contamination, lurks insidiously in each "dull grassblade" (JL, 30). Levertov's perception has been subtly politicized—throughout the lyric she alludes to many of the hazards and problems endemic to contemporary life: environmental pollutants, food additives which wreak as yet unknown havoc with the lives of future generations, the unchecked growth of the world's population, and the mad rush to conquer space:

> bread preserved without
> virtue,
> sweet grapes sour to the children's children.
>
> We breathe an ill wind,
> nevertheless our kind
> in mushroom multitudes
> jostles for elbow-room
> moonwards (JL, 31)

In the meditative journey that takes place between Parts One and Three of the poem, Levertov comes to a striking realization: despite—or more accurately, because of—the poet's insight into the dark, destructive impulse which lies within the human heart, it is his responsibility to actively combat this force by exercising his imagination and celebrating life for the brief duration "while he has it" (JL. 31): "Man's capacity for evil is less a positive capacity, for all its horrendous activity, than a failure to develop man's most human function, the imagination, to its fullness, and consequently a failure to develop compassion" (PW, 53). For Levertov, silence, resignation, and despair are therefore unacceptable responses to present world conditions: the necessary corrective is rather a summoning of numinous energy:

> a singing,
> a beating of gongs, efficacious
> to drive away devils (*JL*, 31)

The poet's virtue (and, by extension, his constructive contribution to society) is simply "to be / what he is" (*JL*, 31)—sentient, sympathetic, humane—to register an unflaggingly truthful response to the increasingly dehumanized circumstances in which he lives. This testimony, according to Levertov, is the "utmost response" that can be expected of any artist.

The concluding lines of "Three Meditations" bring the reader back full circle to its beginning; Levertov echoes Olson's words about the poet "filling his whole space," but at the same time amplifies their meaning by conjoining them to a specific goal—that "no devil/may enter" (*JL*, 31). In this regard, her conception of the poet's role assumes primitive, almost shamanistic, overtones; through the power of song, she not only keeps the "devil" within herself in check, but sets an ethical and aesthetic example for society at large— encouraging others to also "try to equate 'human' with 'humane.' "[9] "Three Meditations" thus establishes a crucial philosophical framework through which to view all of Levertov's subsequent work: her concern with the preservation of life. The practical "effectiveness" of her political poems is ultimately a moot issue; what is of prime importance, however, is her urgent insistence on the need "to stay alive"—to remain human, to reverence life, and to be conscious of the implications of events which occur beyond the small circle of our daily existence. Levertov's work refuses to let us forget that "we are living our whole lives *in a state of emergency* which is unparalleled in all history" (*PW*, 115) by candidly documenting her own unremitting struggle to react to, incorporate, and make sense of the external world. Through the luminous sparks of her poetic language, we begin to comprehend the full "extent of the human range" (*PW*, 52), and to perceive what is lacking in our inner lives. Regardless of the nature of one's political views, Levertov's poems are truly revolutionary in this sense.

Notes

1. One particularly adverse response to Levertov's political writing occurs in Alvin Rosenfeld's "The Being of Language and the Language of Being: Heidegger and Modern Poetics" (*Boundary* 2, no. 4 [Winter 1976]), where he describes the poem "From a Notebook" in *To Stay Alive* in this way:

> This kind of doggerel, a weak imitation of Berkeley Bravura, winds on for some twenty pages. . . . One feels embarrassed for a poet who strains so hard to enlist her language for the revolutionary "cause," a cause that enters her poetry like some tired locomotive, puffing and chugging its way along until it comes to an exhausted halt. (548)

2. Denise Levertov, *The Poet in the World* (New York: New Directions, 1973), 124; hereafter designated *PW* and cited in text.

3. E. G. Burrows, Interview with Denise Levertov, *Michigan Quarterly Review* 7 (Fall 1968), 240–41.

4. Denise Levertov, *Light Up the Cave* (New York: New Directions, 1981), 116; hereafter designated *LC* and cited in text.

5. Denise Levertov, "The Phonecall," *Life in the Forest* (New York: New Directions, 1978), 70.

6. Denise Levertov, *Collected Earlier Poems, 1940–1960* (New York: New Directions, 1979), 25; hereafter designated *CEP* and cited in text.

7. Reflecting on these early poems in her essay, "H. D.: An Appreciation," Levertov states, "I lived in the midst of [the bombing of London] but in a sense it did not *happen* to me, and though my own first book, in 1946, was written during that time, the war appeared in it only off-stage or as the dark background of adolescent anxiety" (*PW*, 245).

8. Denise Levertov, *The Jacob's Ladder* (New York: New Directions, 1961), 29; hereafter designated *JL* and cited in text.

9. Denise Levertov, *Relearning the Alphabet* (New York: New Directions, 1970), 104.

Songs of Experience: Denise Levertov's Political Poetry

Lorrie Smith*

Denise Levertov's large body of political poetry records the vicissitudes of a deeply ethical imagination grappling with the difficult public issues of the last twenty years. At forty-four, Levertov had published six volumes before her first Vietnam protest poems appeared in *The Sorrow Dance* (1967). The seven volumes since *The Sorrow Dance* all contain poems in response to contemporary political issues; in prose and at readings she is an outspoken activist.[1] Though she continues to write many nonpolitical poems and to gather politically topical poems in separate sections within volumes, Levertov's work since the late sixties is infused with the reciprocal beliefs that "only revolution can now save that earthly life, that miracle of being, which poetry conserves and celebrates"[2] and that by its very nature, poetry itself is "intrinsically revolutionary."[3]

The effort to fuse poetry and revolution is more vexed, however, than Levertov suggests in her numerous *ars poetica*. Her evolution as an engaged writer demonstrates the dilemmas facing those poets of her generation who changed in middle age and in mid-career to accommodate a growing political consciousness but whose radicalism is embodied, for the most part, in traditional forms and idioms. Levertov's grounding in what Charles Altieri calls an "immanentist" poetics[4] is initially shaken by the demands of radical activism, and she is faced with the need to speak didactically without sacrificing her earlier lyricism. This dilemma is primarily psychic for Levertov; except for some experimentation with long sequences, her forms and techniques remain essentially unchanged throughout her career. Levertov's maturation

*Reprinted with permission from *Contemporary Literature* 27 (Summer 1986), 213–32.

as a political poet shows in increasingly complex and refined renderings of the political implications of personal life, poetic practice, and, in her latest volumes, religious belief.

Throughout her career, Levertov sustains a devotion to the formalist creed that "poetry is a way of constructing autonomous existences out of words and silences."[5] Her late-romantic poetics amalgamates Keats's Imagination and Negative Capability, Emerson's organic form, and Williams's mediation between "the spirit of here-and-now" and a "supernatural" realm of values. Her early poetry easily bridges the distance between the "inner" self and the "outer" world by uncovering the numinous in quotidian moments, and she negotiates these two poles with an inductive and organic movement: examining an object, event, or feeling to arrive at a larger revelation. She is, like Williams, a poet of the found object and fortuitous epiphany. "The World Outside" contains characteristic images of illumination and a near-mystical transformation of everyday materials. Through leaps of language, a shadow on "the kitchen wall" yields a "pilgrimage," pigeons "spiral" upwards in "celebration," "tenement windows" reflect a lustrous "blaze," and sunset over Hoboken flashes in a Wordsworthian "westering" glow:

> On the kitchen wall a flash
> of shadow:
>   swift pilgrimage
> of pigeons, a spiral
> celebration of air, of sky-deserts.
>
> And on tenement windows
> a blaze
>   of lustered watermelon:
> stain of the sun
> westering somewhere back of Hoboken. (*JL*, p. 4)

Levertov's subjectivity is at home in the sensory world and easily interacts with it through the mediation of the creative, synthesizing imagination. Her prepolitical poems embrace a benign universe whose inherent order is available to the sufficiently perceptive and articulate poet. Though she inscribes the typical romantic obstacles to revelation in many poems—the flow of time, the otherness of nature and people, the clamor of everyday events, the inertia of what she calls, in a favorite quotation from Rilke, "unlived life, of which one can die"—she almost always overcomes them with a tone of celebration, often ending poems with an ecstatic exclamation at the luminous natural world. Neither the autonomy of "the world outside" nor the integrity of the artist's vision is compromised; each is enhanced and made available to the reader through the equally autonomous form of the achieved poem.[6]

Several critics, however, have noted an imbalance that Levertov will explore deeply before redressing it in her political poems. In an early review, Robert Pack qualifies his generally favorable assessment:

She too often seems predisposed to see things as beautiful or holy. At such times she forces her mysticism. . . . Mystic vision without sufficient doubt or terror, without a firm grasp of unequivocal evil, easily becomes sentimental. To me, Levertov's world is not yet complete, for as yet I find in it no unredeemed pain, no aspect of reality that is unsupportable.[7]

Yet the potential for a more complete world view is, in fact, inherent in her early poetry. As early as *The Jacob's Ladder* (1961), Levertov begins to expand her circumference to include specific social and political topics. "During the Eichmann Trial" establishes empathy as a basis for political commitment. Her effort to come to grips with evil, an impenetrable "other," leads to the realization that Eichmann is not a stereotyped monster but a "pitiful man whom none / pity, whom all / must pity if they look / / into their own face" (*JL*, p. 61). In such lines, Levertov attempts to maintain dialogue with an almost incomprehensible "other" and to bind humanity within her poet's vision and language. But she does not allow pity to become forgiveness or pathos, and the poem ends with a depiction of Holocaust horrors and a realization that all are implicated and responsible, "each a mirror / for man's eyes" (*JL*, p. 67). By assuming personal guilt in a context of universal complicity, she is able to assimilate evil into a coherent moral vision without denying its ultimate "otherness." Evil is merely conceived, however, as an absence of compassion and a failure of imagination; its full counterweight is not yet measured.[8] Only with increasing experience and awareness will Levertov's scope expand to embrace doubt and terror as well as praise and wonder. Her confrontation of "unequivocal evil" in the world is contemporaneous with political awakening and activism during the Vietnam war, and her inclusion of explicit political issues in her poetry gives concrete shape to her earlier vague sense of social malaise.

Levertov's evolution as an engaged "poet in the world" naturally follows from her growing involvement in Leftist politics. Though she was active in Ban the Bomb demonstrations during the fifties, her poems from this period rarely reflect political beliefs. But the Vietnam war and the social turmoil of the sixties compelled Levertov and many of her contemporaries to align themselves with younger radicals, question their aesthetic assumptions, and address political issues directly in poems and public readings. The trauma of the war violently disrupts Levertov's unifying vision and psychic integrity: "Reduced to an eye / I forget what / I was" (*RA*, p. 9). Her focus on the numinous surfaces of the "Here and Now" (the title of her first American volume, 1957) proves inadequate for confronting a larger scope of political events, and with *The Sorrow Dance* she begins to question the value of a visionary poetics disengaged from political commitment. The war is an "other" she cannot assimilate because of its real but incomprehensible horror, its unreal sensationalism as portrayed by the media, and its actual distance in a foreign country. The private sanctity of the present moment becomes entangled with the more diffuse public reality of the Vietnam war. Images of blurred vision and distorted language are frequent in this period of traumatic disruption: she sees too well or not at all, is driven to both protest and silence. For a poet of Levertov's sensibility, such disjunctions are extremely distressing, for they threaten the whole foundation of her poetic enterprise.

While political activism provides a structure and an outlet for Levertov's deeply felt moral outrage, it also engenders new dilemmas: an awareness of history as it impinges on the present moment, of reality beyond her direct apprehension, and of unassimilable dualities at odds with innate impulse to synthesize experience through poetic vision. The interpenetration of inner and outer that sustains psychic equilibrium in Levertov's first six books becomes polarized, after the war, in an almost Manichean opposition of good (life as she has known it, human potential as she can envision it, poetic power as she has enacted it) and evil (the knowledge, simultaneously, of war, suffering, hypocrisy, oppression, and ultimate global obliteration). Thus Levertov's growth as a political poet involves the intensely personal working out of the very traditional confrontation of evil in the world, for her political awakening is equivalent to a fall into the world of experience outside her direct line of vision and beyond her control as a poet. The tension of trying to maintain integrity—to balance her fundamentally mystical imagination with a larger sphere of events and issues—is betrayed in recurrent patterns of unresolved polarity and paradox.

Initially outraged at the war and then despairing, Levertov gradually accommodates the disjunction between political anguish and poetic affirmation. Her poetry after *The Sorrow Dance* attempts to achieve equilibrium and earn transcendence in a world that thwarts this effort. Increasingly, her poetry is conceived as an active "counter-rhythm" to chaos and horror. Not until she learns to live with paradox, relinquishing the desire to reconcile good and evil, can Levertov move beyond defeat toward new, though diminished, forms of affirmation. Her deep yearning for synthesis gradually moderates into a sort of detente which eases the polarized tension between personal life and public contingency, lyric revelation and didactic statement. As she has recently written:

> What those of us whose lives are permeated by a sense of unremitting political emergency, and who are at the same time writers of poetry, most desire in our work, I think, is to attain to such osmosis of the personal and the public, of assertion and of song, that no one would be able to divide our poems into categories. The didactic would be lyrical, the lyrical would be didactic. That is, at any rate, my own probably unattainable goal.[9]

Though "inner" and "outer" are often painfully separate in Levertov's fallen world, they are also paradoxically united because one person suffers and records the dissonance. Her most successful political poems neither collapse the distinctions between these terms nor flatly oppose them, but sustain an equilibrium in which the integrity of each is preserved and enlarged by the other.

Levertov's first antiwar poems appear at the end of *The Sorrow Dance* in a section entitled "Life at War." The poem "Life at War" characteristically describes the knowledge of evil in bodily terms: the war feels to her like "lumps of raw dough // weighing down a child's stomach on baking day" (*SD*, p. 79). Likewise, these final poems weight the whole volume with their dark significance. Experience of good and knowledge of evil are split, irreconcilable, indigestible. A pattern of polarity emerges as the emblem of her recurring dilemma:

> the knowledge that humankind,
>
> delicate Man, whose flesh
> responds to a caress, whose eyes
> are flowers that perceive the stars,
>
> whose music excels the music of birds,
> whose laughter matches the laughter of dogs,
> whose understanding manifests designs
> fairer than the spider's most intricate web,
>
> still turns without surprise, with mere regret
> to the scheduled breaking open of breasts whose milk
> runs out over the entrails of still-alive babies,
> transformation of witnessing eyes to pulp-fragments,
> implosion of skinned penises into carcass-gulleys.
> . . . .
> Yes, this is the knowledge that jostles for space
> in our bodies along with all we
> go on knowing of joy, of love . . . (*SD*, pp. 79–80)

Unable to find an appropriate balance between lyric and didactic in these first angry protest poems, Levertov sometimes borders on polemical cliche and sentimentality. But her technique of presenting precise, descriptive details is one she will use continually to "bring the war home" to her readers. Her ironic counterpointing of lyrical metaphors with military diction and graphic depiction gives force to her political critique, and the jarring disjunctions of language mirror Levertov's own disjointed consciousness. The extremity of images in "Life at War," necessary to shock both the reader and herself into full and visceral awareness, is tempered at the end with a more solemn resignation: "nothing we do has the quickness, the sureness, / the deep intelligence living at peace would have." Though she can desire peace, she makes no motion here to heal the split that her fall has caused. Doubt and anger supplant wonder and celebration, and it will take several volumes before Levertov can begin to regain her equilibrium.

Levertov republishes these first protest poems as a preface to her longer, more experimental poems in *Relearning the Alphabet*, which one critic accurately calls a "spiritual autobiography."[10] After the crisis and despair of "Life at War," she needs to rethink her position and reform herself as a poet to make room for all the conflicting "knowledge that jostles for space." These needs provoke a quest for a poetics more adequate to the complexity of her newly politicized consciousness—specifically, new forms and language that will not abstract or aestheticize experience and that will encompass doubt and terror as well as beauty and holiness. Levertov continues to try to absorb the knowledge of war, but her efforts usually end in paralysis and defeat. In the emblematically titled "The Gulf," her imagination of an "other"—a black boy during the Detroit riots—only becomes "useless knowledge in my mind's eye" (*RA*, p. 16); the "gulf" between them, and between imagination and reality, remains unbridged. In "Biafra," she tries "to make room for more knowledge / in my bonemarrow" but can only trail off with an impotent "no hope: Don't know / what to do: Do nothing:" (*RA*, p. 18). Though she can still portray herself in another poem from this volume as "a woman foolish with desire" ("July, 1968" *RA*, p. 64), the optimistic hope that life goes on in this "dark time" is constantly threatened with despair. This painful state of limbo—and its concomitant state of inarticulateness for the poet—is evoked more fully in "A Cloak":

> And I walked naked
> from the beginning
>
> breathing in
> my life,
> breathing out
> poems,
>
> arrogant in innocence.
>
> But of the song-clouds my breath made
> in cold air
>
> a cloak has grown,
> white and,
>   where here a word
>   there another
> froze, glittering,
> stone-heavy.
>
> A mask I had not meant
> to wear, as if of frost,
> covers my face.
>   Eyes looking out,
> a longing silent at song's core. (*RA*, p. 44)

This poem explicitly conceives of her transformation as a fall from "arrogant" innocence into a world of powerless speech and action. Levertov mourns the loss of poetic power that had once been as natural as "breathing in . . . breathing out."

The title poem of this volume, however, regathers energy to counter inertia, discovers new language to replace silent longing. The poem posits an experimental solution to the stasis and despair that attended Levertov's awakening consciousness of evil. She free-associates on the letters of the alphabet in order to reawaken and transform poetic power. The conventional and (for a poet) comforting structure of the alphabet allows both freedom and progression ("All utterance / takes me step by hesitant step towards / / —yes, to continuance" [*RA*, p. 118]). The poem's meditative process recalls her Hasidic-Anglican father's interest in Kabbalah and numerology and Williams's arbitrary but structured process in *Kora in Hell* of writing daily for a year.[11] Following the confusion and questioning of the fragmented work-in-progress, "From a Notebook," "Relearning the Alphabet" feels satisfying and heartening. Though the poem does not address specific political issues, its position as the finale of the volume automatically forces it to encompass and temporarily resolve the crises of consciousness and action in preceding poems.

The dominant tone of "Relearning the Alphabet" is optimistic, even playful, recapturing a child's pleasure in singing the ABC's and in mastering language. The poem begins with "Joy" and ends with "praise"—key words in Levertov's earlier poetry; images of transcendental light recur throughout the poem. The poem is radical in its quest for linguistic roots; the alphabet itself generates verbs that propel the poem's action: the letter *B* is for "being"; *C*, of course, for "seeing." *D* leads to a new genesis for "Denise": "In the beginning was delight" (another pun, as well as the obvious Biblical echo). The fervent desire to recover the mode of celebration that supported her innocent poetic vision is not entirely nostalgic or unqualified, however. The poem records a quasi-mystical quest both forward and back "home to the present." Halting lines and parenthetical asides trace her mythical descent:

> I go stumbling
> (head turned)
>   back to my origins:
> (if that's where I'm going)
>   to joy, my Jerusalem.
> Weeping, gesturing,
> I'm a small figure in mind's eye,
> diminishing in the sweep of rain or gray tears
> that cloud the far shore as jealous rage
> clouds love and changes it, changes vision. (*RA*, pp. 112–13)

The journey towards "caritas, claritas" is always threatened by a paralyzing return to "limbo" and by the distorting gaps between language and reality. The speaker herself falters, but the procession of the alphabet structures her journey and restores her to active "utterance," "continuance," and "vision." She returns from the underworld to the world she has known all along, now dismantled and reconstructed, the alphabet relearned. The poem ends with a familiar "ah! of praise," but this affirmation has now been matured and tested through a descent to an underworld of split psyche, nightmare, and thwarted language—an underworld whose more social and political realities surface in "From a Notebook."

The mystical wonder and celebration recovered in "Relearning the Alphabet" prove to be provisional and perhaps insufficient responses to political reality, for they are replaced with a renewed sense of darkness and paradox in *To Stay Alive*, published a year later (1971)—her only volume devoted entirely to political poetry. She republishes poems already in print and interpolates "From a Notebook" and "Interim" into a longer, more coherent sequence, "Staying Alive." Levertov struggles in this volume with the daily complexities of radical political action, death—both close to home and global—and language that is increasingly recalcitrant to her needs. She does, however, manage to break the paralyzing stasis of earlier poems, and *To Stay Alive* marks a turning point in Levertov's movement toward an "osmosis of the personal and the public, of assertion and of song."[12]

In addition to finding a way to reconcile her various polarities of consciousness, Levertov must discover a form that will include history and envision the future as well as "dig down / to re-examine" ("Staying Alive," Part II, *TSA*, p. 40) the present. The long sequence form of "Staying Alive" allows a meditative breadth and temporal inclusiveness not possible in her shorter lyrics. Like its main precursor, *Paterson*, the sequence mixes lyric passages with prose, conversations, letters, public documents, and diary entries in a kinetic montage of Levertov's "inner/outer experience" during the sixties. Recurring themes and words reverberate like Poundian subject rhymes to give the poem structure and coherence. The formal alternations of prose and poetry allow a large rhythm of expansion and contraction, mirroring the manic-depressive, painful split which is both personal and national. Like *Leaves of Grass*, *Paterson*, and the *Cantos*, Levertov's is "a poem including history" as well as a poem included and inscribed in history: Levertov's personal case history is inseparable from and representative of the public events in which she is immersed.

The opening "Interim," which tells of a trip to the sea while awaiting her husband Mitchell Goodman's trial for war resistance, is now retitled "Prologue: An Interim." Past experience gains new significance in retrospect and in the new context of her ongoing political struggle. The Prologue also invokes Levertov's personal muse on behalf of the fallen culture and sets forth a major theme of the poem:

> O language, mother of thought,
> are you rejecting us as we reject you?
>
> Language, coral island
> accrued from human comprehensions,
> human dreams,
>
> you are eroded as war erodes us. (*TSA*, p. 22)

A primary mission in this poem is to rebuild a strong and healthy language to counter the polemical jargon and officialese assulting the poet from both Left and Right. But this undertaking, fundamentally moral and political, must first be personal for Levertov. To all her other polarizations she now must add the most basic gap between words and action. She clings to the locus discovered in "Relearning the Alphabet": "Without a terrain in which, to which, I belong, / language itself is my one home, my Jerusalem"; yet throughout the poem she gropes for adequate expression: "I choose / revolution but my words / often already don't reach forward / into it— / (perhaps) . . ." (*TSA,* p. 34); "*revolution,*" itself, she laments, is "the wrong word. . . . But it's the only / word we have . . ." (*TSA,* p. 41; second ellipsis in original). Such skeptical explorations reach toward dialogue to replace what Thomas Merton, in an essay written during the same period, calls "definitive utterance, to which there can be no rejoinder."[13] Levertov strains to maintain dialogue with her own conflicting extremes as well as to promote dialogue as a means toward progressive political change.

"Part I" opens with the refrain that pulses through the poem and structures its progression: "Revolution or death." For Levertov, this choice is highly personal, not just rhetorical, and though she must in good conscience answer "Revolution, of course," the long questioning poem explores the implications and complexities of this choice, deconstructing what first seems to be another absolute dichotomy. (There could, she realizes, be revolution *and* death—a possibility she must come to terms with.) Every choice reveals its alternative; all is provisional, qualified, irreconcilable: "And yet, yes, there's the death." The revolution she chooses "is the first that laughter and pleasure aren't shot down in," but it is also peopled by self-immolating and self-starving martyrs and violent demonstrators.

Her meditations on death first seduce Levertov back to Whitman, Swinburne, and Keats, where dissolution and forgetfulness offer tempting relief and intimations of mystical transcendence to the agonized poet: "Death lovely, / whispering, / *a drowsy numbness . . . / 'tis not / from envy of thy happy lot . . . / . . . river / winds somewhere to the sea*" (*TSA,* p. 30; second ellipsis added). In later sections, she elegiacally explores the suicides of two friends—one "trivial," one tragic. Only by contemplating the feel of death can Levertov begin to come to grips with its global significance. Like "revolution," it must be stripped of abstractness before it can be restored as a vital and meaningful term.

The opening of "Part II" plunges into the complexities of the present moment: "Can't go further. / If there's to be a / second part, it's not / a going beyond, I'm / still here. / / To dig down, / to reexamine" (*TSA,* p. 40). Echoing the opening of Book II of *Paterson*—"Blocked. / (Make a song out of that: concretely)"—Levertov takes Williams's earlier American quest as a map for her own, in spirit as well as form. The climax of the poem—the "Diary" ended here in the previous volume—this section recounts her participation in the 1969 People's Park movement in Berkeley, an event that seems to have galvanized Levertov's radical consciousness. As "The War / comes home to us" (*TSA*, p. 45) and her eyes are seared by tear gas, Levertov proclaims her radicalization and rebirth. Collective activism releases the static polarization brought on by her earlier traumas. Her choice of revolution is affirmative, harking back to her earlier celebratory mode and echoing the very early "Overland to the Islands," where "every step" is "an arrival":

> Revolution: a crown of tree
> raises itself out of the heavy
> flood . . .
>
> . . . .
> Maybe what seems
> evanescent is solid.
>
> Islands
> step out of the waves on rock feet. (*TSA*, p. 47)

"I" becomes incorporated with "we" in Levertov's new identity in solidarity and action. The personal does not dissolve in the collective but gains force, definition, and liberation. Revolutionary transformation involves trial by fire and violence, but these are seen as temporary, cathartic stages of progressive political action, and Levertov welcomes them as active counterforces to numb immobility. If the recovery of joy and hope in this section is a bit facile in its Whitmanesque optimism ("O happiness / in the sun! Is it / that simple, then, / to live?" [*TSA*, p. 44]) the poem's continuing immersion in complicated events and emotions tells us that, in fact, it is not "that simple." Later she admits, "I keep / enduring such pangs of giving / / birth or being / born" (*TSA*, p. 52) and "I forget anguish / as I forget joy" (*TSA*, p. 65).

With her newly won "tragic, fearful / knowledge of *present history*" (*TSA*, p. 66), Levertov transforms the choice between "revolution or death" to the conjunction of two life-giving forces: "revolution" and "poetry." Though this fusion does not relieve her pain or solve her dilemmas, it provides a new source of strength: "But when their rhythms/ mesh / then though the pain of living / never lets up / / the singing begins" (*TSA*, p. 74). Levertov uses this affirmation to dig back into the "tunnel of daily life," now able to celebrate daily joys again, in solitude as well as solidarity. The movement back "home" reenacts the climax of "Relearning the Alphabet," which proves, in retrospect, merely to have been a preparation for this real transformation. Thus the core discovery of this long poem is a new politicized identity in the "Here and Now," which incorporates the past (history) and opens up the future (revolution). Levertov rediscovers happiness, love, heroes, song, and dance in a series of brief epiphanies, but her voice is urgent and these consolations are clearly provisional. Her lines step confidently forward until they are pulled back to the margin:

> only conjunctions
> > of song's
> > > raging magic
> > > with patient courage
> > > > will make   a new life:
> we can't wait: time is
> > not on our side. (*TSA*, p. 82)

She comes to understand that struggle—political as well as poetic—must be renewed daily. A new battle looms at the end—"news of invasion of Laos started to be 'official' "—and her poetic diary hangs in elliptical suspension: "O holy innocents! I have / no virtue but to praise / you who believe / life is possible . . ." (*TSA*, p. 84; ellipsis in original). Pragmatism and prayer mingle to form a provisional response to the complexities of good and evil. Her recovery of the luminous present movement, now irrevocably shadowed by the knowledge of evil, forms the foundation of Levertov's integration of personal and political, lyric and didactic in her later poems.

Images and themes of unreconciled duality reappear with renewed force in *The Freeing of the Dust* (1975), written after her trip to North Vietnam with fellow poet Muriel Rukeyser. The war now appears through the eyes of a witness, for Levertov regains the confidence that her refined vision can accurately convey what she observes: amputees, children in hospitals, nervous bomber pilots, the green landscape and business-as-usual ironically bestowing moments of "Peace within the / long war" (*FD*, p. 35). Rather than being paralyzed and benumbed, as before, Levertov has attained a more realistic vision which can include fluctuation and polarity without a nostalgic yearning for complete synthesis. *The Freeing of the Dust* balances divorce ("Divorcing") with reconciliation ("Libation"). It offers a model of dialogue in place of polarized monologue, recreating a contrapuntal conversation between a Russian poet and an American poet mediated by a translator, all of whom smile "in common knowledge" ("Conversation in Moscow"). As in Wallace Stevens's "Sunday Morning," where paradoxical pigeons fly "downward to darkness, on extended wings," Levertov's experienced vision embraces both "grief and delight entwined in the dark down there."

"Modes of Being" extends Levertov's familiar pattern of extreme opposites by exploring more fully the gaps between simultaneous good and evil (*FD*, pp. 98–99). Four lyrical passages about private experience—"Indoors, reading, talking . . . What more / can love be than epiphany!"—alternate with three italicized passages of flat reportage describing men and women being tortured "*Near Saigon, / in a tiger-cage.*" These two "modes of being" are linked by the universal human gestures of stretching and reaching. The speaker and her companion "reach and enter / a new landscape of knowledge," "January's fist / unclenches," and "shadows yawn and / stretch to the east" at the same time an imprisoned man "*tries to stretch out his hand / and cannot*" and a woman "*tries to straighten her / cramped spine / and cannot.*"

Rather than synthesizing these two simultaneous realities, the imagery and discrete formal divisions provide a chilling contrast between "that which is and / that which is." The poem moves beyond absolute polarization, however, as the speaker's imagination reaches toward both extremes:

> Joy
> is real, torture
> is real, we strain to hold
> a bridge between them open,
> and fail,
> or all but fail (*FD*, p. 99)

The emblematic gulf that dominates so many of her earlier political poems is now replaced by a more hopeful "bridge" constructed through imagination, moral vision, and language:

> What wings, what mighty arch
> of feathered hollow bones, beyond
> span of albatross or eagle,
> mind and heart must grow
>   to touch, trembling,
> with outermost pinion tips,
> not in alternation but both at once,
> in one
> violent eternal instant
> that which is and
> that which is . . . (*FD*, p. 99)

Paradoxically, Levertov can both imagine this balance and admit its impossibility. Ending as an unanswered question, the poem stops short of transcendence and projects its conditional, almost sleight-of-hand reconciliation only through a supreme effort of language itself. The ending ellipses leave the reader, implicitly included in the speaker's "we," straining "to hold / a bridge . . . open."

Levertov remains haunted by her own question, however. "Unresolved" (*CB*, p. 103) is structured by the same paradox in "Modes of Being" and extends the attempt to make torture—here in El Salvador—real and comprehensible. Again, the poem juxtaposes grisly newsreel close-up with lyric responses to this other reality. Jostling the same knowledge of simultaneous good and evil, she finds a tone weary and resigned rather than painfully torn. The poem's image of a strangled bird descends from the "mighty arch" of wings imagined in "Modes of Being," frankly representing failure where before there was fragile desire:

> We know so much of daily bread,
> of every thread of lovingly knit compassion;
>
> garments of love clothe us, we rest
> our heads upon darkness; when we wake

> sapphire transparency calls forth our song.
> And this is the very world, the same, the world
>
> of vicious power, of massacre.
> Our song is a bird that wants
> to sing as it flies, to be
> the wings of praise, but doubt
>
> binds tight its wire to hold down
> flightbones, choke back breath.
> We know no synthesis. (*CB*, pp. 104–5)

With this flat denial, Levertov reaches the limits of polarity, whose extremes she has explored obsessively and whose poetic possibilities she has exhausted. Her most recent political poems assume "no synthesis" and move beyond this impasse toward a more complex paradigm of dialogue—both spiritual and social—to bridge her knowledge of evil and her yearning for peace.

In her two most recent volumes, *Candles in Babylon* (1982) and *Oblique Prayers* (1984), Levertov extends the qualified optimism recovered in *The Freeing of the Dust* and relies more strongly than ever on the mysticism underlying all of her work. She has refined both her lyricism and her didacticism and integrates them in her current work with polished, pared-down language. She no longer leaps to the exclamatory epiphanies of her early lyrics or the blunt invective of some previous political poems; transcendence is now muted and provisional, political outrage now tempered by wisdom and experience. Above all, she tells us, poetic vision can no longer pretend to be neutral; yet the poet's gifts of heightened perception and expression offer hope in this "Age of Terror." Though moments of visionary affirmation are never purely innocent in Levertov's fallen world, her knowledge of evil is mitigated by a deep reverence for earthly life.

The set-piece of *Candles in Babylon* is the sequence "Mass for the Day of St. Thomas Didymus"—a contrapuntal exploration of faith and doubt in the nuclear age. The solemn procession of liturgical sections works emotionally as an actual mass does to save the poem from ponderousness. Invocation, confession, praise, blessing, creed, song, and plea are modulated in a whole that, like "Relearning the Alphabet," is at once freely organic and highly structured. As in a mass, private emotions find release in communal ritual and, as in so many of Levertov's later political poems, the lyric voice is a collective "we" rather than a singular "I." Like Christian faith itself, Levertov's poetic mass assimilates a knowledge of evil and counters it with hope and praise, however qualified and diminished. The poem succumbs neither to transcendent ecstasy nor to absolute despair, but rests with an acceptance of fluctuating and irreconcilable extremes: "I believe and / interrupt my belief with / doubt. I doubt and / interrupt my doubt with belief"

(*CB*, p. 110). Language is both divinely incarnate ("very word of / very word, / flesh and / vision" [*CB*, pp. 111–12)] and threatened with extinction ("What of the emptiness, / the destructive vortex that whirls / no word with it?"). At the center of these circular dilemmas lies a "spark / of remote light" (*CB*, p. 115) salvaged from Levertov's original immanentist poetics. She prays not to an orthodox deity but to the spirit infusing "the ordinary glow / of common dust in ancient sunlight" (*CB*, p. 110). The mass inverts Christian hope at the end by placing tentative faith in mankind, who now has the almost overwhelming responsibility to shelter "a shivering God"—the Agnus Dei shorn of symbolism, "reduced" to a "defenseless . . . wisp of damp wool" (*CB*, p. 114).

In *Oblique Prayers,* the political concerns of the poems in the section "Prisoners" merge with the spiritual concerns in the final section, "Of God and of the Gods." The volume is infused with a renewed celebration of nature which, unlike mankind, knows "no clash / of opposites" ("The God of Flowers," *OP*, p. 77) and a rediscovery of immanence in fleeting moments and essential things of the world: "A sorrel grass, / a crust, / water, / salt" ("This Day," *OP*, p. 81). These celebrations, bridging Levertov's early and late poetry, are now more valuable for being less innocent, tinged by the knowledge that it is also "part of human-ness / to enter / no man's land" ("Oblique Prayers," *OP*, p. 82) and tempered by the dark forces compelling human history in a time when "we've approached / the last / the last choice" ("The Cry," *OP*, p. 44). Though she is able to envision transcendent unity in nature, Levertov continues to maintain dialogue with all-too-human oppositions in herself. In "Thinking about El Salvador," she finds silence the only logical and humane response to brutality; yet she overcomes the temptation to be mute in the desperately titled "Perhaps No Poem But All I Can Say And I Cannot Be Silent" and later in "The Antiphon," where "once more / all is eloquent" (*OP*, p. 84). In "Vocation," she praises "martyrs dying / passionately," through whom "we keep our title, *human*, / word like an archway, a bridge, an altar" and shows mature confidence in her own vocation as a "poet in the world" building "an archway, a bridge, an altar" through poetic language and moral vision (*OP*, p. 31).

Levertov's recent poems move beyond polarity to embrace both "anguish" and "affirmation." These terms, the emotional corollaries of good and evil in Levertov's lexicon, are no longer polarized but are yoked together to form the core of Levertov's later political aesthetic: "In our time, a political poetry untinged with anguish, even when it evokes and salutes moments of hope, is unimaginable. Yet—because it creates autonomous structures that are imbued with life and which stir the life of those who experience them—poetry is, in process and in being, intrinsically affirmative."[14] Increasingly, Levertov's affirmations are accepted reverently and offered generously as gifts of grace from a God "in the dust, / not sifted out from confusion" ("This Day," *OP*, p. 80). The poet's task is to allow for both "anguish" and "affirmation" and to flesh out their relations. "Of Being" achieves, in form and thought, a rhythmic interlocking of these impulses, then moves beyond duality to a new realm of the sublime:

> I know this happiness
> is provisional:
>
>   the looming presences—
>   great suffering, great fear—
>
> . . . .
> but ineluctable this shimmering
> of wind in the blue leaves:
>
> this flood of stillness
> widening the lake of sky:
>
> this need to dance,
> this need to kneel:
>   this mystery: ("Of Being," *OP*, p. 86)

The indented stanza makes room for the simultaneous reality of both "happiness" and "great suffering, great fear." The hope of salvation in "unmerited" and fortuitous "grace perhaps" is bolstered by Levertov's reworking of her original immanentist beliefs: "this mystery:" moves ahead of the other lines, and the ending colon points to a future the poet hardly dares to imagine or articulate.

Levertov has recently described the movement from agnosticism to faith evident in her latest poems:

> I have been engaging, then, during the last few years, in my own version of the Pascalian wager, and finding that an avowal of Christian faith is not incompatible with my aesthetic nor with my political stance, since as an artist I was already in the service of the transcendent, and since Christian ethics (however betrayed in past and present history) uphold the same values I seek in a politics of racial and economic justice and nonviolence.[15]

This turn is clearly a natural outgrowth of Levertov's whole poetic endeavor for, as she goes on to say, the "acknowledgement, and celebration, of mystery probably constitutes the most consistent theme of my poetry from its very beginnings."[16] We might recall, as Levertov no doubt expects us to, the Latin root of "religion"—"to tie back." To recover and forge connections, to bridge gaps, has been Levertov's fundamental impulse since her fall into the world of political experience. At once lyrical and ritualistic, poetic prayer bridges personal emotions and larger collective concerns. It seeks communion both horizontally, between humans, and vertically, between the human and the divine—both central modes of dialogue in Levertov's later political vision. Closely related to song and poetry, prayer reaffirms the poet's effort to restore language as a vehicle for political struggle: "Keep writing in the dark . . . / words that may have the power / to make the sun rise again" ("Writing in the Dark," *CB*, p. 101; ellipsis added). Levertov's lyric prayers, read in the context of her political engagment, become a form of activism imploring the reader's own active engagement and response. John Berger finds inherent connections between poetry and prayer and makes explicit their relevance to political action. His statement aptly describes Levertov's efforts to mediate between the spiritual and the political:

> To break the silence of events, to speak of experience, however bitter or lacerating, to put into words, is to discover the hope that these words may be heard, and that when heard, the events will be judged. This hope is of course at the origin of prayer, and prayer . . . was probably at the origin of speech itself. Of all uses of language, it is poetry that preserves most purely the memory of this origin.[17]

Levertov's knowledge of the world and of the word have been deepened and enriched by political activism. She has lost irretrievably the innocent and easy epiphany of her early poems, for "Reason has brought us / more dread than ignorance did" (*CB*, p. 77). She has no illusions about the power of poetry to change political structures or to eradicate evil, and she offers no systematic program for social regeneration. Rather, her strength as a political poet lies in her appeal to celebrate what is valuable and to protest what is unconscionable. Her poems force us to see that both joy and terror are real in our world and challenge us to reconcile them for ourselves. Moreover, she is exemplary in our courage to speak from a clear moral and ideological position when much American poetry remains hermetic and socially disengaged. Levertov counters the unspeakable in our "Age of Terror" with dialogue, song, and prayer.

Notes

1. My discussion focuses on the political poems in seven of Levertov's volumes, all published by New Directions in New York: The following abbreviations will be used in the text: *JL: The Jacob's Ladder* (1961); *SD: The Sorrow Dance* (1967); *RA: Relearning the Alphabet* (1970); *TSA: To Stay Alive* (1971); *FD: The Freeing of the Dust* (1975); *CB: Candles in Babylon* (1982); *OP: Oblique Prayers* (1984). "The World Outside" and "Life at War" appear in *Poems 1960–1967*. Copyright ©1961, 1966 by Denise Levertov Goodman. "Life at War" was first published in *Poetry*. "A Cloak" and "Relearning the Alphabet" appear in *Relearning the Alphabet*. Copyright ©1968 by Denise Levertov Goodman. "Models of Being" appears in *The Freeing of the Dust*. Copyright ©1974, 1975 by Denise Levertov. "Unresolved" appears in *Candles in Babylon*. Copyright ©1982 by Denise Levertov. All poems are reprinted here by permission of New Directions Publishing Corp.

2. Denise Levertov, "The Poet in the World," in *The Poet in the World* (New York: New Directions, 1973), 115.

3. Levertov, "Great Possessions," in *The Poet in the World*, 106.

4. Charles Altieri, "Denise Levertov and the Limits of the Aesthetics of Presence," in *Enlarging the Temple: New Directions in American Poetry during the 1960s* (Lewisburg, Penn.: Bucknell University Press, 1979).

5. Levertov, "The Nature of Poetry," in *Light Up the Cave* (New York: New Directions, 1981), 60.

6. For fuller discussions of Levertov's early poetry, see: Thomas A. Duddy, "To Celebrate: A Reading of Denise Levertov," *Criticism* 10, no. 2 (1968), 138–52; Ralph J. Mills, "Denise Levertov: Poetry of the Immediate," in his *Contemporary American Poetry* (New York: Random House, 1965), 179–96; Diana Surman, "Inside and Outside in the Poetry of Denise Levertov," *Critical Quarterly* 22 (1980), 57–70; and Linda Welshimer Wagner, *Denise Levertov* (New York: Twayne Publishers, 1967).

7. Robert Pack, "To Each Man His Own Muse," *Saturday Review* 45 (December 8, 1962), 28–29, reprinted in *Denise Levertov: In Her Own Province*, ed. Linda Welshimer Wagner (New York: New Directions, 1979), 119–21.

8. For Levertov's own formulation of evil as "good in abeyance," see "Origins of a Poem," in *The Poet in the World*, 53.

9. Levertov, "On the Edge of Darkness: What Is Political Poetry?" in *Light Up the Cave*, 128.

10. James F. Mersmann, *Out of the Vietnam Vortex* (Lawrence: University of Kansas Press, 1979), 102.

11. "Relearning the Alphabet" is dated June 1968 to April 1969 and is almost contemporaneous with "From a Notebook: October '68–May '69," which I will examine in the context of its reworking in the subsequent volume, *To Stay Alive*. These two poems may be viewed as alternative responses to the events of this period, though the expansion and republication of "From a Notebook" as "Staying Alive" demands that they be read sequentially.

12. For a discussion of how Levertov works out the terms of lyric and didactic in *To Stay Alive*, see Paul Lacey, "The Poetry of Political Anguish," *Sagetrieb* 4, no. 1 (Spring 1985), 61–71.

13. See Thomas Merton, "War and the Crisis of Language," in Robert Ginsberg, ed., *The Critique of War* (Chicago: Henry Regnery, 1969), 99–119. Merton writes, "The language of the war-maker is *self-enclosed in finality*. It does not invite reasonable dialogue, it uses language to silence dialogue, to block communication, so that instead of words the two sides may trade divisions, positions, villages, air bases, cities—and of course the lives of the people in them" (p. 113). Levertov refers to dialogue repeatedly in poems and essays, and this paradigm of communication underlies her political as well as aesthetic intents: "The poet develops the basic human need for dialogue in concretions that are audible to others; in listening, others are stimulated into awareness of their own needs and capacities, stirred into taking up their own dialogues, which are so often neglected" ("Origins of a Poem," in *The Poet in the World*, 49); "A poet driven to . . . maintain a dialogue with himself, concerning politics, can expect to write as well upon that theme as upon any other" ("The Poet in the World," 115).

14. Levertov, "The Nature of Poetry," in *Light Up the Cave*, 60.

15. "A Poet's View," *Religion and Intellectual Life*, ms. p. 4.

16. "A Poet's View," p. 6.

17. John Berger, review of *Missing* by Ariel Dorfman, *Village Voice Literary Supplement* (September 1982), p 11.

Denise Levertov's Political Poetry   Jerome Mazzaro*

In the opening poems of *Breathing the Water* (1987), Denise Levertov speaks of a "task" and a "fire . . . replenished . . . while [one] sleeps" as ways in which her muse communicates and she acts as its medium. The message is

*This essay was written specifically for this volume and is published here for the first time with permission of the author.

never bloodless "old loves" or "moments forced / out of the stream of perception / to play 'statue.' "[1] Rather, like the poetry of her early mentor, William
Carlos Williams, the message is *the* stream of perception," and her poems
are not so much an imitation of nature as definitions of conditions and a living
extension of and addition to nature. Writing provides focus and, as such, is
one of several creative actions that, over the years, have consistently countered society's negative impulses. In "Some Notes on Organic Form" (1965),
she identifies the process with a discovery of intrinsic form and Gerard
Manley Hopkins's "inscape," modifying his basic "pattern of essential [sen-
sory] characteristics both in single objects and . . . in objects in a state of
relation to each other . . . to include intellectual and emotional experience
as well" (*PW*, 7). The views are little different from those that she expressed
for Donald Allen's *The New American Poetry, 1945–1960* (1960), where she
also maintains that "poets are instruments on which the power of poetry
plays" and that she longs "for poems of an inner harmony" whose "social
function" would be "to awaken sleepers [to truth] by other means than
shock" (*PW*, 3). The consistency of these and other views suggests the possibility of "one significant, consistent, and developing personality" that T. S.
Eliot finds in "a great poet,"[2] especially since Levertov believes with Paul
Valéry that poetry's form and language should effect a "harmonious exchange
between impression and expression" (*LC*, 129).

Still, in regard to political poetry, particularly "lyrical" political poetry—
"typically . . . short, or fairly short, poems"—she recognizes that it is often
"written without personae: nakedly, candidly . . . in the poet's unmediated
character, often with actual syntactic incorporation of the first person singular, or sometimes the first person plural" (*LC*, 119–20). In any case, she
states, it is "Written from a personal rather than a fictive, and a subjective
rather than objective, standpoint" (*LC*, 120); in a tribute to Pablo Neruda,
she describes its impact in motion picture terms. Her own *Footprints*
(1972), written in reaction to the country's wars at home and in Vietnam,
demonstrates how these political lyrics function. Separate poems complement actual political involvements and collectively shape as much as
readers come to know of a persona. Much like movie images, events are
presented close up ("Hut"), in middle range ("A New Year's Garland for My
Students"), and in long shot ("Man Alone"), and the conscious impact of
their shifting distances is neither consistent perspective nor personal language but, as in motion pictures, calculated intersections of montage in
order to reinforce subjective truth or conviction. Although circumscribed
by an "I," there is neither Eliot's "developing personality" nor the separate
impersonal objective truths that Williams pursues with his cubist "intersec-
tion of loci" and coincidences of "several sense experiences of differing
sorts."[3] There is, instead, a sacrifice or submergence of self to larger linguistic and social issues. In this submergence, the reluctance of the "I" to ally
identity with personal involvement and rigid perspective contrasts with the
often coercing personae of contemporary male writers. Readers are left

with no clear or vested realized imaginary world through whose values they may rummage to discover the "poet" underneath.

That no fictive persona emerges is consistent with a conventional view of three voices in poetry. The "lyric," as James Joyce points out in *A Portrait of the Artist as a Young Man* (1916), is "the simplest verbal vesture of an instant of emotion. . . . He who utters it is more conscious of the instant of emotion than of himself as feeling emotion." It offers what Eliot calls an "objective correlative" to the speaker's state and differs from epical and dramatic voices by the artist's disregard of himself "as the centre of an epical event" and self domination of others by their assuming "a proper and intangible esthetic life."[4] The tests and reconciliations of lyric are with external "realities" rather than with internal consistency, controls, and resolutions, even when these external "realities" are made surrealistic by circumstance. Thus, in "Hut," the items named—mud, wattles, moss, earth—present for their coincidence with the items that make up real huts the vehicles for accepting the validity of the poem's action. At the same time, the diction, line divisions, and placings of words constitute a key to and an acceptance of the speaker. The blending of impression (mud, wattles, etc.) and expression (diction, line division) is the basis on which the whole poem is evaluated and accepted by its congruence to a reader's imagined and/or real experience of huts. There is no separable, internalized meaning-point or contest about which "fictive" realities form and appropriate sets of objects, situations, and chains of events become particular emotions. As in traditional lyrics, by mere virtue of being sung, the subject becomes different from its unsung counterpart. The singing is the assertion of its value and transportation into a dimension peculiar to song, where by inscape it becomes whole, more permanent, and part of a universal harmony.

Aesthetic shiftings like those that Levertov employs are similarly not new to poetry, and within poems, they serve broadly different ends. They occur regularly in narrative and quasi-narrative works to allow poets to move from large opening scenes to more specific identifications, intensifications, and memorializations. Thus, from a description of a political protest as "scaffolding set up for / TV cameras" and "100,000 reddening / white faces," one closes in without disruption on the voice of Judy Collins bleating, "We must *not* be angry, we must / L-O-O-O-V-E!" (*P3*, 165). So, too, in the musically modeled suites that are common in contemporary poetry, aesthetic shifts provide variety and renewed interest by changes in rhythm, form, and theme that are comparable to sonata movements or songs of a song cycle. The interplay of letter and journal entries and lyric lines throughout *To Stay Alive* (1971) offers one example of this shifting, as do the differing rhythms in and themes of Levertov's multisectioned poems. Also common are the aesthetic shiftings associated with meditative poetry. John Pick has described their presence in Hopkins's poetry, and Louis Martz traces their impact on seventeenth-century English metaphysical poems. In Levertov's work, they occur most often in poems that identify and then summon distant or dead figures into a speaker's presence or transport her to places where these absent figures or landscapes abide. Third-person narrative or description turns in these shiftings into first- and second-person colloquies as the distance closes. At times, the figure is a younger version of the poet as, in the manner of Williams, she appears to seek that fusion of the dream that a poet dreams "when he was young [with] the phenomenal world of his later years." This fusion must occur if the poet "is to be rated high as a master of his art."[5]

Levertov's use of these shiftings comes into fullest play in *To Stay Alive,* where in donning the semblance of a unified persona she offers the poetic equivalent of a movie or video documentary. The volume records her life from the identification of her dead sister Olga "with the pacifists 'going limp' as they are dragged to the paddywagon in Times Square in 1966" to an understanding "by 1970 that 'there comes a time when only anger / is love' " (*P3*, 106). The record spans two successive broad movements—"Preludes" and a multisectioned "Staying Alive." The Preludes are seven short works, four drawn from *The Sorrow Dance* (1967), two from *Relearning the Alphabet* (1970), and the last appearing in a book collection for the first time. "Staying Alive," likewise, divides into seven parts: four longish episodes separated by "Entr'actes" and an eighth introductory "Prologue," taken along with the opening two parts and first Entr'acte from *Relearning the Alphabet*. Within these movements at least four different kinds of distancing occur: temporal (then and now); personal (I and others); emotional (personal and impersonal); and generic (poetry and prose). Distancing occurs between poems, as between "Life at War" and "What Were They Like?" as well as between segments of a poem, as in segments of the "Olga Poems," or within segments, as in the shifts between prose and poetry in the Prologue. The shifts not only collapse "then" into "now" but, in the Prologue, work to reinforce an image of freedom as the freedom of conscience associated with a flowering nature rather than with a copresent destructive war. As Levertov says in Part Three of the Prologue, "To repossess our souls we fly / to the sea" (*P3*, 130), the same sea that in the next part she is taken to by her mother when she is fourteen, and whose peace she remembers "years later." She will ally this soul repossession to personality development and the world's need "to go on / unfolding" by no human "blueprints" (*P3*, 137), at the same time that she will insist that revolution can begin with one-man revolutions "of peace and mutual aid" (*P3*, 151).

To increase the book's similarity to a documentary of social engagement, Levertov keeps, within the book's developing persona, to a chance, associational order in which dates of events and of composition appear, as well as to orderly rhetorical unfoldings of definition, example, and illustration-as-proof. The actual identification of Olga with the pacifists occurs in "A Note to Olga (1966)," which is preceded in the sequence by the Olga Poems and their delineation of the same opposing forces of nature and war that occupy the poet's earliest preserved lyric, "Listening to Distant Drums," written in 1940. As in that poem, a creative thrust identified with nature resists threats from the "distant drums" of war. Indeed, by identifying herself as again sixteen in the opening section of the Olga Poems, Levertov locates its initial scenes in 1939–40, and one may argue that *To Stay Alive*, in its various recapitulations, consciously seeks, by backward expansion, a more aware, projectable persona that encompasses the whole of the poet's writing history. Now two months dead, Olga was during the war sensuously alive in the "camera" of the poet's mind. Once "the loveliest woman ever born," she becomes in these early sections like W. B. Yeats's Maude Gonne: "an old bellows full of angry wind"[6] in her attempts to convert others to her vision by browbeating "the poor into joy's / socialist republic" (*P3*, 112). It is a likeness to this strongly willed, fierce commitment that immediately prompts Levertov to link the pacifists to Olga.

Having established a generative figure of Olga by Wordsworthian recollection, the poet returns to childhood memory and Heraclitus' view that "everything flows." Memories occur changed to assist and reflect the present. Summoning those life-furthering images upon which Olga's seemingly draining political passion intruded, the poet constructs a world shaped by a twofold dialectic of flowering and destruction, activist and resistant audience. This dialectic ends on Olga's deathbed as her political passions are identified with and subsumed into the religious "everlasting arms" underneath all life. Having witnessed "history" burning down to a "kind candle" (*P3*, 115), Levertov values Olga for contributing to her own inner self-transformation. In this discovery, the poet begins to examine the relation of art to life and political action, repeating in her imagination actions identified with her sister. Rather than forcing transformations from without by insistent direct persuasion (advocacy), art and Olga work better by providing examples for other, inner individual reformations. Preserving those examples through imagined recollection and reenactment, Levertov presents the poem's final revelations of understanding and union, indicating that such union for the purpose of understanding is a task of poetry. This task becomes more clearly felt in "A Note to Olga (1966)," as memory becomes encased in a lead-and-emerald reliquary hung about the poet's neck and what was once an imagined reliving of events in Olga's life becomes an unconscious reenactment of them in a protest that leads to both the arrest of the pacifists and the confirmation of individual, inner religious reformations.

This witnessing of art to life continues in the other Preludes. "Life at War" and "What Were They Like?," the two other poems from *The Sorrow Dance*, speak directly to the effects of war. The first describes not the wearing away of vitality by passion but the poisoning of life. Even the "imagination [is] / filmed over with the gray filth of [war]" (*P3*, 121). The poem implores men "whose language imagines *mercy* [and] *lovingkindness*" to seek "the deep intelligence living at peace would have" (*P3*, 122), for proper language (i.e., poetry) embodying man's noblest ideals offers possibilities for reformation. The second poem poses a series of six questions whose answers relate what the people of Vietnam were like. Accurate memory of them, however, is gone, for their song "is silent now" (P3, 123). The poems lead into "Advent 1966" and "Tenebrae," which continue the religious currents in the Olga Poems and "A Note to Olga (1966)." Drawn from *Relearning the Alphabet*, the first uses a Robert Southwell poem to link the burning children of Vietnam to his famous image of Christ as a burning infant, "prefiguring / the Passion upon the Eve of Christmas." Their burning is "wholly human and repeated, repeated, / infant after infant." "Through the cataract filming over / [her] inner eyes" (P3, 124), she sees not redemption through imitation, as one may achieve by truly imitating Christ, but either more children burning or others being prepared for burning. These links of the Passion and Christmas with the destruction of Christian ideals by materialism are repeated in "Tenebrae," also drawn from *Relearning the Alphabet*. The darkness at Christ's death that gives the poem its title is now associated with religious collapse; the poet is trying to encourage positive religious reformation by dramatizing the results and future of unreformed behavior. "Enquiry," which concludes the segment, depicts a victim of the war forever watching over the man who burned her eyelids off. Her look becomes the look of history and the poet's equivalent of damnation.

In its mix of poetry and prose, the Prologue seems immediately to invite comparison with Williams's *Paterson* (1946–62), but whereas the Williams poem identifies a place, the Prologue identifies a spiritual state. It opens with the dwindling of the soul brought on by war and the concomitant collapse of meaning into Orwellian doublethink. "Yes means no," and towns are destroyed in order to "save" them (P3, 129). Language, that "coral island / accrued from human comprehension, / [and] human dreams," is eroding "as war erodes us." The effort "to repossess our souls" and our language begins disjointedly in the poet's retreat to more peaceful times and places and in excerpts from her diary concerning de Courcy Squire. Squire had prevented the arrest of her fellow war resisters and is now fasting in jail, ostensibly because she questioned in court the roles of "judge and defendant" (P3, 130). Haunted by the passion of Squire and the indictment of her own husband, Mitchell Goodman, the poet speaks out about supportive, misconceived sympathies, interweaving poetic lines with excerpts from a Puerto Rican letter and more prose diary entries. The interplay of genres augments an already established interplay of distancing in which the reader has seen an impersonal, didactic opening turn descriptive and then become a play of "I" and "others" that sometimes expands the "I" into a collective, transpersonal "we." Rejecting certain sacrifices and self-immolation for herself, the poet comes to acknowledge the impact of those "who could bear no more" and will try anything "to show us / the dark we are in" (P3, 135–36). Like those "human dreams" preserved by language, their acts lead to expansion, memorialization, and that spiritually transforming "cure" of "freedom of conscience" that Squire senses will solve her own situation.

The parts of the main body of "Staying Alive" that Levertov takes from *Relearning the Alphabet* define the meanings of the opening cry, "Revolution or death." What is "revolution"? This one, she acknowledges, "has no blue-prints." It is fired by a desire for "the world to go on / unfolding" (*P3*, 137). One chooses it because one does not want "death." Not biological death, which she concedes is inevitable, but spiritual death, "the obscene sell out" of the soul and its impulse to unfold. This "death" preoccupies her and colors her thought as she focuses on Lorie, who like past mythological heroes "has died and risen." Lorie is pulled by her "psychic energy" into fulfillment through sculpture, poetry, painting, psychology, photography, teaching, cookery, love, Chinese philosophy, and physics (*P3*, 138). If Lorie can "live" thusly, she concludes, so can she. Lorie's heroic resurrection is followed by that of Bill Rose, whose living words on a postcard still speak three weeks after his death. He lives, too, in heroic return as well as in the memories of friends and students, generating for the poet echoes of Hopkins's "Spring and Fall" and its corollary heroic survival through art (language). As a poem that still resonates, Hopkins's words live even longer than Rose's. It is this survival and heroic rebirth that Levertov does not yet recognize as "revolu-tion" and that she seeks and examines in the last section of Part One. She grants that her own "roots" are "in the 19th century" and that her own home—the Jerusalem that she possesses in her soul and promises to visit each Passover—is language (*P3*, 141). This home, at times, makes her "un-true to [her] time," but changing it will make her untrue to herself, another form of death (*P3*, 143). Somehow she must resolve these contradictions.

A brief, meditative Entr'acte takes her out of the busy traffic and Sar-trean nausea that surrounds, distracts, and threatens her survival into a realization that her "task" is not destruction but "to make / of a song a chalice[;] / of Time, / a communion wine," (*P3*, 147). Her choices are to be made positively *for* something, not negatively from fear. She sees "revolu-tion" as a way of holding on to or recapturing; it resembles revolving seasons or the re-membering of experience by art. Her own efforts, however, are stalled by confusion. In nature, revolution shapes a sensuous realization of fullness, and by lamenting that it is not so "for us," she draws a different revolution for man. She rejects immediately the idea of revolution as "an exchange / of position, the high / brought low, the low / ascending," (*P3*, 149). It is the "wrong word" for the "new life" that she seeks. Revolution is, rather, an outer change brought about by an inner transformation. The outer conver-sion of an empty lot into the People's Park in Berkeley offers an example in action. She celebrates its creation, as the "old system" seeks with helicop-ters, bulldozers, and police to reclaim the land and its former fallow state. The war that she thought was abroad has come "home to us." This realization prefaces in *Relearning the Alphabet* both the volume's title poem, in which the poet discovers that "in-seeing . . . may not be forced by sharp / desire" (*P3*, 97), and a concluding "Invocation," in which she prays that her house-hold gods will guard her house's "profound dreams," allowing the dreams to return when she returns from abroad (*P3*, 101). The expanded detail or Sartrean nausea leading to the inscape or "freedom" of the poem's final form suggests that the poet may have felt that her original conclusions were overly pat and lacking in the felt anguish whose absence from political poetry she finds "unimaginable" *(LC*, 60).

The new, second Entr'acte begins the delineations of these details and anguish. It examines the options of active versus passive resistance and the poet's growing desire for violence. She blames the desire on "the devil," and unable to see him in others, she asks if, perhaps, he is not in "her eyes" *(P3*, 16–62). Her participation in protests has led her to a world that she did not know existed, and it has let loose a blind anger that leads her, too, to want to "smash the state" (P3, 163). Trying to restrain this anger and return to sane, creative inner reformation defines her present anguish. She goes to Europe and England not as a "cop-out" so much as a Kore-like retreat to regain energies that will revive her soul to positive social action. Abroad she learns that she must "get down into [her own] well" and "depth as into a poem" *(P3*, 179). A brief Entr'acte introduces the idea of merging "revolution" (passion) and "poetry" (creativity) into "new song" *(P3*, 180); then Part Four recounts her return to America where "daily life / is not lava" and "home" is again "language" (books, photos, rooms, and an old bread knife). She realizes that "the reason for happiness is" *(P3*, 182–83). It serves no further purpose, and repeating Albert Camus' discovery of "an invincible summer" inside her "winter" *(P3*, 184), she returns mentally to the building of People's Park. Its defeat influenced the suicides of Judy and Grandin. Remembering them amid the painful daily realities of East Boston brings the knowledge that she wishes "revolution, not death." *(P3*, 187). "There is no suicide in our time," she concludes, "unrelated to history." Yet, she is no vengeful Kali; she cannot "sustain for a day / that anger" *(P3*, 188). Rather, she must try "to learn / that other kind of waiting" that is not "a preparation for life" but patient, natural growth. She begins to "knit / idiom with idiom" in a new song of revolution and poetry. This song will record love of those "who do dare / to struggle" and "reject / unlived life" rather than die of it *(P3*, 189–90). Her task is not destruction but praise of those "who believe / life is possible" *(P3*, 191).

The persona of *To Stay Alive* is defined not only by the emotions in and surrounding the work's concerns but also by the techniques that poetry uses to express these emotions and concerns. Levertov notes that her own line is "based on speech rhythms and on the way speech affects, and is affected by, thought rhythms" *(LC*, 54). It is individual to and expressive of the particular inner voice that she senses framing it. Lines like "The waves / break on the packed sand" *(P3*, 131) break physically to reinforce a sense of the waves' motion, and their direct word order—or sometimes lack of it—embodies the writer's own diction and thought process. So, too, does what a writer chooses to leave out. The elimination of verbs, for example, in lines like "Peace as grandeur. Energy / serene and noble" *(P3*, 131) conveys an immediacy of apprehension. Similarly, the elimination of metaphor, the naked use of cinematic dissolve or segue to convey similarity, difference, contiguity, and cause-and-effect adds to the quickness of a speaker's temperament. It becomes a temperament that refuses to distance its impressions or to impose connectives and priorities on experiences that imprint themselves para-tactically and only in interpretation and deflection take on coordinating and subordinating significance. Still, in these refusals, the thought rhythms go beyond projecting chaos or hysteria by conveying, in what seem chance and chronological orders, underlying patterns and, with them, a belief in magic, symbolism, spiritual realms, and depth psychology. Thus, without a direct mention of Kore, the poem's speaker undergoes the mythic pattern of the goddess's creative and vegetative death and resurrection by simply express-ing a life juxtaposed with nature and seasonal revolution. In the discovery and recurrence of these latent patterns lie the poet's various appeals to inspiration, inscape, insight, and change.

In a similar way, Levertov's references to the German poet Rainer Maria Rilke in essays and talks make clear the indebtedness of both the persona and the poem to his views of the poet's role. One can see this indebtedness not only in the volume's resolving in praise but in the location of its action at the juncture of life and death. Early in the *Sonnets to Orpheus* (1922), Rilke announces that "praising is it" (*Rühmen, das ists!*), and in "Line-Breaks, Stanza-Spaces, and the Inner Voice" (1965), Levertov cites him as the source for beliefs like the "unlived life, of which one can die" (*PW*, 20), which appear in various poems, and, in "Dying and Living" (1975), for the practice of locating poetry at the conjunction and synthesis of "life/death or death/life" (*LC*, 99). The indebtedness begins seven or eight years before her arrival in America and her first reading of Williams (*LC*, 633); she alters Rilke's "praise of intense, bold, essentially death-defying acts and attitudes" (LC, 99), which is dependent on a view of disappearing beauty, to praise that is dependent on a view of disappearing morality. Praise is due "the deadly and the violent days" (*LC*, 93) as well as "the unnameable," "the stillness" as well as "the storm" (*LC*, 99). As much as Kore and her seasonal myth, his statements define the speaker and her experiences as poetic and shape the work's medi-ating epical images and claims on poetry audiences. By Levertov's attention to these images, seemingly spontaneous, "naked," and "candid" experiences unify, having become, as Rilke says, not only blood, glances, and gestures no longer to be distinguished from the growth of the "I" but also bridges to the impersonal. Their simultaneously personal and transpersonal merging pre-vents the mechanical and surface similitudes of banal poetry and bad movie documentary realism and underpins the book's coalescing concerns.

More personally, the persona of *To Stay Alive* may be seen as individu-ally sensitive to and thoughtful about the positive and negative directions of American life during the late 1960s and early 1970s. These directions impose themselves, initially turning a woman who shapes conditions into a person being shaped by circumstances. Often her first responses are to physical conditions, although, as in "Staying Alive," she may also respond to catch-phrases and people. Regressions occur that force reexaminations by means of art, dream, and past experience. The course of these regressions reveals living conditions, friendships, past readings, phrases of song, habits, and religious training and equips her for reestablishing order through insight. The sanity, intelligence, and generosity that emerge in the process engage readers' sympathies in the conditions that unfold, and however nightmarish and disordered things become, the speaker knows to keep herself trustworthy by keeping her accounts accurate, believable, and realistic. This trustworthiness is reinforced for readers by the trust that others within the work place in her. Also contributing to this trust is the poet's perceived engagement or commitment, which, at times, narrows her enemies ungenerously to dehumanized, detestable, one-dimensional "soldiers" or "police" or "authorities." At other times, as in the cases of suicide and the statement of Mahatma Gandhi, her commitment generates a weighed, complex mix of the appeal of and the revulsion toward self-destructive and violent behavior in the causes of liberation. Accompanying these out-of-hand rejections of her enemies are the often uncritical and automatic acceptances of fellow sympathizers. Readers are to embrace, for instance, Dennis Riordon, Squire, David Worstell, Chuck Matthei, Jennie Orvino, Lorie, Rose, and others merely by virtue of their participation in anti–Vietnam War actions.

Despite the believable details, students of political science may find the realpolitik of both Levertov's political lyrics and *To Stay Alive* lacking in sophistication. Nonetheless, like the persona of *To Stay Alive*, the politics has a literary antecedent. Not so different from the politics articulated by Walt Whitman's *Democratic Vistas* (1871), Levertov's may gain some acceptance among readers from the similarity. Whitman's vision of an evolutionary dialectic of "political" and "social" democracies resolving into a "religious" democracy is consistent with ideas in the circular that Matthei distributes and Levertov reprints. She, too, believes in "the theory or doctrine that man properly trained in sanest, highest freedom, [can] and must become a law, and a series of laws unto himself, surrounding and providing for, not only his own personal control, but all his relations to other individuals and to the State." Moreover, like Whitman's vision, hers suffers from a contradictory emphasis on "individualism" and "comradeship" or mutual aid; the clash is resolved, as is Whitman's, by inner religious reform. For both, love is the force that brings about the reform, even if that love gains expression as "anger" and sometimes hides under the name of "justice." But, again, in keeping with her intention not to create arrested artful moments (statues), Levertov resists Whitman's precisely formulated Hegelian stages, preferring to accept and object to the confusing nausea of "what is" than to provide an abstract plan. She also resists his placing ultimate responsibility for the plan's completion on something like divine will, insisting, rather, on human participation and responsibility in the process; although, again, like many modern theologians, she is unclear where determinism ("no [human] blueprints") and human will begin and end. One may wonder, for instance, whether the returns or drifts to universal harmony in her vision are humanly, divinely, or mutually motivated, and to what extent. Certainly the natural modes that she uses suggest changeable realizations of a fixed order.[7]

Nor is Levertov's political vision confined only to the United States and Vietnam. It is rooted in an ideal of government similar to that which she quotes in her second essay on the South Korean poet, Kim Chi Ha (1980). This government would uphold "the right of revolution . . . the ongoing and inextinguishable possibility of overthrowing illegitimate authority," and would be "indivisible from an uncompromising rejection of oppression" (LC, 145). In Candles in Babylon (1982), El Salvador: Requiem and Invocation (1983), Oblique Prayers (1984), and Breathing the Water, she applies that principle to El Salvador and South Africa. Proclaiming that injustice in any land "is one with injustice anywhere. / All of us are / our brother's keepers, / members one of another, / responsible, culpable, and— / / able to change" (ES, 16), she describes decapitations and the cutting out of tongues in El Salvador, repeating in "Thinking about El Salvador" the image in "Enquiry" of victims passing judgment on their oppressors. Like the dead Vietnamese of "What Were They Like?" their song is mute. El Salvador: Requiem and Invocation mourns the murders of Archbishop Oscar Romero and four American nuns "gunned down / in the hospice for incurables" and "ambushed, / raped, killed, [and] flung in a pit" (ES, 12). "Unresolved" returns to "Advent 1966" and its theme of repetitive murder; "Carapace" presents a twelve-year-old's account of the murder of his father who "preached the Gospel" and was deemed subversive by the Guardia Civil because he knew his rights (BW, 36). "From the Image Flow" and "Making Peace" move to South Africa and its ascent from the darkness of slavery to the fire of revolution. In them, Levertov again calls for an "imagination of peace to oust the intense, familiar / imagination of disaster" (BW, 40).

The religious awakenings on which Levertov predicates the inner reformations that will bring about her "religious" democracy are often settled in the closing pages of her books, as if the process of their fruition is either a hieratic Neoplatonic ascent from earlier positions or a late stage of evolution. "Psalm: People Power at the Die-In" and its briefer "About Political Action in Which Each Individual Acts from the Heart" from Candles in Babylon mention its appearing in a "communion" of solitaries generating "great power" for change (Whitman's "social" democracy?). Her "Mass for the Day of St. Thomas Didymus" would collect such solitaries in communion and keep active a hope lying in the "unknown . . . which imagined us" and "stays . . . our murderous hand" (CB, 109). For all his omnipotence, this "lover of making," whose name "is written" in both the imagination and Creation, must not be abandoned. Nor should the perceived ability of individual pasts to recapitulate a single multiform radiance be lost. Ontogeny must recapitulate phylogeny (CB, 110). "Of Rivers" in Oblique Prayers presents a force in one of these individual pasts—"the pulse of [rivers'] springs"—as "a god or goddess" in whom the rivers' fealty rests and "their way / to know, in unknowing flowing, / the God of gods, whom the gods / themselves have not imagined" (*OP*, 71). These lesser "earth-gods," Levertov goes on to say in "Of Gods," gain power through the radiating present, the "spontaneous shimmering of fact— / brilliant wings with no history" (*OP*, 72). Their radiance, at times, is all that humans respond to experientially and imaginatively, ignoring the true, single creative unknowability that, in "The God of Flowers," she hopes man will seek out in "the unknown God of the gods." Although not easily manifest, he "watches and smiles" (*OP*, 77).

From the exchange of this individual "great energy" and collective "great power" comes that transforming insight and change embraced in "St. Peter and the Angel." Having been transformed, Levertov's individual finds himself "the key . . . to the next door, / the next terrors of freedom and joy" (*OP*, 79). Freedom and joy are terrors because man must for his own fulfillment protect "the God of the gods," even if he must, as Gandhi says, "cultivate the art of killing and being killed." He must not "in a cowardly manner" flee from his duty because of "danger" (*P3*, 106–7). Her own reformation in "This Day" and "Oblique Prayer" leads not to unusual insight but to the perception of a harmony in "the world, a word / intricately incarnate," a gray "place / without clear outlines" (*OP*, 81–82), in which she can remember "blesséd light." In a final affirmation of the creative flow as a manifestation of deity and awareness of it as proof of reform, "Passage" describes the curative spirit entering "wind from the compass points, sun at meridian" (*OP*, 87). In *Breathing the Water*, "Caedmon," "The Servant-Girl at Emmaus," and "Variation on a Theme by Rilke" also identify artists with the expression of this spirit; their "inspired depictions" show "us exactly / the manifold countenance / of the Holy One, Blessed be He" (*BW*, 71). Like artists, mystics and Julian of Norwich also provide media for divine revelations in "On a Theme from Julian's Chapter XX" and "The Showings: Lady Julian of Norwich, 1342–1416." Much as in Whitman, the reformations render existing political institutions "no account." Nonetheless, if their means and contents and tests are known, the reformations are not yet described as having widely happened, except negatively by an occasional rejection of what presently is (*via negativa*) or positively by musical analogues (*musica mundana*).

One might argue in defense of Levertov's positions that she does not intend in any of her political poems to overthrow immediately the government of the United States. Rather, she seeks to win over its mind and heart in limited areas: atomic bomb testing and use, civil and human rights, wars of oppression, and negative views of women. Like Ezra Pound, she sees the problem of bad government as one of language, and as an expert on language by virtue of her poetic sensibility and training, she seeks to replace bad language and bad government with properly used language and good government. The "badness" of bad language is not, as Levertov makes clear in her own case, simply a matter of outdated diction or usage. Rather, bad language corrodes man's need to go on unfolding spiritually, either by not being in touch with spiritual expansion or by preventing it. Like poetry, proper language illuminates the inscape of what it embraces and, in doing so, assists man in the universal drive toward fulfillment. It thus differs from doublethink, which is employed by governments to prevent inner reformations and which cloaks as magnanimous inhibiting and self-serving actions. Such cloaking is reversible. Still, Levertov recognizes that, despite government's conspicuous corruptions of language, the hidden source of corruption is a "capitalist-imperialist system" (*PW,* 121). She attacks this system directly in "Speech for a Rally, 1970" (1970) and in the libretto for El Salvador. In the *Requiem,* she describes an original harmony disrupted by "men from a far place" who "come seeking gold" and "denying / the mystery of the land" (*ES,* 8). Their exploitations of the land and people are perpetrated by the modern-day planters converting money from exported crops into arms. The planters pay the military, who join them in inhibiting and enslaving the people.

Being an autodidact without formal instruction "after the age of twelve" (*LC,* 207), Levertov evades easy attributions of formal influences on her work. From her own statements, one suspects that the deep feelings for nature that are part of her politics are linked psychologically to her mother and that her father accounts for the mystical and more traditional religious dimensions. Nonetheless, besides the already mentioned debts to Rilke, Williams, Pound, Neruda, and Hopkins, one can also argue the influence of D. H. Lawrence, whose poetry, which she mentions having taught at Vassar, she quotes in "The Sense of Pilgrimage" (1967). She shares Lawrence's belief in a "spirit of the place" and his sense that the intellectual "has been too much favored" (*LC,* 52). "Sensuous apprehension" is for both "a way of receiving" and a "way through" the poem (*LC,* 48). Similarly, there are in her evolutionary and mystical tendencies equally strong but less easily fixed affinities to the thought of Henri Bergson. She shares with him the belief that God "has nothing of the already made" but, instead, is constantly changing. He is both love and the object of love, and the universe's ordained evolutionary process creates "creators" that he may have "besides himself, beings worth his love." Again, as in Lawrence, God's reality is not found through intellect but by intuitions or mystical experiences that impel men to actively advance divine purpose (Levertov's harmony) by helping to complete their own full development. At first the spirit of these mystics or activists will be achieved and maintained by a few (for Bergson, the contemplatives; for Levertov, the true poets), but eventually the whole of mankind will participate in the process and the world that it brings into being (her religious democracy).[8]

How many of Bergson's ideas may have influenced Levertov by way of the popular English translation of Pierre Teilhard de Chardin's *The Phenomenon of Man* (1959) is difficult is know, but Levertov shares with the Roman Catholic priest and paleoanthropologist the beliefs that consciousness is "spiritual energy," that its inner force duplicates a material external force (Valéry's harmonious "impression and expression"), and that self-consciousness is a stage of inner evolution that will eventually embrace, as a further transformation, "hyperpersonal consciousness" or mysticism. Levertov avoids, however, the charge of determinism sometimes leveled at Teilhard by making her stages of improvement related not to biological changes but to acts of choice and, hence, free will. In this, she seems closer to older naturalists like Alfred Russel Wallace who argue that certain human improvements cannot be explained on the basis of bodily changes brought about by natural selection and the struggle for existence, and that man has transferred to his machines and tools some of what had been alterations of body parts.[9] With increasingly higher stakes, civilization has moved creatively nearer and nearer to fulfillment. It has also moved for Levertov—at times by virtue of the same creativity that aided its advancement—closer to total destruction. Choice in both movements has been individually constant—"life" or "death"—and in choosing "life," one chooses fulfillment in a scheme of divine purpose that appears to resemble Augustinian choice. But, again, the means by which individual choice turns through imitation into permanent collective improvement is not specified. Nor is the time required for the change given. Thus, Teilhardian evolution is no better than Whitmanian or Marxist (not "an exchange / of position") dialectic for clarifying the relations between ontogeny and phylogeny and fixed and changeable character, especially since the vital dialectic of creativity and destruction remains.

Equally or, perhaps, more important poetically to the shaping of Levertov's political views are the impacts of the Cambridge classical anthropologist Jane Harrison and depth psychologists C. G. Jung and Carl Kerényi. They speak of a relation of art to ritual, ritual to mythology, religion, and thought, and the appearances of identifiable permanent patterns on whose recurrence are shaped theories of personal individuation or fulfillment. Although thought up for the purpose of explaining how things "are at the right and proper distance," the myths that assist art and flesh out these patterns paradoxically possess "among other things the property of being [themselves] explanatory." Their symbols contribute to understandings of historical epochs and the "collective unconscious" that entertains superpersonal forces and "transmits the common psychological inheritance of mankind." This transmission aids in establishing individually healthy personalities and socially collective identity. In regard to the Kore myth, which contributes to the inscape of "Staying Alive" and is also a part of Williams's poetry, Jung notes that the figure "when observed in a man" is related to the "anima," or helpful female element in the male unconscious, and when observed in a woman, to "the type of superordinate personality or self." For Williams, the figure is associated with a sense of his being "buried under the earth . . . but as any plant is buried, retaining the power to come again." It represents a need for an endopsychic automatism to rescue him by putting him in communication with a whole self and restoring him to creativity. For Levertov, the figure is the type of total woman—woman as she really is, not as she appears to herself. It puts her in touch with all women and gives her the feeling that her life spreads out backward and forward over time. It allows the recovery of that universal harmony that she feels in her positive contacts with nature.[10]

It is Levertov's reliance in works like "Staying Alive" on the permanent pattern of these individuating myths that prevents her poems' turning into "statues." Continually radiating out in diverse manifestations, these myths avoid the "deaths" of language that Sartre sees occurring when the beliefs that vitalize choice are no longer options.[11] One would expect, for example, that normally to a generation of readers who did not live through the 1960s many of the issues and choices of *To Stay Alive* would be "remote" and "dead" and, hence, "artistic" by virtue of their no longer being possible. By having attached their continuities to myths like that of Kore's perennial descent and return, Levertov hopes to blunt some of this loss. In choosing "life" or creativity, she discovers, as part of the myth, that others are the condition of existence and, therefore, she chooses for everyone. Moreover, by actively involving readers in bridging the gaps of montage and stimulating their imaginations with striking and startling images, she draws them, too, into the myth and "that self same creative road" that Sergei Eisenstein notes the montage author travels "in creating the image."[12] As she indicates, it is for readers to discover in the poems and choices of politically active writers "something that culminates a process of thought and feeling already under way, and propels them [too] into some form of action" (*LC*, 125). In political lyrics, the propulsion and choice are outward into life. In the more apical *To Stay Alive*, they are, at first, inward toward accepting the persona on which the volume's issues and choices center. However, singly and in combination, the strategies contribute ultimately to the poet's and readers' making sense of an outward reality and assist them in living fuller lives. The concurrences of these lives with "messages" from dream states mark the joint artistic and political fulfillments that the "I" embraces.

Notes

1. Denise Levertov, *Breathing the Water* (New York: New Directions, 1987), 3, 4, 8. The following abbreviations of Levertov's books have been adopted for internal citation: *PW—The Poet in the World* (New York: New Directions, 1973); *LC—Light Up the Cave* (New York: New Directions, 1981); *P3—Poems 1968–1972* (New York: New Directions, 1987); *CB—Candles in Babylon* (New York: New Directions, 1982); *ES—El Salvador: Requiem and Invocation* (Boston: Back Bay Chorale, 1983); *OP—Oblique Prayers* (New York: New Directions, 1984); and *BW—Breathing the Water*. The abbreviations are accompanied by page citations.

2. T. S. Eliot, *Selected Essays*, 3d ed. (London: Faber & Faber, 1951), 203.

3. William Carlos Williams, "The Great Sex Spiral," *Egoist* 4 (August 1917), 110.

4. James Joyce, *The Portable James Joyce*, ed. Harry Levin., rev. ed. (New York: Penguin Books, 1966), 482.

5. William Carlos Williams, *Selected Essays* (New York: Random House, 1954), 236. For the treatment of meditative poetry in Hopkins and the seventeenth century, see John Pick,

Gerard Manley Hopkins: Priest and Poet, 2d ed. (New York: Oxford University Press, 1966), and Louis L. Martz, *The Poetry of Meditation* (New Haven: Yale University Press, 1954).

6. W. B. Yeats, "A Prayer for My Daughter," in *Collected Poems* (New York: Macmillan, 1956), 187.   .

7. For Whitman's stages of democracy, see Jerome Mazzaro, "Whitman's *Democratic Vistas:* The Vast General Principle and Underlying Unity," *Walt Whitman Review* 8 (1962), 89–90.

8. For an excellent, brief summary of Bergson's evolutionary views, see "Henri Bergson" in *The Encyclopedia of Philosophy,* ed. Paul Edwards (New York: Macmillan, 1967), I:287–294.

9. Pierre Teilhard de Chardin, *The Phenomenon of Man,* trans. Bernard Wall (New York: Harper & Row, 1959). For analysis of Wallace's positions, see Loren Eiseley, *The Immense Journey* (New York: Random House, 1955).

10. André Akoun, et al., "A Conversation with Claude Lévi-Strauss," *Psychology Today* 5 (May 1972), 94; C. G. Jung and C. Kerényi, *Essays on a Science of Mythology,* trans. R. F. C. Hull (New York: Pantheon Books, 1949), 6, 217, 219, 225; Carl G. Jung, ed., *Man and His Symbols* (New York: Doubleday, 1964), 107; William Carlos Williams, *I Wanted to Write a Poem,* ed. Edith Heal (Boston: Beacon Press, 1958), 21.

11. Jean-Paul Sartre, *Literature and Existentialism,* trans. Bernard Frechtman (New York: Citadel Press, 1965), 7–37.

12. Sergei Eisenstein, *The Film Sense,* ed. and trans. Jay Leyda (New York: Harvest Books, 1947), 32–33.

The Poetry of Political Anguish   Paul A. Lacey*

When she spoke at Earlham College recently, Denise Levertov read a piece she called "Perhaps No Poem, But All I Can Say and I Cannot Be Silent." In the question period, when a student asked her why she gave the piece that title, she answered that, though she felt what she was saying intensely, she was not yet sure that the piece had the form and control which a poem required. That form she related to the inwardness of a poem. It has to be not merely addressed to a person or problem *out there,* it must come from *in here,* the inner being of the poet, and it must address something *in here.* In "Origins of a Poem" she speaks of the need for the poet to maintain dialogue with the heart, or with the reader within. "Every art needs two— one who makes it and one who needs it." For Levertov, both are the poet.

In her latest book, *Candles in Babylon,* she includes "A Speech: For Antidraft Rally, D.C., March 22, 1980" and a note which says that this *is* a speech, not properly classifiable as a poem but not prose, either. She includes it because draft counselors and high school teachers have requested it. In each of these cases, Levertov has offered a work significant for its intensity of comment on a political or social problem; and in each case, without apologizing for either the form or the content of the piece, she has wanted to distinguish it from poetry. Behind this problem of classification lies the issue of the connections between poetry and politics, an issue which

*Reprinted with permission from *Sagetrieb* 4, no. 1 (Spring 1985), 61–71.

Levertov addresses extensively in both her collections of essays, *The Poet in the World* (1973) and *Light Up the Cave* (1981).

Few poets of our time have devoted more intellectual energy to exploring the nature of poetic form—the way poems happen, the nature of inspiration, ways to "invite the muse," the discipline behind open forms, how one discovers the shape a particular content must assume, the significance of line-breaks, and the like. A substantial part of her two collections of essays is devoted to such shop-talk about the poet's craft. At the same time, few poets have devoted more intellectual energy to exploring how political themes and commitments might find appropriate expression in poetry. She pursues these questions in her essays, but even more powerfully and intensely in the poetry itself.

In literary history there has not always been a question how politics and poetry connected. From classical times the main tradition of Western literary criticism asserted that poetry ought both to delight and instruct, to be sweet *and* useful. Such criticism subsumed political, religious, social or philosophical content under the description of genres. A poem, such as the *Iliad* or the *Aeneid,* which recounts a people's history as an explanation of its future destiny, is an *epic.* A poem, such as Pope's "Essay on Man" or Mandeville's "Fable of the Bees," which offers a philosophical or religious account of human nature so as to recommend a particular social or economic order, is *didactic.* The possibility of a political stance is presupposed in the poet's choice of genre. It is an aspect of how the poem is to be *useful* or *instructive.* To speak of a political epic or a didactic political poem is redundant. As long as critical theory addressed questions of form and content separately and conceived of form as the decoration of content, there was not much reason to worry about whether politics and poetry belong together.

Essentially two things have to happen before the relation of politics and literature becomes a controversial issue. First, political process must develop to the point where party politics emerge. That is to say, factions develop in opposition to one another in a framework where competition for the power to govern takes the form of influence with a ruler or an electorate. "Politics" as we understand it does not emerge as a subject of discussion until it is *partisan* politics; before that it is simply patriotism, if it has any name. When the *partisan* nature of political views becomes obvious, the relation of politics to literature becomes a matter of debate. The English Civil War, the Commonwealth period and the Restoration give us compelling examples of intense political activity among writers and of their self-awareness of their writing as a form of political activity. We need only think of Milton's sonnets to illustrate the point.

Second, to put the matter in the terms used by Meyer Abrams in *The Mirror and the Lamp,* before the relation of politics and literature becomes controversial, literary criticism must shift away from *imitative* or *pragmatic* theories of literature to *expressive* ones. With the beginnings of Romanticism, then, there begins the debate about the connection of politics and literature—not merely because the great English Romantic writers responded to the French Revolution and the Napoleonic era but because their most characteristic form came to be the lyric. And as the lyric came to be valued as the most *expressive* and therefore the most genuine of poetic forms, the didactic came to be correspondingly distrusted, so that Shelley, one of the most politically engaged of English poets, would say in his Preface to *Prometheus Unbound,* "Didactic poetry is my abhorrence. . . ."

First, *politics* becomes *partisan politics*—taking sides; later on, poets give a political dimension to their alienation from society by their sympathy for revolutionary or other extreme political positions; both these developments are going on at the same time that the most intensely personal, self-expressive forms are becoming accepted as the norm for what poetry ought to be. Politics and poetry come to a parting of the ways: "Out of our quarrel with others we make rhetoric," says William Butler Yeats, "out of our quarrel with ourselves, poetry." Rhetoric is the stuff of partisanship, of propaganda, of persuasion and instruction in what is already known, of politics. Poetry is the quarrel with the self, the exploration of what the poet believes and the discovery of what he knows. Rhetoric is didactic; poetry is lyrical.

In Denise Levertov all the elements of the controversy meet. She is the inheritor of this literary tradition. She believes that poetry creates "autonomous existences out of words and silences" by finding the organic form which reveals the inner meaning of experience. Poetry aspires to the autonomy of Song, but its musicality arises from "fidelity to experience." The fully realized poem is a world in itself." Because it creates autonomous structures . . . poetry is, in process and in being, intrinsically affirmative." In finding the form which is the revelation of content, the poet makes clear to herself "and thereby to others, the temporal and eternal questions." The poet finds the right form *out there* by internalizing those temporal and eternal problems, holding dialogue with the heart. "What the poet is called on to clarify is not answers but the existence and nature of questions."

But precisely because poetry is what it is, all aspects of human experience can rightly find a place in poetry. The temporal and eternal questions can have a political content as well as any other kind of content. "For the poet . . . there is no such thing as an isolated study of literature. . . ."

To allow that political themes may be appropriate to poetry does not solve the problems of form, however, for the lyric is still the most commonly expected poetic genre in our time. The political poem, Levertov says in "On the Edge of Darkness: What Is Political Poetry?" (1975) is "ostensibly lyric," it consists of short poems written in the poet's own voice, "markedly, candidly, speaking in the poet's unmediated character . . . written from a personal rather than a fictive, and a subjective rather than objective, standpoint." Yet the political poem must deal with social observations, descriptions of events, expressions of opinions such as the lyric has not typically addressed. "The poetry of political anguish is at its best both didactic and lyrical."

As Levertov has made these ideas clear in her prose, she has been struggling to realize their meaning in her poetry. She has become ever more skillful in achieving the goals she sets for the political poem, "to affect our senses and engage our aesthetic response just as much as one with whose content . . . we can have no argument." But that achievement has been hard-won, starting with *The Sorrow Dance* (1967) and *Relearning the Alphabet* (1970), the two books in which her "poetry of political anguish" first appeared. The accomplishment of both those books was high, but a number of poems felt obsessive, fragmented, unfinished. In *Relearning the Alphabet*, particularly, works seemed imperfectly realized. Both "An Interim" and "From a Notebook: October '68–May '69" seemed to be works in progress rather than finished poems.

To Stay Alive (1971), her most significant exploration of political themes in her poetry, gave her a base on which all her subsequent political poetry rests. In that book she succeeded in enunciating for herself a politically revolutionary position through the medium of poetry which remains open-ended and exploratory. She expresses her commitment to partisan political questions, but in ways which clarify "not answers but the existence and nature of questions." How she accomplishes this will emerge from a close examination of the re-organizing and completion of the long poem-sequence called "Staying Alive."

To Stay Alive is made up of two sections of poems, "Preludes" and "Staying Alive," containing poems drawn from four different sections of the two previous books. The ordering of the poems has changed substantially, and the final poem sequence has almost tripled in length. In her Preface Levertov says that the justification for bringing these poems together is esthetic: "It assembles separated parts of a whole." As "a record of one person's inner/outer experience in America during the 60's and the beginning of the 70's," the book presents a search for integrity in both political utterance and poetic form. For Levertov, however, the only valid test of the book is esthetic: whether it creates that sense of wholeness, that intensity of inner experience and reflection upon it which alone satisfies the "reader within."

"Staying Alive," the long multi-sectioned, multi-form poem which makes up three-quarters of the book, is the test case for how Levertov successfully brings politics and poetry together into an esthetic whole. In it she has set herself the hardest imaginable task, for in what seems like a sprawling, loosely associational form—"Prologue—An Interim" and four "Parts," the first three each followed by an "Entr'acte"—she draws on political and personal events from late December, 1967 through November, 1970, criss-crosses America, Italy, Yugoslavia and England, circles back in time from childhood to young adulthood to the present, and intersperses prose journal entries, excerpts from newspaper reports, political leaflets, popular song lyrics, passages form letters, quotations from Rilke, Gandhi, Brecht and Camus and echoes of poems by Keats, Hopkins and Swinburne.

But the poem is neither loosely sprawling nor merely associational. Its strategy is what it has always been for Levertov, to move from Reverence for Life to Attention to Life, from Attention to Seeing and Hearing, which leads to Discovery and Revelation of Form, and from Form to Song, which is how she describes the process in "Origins of a Poem" in 1968. For her, knowing and making are inseparable. "Staying Alive," however, begins in *interim*, in-between-time—the immediate occasion for which is the impending draft-resistance trial of Mitchell Goodman—when everything appears temporary and provisional. Alienation from American society has its counterpart in increasing doubt about the poet's past: where the present lacks meaning, neither a usable past nor a desirable future are easily discovered. The poet's "clear caressive sight" is blurred; language, "virtue of man," erodes, rejects us as we reject it. The thread of connection which ran from Reverence for Life to Form and Song has been broken; no fabric stands whole. Consequently, a new fabric must be made, every strand twisted, pulled and tested.

The poem cannot be woven until the unweaving has occurred. We find our way through it by following the broken threads, by discovering how they are reconnected, and by finding the new, whole threads which draw the pattern together.

The first pattern, then, is disjunction. Life or death. The dwindling of the soul or the immensity of sky and sea. "Peace as grandeur. Energy / serene and noble." The self-immolation of "the great savage saints of outrage." The coral island of language, eroded by war; the witness of resisters who "make from outrage / islands of compassion others could build on." Restoration has begun, but devastation still dominates the poem, as it dominates the society in which the poet lives. That disjunction continues in "Part I (October '68–May '69)," which explores the stark choice of "Revolution or Death." That phrase acts on us as though the throb of train wheels repeated it. Working into that rhythm are those suggested by *"Which side are you on?"*—the old labor song—and the first question at Passover, "What makes this night different from all other nights?" Everything speaks of choice: choosing a side, being of the chosen people, choosing life with the young because "Death is Mayor Daley." Death is also *Unlived life / of which one can die.* This exploration of choice proceeds on several levels: the political and the social are the most obvious, but the personal is even more influential, signaled by the weaving of nineteenth century poems about death into the pattern of the poem's reflections. At stake is not only how the world might be revolutionized but how the poet can grow into the second half of her life.

Death is not merely "the obscene sellout." It is also lovely and soothing, as the phrases from Keats and Swinburne remind us. Over against the longing for death, we have the image of the pulsing brain:

> The will to live
>
> pulses. Radiant emanations
> of living tissue, visible only

> to some photo-eye we know
> sees true because mind's dream-eye,
> inward gage, confirms it.
>   Confirmation,
> a sacrament.

Part I circles its subjects, exemplifying in its method what it "discovers" as its conclusion: that revolution must not be merely circular and life not merely linear, but that both must radiate from a center. This revolution becomes "prismatic radiance pulsing from live tissue," the photographic image of the living human brain. Objects, events, memories cluster around an unknown, shifting center which gives them "a character that throughout all transformations / reveals them connatural." "Revolution or death" speaks simultaneously of the political and the psychic life.

Time, place and language serve as images for what is happening to the poet. Her roots are in the nineteenth century, so she is out of touch with those—the young—she most wants to know. She chooses revolution, but fears that her words do not reach into it. "Language itself is my one home, my Jerusalem," but in this age of refugees she too has been uprooted.

> My diction marks me
> untrue to my time;
> change it, I'd be
> untrue to myself.

"Entr'acte" is indeed an interval between acts. It is, first of all, a return to a beloved landscape, to a former way of living, and to the pleasures of the body. In "Life at War" she writes:

> Yes, this is the knowledge that jostles for space
> in our bodies along with all we
> go on knowing of joy, or love:

and that remains a characteristic way for her to represent what has most meaning for her. For Levertov, deep knowledge has to be known *in the body*, literally incorporated. Even memory is bodily knowledge for her. "What pain! What sharp stabs of recall! What revelations." This interval, like the earlier interim, offers a time of renewal and re-collection:

> Again to hold—"capture" they say—
> moments and their processions in palm
> of mind's hand.

The recursive nature of "Staying Alive" is further emphasized in Part II, where there is no "going beyond" but a digging down and re-examination of already stated themes: the meaning of revolution; the inadequacy of language—revolution is "the wrong word"—the incomplete images and gestures which offer "A beginning" for living a life. She finds hints of the new life in the witness of Mitchell Goodman, A. J. Muste, other pacifist and resister friends, and in the making of the People's Park in Berkeley. In the clearing of that land she has seen "poets and dreamers studying / joy together," making the "place, locus, of what could be our / New World even now, our revolution. . . ."

Even as "The War / comes home to us . . ." the poem has begun to enrich the images on which a life can grow. Time becomes not a sequence but a radiating from a center, "pulsations, as from living cells." Place becomes valorized anew, in a People's Park. Revolution becomes like a force of nature, a tree rising out of a flood, a sea full of swimmers, islands—like the islands of compassion—"which step out of the waves on rock feet."

The second Entr'acte takes us back again to bodily knowledge of the cost of revolution, "the grim odds we're / up against." What the body knows is the nausea of tear gas, feeling a kind of death which is also "a kind of joy" as the mind remains "clear in its despair." In "the interim" the poet fled to the sea to repossess her soul; in the first Entr'acte she went back to a Maine home in winter to "capture" moments in memory; now in the clarity of anguish "Nothing / will do but / to taste the bitter / life."

With Part III the poet returns to Europe after ten and England after twenty years. This marks another turn inward and a new recovery of resources. "What gentleness, what kindness / of the *private life* I left, unknowing / and gained instead the tragic, fearful / knowledge of present history. . . ." The reader cannot tell how to balance the loss and gain represented here: so much of "Staying Alive" is a lament for what has happened to the inner life, yet it is impossible to believe that the poet would prefer to have remained ignorant of the "tragic, fearful knowledge" of our times. When she returns to the "writhing lava" of America, it may be with "fierce hope" or no hope, but she will continue to struggle. The poet's spiritual condition becomes clearer to her in a friend's account of a dream of being entrapped in a tunnel with great dogs barking at either end. This image from the unconscious mirrors the poet's own feeling of being unable to move forward but needing to dig down and re-examine. The dreamer remains the victim of her dream until she brings imagination to her aid: "The dogs / will not go away. / They must be transformed." She imagines herself sitting quietly in the middle of the tunnel, using the "fiery stillness" of her being to transform the images of fear into something else. The dream therapy acts as a parable for the poet, whose friend shares what she has learned with her: "Get down into your well / it's your well / go deep into it / into your own depth as into a poem." At the end of Part III, the poem has turned from *places* to the process of making a place for oneself, from images of terror and emptiness to what Jung calls "symbols of transformation."

The third Entr'acte returns to the image of the pulse, which appears so significantly in earlier parts of the poem—in the radiant pulsations of the living brain, the pulsing rhythm of "revolution or death," the pulsation of time from a center—and makes it the primary symbol of how to stay alive. It is a sign of bodily wisdom, echoing Keats' "axioms in philosophy are not axioms until they are proved on our pulses," and it is a sign of attunement to "the great pulse."

> Peace could be

> that grandeur, that dwelling
> in majestic presence, attuned
> to the great pulse.

Now the poet further deepens the meaning of the image by bringing together two dominant themes of the poem, "revolution" and "poetry," and describing each as a throbbing pulse. Revolution is a "flame-pulse" which sustains life; poetry is "living water" which refreshes the parched soul. Fire and water are contraries; if they are pitted against one another, both will be destroyed. They are also two of the four elements, the primary building-blocks of creation; brought together they help make a life. Revolution and poetry, if they are pitted against each other, will each perish.

> But when their rhythms
> mesh
> then though the pain of living
> never lets up

> the singing begins.

Part IV begins "I went back." Going back is the dominant theme of this final section of the poem, and with it Levertov gathers up and reconciles the conflicts which have provided the dialectic of "Staying Alive." She has gone back to her past in England, to recover some of the gentleness and kindness of that life; she has gone back to America, her literal home, filled with the "objects of dailiness" which pull her there; she has gone back to her memories of her sister; she has gone back to the wild zigzagging pace of airplane life, "the push and shove of events," but no longer as "a defective migrant," for she knows where she longs to be; most important, she has gone back down into the depth of her own well, the inner place where all those experiences can find a resolution and a home.

From "interim," the time of waiting, the poet has returned to the dailiness of life, which has its rhythm of expansion and contraction, its pulse of happiness and sorrow. For the first time in this long poem, happiness explicitly emerges as a theme. The poet experiences it unalloyed in dancing, in looking at Zen paintings, in the momentary community of clearing People's Park and dodging police clubs and in the close fellowship with revolutionaries in Europe. What had been only threads of happiness, forgotten or unvalued in the long, grinding struggle against death, now appear as a strong, connecting strand in the pattern of her life. Happiness comes in those moments, but the capacity to be happy resides within the self.

Camus wrote:
"I discovered inside myself, even in the very midst of
winter, an invincible summer."

The choice is not simply between revolution *or* death: "Staying Alive" is punctuated by deaths. Some are natural deaths; some the political statements of Buddhist monks and "the great savage saints of outrage," Norman Morrison and Alice Herz; some are the inexplicable suicides, the gestures of ultimate, hopeless alienation. One dead friend ignored the world outside of herself; another was flooded by it. Each is a suicide.

There is no suicide in our time
unrelated to history, to whether
each before death had listened to the living, heard
the cry, "Dare to struggle,
            dare to win."

The poet must come to her terms with each of these deaths, to grieve, to regret, to rage, to discover how she might incorporate into her own life the abiding values of those lost or wasted lives.

Life comes to the poet in moments, flashes, pulses—brief throbs of love, hate, rage or happiness. What we learn with her is not that happiness does not last but that it can return again. Meanwhile there is the kind of waiting which is restorative. The pulses of insight or experience can be taken into the dark well, the middle of the tunnel, stored there until they are transformed into sustaining energy.

Get my head together. Mesh. Knit
idiom with idiom in the
"push and shove of events."

"Staying Alive" took its start in broken connections and unraveling threads. The pulse of life was low and irregular. At its conclusion, the knitting and meshing continue, but death has broken some connections forever. Some have found death in the revolution itself. Some have been unable to stay alive. New connections are forming, however; language is regaining its integrity, through the acts of those whose word is good and through the struggle of the poet to unite the two pulses of revolution and poetry so that the singing can begin. The fabric of resistance communities has been tested and borne the strain. The poet has come back to the places which restore her, where her inner life finds a home.

Characteristically, what Levertov has accomplished in comprehending the revolution she has achieved in and through the making of the poem. It is an exemplar of what she has called the poetry of political anguish at its best, both didactic and lyrical. In the pulling together of the poems in *To Stay Alive*, and particularly in the completion of the fragmentary Notebook poem in "Staying Alive," Levertov has substantially enlarged her range as a poet and helped revitalize political poetry in English. She has learned how to weave together private experience and public event so that both are available to the reader, to show us the inner and outer lives in conflict and in reconciliation, to integrate *reportage* and documentary into lyrical form and find a genuine inscape. At the end of "Staying Alive" we have affirmation but not final resolution. That is as it should be; we could trust no other conclusion. The poem remains open-ended, like the life it celebrates.

Levertov: Poetry and the Spiritual   Linda Wagner-Martin*

At what point does the overtly political become a more enclosing, less compartmentalized angst? Levertov's essays on Kim Chi Ha, Solzhenitsyn, Neruda, and others, as well as her important 1960s and 1970s poem collections that were often described as "political,"[1] have prompted a great many of her readers to characterize her work in that way. Yet running concurrent with that perhaps more easily labeled theme has always been a pervasive spiritualism. Joyce Beck points to the " 'natural supernaturalism' of her romantic poetics," her rearing as the child of a Church of England clergyman, and her ancestral roots in Judaism. Harry Marten finds Levertov's poems of the last ten years to be conclusive proof that the poet has become "increasingly convinced that the exercise of the imagination moves one toward faith."[2] From her earliest writing to the most recent, Levertov has revealed her fused Christian and Hasidic beliefs in the joys of the immediate world, supporting the holistic "I" that is itself a part of the divine, as well as the compelling and nourishing community of shared belief.

Indeed, Martin Buber's *I and Thou* is probably one of the routes to Levertov's politics. The person actively involved must speak aggressively, for the purpose of her involvement is to effect change, to better the community, the polis. Even though Levertov in her early work was not influenced by Charles Olson—and tried to avoid the kind of mesmerizing contact with him that she had seen absorb her good friend Robert Creeley[3]—she shares with Olson his deep reverence for the good, the beneficial, the constructive, not in any platitudinous sense but with the most profound recognition of affinities among people, in their specific places. It is this reverence for the human body and spirit, for capabilities both mental and physical, that has marked Levertov's art. She cannot bear—literally—the fact that humankind keeps refusing its potentials for understanding, for greatness. She refuses to bear the fact that human beings become vessels of violence and degradation. And her refusal is often angry, vehement, strident—"political."

*This essay was written specifically for this volume and is published here for the first time with permission of the author.

Levertov's poem "Continuum" from her 1978 collection *Life in the Forest* expresses that connecting, joining belief—both in human faith and in the anger that human beings' lapses from faith provoke. Another dimension of her sense of life as process, life as testing ground, is her belief that humankind draws from, and in turn sustains, the natural world. Many of her metaphors are drawn from nature, and many of her most effective allegories conjoin the natural and the human. "Continuum" begins with a description of a fragile part of the natural world, representative of the fragile voice of the commonplace poet:

> Some beetle trilling
> its midnight utterance.
>
> Voice of the scarabee,
> dungroller,
> working survivor. . . .[4]

Hardly pretentious, this creator of voice is menial, hard-working, a survivor; and its voice "trills"—an unexpectedly aesthetic verb, given the rest of the description of the beetle—during the night. Never visible, then, because of the natural darkness, the creator makes his or her intentions known only through sound. Levertov's opening connects the reader to the epigraph for the entire book, the Henry James quotation that privileges the unheralded work of the artist: "We work in the dark. We do what we can. We give what we have. Our doubt is our passion. Our passion is our task. The rest is the madness of art."

Levertov's opening description of the Kafkaesque dung beetle (surely we are meant to hear Gregor's voice from "The Metamorphosis" in that choice of noun, which also pays homage in an Egyptian sense to the earthly sacred) echoes James's passionate definition of the artist and expands that identity to include the larger community of people risking danger, separation from their culture, health, and perhaps madness in order to speak truthfully. In the central stanza of the short poem, Levertov speaks of herself as a parallel creating voice, assessing her years of travel and work in search of the knowledge that the beetle possesses innately:

> I recall how each year
> returning from voyages, flights
> over sundown snowpeaks,
> cities crouched over darkening lakes,
> hamlets of wood and smoke,
> I find
> > the same blind face upturned to the light
> > and singing
> > the one song. (p. 63)

Levertov's travels took her wherever there was human anguish, from Vietnam to Central America and the American South. Cities, hamlets, mountains, lakes—and yet in every case, her voyages became "flights" because they awakened her imaginative energy. She was never merely traveling: she was re-creating the importance of what she saw before her. Of course, her work was "political." It charted the actual that she had seen. More importantly, it gave her material from which to create the philosophical themes of endurance, of the need for change, of the need to recognize humankind's sinister bent as well as its greatness. So from her own countless travels, she as poet returns to the quiet natural world—whether in Boston, Mexico, or Maine—where the sim-ple, eternal dedication of the beetle keeps her singing truthfully.

The closing three-line stanza, which follows the description of the bee-tle or poet ("the same blind face upturned to the light"), or rather, of beetle/poet made one, both still singing an eternal song—"the one song"—describes a scene that draws together the dichotomies of nature: "the same weed managing / its brood of minute stars / in the cracked flagstone" (p. 63). Human effort—"managing"—rises above the evidence of damage and waste, "cracked flagstone," in order to sustain the "brood of minute stars." The product itself is diminutive—shaped to reasonable size but given the luster that Levertov's belief in the efficacy of art allows. From the simple, the primitive, the natural, comes brilliance, a word not in the poem but sug-gested through its near-rhyme with the opening word *trilling*. The whole experience is brought to a finish through the reflecting title, "Continuum." Year after year, travel after travel, seasonal happenings occur—for nature and for the poet—while the song, the "one song," goes on, changing slightly with events and with the singer's capacities, but forming a continuum, with no abrupt shifts or changes.

One of the ways Levertov has maintained the sense of continuity within her many poems is her constant voice. Her best poems work from the impulse of her natural voice, a slightly staged, quasi-British voice, speaking in a rhythm that demands—insists—that listeners attend to it. In its quietly emphatic way, Levertov's voice forces the reader to give full value to line arrangement, to the isolation of a few words in a line, so that the rhythms of the poet-persona's voice carry their meaning into the ear of the reader. The effect of Levertov's poetry is as much aural as it is visual. The reading process makes use of the visual in order to create the aural.

These segments of the reading process are interrelated because of the skill with which Levertov has written her poetry. Her principle of design is that line division signals pause and enjambment. Through visual design she creates a flow of voice that allows the reader to participate—to speak the poetry after her. She uses punctuation carefully, always meaningfully com-bined with line endings, so that the reader has ample information about where the meaning units of each poem lie. Once into "Continuum," for example, the reader is relieved that the second line ends with a period and therefore separates the opening couplet from the rest of the poem. The only other period occurs at the end of the poem. Through her punctuation,

Levertov creates a two-part poem, rather than a six-stanza poem. The first two lines—the beetle singing—become the crystallizing image for the meaning of the rest of the poem.

The opening tercet of the longer part of the poem is obviously modifying the initial image, so it, too, is easy for the reader to apprehend. The ellipsis that follows gives another clear signal to the reader: these two segments are joined together, but they are also being fused with the body of the poem. The ellipsis acts as a glide, a verbal fall into the more matter-of-fact phrasing of the central segment, the heart of the poem—which also looks like the heart in its blocked appearance. There is a kind of assurance both in its simple shape and in the poet's use of the "I": "I recall how each year. . . ." Rather than seeming egotistical, this statement exudes a tone of confidence (of course, reader, you will want to hear about my travels, and I assume the role of speaker so that you can rest into the role of hearer, the classic narration of journeys creating the traditional symbiosis of language and response.)

The reader is consequently compelled to listen, and to accept the seemingly more personal middle section of the poem as only another plane of the poet's expression. Juxtaposed with the visual description of the beetle, this section also tells us that life gives us experiences we need to express. And it is this knowledge that appears in the poem's shorter fourth division, which contains a description that can be applied to both the beetle and the poet. While the poignance of a "blind" face is clear, the metaphoric import of the sightless turning to the light is perhaps the most important statement the poet makes. Following instinct, the beetle trills, the blind face looks for light, the poet speaks, and the artistic product—"one song"—is the result of this untutored creativity. No matter what the world of humankind experiences, the drive of the artist—both natural and intellectual—is to reach for the positive, the light beyond the earthiness of the human.

Levertov's concluding image goes further than her opening one, which is humbly realistic except for the word *trilling* that foreshadows the artistic accomplishment to come. In the ending, even "weeds" can manage to affect life, faced with the problems of that enigmatic brood of stars.

"Continuum"—for all its brevity and modesty—becomes a key poem within *Life in the Forest;* it is the title of the second section of the book. By choosing to end this section with its title poem, Levertov emphasizes its importance. There are poems within the section—and within the collection as a whole—that question this expression of difficult faith, of the premise of continuity. In her poems about the bombing of Hiroshima and Nagasaki, about the misery in Chile in 1977, and about racist America, she uses nature to show the depletion of the human spirit. She is following the same process her beetle does as she recognizes the real and moves beyond it into her song. Her song fuses both acknowledgment of the real and the primacy of the ideal.

In *Life in the Forest,* as in all Levertov's collections, her arrangement of the poems is crucial. Each book must be read as a narrative of emotion if not of fact, and the poems that are placed at the opening and closing of each section—as of each collection—are particularly important to Levertov's oeuvre. Despite her attention to some overtly political themes in *Life in the Forest*, its organization shows the reader that it is not intended to be primarily a political book. It is more often a book about Levertov's mother—her life and death—and about Levertov's understanding of her mother and her mother's life, which had been given to nurturing, to gardening, to appreciating beauty and knowledge and music. Finally, it is also a book about Levertov's own coming to knowledge of herself as woman, a woman of the 1970s seen through the grid of her mother's life in Mexico in her nineties, the poet's memories of life in England, and her more recent history as a divorced American woman. Through her understanding of her mother's waning but wise life—at ninety, ninety-one, ninety-two, ninety-three—Levertov reaches toward the whole continuum of life experience.

Her more characteristic image for that understanding of life experience had been the sharing of language. In "Writing to Aaron," she encapsulates years of experience in a structure that questions its own possibility but affirms that their meaning to each other—and the story of their separate lives—existed in words. The poem closes: "The Word itself / is what we heard, and shall always hear, each leaf / imprinted, syllables in our lives" (p. 6). Art as aesthetic connection, human meaning as poetry: these were the stances Levertov developed in her poems. But much of *Life in the Forest* is physical rather than intellectual, and the poet writes in her Introductory Note that she has tried to follow the aesthetics of Cesare Pavese. What she admires about his poems is twofold: that they are "about various persons other than himself," and that his aim is "suggesting a narrative through the depiction of a scene, a landscape, rather than through direct recounting of events as such" (p. vii). The change in focus is clear.

Levertov's mother becomes an external persona used to break out of the autobiographical mode so common to contemporary poetry—but the choice of her mother as subject, though natural and important, posed some problems for Levertov. Levertov had never been interested in being a "woman" poet, or—heaven forbid—a "poetess." She spoke frequently about the position of the gendered poet, always insisting that she be seen as *poet*, not *woman* poet. But the 1960s and 1970s brought new recognition of the valuable differences between men's and women's selves, and Levertov was absorbing those recognitions as she lived the life of a prominent woman poet during those decades. The crucible of her mother's death in 1977 seems to have brought her to yet another kind of realization of what women's lives could mean, however, so when she wrote the poems collected in this 1978 book, her attitude had been subtly changed by her own circumstances. Levertov's recognition of her poems as art created by a woman keeps one foot in her former stance. As she said in *American Poetry*, she is first of all a poet: "I don't believe I have ever made an aesthetic decision based on my gender." Although she admits, "Obviously many of my poems . . . were written by a woman," she still insists that there is a difference between gender as aesthetic and gender as subject. "If a woman poet writes poems on what her female body feels like to her, what it's like to menstruate, to be sexually entered by a man, to carry and bear a child and breast-feed it, her *subject matter* derives directly from her gender; but it will be the *structure* of the poem, its quality of images and diction, its details and its totality of sounds and rhythms, that determines whether or not it is a poem—a work of art." And if it is a successful work of art, Levertov concludes, it will transcend a range of "inessential" factors—"including gender."[5]

Much of Levertov's 1980s poetry tentatively refutes that intellectual position, because the core of her conviction as poet—and, recently, as poet of spiritual and mystical voice—stems from her involvement with her mother's life and death. The metaphor she chooses to express the fulfilling quality of her mother's life is itself a feminine one, that of the garden. Such a metaphor makes Levertov's poems about the mother/the feminine reach past gender into both the specific and natural, as well as the universal. In "A Daughter, II," Levertov creates the image of "a garden / of recognitions and revelations. Eden / of radiant comprehensions" (p. 30). She juxtaposes this external frame, in "A Daughter, I," with her memory of the mother—young and caring—as she longs

> for her mother to be her mother again,
> consoling, judging, forgiving,
> whose arms were once
>   strong to hold her and rock her,
> who used to chant
>   a ritual song that did magic
> to take away hurt. Now mother is child, helpless. (p. 27)

The several poems culminate in "Death in Mexico," a poem with a purpose-fully ambiguous title. Yes, her mother is dying. But contrary to the reader's expectation, Levertov emphasizes the death of her mother's garden—uncared for, unwatered: "three weeks before she died, the garden / began to vanish." Despite the fact that her mother had nurtured English and Welsh flowers in this Mexican location for twenty years, in less than a month the garden becomes "a greenish blur" complete with "weeds, flowerless rose-bushes, broken stems of the canna lilies and amaryllis," hedged inside a rickety and broken fence. The destruction of her mother's garden becomes a means for the poet to lament her personal, inexpressible loss:

> . . . by then for two years
> you had hardly been able to hear me,
> could barely see to read.
>   We spoke together
>   less and less.

> There's too much grief. Mother,
> what shall I do with it?
> Salt grinding and grinding from the magic box. (p. 42)

The grief that accrues from her mother's death shapes the later sections of *Life in the Forest*. One long sequential section, "Modulations for Solo Voice," traces the end of a love affair; more important, it establishes the paradigm of speaker and listener, voiced expression and unvoiced. The "one song" from "Continuum" becomes a forceful image in the later poems of this collection, so forceful that Levertov can close the book with the simple, runic "Magic," a poem that resonates in shape and language with the hum of "The brass or bronze cup, stroked at the rim, round and around" (p. 135). When the sound dies away, it is because the two listeners have ceased to respond to it. Throughout Levertov's poems, the inattentive hearer—or the hearer whose capacity to listen is marred or broken—constitutes a major disappointment, one sure cause of her grief.

The poet turns from this pervasive grief to the search for the light, often finding its radiance coupled with the song—both key images from "Continuum." As she writes in "A Pilgrim Dreaming," the poet can come to knowledge of herself:

> By the fire light
> of Imagination, brand
> held high in the pilgrim's
> upraised hand, he sees,
> not knowing what boundaries it may have. (p. 124)

In Levertov's collections during the 1980s, the image of light intensifies, while grief—submerged and in some ways placated—becomes the means to that light. *Candles in Babylon* (1982), *Oblique Prayers* (1984), and *Breathing the Water* (1987) convey a deeper sense of Levertov's acceptance of a presence that defies rational understanding. The tone of much of this poetry resembles that of Levertov's effective "A Woman Alone" from *Life in the Forest*. As the divorced woman faces her life separate from others, she learns to work her way toward individual wholeness. To choose—that is the essence of the poet's definition of living alone—to enjoy the great freedom of single-ness, "her time / spent without counting the change" (p. 16). Levertov's spiritual quest seems to have followed the same patterns as her coming to terms with her self alone: realization, choice, commitment. While it is probably too soon to describe explicitly what her spiritual vision consists of, her readers have parts of that image in these last three collections of poems. Her six-part penultimate poem from *Breathing the Water*," The Showings: Lady Julian of Norwich, 1342–1416," is a powerfully satisfying expression of Levertov's most recent thematic concentration, the speaker's search for faith and vision.

As the title suggests, Julian's vision is the core of Levertov's poetic recreation of the miracle—of Julian's vision and her life. It begins with the concrete evidence of that vision, "a little thing, the size of a hazelnut, held safe in God's pierced palm."[6] Levertov's choice of the indefinite noun *thing* bears witness to her dedication to William Carlos Williams's "No ideas but in things," the battle cry of those imagists and objectivists of the twentieth century who have believed in the efficacy of the object. It also echoes natural speech, and one of the projects of her poem is to humanize the mystical process, to give life to Lady Julian of Norwich.

To that end, she describes Julian's choice not to marry, her learning, her naming—making the saint into a "real" woman ("Thirty was older than it is now," "Somehow, reading or read to, she'd spiralled up within tall towers of learning"). And her childhood becomes a part of Levertov's evocation, expressed again through lush if typical country images, their completeness tied to the full life of the saint as woman: "the dairy's bowls of clabber, of rich cream, / ghost-white in shade, and outside / the midsummer gold, humming of dandelions" (p. 77). When God appears to her, that expression is also given naturalness: God is imaged as both human father and, through the metaphor, human mother:

> God's wounded hand
> reached out to place in hers
> the entire world, "round as a ball,
> small as a hazelnut." Just so one day
> of infant light remembered
> her mother might have given
> into her two cupped palms
> a newlaid egg, warm from the hen; (p. 78)

Naturalness, ease of understanding, ease of expression, and acceptance of whatever miracle: these are the emphases of Levertov's poem about the mystical happenings. Accordingly, her diction itself becomes matter-of-fact, as tied to earth and fact as the description of the hazelnut:

> brown hazelnut of All that Is—
> made, and belov'd, and preserved.
> As still, waking each day within
> our microcosm, we find it, and ourselves. (p. 78)

The horror of the rest of Lady Julian's story is understated, compressed into the last two poems, and set in our own times when the poet's voice reminds us,

> She lived in dark times, as we do:
> war, and the Black Death, hunger, strife,
> torture, massacre. She knew
> all of this, she felt it
> *sorrowfully, mournfully,*
> *shaken as men shake*
> *a cloth in the wind.* (p. 81)

Her experiences were judged "delirium," "hallucination," but she persisted, and her final vindication gives Levertov the closing image for the poem— another crystallization of light and song that places Lady Julian in one of the highest positions in Levertov's "continuum" of moral greatness. Her readers have come to expect change and affirmation in Levertov's later poems, and these qualities are the touchstones for her future work. Through the particular to the universal, Levertov's intensely concrete and personalized poems take her readers to places, and visions, unexpected in both contemporary times and contemporary poems.

Notes

1. See Levertov's essay collections, *The Poet in the World* (1973) and *Light Up the Cave* (1981) (New York: New Direction), as well as Liana Sakelliou-Schultz, *Denise Levertov: An Annotated Primary and Secondary Bibliography* (New York: Garland, 1988).

2. Joyce Lorraine Beck, "Denise Levertov's Poetics and Oblique Prayers," *Religion and Literature* 18, no. 1 (Spring 1986), 45; Harry Marten, *Understanding Denise Levertov* (Columbia: University of South Carolina Press, 1988), 17.

3. Comment by Levertov to the author at the University of British Columbia Poetry Conference, July 1963.

4. Denise Levertov, *Life in the Forest* (New York: New Directions, 1978), 63; hereafter cited in text.

5. Denise Levertov, "Serving an Art," in "Sexual Poetics: Notes on Genre and Gender in Poetry by Women," *American Poetry: A Triquarterly* 1 (1984), 74–75.

6. Denise Levertov, *Breathing the Water* (New York: New Directions, 1987), 75; hereafter cited in text.

Metaphors of Life and Death in the Poetry of Denise Levertov and Sylvia Plath

Sophie B. Blaydes*

According to Aristotle, metaphor is "the greatest thing by far. . . . It is the one thing that cannot be learnt from others; and it is also a sign of genius. . . ."[1] Metaphors compare; in good metaphors, the comparisons enable us to see more clearly. The poetry of Sylvia Plath and Denise Levertov possesses the sign of genius and provides us with insights into life and death. Their poems are metaphors, emblems of their lives. Plath's poems are violent—they negate life; Levertov's are contemplative—they celebrate life. Plath justifies death through art; Levertov awakens to life through art. For each, poetry is not only the way to understand life, but it is life itself. Through their work, the two poets present an odd congruity, one as a victim, the other

*Reprinted with permission from *Dalhousie Review* 57 (1976), 494–506.

as victor. Where Plath sees and absorbs the sickness of a sick world, Levertov discovers and applies the antidote for that sickness. Both describe the diseases of our time through personal yet universal metaphors; Plath's are metaphors of violence and defeat; Levertov's are of anguish and endurance.

In Plath's poetry, the metaphors are painful and destructive, They are of ". . . a cut, a contusion . . . thalidomide, fever, an accident, a wound, paralysis, a burial, animal and human sacrifice," heretic burning, wartorn lands, extermination camps. One critic called her poetry a "garden of tortures."[2] That garden is defined by a rigid metaphorical scheme where life is represented by color, rhythm, and heat and where death is antithetically black, white, stasis, and cold. Plath has used her metaphorical scheme to translate and absorb events in her life; she has re-ordered and interpreted her life through her poetry and has then come to control its events through a personal mythos of metaphors and images. For Plath, the "blood jet is poetry," and it leads to death.[3]

For Levertov, poetry "reverberates through . . . life . . .";[4] her images and metaphors celebrate life. She too responds through her poetry to her experiences, but her response has a vitality because poetry to Levertov is a life force. She has said that "the interaction of life on art and of art on life is continuous. Poetry is necessary to a whole man . . . [it must not be] divided from the rest of life. . . . Both life and poetry fade, wilt, shrink, when they are divorced."[5] She says of the true artist that he

> . . . draws out all from his heart,
> work with delight, makes things with calm, with sagacity,
> . . . composes his objects, works dexterously, invents;
>
> arranges materials, adorns them, makes them adjust.[6]

She says in another poem, "Pleasures,"

> I like to find
> what's not found
> at once, but lies
>
> within something of another nature,
> in repose distinct.[7]

And so she can find "imagination made fur" in a cat, or affirm her identity by rejecting a limp, clean, empty dress, or describe innocence through a Mexican family going to a movie.

Both Plath and Levertov question the nature and value of man's life, and they convey their contrasting visions of reality in clear, vigorous images and metaphors. The poets' antithetical answers arise paradoxically from corresponding experiences. Plath was born in Boston in 1932 and died in London in 1963, a suicide; Levertov was born in London in 1923 and lives now in New England. Both married writers.[8] Comparable worlds have for these two women generated opposite responses. Yet, despite their differences, the two women speak to the reader, who is caught by the truth of the images; their duality suggests the complexity of life and our ambivalence in responding to it. The poets define the contradictory moods and attitudes of modern man through their metaphors.

Plath's poem "Daddy" and Levertov's "During the Eichmann Trial" demonstrate the poets' contradictory views of a modern reality. Plath's vision is negative and violent; Levertov's is positive and vital. Where one sees life, the other sees death. Where one feels hope, the other feels despair. Where one teaches, the other destroys. Plath's poem "Daddy" becomes a persuasive polemic for death through her metaphor. As she suggested of her later poetry, "Daddy" should be read aloud because its strength increases through the sound of the words and the rhythmic patterns of the stanzas. The cumulative sound of the poem becomes a metaphor for the harsh, implacable message which is death by murder.

The effect of metaphorical sound is not accidental. Plath may speak unconventional ideas of vampires and group murder, but they are presented in traditional, albeit personalized forms. The poem has sixteen stanzas of five lines each. Plath characteristically uses a stanza, but her ideas threaten to break through the restrictions and undermine the ordered form of the stanzas. Such a traditional poetic device as the stanza becomes a container for her insane world.

While it has no conventional rhyme scheme, the poem is dominated by rhyme. The long—*oo* sound appears six times in the first line: "*You do* not *do. You do* not *do.*" The sound increases in frequency until it appears in the last five stanzas clearly twenty-five times and four times in off-rhymes. The repeated—*oo* sound increases the tempo; it intensifies the impact by charging the poem with the pain and power of its restrictive sound,—*oo*. The sound not only increases the tempo and intensifies the tone of the poem, but it also becomes a metaphor of the pain and frenzy of the poet's experience.

Adding to the sound pattern is Plath's effective use of rhythm. The poem is comprised basically of iambs, with some anapests and spondees. Aristotle was the first to tell us that the iamb is the rhythm closest to ordinary speech—a fact that coincidentally applies to both Greek and English. Plath has used conventional rhythm for the poem, yet the effect of the rhythm is unconventional. The first lines of "Daddy" are startling. They contain the certainty and the simplicity of a nursery rhyme.

> You do not do. You do not do
> Any more, black shoe
> In which I have lived like a foot
> For thirty years, poor and white,
> Barely daring to breathe or Achoo.

The rhythm is reassuring, and, like the odd horrors of the nursery rhyme, the bizarre situation of "Daddy" is accepted because a sense of order is imposed on a hideous reality.

Plath's diction adds to the hideous reality; it is startlingly simple. Specifically, of the 515 words in the poem, only 75 are polysyllabic; 85 percent of
the poem is monosyllabic. In addition, the word order of the statements is
normal. Plath uses few adjectives—about three per stanza. The words are
not extraordinary, but they are highly charged by the rhythm, the sound
patterns, and the context in which they are placed. The simplicity of the
poem's diction is timeless and lends an air of universality to a highly personal
dilemma.

"Daddy" may open simply and directly as a nursery rhyme,[9] but it closes
with the intensity of a martial air or the frenzy of a religious ecstasy. The
poem's movement may be compared to a military cadence that grows louder
and becomes more emotional or to a religious exaltation that carries the
curse of vengeance and death. The tempo and intensity of the poem become
metaphors for Plath's association of the world of the poem with the world of
the nursery. In the poem, the rhythm and tone vie against the content, just
as the speaker struggles and loses her identity as she gives herself to a force.
In the poem, the poet becomes part of an ordered, ecstatic experience that
denies individuality and reason.

Plath's poem is psychologically persuasive through its sound and rhythm;
it is intellectually persuasive through its imagery. The images in "Daddy" are
startling, yet consistent with Plath's personal mythos and the tone of the
poem. Black—her emblem for death or evil—occurs in "black shoe," "black
swastika," "blackboard," "the black man," "a man in black," "black telephone,"
and, finally, "your fat black heart."

The shoe is one of the first of many highly charged images; it moves in
two compelling directions: on the one hand, it supports the nursery rhyme
motif that is suggested by the rhythm, "You do not do. You do not do / Any
more, black shoe. . . ." We are in the world of the old lady who lived in a
shoe, a world where one calls one's father "Daddy." But "black shoe" quickly
becomes part of the sinister Nazi motif that builds throughout the poem. The
black shoe is the Fascist boot, the Fuerher, that father who has controlled her
for thirty years. In the first stanza, the poet rejects the black shoe that has
contained her, "barely daring to breathe or Achoo." Her life and her will
have been subjugated to those of her father. The black shoe is then a metaphor for her past, her suffocated spirit.

The black shoe is the first of a series of metaphors of Fascism that build the
argument of the poem. Plath uses words with Germanic sounds of Fascistic
nuances, although she begins with a kind of nursery innocence with the word
"Achoo." The child-like tone of that first stanza is completed by "Achoo," a
word that carries a double suggestion: it is the child's word for sneeze, but it is
also a hint of the heavier, more sinister Germanic sounds that follow: "Ach,
du," "Ich, ich, ich," "luftwaffe," "Panzer-man," "Meinkampf."

As she loses her child-like tone, the poet becomes a Jew, and the basic
metaphor is now more threatening and violent. The images include "Polack,"
"barb wire snare," "Dachau, Auschwitz, Belsen," "gypsy," and "Jew," "Jew,"

"Jew." As we move with her through the poem and see her assume these identities, Plath becomes a victim, a woman without will. She is tortured; she becomes an individual without identity. Through the poem Plath forces her personal plight into a public trauma so that she, like the Jews, is abandoned. She was abandoned by her father, her daddy; the Jews were abandoned by the Fuerher. They were destroyed by him, their father; so she continues the parallel, whereby she too is carried by a wave of murder and destruction. Her father had "bit my pretty red heart in two." When she was ten, he died; at twenty, she tried suicide; then she married another Fascist: "A man in black with a Meinkampf look / And a love of the rack and the screw." Inevitably, she identified with the Jews, who are victims, because she, like them, is tortured and persecuted.

She is ambivalent toward her father, whom she loves and hates. She knows she is a victim, but she detaches herself from her experience, with the shadow of a will. By the end of the poem, she is violent as she rejects and kills, but her actions are part of a mass response where she loses her individuality. The violence of the action is propelled by the incantatory tone and form of the poem—she is part of a selfless motion that builds hypnotically, with frenzy, until she is driven to an act of passion. But even that act is a group act—when she kills, she kills facelessly in a vengeful, hating crowd.

If there is love in the poem, it is painful: "Every woman adores a Fascist." To Plath, love is brutal, and it is mixed with hate. It is "the rack and the screw." At the end of the poem, she joins a village in a primitive ritual.

> There's a stake in your fat black heart
> And the villagers never liked you,
> They are dancing and stamping on you,
> They also *knew* it was you,
> Daddy, daddy, you bastard, I'm through.

The poem ends hopelessly. The counterpoint of the child's cry with the bitter accusation "Daddy, daddy, you bastard . . ." is hideous, startling, compelling. The poem contains no hope, unless death is that hope.

Aristotle defined tragedy in therapeutic, positive terms. Tragedy to him has a social function because it provides an emotional release, a catharsis, for the members of an audience. The individual pities the dilemma of the tragic hero and fears that he too could suffer excessive punishment. Plath's dilemma, her tragedy, is described in pitiless terms; she presents an individual's tragedy but in artificial or large terms. The artifice of the nursery rhyme and the absorption of the Fascist victimization of the Jews provide bases that do not invite catharsis. Plath, however, effects her own catharsis through death. The ritual death of Daddy, alone, will free her from the pain and persecution of love which was caused by her father's actual death twenty years earlier.

The poem is intimate and terrifying, and according to A. R. Jones, it ". . . is committed to the view that the ethos of love/brutality is the dominant historical ethos of the last thirty years."[10] So, her tortured mind reflects the tortured age through the historical events of concentration camps, Fascism, and violence. To some, then, the poem is an emblem of our age, which is defined as "schizophrenic, torn, between brutality and love."[11] The love that Plath presents in the poem denies life; she seeks a release from love and discovers that death alone can provide it.

The poem is metaphorically charged in its form and its imagery. Through its structure and cadence and its monosyllabic diction, "Daddy" presents the reader with a violent act of passion in traditional and universal terms. As Jones writes, ". . . we are persuaded almost to cooperate with the destructive principle—indeed to love the principle as life itself."[12] He sees Plath's poetry as the product of a deranged mind because "in a deranged world, a deranged response is the only possible reaction of the sensitive mind."[13] Such a statement denies that we may find beauty, order, and health in our time. That view leaves us with the visionary who perceives chaos and then self-destructs. To A. E. Dyson, Plath's "amazing poems . . . are not the expression only, but the transmutation, of suffering. . . . They are in the highest degree creative art, and . . . in art, there is healing of a kind."[14] But Plath's healing in "Daddy" is murderous. Even after the ritual murder, the apparent purgation at the end of the poem does not resolve her dilemma. She remains a victim-murderer.

Yet most of us would agree with Aristotle that poetry provides aesthetic outlets for our emotions—not only our rage or frustrations but also our love and joy. To embrace a negative, destructive vision of love and life is to ignore the variety of man and his resilience—his capacity for pain, his ability to find beauty and joy in life. Just as Plath's work should not be celebrated because she is a suicide, Levertov's should not suffer critically because of her psychic health. Instead of using her poetry for exorcism of demons or affirmations of destruction, Levertov finds meaning in life, ". . . a form in all things (and in our experience) which the poet can discover and reveal."[15] To Levertov, the poet is a seer, an interpreter. She has said that ". . . the poet stands open-mouthed in the temple of life, contemplating his experience [and] there come to him the first words of the poem: . . ."[16] The poet, to Levertov, transforms experiences into words with "a religious devotion to the truth, to the splendor of the authentic, [involving] the writer in a process rewarding in itself; but when that devotion brings us to undreamed abysses and we find ourselves sailing over them and landing on the other side—that's ecstasy."[17]

Both Plath and Levertov suggest through their poems an ecstasy that encompasses them and the reader, but one reaches a frenzy of death and murder, the other an impetus and a commitment to life. Levertov's affirmations of life are clearly revealed even in the titles of her anthologies: for example, one is *To Stay Alive* (poems), another *The Poet in the World* (essays). In these works, subjects range from her sister's death to protests against the Vietnamese War to her poetic credo. Each becomes a metaphor for the significance of man and the need to live. Her short poem "The Tulips" demonstrates her use of the imagists' techniques.[18] The poem is also the subject of one of Levertov's essays where she explains her creative process.[19] Like the imagists, she strives for the utmost concentration.

> Red tulips
> living into their death
> flushed with a wild blue
>
> tulips
> becoming wings
> ears of the wind
> jackrabbits rolling their eyes
>
> west wind
> shaking the loose pane
>
> some petals fall
> with that sound one
> listens for

The images in the poem arose from a simple experience. She had received a "bunch of red tulips."[20] The first lines suggest the basic thesis; the tulips were fully alive up to "their last moments. They hadn't given up before the end." The third line recalls that tulips turn blue as they die, which reminded Levertov of the flush on the cheeks of a fevered person. "Wild blue" seemed appropriate because it suggested the color of a wild sky at sunset. The next four lines describe the movement of the tulips' petals; as they darken, they also turn back. The petals seemed to be like wings; and they also became the long ears of the jackrabbits, who in a state of ecstasy would roll their eyes. The "west wind / shaking the loose pane" was, she said, "pure observation." "The flowers were on the window sill, and the pane of glass was loose, and the wind blew and rattled the pane."[21]

The last three lines simply describe that loosening of the petals in death; ". . . perhaps that death was hastened by the blowing of the west wind." She had noticed that "there is a little sound when a petal falls . . . a sound like the breath of a human being who is dying; it stops, and one has been sitting by the bedside, and one didn't even know it, but one was in fact waiting for just that sound, and the sound is the equivalent of that silence."[22] The line then is broken where the silence is.

The poem is more than an image for her reality; for Levertov, it becomes a metaphor for life translated from her experience. It, too, may teach and persuade because it demonstrates a life force. She said that

> . . . a poet, a verbal kind of person, is constantly talking to himself, inside
> of himself, constantly approximating and evaluating and trying to grasp his
> experience in words. And the "sound," inside his head, of that voice is not
> necessarily identical with his literal speaking voice, nor is his inner vocabu-

lary identical with that which he uses in conversation. At their best sound and words are song, not speech. The written poem is a record of that inner song.[23]

The poem is carefully, skillfully articulated. Levertov, like Plath, uses charged language that is simple and direct. Both achieve comparable effect by monosyllabic diction and by traditional but unconventional rhythmic sound patterns. Plath uses iambs and anapests; Levertov uses spondees, trochees, and pauses. There is a music to "The Tulips," but it is a gentle, quiet music that alerts and soothes us, just as we are alerted to death in life and yet are soothed by death when death is a silence or a stillness that holds no terror. It is only an absence of sound and motion. The music is effected by the sounds of the words as well as their emphasis. *Tulips* is repeated in the fourth line, reminding us of the flower and providing an odd rhyming pattern from line 1 to line 4. The short *i* of tulips is repeated in w*i*nd/w*i*nd/w*i*th. The *w* is repeated, in *w*ings/*w*ind/*w*ind/*w*ith/*w*est. The *n* is repeated in wi*n*d and wi*n*gs. The rhymes or repeated sounds are not prominent. They suggest a continuity, but they do not stress through rhyme, rhythm, or image. Instead we find a quiet affirmation of life and an easy acceptance of death through a poem that is natural. It is a metaphor of Levertov's basic thesis—we live until we must die, until a wind, an event, shakes us from our hold on life. We break loose into death silently.

That same individualistic view of life that humanizes every object, whether it is a tulip or a dress, significantly persists when Levertov observes Adolf Eichmann. While Plath uses the Nazis for her metaphors of death, Levertov turns to Eichmann's trial to validate man. In the first five lines of her poem "During the Eichmann Trial," Levertov extends her vision of humanity so that it includes the Fascist who epitomizes evil during the days of his trial. For most who wrote of Eichmann or who saw him, he was a monster. For Levertov, he was a man:

> He had not looked,
> pitiful man whom none
>
> pity, whom all
> must pity if they look
>
> into their own face. . . .[24]

In order to understand Eichmann and his murder of five million Jews, Levertov defines him in terms that are compatible with her vision of life. She is struggling to identify the individual in Eichmann, the "I" that could destroy obediently and mindlessly. Her poem strangely uses the same images, even the same metaphors, that Plath used in "Daddy," but Levertov's are invested with the questions that lead to understanding, not with Plath's arguments that lead to final solutions.

The poem insists upon the connection between Eichmann and herself and others—the synapse is of pity. We must pity if we look at Eichmann and at ourselves.

> Here is a mystery,
>
> a person, an
> other, an I?

Is he a man? Did he kill five million? "Count them," she says. Eichmann's answers to the question of his behavior oddly recall Plath's poem:

> "I was used from the nursery
> to obedience
>
> all my life . . .
> Corpselike
>
> obedience."

Eichmann's justification reminds us of the child-like tone of "Daddy" and then of the mindless, depersonalized action that moves Plath to group murder.

Later in the poem, Levertov refers to blood in almost the same phrase that Plath used to explain poetry: "the blood jet." She says of all those deaths in the German camps,

> "A spring of blood
> gushed from the earth."
> Miracle
>
> unsung. I see
> a spring of blood gush from the earth—
>
> Earth cannot swallow
> so much at once
>
> a fountain
> rushes towards the sky
>
> unrecognized
> a sign—.

The blood of the Jews is a road to heaven—a sign of spiritual life from an anonymous death. And what of Eichmann?

> Pity this man who saw it
> whose obedience continued—
>
> he, you, I, which shall I say?
> He stands

> isolate in a bulletproof
> witness-stand of glass,
>
> a cage, where we may view
> ourselves, an apparition
>
> telling us something he
> does not know: we are members
>
> one of another.

Eichmann, the Fascist, the man in the glass booth, becomes in Levertov's poem a startling metaphor: he teaches a lesson he has not learned, that we are bound by humanity, that we share our humanity, that we must pity one of our own "whose obedience continued." Eichmann, the monstrous killer of the Jews, the unrepetant, unthinking murderer is yet another mode of experience for Levertov, who wonders about his crime and yet perceives in him what we too possess, humanity. Our function is to pity.

The tone is contemplative. Yet it contains allusions to the worst crime of our era, but the crime is modulated by the thesis that we are part of one another. The thesis is supported by the simple form and direct diction that characterize Levertov's other poems. The basic form of the poem is the couplet, with short lines of two or three feet. The rhythm of the poem is not abrupt or staccato, because Levertov uses run-on lines between the couplet stanzas. She both exploits and ignores the limitations of the stanza by using the run-on lines and by repeating sounds, words, and phrases without accentuating them. For example, "pitiful," "pity," and "pity" occur in the first four lines. "Whom" is repeated twice in the same lines. The continuity from one stanza to another is effected quietly, just as the main thesis of the poem is emphasized by the repetition of a few words. The repetition of sounds and phrases creates a unity and flow in the poem that sustain and extend the thesis of the poem. The diction is comparable also to the other poems by Plath and Levertov: 77 percent of the words are monosyllabic, creating a simplicity and directness that support the simplicity and directness of her thesis.

Where Plath used the Jew-Fascist motif to persuade us to kill, Levertov uses the same motif to teach the brotherhood of man. Where Plath's metaphors enabled her to lose her identity and become a faceless killer in a group, a victim who retaliates, Levertov's metaphors enabled her to reaffirm her identity even through Eichmann, who victimized so many. With Plath, the self is lost; with Levertov, it is affirmed. With one there is only death; with the other, life.

That Levertov and Plath saw the same world in antithetical terms may not surprise us, but when their experiences and the metaphorical expression of those experiences are so close in time and place, we do wonder at the differences. Plath translated her experiences into an argument for death; she used a compelling, riding structure and a metaphorical design that forced us to agree with the murder of her father and, by extension, to affirm her death. She was not a Jew, and her father was not a Nazi, but those metaphorical identities gave her the facelessness that violence demands. Her anonymity is strengthened by a rhythm that builds to a martial cadence or a ritualistic frenzy, in either case justifying a loss of self and a move to murder and eventually to suicide.

Levertov translates her experiences into an adoration of life; she uses a looser structure that is defined by her in a traditional fashion, i.e., through rhythm, sounds, and pauses that function as vehicles of the theme. She is emblematic, choosing a tulip to verify her idea that we live fully until we die. We want to agree with her lesson, because her metaphors are common and comforting. Unlike Plath, Levertov is a Jew; yet, paradoxically, it is Plath, not Levertov, who is persecuted. Somehow the sense of victimization is part of Plath but not of Levertov. Instead, Levertov finds through Eichmann another explanation of the nature of man by identifying him as an individual, an "I," who is pitiful. His inability to comprehend his crime is pitiful. Levertov does not seek vengeance or even a catharsis from that tragedy. She takes it in, absorbs it into her scheme of life, and affirms through Eichmann the brotherhood of man. Anything that denies her individuality is rejected, whether it is a dress or her Jewishness. She is an "I."

The visions of Plath and Levertov are contrary. One wrote as a Jew and was not; the other was a Jew and wrote as an Everyman. One saw in her life despair, death, destruction; the other hope, life, a lesson. Both conveyed their experiences in concentrated language, in stunning images, compelling metaphors. Both used the rhythm and sounds of words to impress us subliminally with their contrary theses.

Notes

1. Aristotle, *De Poetica*, transl. Ingram Bywater, *Poetics*, chap. 22, 1459ᵉ lines 53–57, in *The Basic Works of Aristotle*, ed. Richard McKeon (New York: Random House, 1941), 1479.

2. Annette Lavers, "The World as Icon—On Sylvia Plath's Themes," *The Art of Sylvia Plath*, ed. Charles Newman (Bloomington: Indiana University Press, 1971), 104–105.

3. Sylvia Plath, "Kindness," *Ariel* (New York: Harper & Row, 1965), 82.

4. Denise Levertov, "The Poet in the World," *The Poet in the World* (New York: New Directions, 1973), 116.

5. Ibid., 112.

6. Denise Levertov, "The Artist," *With Eyes at the Back of Our Heads* (New York: New Directions, 1960), 4.

7. Levertov, "Pleasures," *With Eyes . . .* , 17.

8. Plath was married to the poet Ted Hughes; Levertov was married to the novelist Mitchell Goodman. Levertov's volume of poetry *The Freeing of the Dust* (New York: New Directions, 1975) affirms her resilience despite the separation from her husband.

9. A. R. Jones, "On Daddy," in Newman, *The Art of Sylvia Plath*, 230–36.

10. Ibid., 236.

11. Ibid.

12. Ibid.

13. Ibid., 231.

14. A. E. Dyson, "On Sylvia Plath," in Newman, *The Art of Sylvia Plath*, 209.

15. Denise Levertov, "Some Notes on Organic Form," *The Poet in the World*, 7.

16. Ibid., 8.

17. Ibid., 13.

18. Denise Levertov, "The Tulips," *The Jacob's Ladder* (New York: New Directions, 1961), 53.

19. Denise Levertov, "Line-Breaks, Stanza-Spaces, and the Inner Voices," *The Poet in the World*, 20–24.

20. Ibid., 20.

21. Ibid., 21.

22. Ibid., 22.

23. Ibid., 24.

24. Denise Levertov, "During the Eichmann Trial. i. When We Look Up," *The Jacob's Ladder*, 61–63.

Exploring the Human Community:
The Poetry of Denise Levertov and
Muriel Rukeyser
Harry Marten*

"I am insisting," David Reisman wrote some thirty years ago, "that no ideology, however noble, can justify the sacrifices of an individual to the needs of the group."[1] An assertion of the primacy of what Quentin Anderson has called "The Imperial Self" is, of course, an old sweet song sounded to celebrate privacy, self-sufficiency, ingenuity, energy and variety. "Elbow room," cried Dan'l Boone, who finding himself in legal trouble in old Kentucky, began again in Missouri. After experiencing life along the Mississippi, Huck Finn lit out for the territories. And Emerson assured us that nature's uncorrupted richness was a reflection of the beauty of our souls. Responding not to others in communities, but to the cosmos around us, we would become aware of the cosmos within us. An American poem was to be lived and the solitude of the wilderness would reveal its rhythms.[2]

But songs of the private man also have their own rough rhythms, dissonant meters of a desocialized imagination. Describing "the American flight from culture, from the institutions and emotional dispositions of associated life,"[3] Quentin Anderson tells us that:

> the term "individualism" has substituted for an investigation of the imaginative consequences of an increasing measure of personal isolation. . . . Indi-

*Reprinted with permission from *Sagetrieb* 3 (Winter 1984), 51–61.

vidualism, insofar as it stands for the energy, inventiveness, and adaptability of Americans committed to commercial or industrial enterprise, is a name for those personal qualities which foster impersonality in social and economic relations; the individualist is . . . the man who subjects others to himself through his shrewdness in gauging their appetites or anticipating their needs. . . .

In Emerson, society was not spurned; it was judged irrelevant to human purposes in the measures that it forced or encouraged each of us to assume a distinct role. (*IS*, pp. 4–5)

Paul Goodman puts it more bluntly: "[Our society] thwarts aptitude and creates stupidity. It corrupts ingenuous patriotism. It corrupts the fine arts. It shackles science. . . . It has no Honor. It has no Community."[4]

Still, the issue is not simply that we are a people who are infatuated with difference, throwing together ambition and daring with irresponsibility, indifference, avoidance and escape. Too, as Muriel Rukeyser has written, "We suffer from . . . [a] hunger for uniformity, the shared norm of ambition and habit and living standard. The repressive codes are everywhere."[5] For Philip Slater, charting the stress lines of "American Culture at the Breaking Point," the paradox is clear: "The desire to be somehow special sparks an even more competitive quest for progressively more rare and expensive symbols—a quest that is ultimately futile since it is individualism itself that produces uniformity."[6]

Comfortably conformist, embracing rules and systems, we fantasize and mythologize individuation which in turn often simply sustains our national sameness. As we now recognize, much of the poetry of our time, reflecting aspects of the duality, has typically followed directions that lead at one extreme to what Conrad Aiken called "the jejune precisions of artifice and formalism, the snug enclosures of wit and irony,"[7] or at the other to what Louis Simpson not long ago labeled the "Revolution in Taste," in which "we are stuck with our sweating selves" while poetry becomes "almost exclusively a means of self-expression."[8] Recently, perhaps inevitably, a reaction to these extremes of detachment and disclosure has set in, offering a poetry of rhetoric of discourse that according to Robert Pinsky, "is primarily neither ironic nor ecstatic."[9]

With so much recent poetry alienating readers in its extreme privacy, its too brittle displays of wit, and its use of rhetoric to avoid both self-absorption and irony, we might wonder if there is a meaningful alternative. Can there be something other than a self-centering verse that seems to find authority beyond the poem itself, simply in the fact and fervor of its utterance coupled with an insistence on the poet's special power as seer? Is there an alternative to systematically detached verse which seems to claim its authority strictly in the intricacies of its formal surfaces? Or to a poetry that claims the virtues of "civilized . . . communication"[10] and the authority of well-executed rhetoric? An art that answers these questions must, I believe, affirm both self and nonself, must be impassioned and scrupulously controlled, must find its authority in the ways both feeling and thought, form and statement conjoin. It must in fact be an art of community, of relationships both inside and outside of the poem. In our time this art has been most visible in the work of Denise Levertov and Muriel Rukeyser, friends who shared imaginative sympathies.

"Poetry depends on the moving relations within itself" Rukeyser wrote in an introductory note to *The Life of Poetry:*

> It is an art that lives in time, expressing and evoking the moving relation between the individual consciousness and the world. The work that a poem does is a transfer of human energy, and I think human energy may be defined as consciousness, the capacity to make change in existing conditions. . . . To accept poetry in these meanings would make it possible for people to use it as an "exercise," an enjoyment of the possibility of dealing with the meanings in the world and in their lives.

The poet's task is neither simply to explore nor eschew self, but to uncover and make known through poetic form and content aspects of the relation I:world.

"Art is action" for Rukeyser, though "it does not cause action: rather, it prepares us for thought" (*LP*, p. 24). And action, Rukeyser suggests in a discussion of the work of Karen Horney, is defined "in terms of relationship, so that the individual is seen not only as an individual, but as a person moving toward other persons, or a person moving away from other persons, or a person moving against other persons" (*LP*, pp. 8–9). In art, as in life, what fascinates are the complex ways that individual entities together constitute a whole. "Art is not a world, but a knowing of the world" (*LP*, p. 24); it offers knowledge of correspondences, and in such knowledge, Rukeyser tells us, "imaginative experience . . . will have meaning. It will apply to your life; and it is more than likely to lead you to thought or action, that is, you are likely to want to go further into the world, further into yourself" (*LP*, p. 24). The lesson is always one of contraries: the way into self and the way toward others are inseparable; the way of thought is the way of feeling, the way of form the way of content: "A fine poem will seize your imagination intellectually—that is, when you reach it, you will reach it intellectually too—but the way is through emotion, through what we call feeling" (*LP*, p. 8). In Rukeyser's best poetry, "form and content, relation and function, reach and merge" (*LP*, p. 39).

"After my mother died," Denise Levertov wrote in a 1980 essay remembering Rukeyser, "when I told Muriel forlornly that I felt myself to be a middle-aged orphan, she said, 'Oh, I'll adopt you. You'll be my Adopted Something.' She meant that and I felt it, felt . . . strengthened."[11] The declaration in all its spontaneous supportive warmth, humor, and vagueness points us to the complexity and fullness of the relationship of the two women. Not simply friends and political allies, not feeling like sisters, but "Something," Levertov and Rukeyser were "fellow Votaries of Poetry" (*LC*, p. 194), kindred spirits sharing almost seamlessly their principles for the "Life of Poetry."

Rukeyser's words, ideas, feelings, resonate in Levertov's work. "The great power of art is to . . . activate" (LC, p. 9), Levertov explained not long ago, echoing her friend. And this is accomplished by acknowledging that "internal and external work, the self-directed . . . and the . . . extroverted, must be concurrent, or at least rhythmically alternating. They are complementary, and neither can be substituted for the other" (LC, p. 96): "The self will surely suffer if egotism leads a person away from the experience of the Human Communion. And the commonweal, as surely, suffers if those who work for its betterment are hollowed-out self-neglecters whose imaginations are atrophying" (LC, p. 96).

For "There can be no self-respect without respect for others, no love and reverence for others without love and reverence for oneself" (PW, p. 53). Both poets offer close attention to the objects they observe, as well as to "the mind as it feels its way through . . . an impression" (LC, p. 72). And each attends not so much to the qualities of the world perceived, or alternatively to the perceiver's mind, as to the relationship between the two. The poems of both women reveal a process of discovery in which interiors and exteriors are mutually defining.

In presenting what Levertov has called "the mind's dance among perceptions" (LC, p. 62), each poet believes that art is "valuable both as human testimony and as aesthetic experience" (LC, p. 62), and each finds for herself the lines of force and form that will give such experience authority. Central to comprehending the achievement of both is a recognition that they are neither lyricists, nor polemicists, but storytellers.

Sometimes the simple selection of a subject for tale telling may go far toward revealing the relationships of the twinned inner and outer worlds of writer, reader, fictive characters. Rukeyser, for instance, often a poet-biographer, offers portraits of lives which become "an image reaching backward and forward in history, illuminating all time" (LP, p. 34), lives that "in their search and purpose, offer their form, offer their truths . . . reach us as hope" (LC, p. 34), collapsing distinctions of self and non-self, time and place. These are telling lives of men and women as disparate as the Jewish scholar "Akiba"—revealed in "Music of those who have walked out of slavery. . . . / The song of the way in" (CP, pp. 474–75)—or the artist Kathe Kollwitz, of whom the poet has written "my lifetime / listens to yours" (CP, p. 479). But most often for Rukeyser and Levertov the manner of narration as much as its subject reveals the intricate choreography of the dance of objective and subjective perceptions, directing the reader not just to what is seen, but isolating for thought and feeling the relation between things observed and the observer.

No poem of Rukeyser's, I believe, can tell us more than "The Gates." The end piece of Rukeyser's final book, it is conclusive and convincing, seeming both in its themes and in their presentation to sum a lifetime's writing. Beginning with a prose statement ironically entitled "Scaffolding" which indicates that the poem has a framework in facts—"An American woman is sent to make an appeal for [the South Korean poet Kim Chi Ha's] life" (CP, p. 564)—and suggests simultaneously the imminence of Kim's execution for having "written his stinging work" (*CP*, p. 564), the poem promises to be a clear narrative of Rukeyser's 1975 journey to Seoul as president of American P.E.N. But before even two of the poem's fifteen sections are complete, definite outlines of the event have been blurred to include moments of memory and meditation that confuse our sense of place; and narrative point of view slips in and out of focus, one time seeming to represent the poet Muriel Rukeyser, another the poet Kim Chi Ha, and yet another "we," the half perceiving, half creating reader. Amidst the deliberate ambiguities we are not allowed to lose sight of Muriel Rukeyser's centrality or the horrifying predicament of the Korean poet, but the work modulates toward being a tale about seeing as well as an account of things seen.

The poem's first line—"Waiting to leave all day I hear the words"— provides the sort of sharply declarative opening which we can expect to be followed by lines that tell us more about who is waiting, and where, and what words are being heard. And though that information has been in part re- vealed by the prose note (Muriel Rukeyser waits "in the mud and rain at the prison gates . . . before the house of the poet. He is in solitary" [*CP*, pp. 564–65]), and the lines that come do seem to offer concrete information ("That poet in prison"; "I and my son"; "The new friend comes into my hotel room"), what immediately follows is, by and large, an exercise in studied ambiguity. Rukeyser envelops her tale in a rhythm of perception that alter- nately expands beyond any particular moment to include far-ranging territo- ries of thought and emotion, and contracts to a precise event recreated with physical and emotional immediacy. The poet Kim Chi Ha, who we know to be living, whose words we can read, becomes mysteriously for a moment "that poet newly-died / whose words we wear" as Rukeyser conjures not one man suffering for his power of perception, but any true poet's legacy of language that lives beyond a moment, passed on through generations, "link- [ing] us in our variousness" (*CP*, p. 565). Paradoxically locked up by being locked out of the poet's prison, compelled to wait for word of the poet for the poet's words, we can still, in memory and in anticipation, be "Walking the world to find the poet of these cries. . . . flying the streets of all the air" (*CP*, p. 565) as physical places give way to interior spaces before the tale brings us back to the land of bugged hotel rooms and restricted speech ("Turn on the music so we can talk" [*CP*, p. 566]).

Mixing and merging poetry of direct statement and poetry of evocation, the narrative, by turns deeply personal and broadly general, slowly finds its way. The poem now centers on Rukeyser's intense moments of confronta- tion, now collapses as if under pressure into both individualized and general- ized glimpses of associated experiences of repression, solitude, and suicide, or of sexual love, childbirth and mothering—experiences reconstructed anec- dotally: "then Mary said, / . . . / 'Never mind, Muriel. / Life will come . . . / knocking and coughing and farting at your door' " (*CP*, p. 570); or as myths involving such elemental figures as "grief woman" and "vigil women" (*CP*, pp. 568–69); or as dreams of "massacres, the butchered that across the fields of the world / lie screaming" (*CP*, p. 569); or as metaphysical nightmares of children "crucified," "spiked on time" (*CP*, p. 571). The verses, pushing back the boundaries of the physical, making palpable the fears, questions, hesitations, and hopes stirred by the drama of imprisonment, teach us with their multiplicity of narrative modes and direct and indirect perceptions, that one man's incarceration, one woman's story, however vivid, are not one individual's experience alone.

"Among the days / among the nights of the poet in solitary," our narrator informs us, "a strong infant is just beginning to run" (*CP*, p. 566). The last crucial questions of this poem filled with questioning are for that infant—Kim's son, Rukeyser's, the reader's: "How shall we tell each other of the poet? / . . . / How shall we speak to the infant beginning to run? / All those beginning to run?" (*CP*, p. 573). There are no simple answers, but if we have accepted Rukeyser as our guide, we will have begun to find a voice that records things as they are but is not detached, that affirms the self but is not self-enclosed, that records variety of relationships in an effort to "Seize structure. / Correspond with the real. / Fuse spirit and matter / . . . / Announc-[ing] [its] soul in discovery" ("The Six Canons," *CP*, p. 439).

If Muriel Rukeyser's poems mix modes of narration, points of view, perceptual boundaries, to explore human community, Denise Levertov's are even more emphatically exploratory. Interested in revealing "the *process* of thinking/feeling, feeling/thinking, rather than focusing more exclusively on its *results*" (*LC*, p. 62), Levertov finds that her "crucial precision tool for creating this . . . mode is the linebreak" (*LC*, p. 62) which can rhythmically record brief pauses among perceptions:

> Regular punctuation is a part of regular sentence structure, that is, of the expression of completed thoughts. . . . But in poems one has the opportunity . . . to make manifest, by an intrinsic structural means, the interplay or counterpoint of process and completion—in other words to present the dynamics of perception *along with* its arrival at full expression. The linebreak is a form of punctuation *additional* to the punctuation that forms part of the logic of completed thoughts. . . . To incorporate these pauses in the rhythmic structure of the poem . . . allows the reader to share more intimately the experience that is being articulated; and by introducing an alogical counter-rhythm into the logical rhythm of syntax it causes, as they interact . . . the dance of alogical thinking/feeling in process. (*LC*, pp. 62–63)

Even when she is at her most objective, scene setting or simply reporting an event, the technical grammar of Levertov's tale-telling marks for us the perceiver's presence as well as the things described. For the mind "as it feels its way through a thought or an impression often stops with one foot in the air, its antennae waving, and its nose waffling" (*LC*, p. 72).

Mixing long narrative lines with imagistic fragments that clarify intense experiences ("A Tree Telling of Orpheus," "An Interim," "A Daughter [I] [II]," "Mass for the Day of St. Thomas Didymus"), Levertov works logical syntax against the pauses of perception that determine line ends. And the resulting complexities of comprehension transform detached observation into active participation in the selecting and seeing process.

"A Solitude," the beautifully made and felt poem about blindness and sight published in *The Jacob's Ladder* (1961), and the wrenching mother-daughter remembrances, "A Daughter (I)," and "A Daughter (II)," published seventeen years later in *Life in the Forest*, form a revealing outline around the development of Levertov's use of line break to capture varieties of perceptual discoveries.

The brief narrative of "A Solitude" describing the poet's encounter with a blind man on the subway is neither about absence of vision nor "solitude." Rather it concerns that aspect of human relationship which Rilke once explained as "the mutual bordering and guarding of . . . solitudes" (*LC*, p. 286). As Levertov came to see, "solitude, and the individual development for which it is a condition," provide "the only valid ground on which communion of the many, the plural Other of brother-and-sisterhood, can take place" (*LC*, p. 286).

Syntax is strained throughout the poem and is delayed by line endings, rest stops that momentarily isolate units of thought, feeling, or perception for our contemplation before combining into larger units of observation. Discrete impressions are never lost in a final gestalt. As Levertov seems to suggest both with her subject and her technique of presentation, any idea of wholeness must take into account the variety and complexity of the relationships of individual parts.

The poem begins not with a simple sentence that establishes coherent structure, but with a series of fragments unraveling structure, revealing its various lines of interconnection:

> A blind man, I can stare at him
> ashamed, shameless. Or does he know it?
> No, he is in a great solitude. (*JL*, p. 68)

By refusing to allow regular syntax to determine definitive meaning among several options, Levertov offers us a glimpse of the nature of meaning itself—something to be assembled and reassembled by participants and observers alike, establishing relationship amidst the discrete juxtapositions that experience provides. The seemingly simple lines, then, demanding that the reader take an active role in making meaning, leave a variety of impressions: an ashamed speaker (nervously impolite but compelled by inner need or curiosity) stares at a blind man; a shameless speaker (protected by indifference, or by the other's failure to know) stares at a blind man; a speaker's stare, somehow unsettlingly disconnected from the rest of the speaker's self, is ashamed and/or shameless. The first line ending "him" without any punctuation, and the second beginning "ashamed, shameless," even gives us a moment's pause to consider that the shame or lack of it is the blind man's, not the speaker's. Of course even as the reader recognizes a multiplicity of meanings, he or she is discovering that some possibilities are strained, others more explicit. Surely the opening is meant to reveal its speaker's state of mind when confronted by a situation ("a great solitude") which, promising to make few demands of self or relationship, makes many. Still the ambiguities have shown the encounter on the subway to be a complicated experience for both narrator and reader.

A poem of process as well as pattern from the first, "A Solitude" continues to present and explore perceptual possibilities. Following an irregular path to meaning by moving forward and backward from ambiguous and dislocating key words and linebreaks, Levertov reveals a situation filled with surprising correspondences and contraries. As the blind man "trembles" with self-absorbed motion, the train lurches into movement, "moves uptown, pulls in and / pulls out of the local stops. Within its loud / jarring movement a quiet" (*JL*, p. 68),

> the quiet of people not speaking
> some of them eyeing the blind man,
> only a moment though, not thirsty like me,
>
> and within that quiet his
> different quiet, not quiet at all, a tumult
> of images, but what are his images,
>
> he is blind? He doesn't care
> that he looks strange. . . . (*JL*, p. 68)

This is a fluid world where inscapes and exteriors now reflect, now contrast one another, where facts suddenly and surprisingly lose their assurance ("he is blind?") and statements are juxtaposed or broken in such a way as to render disparate meanings almost simultaneously ("he is blind? He doesn't care"; "He doesn't care that he looks strange"). Here where interrupted definitions of self and non-self are unavoidable and unpredictable, we must take nothing for granted as we discover the many meanings of the expression, "I am":

> "A nice day,
> isn't it?" says the blind man. Solitude
> walks with me, walks
>
> beside me, he is not with me, he continues
> his thoughts alone. But his hands and mine
> know one another,
>
> it's as if my hand were gone forth,
> on its own journey. . . .
> and now he says he can find his way. He knows
> where he is going, it is nowhere, it is filled
> with presences. He says, *I am.*

"Facing and communicating," Muriel Rukeyser once wrote, "that will be our life, in the world and in poetry" (*LP*, p. 40). If Denise Levertov presents the knowledge of communication quietly in "A Solitude," she represents similar knowing more urgently in "A Daughter (I)" and "A Daughter (II)," intense and poignant, deeply personal evocations of her mother's death. The message and technique of discovery is largely unchanged. Levertov once again explores the process by which self and non-self meet in mutual opposition and definition, each becoming other:

> Now mother is child, helpless; . . .
>
> . . . .
>   at the mercy
> of looming figures who have the power
> to move her, feed her, wash her, leave or stay
> at will. And the daughter feels, with horror,
> metamorphosed: *she's* such a looming figure—huge—a
>   tower
> of iron and ice. . . . (*LF*, p. 27)

But now syntactic disruptions are more profound, the pressures of mid-line and end-line rhythmic pauses more severe. The reader, forced by the tensions in the lines to read actively so as to shape the fragments into more complete logical perceptions, cannot help but feel immediately in the choppy rhythm, as well as apprehend intellectually, that relationship, expressed in a variety of combinations of part to part and parts to whole, defines the people we are and the world we inhabit:

>   A day later begins
> the witnessing. A last week of the dying.
> When she inserts
>   quivering spoonfuls of violently
> green or red *gelatina*
>   into the poor obedient mouth,
> she knows it's futile.
> . . . .
> Each dawn the daughter, shivering,
> opens the curtained door
> and steps out on the balcony; and from time to time
> leans there during the days. Mornings,
> emphatic sunlight seizes the bougainvillea's
> dry magenta blossoms. Among sharp stones, below,
> of the hospital patio,
>   an ugly litter of cigarette stubs
> thrown down by visitors leaning, anxious or bored,
> from other balconies. No one sweeps up.
> Sobs shake her—no tears. (*LF*, p. 29)

"In the best poetry of your time," Stanley Kunitz wrote more than twenty years ago, one is aware of a moral pressure being exerted on the medium in the very act of creation. By "moral" I mean a testing of existence. . . . What does it feel like to be totally one's self?; an awareness of others beyond the self; concern with values and meanings rather than with effects . . . a conviction about the possibility of making right and wrong choices.[12]

Without this pressure "we are left with nothing but a vacuum occupied by a technique,"[13] or, perhaps worse, by a voracious ego "starved of the experience of community" (*LC*, p. 83). But amidst the formalists, the confessors, the discoursers of our day, Denise Levertov and Muriel Rukeyser have always stood fast and stood out. Responsive to demands of technique, of feeling, of individual expression and community concern, like all "true artists" they have been *"abundant, multiple, restless . . . capable, practicing, skillful"* ("The Artist," *WE*, p. 4), creating with delight for our pleasure, crafting with sagacity to help us know better ourselves and our worlds.

Notes

1. David Reisman, *Individualism Reconsidered* (Garden City, N.Y.: Doubleday Anchor, 1954), 27.

2. See Harry Marten and Wayne Fields, "The Wilderness Dream," *Mississippi Valley Review* 3 (1974), esp. 45–48, for a discussion of self and the wilderness on which I draw here.

3. Quentin Anderson, *The Imperial Self: An Essay in American Literary and Cultural History* (New York: Alfred A. Knopf, 1971), 3; cited in text as *IS*.

4. Quoted in Allen Guttmann, "The Conversions of the Jews" in *Contemporary American-Jewish Literature*, ed. Irving Malin (Bloomington: Indiana University Press, 1973), 55.

5. Muriel Rukeyser, *The Life of Poetry* (New York: A. A. Wyn, 1949), 15; hereafter cited in text as *LP*. All references to Rukeyser's poems are from *The Collected Poems of Muriel Rukeyser* (New York: McGraw-Hill, 1978); cited in text as *CP*.

6. Philip Slater, *The Pursuit of Loneliness: American Culture at the Breaking Point*, rev. ed. (Boston: Beacon Press, 1976), 14.

7. Conrad Aiken, *Collected Criticism* (Oxford: Oxford University Press, 1968), 101.

8. Louis Simpson, *A Revolution in Taste* (New York: Macmillan, 1978), 169.

9. Robert Pinsky, *The Situation of Poetry* (Princeton: Princeton University Press, 1976), 134. For further discussions of recent discursive poetry, see Stanley Plumly, "Chapter and Verse," *American Poetry Review* 7, no. 1 (1978), 24, and Charles Altieri, "From Experience to Discourse: American Poetry and Poetics in the Seventies," *Contemporary Literature* 21 (1980), 192–93.

10. Altieri, 193.

11. Denise Levertov, *Light Up the Cave* (New York: New Directions, 1981), 194; hereafter cited in the text as *LC*. Other works by Levertov will be cited with the following abbreviations: *Life in the Forest* (1978): *LF; The Poet in the World* (1973): *PW; The Jacob's Ladder* (1961): *JL; With Eyes at the Back of Our Heads* (1960): *WE*. All are published by New Directions.

12. Stanley Kunitz, *A Kind of Order, A Kind of Folly: Essays and Conversations* (Boston: Little, Brown, 1975), 17.

13. Kunitz, 17.

Edge of the Transcendent: The Poetry of Levertov and Duncan

Rudolph L. Nelson*

Sometimes, after staying in a village parlor till the family had all retired, I have returned to the woods, and, partly with a view to the next day's dinner, spent the hours of midnight fishing from a boat by moonlight, serenaded by owls and foxes, and hearing, from time to time, the creaking note of some unknown bird close at hand. These experiences were very memorable and valuable to me, anchored in forty feet of water, and twenty or thirty rods from the shore, surrounded sometimes by thousands of small perch and shiners, dimpling the surface with their tails in the moonlight, and communicating by a long flaxen line with mysterious nocturnal fishes which had their dwelling forty feet below, or sometimes dragging sixty feet of line about the pond as I drifted in the gentle night breeze, now and then feeling a slight vibration along it, indicative of some life prowling about its extremity, of dull uncertain blundering purpose there, and slow to make up its mind. At length you slowly raise, pulling hand over hand, some horned pout squeaking and squirming to the upper air. It was very queer, especially in dark nights, when your thoughts had wandered to vast and cosmogonal themes in other spheres, to feel this faint jerk, which came to interrupt your dreams and link you to Nature again. It seemed as if I might next cast my line upward into the air, as well as downward into this element, which was scarcely more dense. Thus I caught two fishes as it were with one hook.

—Thoreau, *Walden*

Denise Levertov and Robert Duncan are invariably classed together as members of "the Olson group," poets influenced by the projective verse theories of Charles Olson. M. L. Rosenthal sees this group producing "a serious body of non-traditional verse" and foreshadowing "the more dynamic directions of the future." Stephen Stepanchev adds that the Olson poets share also in common a poetry rooted in American experience and reflecting the American idiom. Duncan himself says that since 1951 his work has been classed in his own mind with "a larger work" that appeared in the writings of Olson, Levertov, and Creeley. Although Linda Wagner, in her recent book, *Denise Levertov* (1967), maintains that "the Olson group" is tied together only very loosely by personal association and certain theoretical beliefs held in common, it seems clear that Levertov and Duncan are more closely related to each other, both personally and professionally, than are the members of the group as a whole. The fact of their personal friendship is essentially irrelevant to a comparison of their poetry, but the similarity of their views and their estimate of each other's poetry are not.

Duncan, although only four years older than Levertov, had been producing his mature poetry for many years before Levertov, in 1957, published her first book of American poems (her first book, *The Double Image*, had been

*Reprinted with permission from *Southwest Review* 54, no. 2 (1969), 188–202.

published in England in 1946); so it is not surprising that Duncan does not claim Levertov as one of the poets who has helped shape his own style. He does credit one of her poems, "The Shifting," with first releasing his "sense of a new generation in poetry" in 1952. He has expressed great admiration for her work. In a prefatory note to her *Overland to the Islands* (1958), he says that her poems bring him again and again

> to the most intense thing, to that crossing of the inner and the outer reality, where we have our wholeness of feeling in the universe. She catches it as only the craftsman devoted to the language can catch it that has her genius there so that the thrill of adrenaline comes at the nape of the neck. . . . In the dance of word and phrase to express feeling, in the interior music of vowels, in subtlety of changing tempo within the form, in the whole supple control in freedom, she excels.

Levertov has not only been lavish in her praise of Duncan's poetry, but has also cited him as one of the major forces in the evolution of her own poetic style. As Linda Wagner puts it, "of all poets contemporary with her, she most respects Duncan." In a biographical note in Donald M. Allen's anthology, *The New American Poetry* (1960), she mentions "conversations and correspondence with Robert Duncan" as one of the major influences on her. In the essay "Some Notes on Organic Form," which appeared in *Poetry* (September 1965), she indicates one specific thing she learned from Duncan; namely, that one must leave "rifts" in the poem, "gaps between perception and perception which must be leapt across if they are to be crossed at all." In a poetry seminar at Brown University in November 1967, she included Duncan with Yeats, Wallace Stevens, and William Carlos Williams as four poets whose work she goes back to constantly for creative inspiration.

But with all the identical classifications, the common poetic convictions, the personal relationships, the mutual esteem, one comes away from the poetry of Levertov and Duncan with the distinct impression that their differences are more crucial than their similarities. Both comparisons and contrasts can be clarified by looking at their poetry as organic in form, as religious in content, and as resident in that borderland between the temporal and the eternal, the common and the mysterious—poetry at the threshold between the mundane known and the transcendent knowable.

The metaphor of the threshold or border or boundary dividing realms of experience is common in the writings of both poets. In fact, one could call it a dominating metaphor of their poetic imaginations. Duncan gives the figure its most explicit statement when he refers to the locus of the poet's attention at "the threshold that is called both *here-and-now* and *eternity*," where "identity is shared in resonance between the person and the cosmos." Less explicit but more evocative are references from his poems. In "The Song of the Borderguard," it is the poet who stands guard at "the beautiful boundaries of the empire"—"the borderlines of sense." In "The Structure of Rime

VII," the poet is told: "The streams of the Earth seek passage through you, tree that you are, toward a foliage that breaks at the boundaries of known things."

Perspective changes at the threshold of the transcendent; in paying homage to "the old poets" Duncan says: "In time we see a tragedy, a loss of beauty / the glittering youth / of the god retains—but from this threshold / it is age / that is beautiful." One can sometimes hear a "god-step at the margins of thought." "Flickers of unlikely heat / at the edge of our belief bud forth." The poet is referred to as an Outrider who comes "to the threshold of the stars, to the door beyond which moves celestial terror." "Often I am permitted to return to a meadow," the poet says, "as if it were a given property of the mind / that certain bounds hold against chaos." There are those who wish to cut off access to the fields of poetic vision: "In the caves of blue within the blue the grandmothers bound, on the brink of freedom, to close the too many doors from which the rain falls."

Finally, in his play on theosophical themes, "Adam's Way," Duncan dramatizes the encounter of the pure and innocent Adam and Eve with the temptation of Samael. He tells them: "God has removed you from your own ground / into a silly magic of Eternity—it's but a word—in which you are nothing and you rejoice." Adam and Eve give up their natural and holy love for the selfish love which Samael shows to them, a life which he admits is not the Tree of Life but instead what he calls "the Tree of the Other Side, of what is more." Samael kisses Eve, "awakening in her the grievous knowledge of the denial of love in which he dwells." Duncan implicitly acknowledges, as we all must, that he has partaken of the fruit of the Tree of the Other Side, that he does not dwell in the eternity of perfect love and innocence. But in his poetry he is trying always to break through into the transcendent realm.

In Levertov's work too we confront the image of the threshold or boundary. In his headnote to *Overland to the Islands,* Duncan placed Levertov's work in a sort of borderland: "that crossing of the inner and the outer reality, where we have our wholeness of feeling in the universe." That borderland becomes more readily identifiable as the same territory Duncan is exploring when we look at some of the relevant images in Levertov's poems. In the poem entitled "Threshold," a particular visual impression of form from the natural world excites the mind and raises the question of how that form can be captured in the pulsebeat of poetry. When she asks what stone hands turn "to uncover / feather of broken / oracle—" we become aware that the threshold leads to some sort of transcendental insight, a state which she labels "wonder." Much the same thought is expressed in "The Illustration," in which she speaks of learning "to affirm / Truth's light at strange turns of the mind's road, / wrong turns that lead / over the border into wonder." Another poem from *The Jacob's Ladder* refers to the gist of an insight "not quite caught, but filtered / through some outpost of dreaming sense." In an earlier poem, this borderland, identified as "the edge," is the source of the poem as true revelation, although it may not be the poem the poet expected to find there. And of course the Jacob's ladder image is borrowed from the Hasidic literature, where it represents a means of access between earth and heaven, the human and the divine. Even the colors on a brick wall, when properly perceived, can provide an entrance to the world of wonder: "archetype / of the world always a step / beyond the world, that can't / be looked for, only / as the eye wanders, / found." In the closest thing to a detailed statement of her poetics, "Some Notes on Organic Form," Levertov has referred to poetry as containing rifts, gaps between perceptions, which often span different realms of experience and understanding.

> The X factor, the magic, is when we come upon those rifts and make those leaps. A religious devotion to the truth, to the splendor of the authentic, involves the writer in a process rewarding in itself; but when that devotion brings us to undreamed abysses and we find ourselves sailing slowly over them and landing on the other side—that's ecstasy.

This is one thing, then, that Denise Levertov and Robert Duncan have in common. For both of them, poetry is a dynamic means of exploration beyond what we already know into a realm of wonder or eternity which at this point we shall call transcendent. Whether Levertov's concept of the transcendent is the same as Duncan's is a key question. Clues to the answer may be found in the theories of organic form espoused by the two poets and practiced in their art.

The common denominator in all theories of organic form in poetry is the conviction that the form of a poem must emerge from the subject matter itself rather than from arbitrary predetermined structures and styles. Emerson's "ask the fact for the form" is usually cited as an authoritative precedent. With many contemporary poets, organic form simply means the freedom to be experimental in technique; it has no implications beyond style. With Duncan and Levertov, organic form goes much deeper; it has implications which can be called broadly theological. According to Levertov, organic form is "a method of apperception, i.e., of recognizing what we perceive, and is based on an intuition of an order, a form beyond forms, in which forms partake, and of which man's creative works are analogies, resemblances, natural allegories."

So far, this seems more philosophical, in a Platonic sense, than theological. But how is the poet to go about his task? A poem is demanded of him by the experience of a moment in life. To fulfil the demand, he contemplates, which means, says Levertov, "not simply to observe, to regard, but to do these things in the presence of a god." It demands an act of religious dedication to be able to see beneath the external characteristics and discern the form at the heart of creation. In "The Novices" a man and a boy go deep into the woods, "knowing some rite is to be performed." When they have shown their willingness to give themselves to nature in this way (much as Ike McCaslin did in Faulkner's *The Bear*), the gentle but awesome spirit of the forest appears and reveals his will—the rite was merely to enter the forest; now they are to look around them and see nature in a new way, "intricate branch and bark, / stars of moss and the old scars of dead men's saws." As the spirit recedes among the forms, "the twists and shadows they saw now, listening / to the hum of the world's wood."

Duncan contributed to Howard Nemerov's book *Poets on Poetry* (1966) an essay entitled "Toward an Open Universe" in which is perhaps his clearest statement on organic form. The poet seeks to discover the divine order in things, "to penetrate to that most real where there is no form that is not content, no content that is not form." It is form which stirs the poet. Finding proper form for his poetic vision is certainly not a matter of adhering to established traditions; it hardly seems even to be consciously chosen. The poet follows his consciousness of "orders in the play of form and meanings toward poetic form." "We have only to listen and to cooperate with the music we hear." There is clearly a supernatural factor in this process. "There is not only the immanence of God, His indwelling, but there is also the imminence of God, His impending occurrence."

As one of Duncan's primary poetic subjects is poetry itself, one is not surprised to see the same convictions appear in his poems. In one of a series called "The Structure of Rime," he voices this apostrophe: "O Lasting Sentence, sentence after sentence I make in your image. In the feet that measure the dance of my pages I hear cosmic intoxications of the man I will be." In "Four Pictures of the Real Universe," he concludes: "Were it not for the orders of music hidden / we should be claimed by the preponderant void." In another poem from *The Opening of the Field* he says: "Poems come up from a ground so / to illustrate the ground, approximate / a lingering of eternal image, a need / known only in its being found ready."

While it would be unwarranted to use these statements on organic form as evidence that either Duncan or Levertov is supporting classical arguments for the existence of God on teleological grounds, it is undeniably clear that both of them conceive of an orderly and purposeful universe. It is clear as well that neither is a philosophical naturalist; neither shies away from the dimension of mystery and wonder in existence.

Beyond this significant similarity, however, the criterion of organic form reveals also a key difference between these two poets. Robert Duncan has used the freedom of organic form to write poetry that is considerably more experimental and esoteric than the poetry of Denise Levertov. I am not at this point making a value judgment on complexity and simplicity. Nor do I mean to imply that free form is the only poetic medium in which one can be obscure. But the notion of organic form is naturally more hospitable to the esoteric. Much of Duncan's poetry is not accessible to even the educated reader without considerable effort. Some critics and fellow poets as well have judged his work to be discouragingly dense. Perhaps the most severe attack has come from D. R. Slavitt in a review of *Roots and Branches* which appeared in *Book Week* (14 March 1965):

> He writes a toned-down imitation of Ezra Pound, full of private allusions to his chums and their books, undigested clots of autobiography, puerile incantations, improbable allusions, and insufferable arrogance in its privacy. What is not obscure is slovenly, and does not give much incentive to go back and puzzle out the rest.

Perhaps these comments reveal more about the reviewer than about Duncan's poetry. But Louis Simpson, writing in the *Hudson Review* (Autumn 1961) and finding in Duncan an "extraordinarily lyrical talent," criticizes him for the fragments of in-group talk and theory that litter his poems "as though their lodgment in his mind were enough to make them poetic." Of *Roots and Branches* James Dickey said in the *American Scholar* (Autumn 1965): "One brings away from it only a sense of complicated inconsequence, of dilettantism and serene self-deception, of pretentiousness, of a writer perhaps natively gifted who has sold himself the wrong bill of goods." X. J. Kennedy, while generally very favorably inclined, feels the need of advising the reader of his *New York Times* review to use a bit of "blind faith" which will enable him to surmount a few private allusions, mysterious gaps in syntax, and quirky spellings. It need hardly be said, of course, that some critics have lavished praise on Duncan and acknowledged no problem on the grounds of obscurity. Perhaps the most favorable responses have come from Hayden Carruth and Kenneth Rexroth, both writing in *The Nation*.

Duncan himself, however, seems to be conscious of a distance between himself and his readers. In a biographical note in *The New American Poetry*, he explains exactly how the poet Helen Adam has been an influence on him. Admitting her genius, he was able to

> shake off at last the modern proprieties—originality, style, currency of language, sensibility and integrity. I have a great appetite for approval from whatever source, and only the example of this poet who cares nothing for opinions but all for the life of the imagination, for the marvellous that is the grain of living poetry, saves me at times.

In short, being true to one's own vision of poetic form may alienate a poet from his audience. In "Pages from a Notebook," after commenting that since Freud "we are aware that unwittingly we achieve our form," Duncan refers to readers of poetry as "our hunters." Then he changes the image and refers to the poem as "an occult document, a body awaiting vivisection, analysis, X-rays." And yet, his is not a reader-be-damned attitude.

> Yes, though I contrive the mind's measure
> and wrest doctrine from old lore,
> it's to win particular hearts,
> to stir an abiding affection for this music,
> as if a host of readers will join the Beloved
>
> ready to dance with me, it's for the
>   unthinking
> ready thing I'm writing these poems.

Duncan wants sympathetic readers, but he demands that they come on his own terms.

It is not, then, that he is turning the liberty of open form into license for deliberately perverse obscurity. It is rather that Duncan conceives of poetry (as have many before him) as an attempt somehow to say the unsayable. If one is feeling a bit testy, he might say with James Dickey: "As he keeps telling us, he is a mystic, which of course allows him to say anything in any order." If one is feeling more charitable, he might say instead that Duncan's poetry "makes sense" when it is seen as the serious attempt of a mystical personality to capture in words the emotional subjectivity of an ineffable experience. When one crosses the threshold into the transcendental, one is faced inevitably with the problem of communication. As Duncan sees it, there is an obscurity in the nature of things.

> There is a wholeness of what we are that we will never know; we are always, as the line or the phrase or the word is, the moment of that wholeness—an event; but it, the wholeness of what we are, goes back into an obscurity and extends to and into an obscurity. The obscurity is part too of the work, of the form, if it be whole.

But I do not think we should let Duncan off the hook quite this easily. It seems to me that there is a seriously limiting factor in his theory and his poetry which stands out in bolder relief when the contrast with Levertov is pursued. Duncan seems to create a radical discontinuity between the world of poetic vision and the world of everyday reality—what Wallace Stevens called the quotidian. As Duncan put it in his statement on poetics for the Allen anthology:

> A child can be an artist, he can be a poet. But can a child be a banker? It is in such an affair as running a bank or managing a store or directing a war that adulthood counts, an experienced mind. It is in the world of these pursuits that "experience" counts. One, two, three, times and divided by. The secret of genius lies in this: that here experience is not made to count. Where experience knows nothing of counting, it creates only itself out of itself.

In terms of the dominating metaphor of the threshold, Duncan has created a clear dichotomy in the universal dwelling-place—between genius and experience, the one and the many, eternity and the here and now. It is at this point that a significant difference appears between the poetry of Duncan and Levertov.

Earlier I said that I was making no value judgment on simplicity and complexity. But now such a judgment must be made. We may grant that the world contains people who tend to simplify complex problems and people who counteract oversimplification by revealing the complexity of life—and that we need both kinds. We may grant that the history of human thought seems to be a pendulum swing between these tendencies. We may grant Thoreau's point in *Walden* (however overstated) that "it is a ridiculous demand which England and America make, that you shall speak so that they can understand you. Neither men nor toadstools grow so." And we may grant that Robert Duncan's complex vision is essentially mystical and ultimately ineffable. But when we contrast him with a poet whose poetic vision also crosses the threshold into transcendental wonder, who does not oversimplify the complexity of existence, but whose poetry, with all its profundity, must be classed for the most part as accessible to the under-standing of the common reader, then I think we have grounds for conclud-ing that Denise Levertov emerges as the superior poet. The key to that superiority is that in the Levertov universe there is no radical discontinuity between the worlds of poetic vision and everyday reality. In her vision the threshold between eternity and the here and now does not seem to be so well defined a boundary as it is in Duncan's. And while Duncan stresses the poet's transcendental vision almost exclusively, Levertov remains sol-idly anchored in the common life and enables the reader to see mystery within the here and now.

Ralph Mills, Jr., in a perceptive article in *Tri-Quarterly* (Winter 1962) on Levertov's work, says that "she plumbs the depths of the proximate." "The quotidian reality we ignore or try to escape Denise Levertov revels in, carves and hammers into tight, precise lyrics." In doing so, "what she no-ticed so shrewdly was that the ordinary is extraordinarily mysterious." There are evidences all through Levertov's poetry that justify Mills's generaliza-tion. The title of one of her books is *Here and Now*. The title poem of *O Taste and See* begins: "The world is / not with us enough." In a poem entitled "Seems Like We Must Be Somewhere Else," she says, "If we're here let's be here now." In "The Goddess," she does not experience the Muse's power until she is thrown out of Lie Castle and tastes on her lips the mud of the ground outside. She quotes approvingly as a headnote to the poem "Joy" some words of Thoreau: "You must love the crust of the earth on which you dwell. You must be able to extract nutriment out of a sandheap. You must have so good an appetite as this, else you will live in vain." She finds metaphors from nature that reinforce this truth. The earth worm, "by pas-sage / of himself / constructing," pays "homage to / earth, aerates / the ground of his living." As with the bee, "Bee-spittle, droppings, hairs / of beefur; all become honey," so in our lives the "honey of the human" emerges from the experiences of the common life. Borrowing a Joycean term, Robert Pack, writing in *Saturday Review* (8 December 1962), says that her best poems move "toward epiphanies, the intense rendering of a moment." He calls her poetry mystical and commends her for her freedom from the kind of self-consciousness that is prevalent in contemporary mysticism. The reason for this, he says, is that she begins not with dogma, but with perception. "Her sense of the invisible spirit of things is rooted in what she sees, and through precise description, through intimation and evocation, she leads the reader to the brink of mystery without trying to push him into the abyss."

Levertov, in her ability never to lose touch with the stuff of the common life even when her poetic vision leads her across the threshold into the realm of mystery, reminds one of Thoreau fishing at midnight on Walden Pond. Close to nature as he was, he found himself thinking transcendental thoughts. But then some horned pout would pull at his line. "It was very queer, especially in dark nights, when your thoughts had wandered to vast and cosmogonal themes in other spheres, to feel this faint jerk, which came to interrupt your dreams and link you to Nature again." Levertov keeps her own grip and ours firmly on the line. In searching out "the authentic," she even takes the poetic risk of making an observation "rising from the toilet seat." Even if she had not said this, we would have known intuitively that the poetic world of Denise Levertov contains toilet seats. We are not quite sure whether Robert Duncan's does or not. Levertov's Jacob's ladder from earth to heaven has solidly built steps with sharp angles that scrape the knees and console the groping feet. We are told to "taste and see" not only tangerines and weather, but "all that lives / to the imagination's tongue." And this includes the emotional experiences of life—grief, mercy—even our own deaths. It is Thoreau's "faint jerk" that is missing from Duncan's poetry. He loses hold of the line that stretches from the private world of his mystical vision to the here and now.

One could argue that Denise Levertov's concept of the transcendent is not the same as Robert Duncan's. It could be maintained that although both of them operate at the threshold, in Duncan's poetic world the other side is clearly a divine realm, whereas the other side of Levertov's world is merely the dimension of mystery within the human. It is quite true that Duncan uses "God-talk" freely and equally true that Levertov tends to avoid the language of traditional transcendence. On the few occasions when she does use it, it is clear that she is not making conventional metaphysical statements. For example, when she quotes the subway poster slogan, "O taste and see," she adds that it obviously is intended to mean the Lord. But then she gives her own interpretation: "meaning / if anything all that lives / to the imagination's tongue," the full range of our human experiences.

In other words, if theological statements are to have any meaning at all, they must be understood in anthropological terms. Mills seems to take this tack in dealing with her poetry. While he acknowledges, in a poem like "The Instant," the presence of "a spiritual revelation of a nearly ineffable sort," he contrasts Levertov's handling of such an illumination with the way the tradition of post-Symbolist literature (by this he means Eliot, Pound, Yeats, Auden) would objectify it "into the order of a larger metaphorical universe." In Levertov's poetry, the experience stands alone, is viewed in its own terms. Then Mills likens her form of illumination to that of Blake and Rilke, "though with them it gives foundation to a whole mythological scheme."

Mills is correct, I think, in finally differentiating the Levertov vision from the Blakean. It is a distinction similar, though not identical, to the one I have been attempting to draw between Levertov and Duncan. But in correctly stressing Levertov's poetry of the immediate, Mills has not sufficiently clarified the dimensions of her "spiritual revelation."

I believe we are dealing with two different kinds of genuine transcendence here. Theologically, transcendence is much less of a problem for Duncan. Though it is certainly true that he does not "believe" in any orthodox creedal sense (he writes that "if Christ, heaven or hell are real, in the sense that Christian belief demands, then we are all damnd"), he has no trouble whatsoever in the concept of the supernatural, making room in his world for fairies as well as Christs. He speaks in *Roots and Branches* of two returns of his mother's presence after her death. Levertov's calculated avoidance in her poetry of the language of traditional transcendence is evidence that she, much more than Duncan, is a product not only of the real world of immediate sights and sounds but of the equally real world of twentieth-century science, philosophy, and theology.

In her avoidance of "God-talk" which is less and less meaningful to the modern mind, while at the same time she steadfastly refuses to capitulate to a naturalistic view of the universe and probes into the wonder and mystery of existence, Denise Levertov has produced a body of poetry particularly congenial to the outlook of contemporary radical theology.

The recent popularizing of "death of God" theology obscures the fact that the traditional concept of a transcendent God has not been a viable option to many thoughtful people for a hundred years or more. The Altizers, Hamiltons, and Van Burens have simply called attention to the fact that such intellectual soul-searching has been going on within the province of theology itself. Without getting involved in any bizarre notions that a God who was once alive has somehow recently died, we can take seriously the redefinition of transcendence that has been going on as a result chiefly, though not exclusively, of the works of Paul Tillich and Dietrich Bonhoeffer. In *Honest to God,* John A. T. Robinson summarizes these insights:

> Statements about God are acknowledgements of the transcendent, unconditional element in all our relationships, and supremely in our relationships with other persons. Theological statements are indeed affirmations about human existence—but they are affirmations about the ultimate ground and depth of that existence.
>
> There are depths of revelation, intimations of eternity, judgements of the holy and the sacred, awarenesses of the unconditional, the numinous and the ecstatic, which cannot be explained in purely naturalistic categories without being reduced to something else. . . . The question of God is the question *whether this depth of being is a reality or an illusion,* not whether *a* Being exists beyond the bright blue sky, or anywhere else.

It is in this sense that Denise Levertov is a poet at the threshold of the transcendent. In the poem "Who Is at My Window?" a blind cuckoo sings a song of fear about the future. The poet responds: "I want to move deeper into today; / he keeps me from the work. / Today and eternity are nothing to him." Note that today and eternity are classed together, both being distinguished from the fear the bird directs toward the future. Clearly one reaches eternity by going deeper into today. Levertov often uses religious imagery to celebrate human life: a city "avenue's / endless nave echoes notes of / liturgical red." She sings a psalm praising the hair on man's body. When she gains insight into herself, the world stirs "with unheard litanies." Respect for the transcendent within the here and now involves not only the realization of the full dimensions of one's own humanity, a major theme in her poetry, but respect for the humanity of others. Her echoing of the biblical truth that "we are members one of another" takes on special impact, rising as it does from a consideration of the grotesque yet haunting figure of Adolf Eichmann on trial.

What then is the transcendent for Levertov? In "The Well" she stands on a bridge and in her mind's eye sees the Muse glide across the dark lake—"and I know / no interpretation of these mysteries." But her heart leaps in wonder as the doors of the world are opened to her. And like Thoreau, who saw the water of Walden Pond as connected underground with the sacred water of the Ganges, she looks into her river and realizes "that the humble / tributary of Roding is / one with Alpheus, the god who as a river / flowed through the salt sea to his love's well." This is as close as Levertov comes to defining the transcendent. God *is* mystery, the depths, wonder. That is all we know on earth and all we need to know. In "The Novices," the man and boy were enabled to see with new eyes when they enacted the rite of going deep into the woods. Our earlier discussion left out one important detail in the poem. Knowing that some rite was to be performed, before the spirit of the woods came to them, they found a chain running at an angle into the earth from an oaktree, "and they pit themselves to uproot it, / dogged and frightened, to pull the iron / out of the earth's heart." Then the wood-demon appeared and told them they need not perform any rite of obscure violence. They were not even to ask what the chain was. "Knowing there was mystery, they could go."

I began by referring to Levertov and Duncan as poets on the threshold of the transcendent. For Duncan the image can stand unchanged. It does not seem appropriate, however, to say that Levertov crosses the border into transcendence in a horizontal sense, as if she were leaving the country of immediate experience for some special mystical realm. Rather, one might say, borrowing the Tillichian notion of depth, that Denise Levertov probes beneath the threshold of the here and now and finds the transcendent within the stuff of immediate experience.

Poetic and Political Consciousness in Denise Levertov and Carolyn Forché
Joan Dargan*

> To sing of wars, of captains, and of kings,
> Of cities founded, commonwealths begun,
> For my mean pen are too superior things . . .[1]

Even as she declines to bring it into her song, Anne Bradstreet, our first poet, acknowledges the political dimension of American poetry; "When Lilacs Last in the Dooryard Bloom'd," Whitman's moving tribute to Lincoln, and more recently, Frost's "The Gift Outright," read at John F. Kennedy's inaugural, confirm the close traditional connection between poetry and politics in the United States. At least two of our presidents, Jefferson and Lincoln, have made enduring contributions to our literature. More typical of the years since World War II, however, is the troubled relationship between poets and the government, symbolized, for example, by Robert Lowell's refusal to accept Lyndon Johnson's invitation to the White House and Allen Ginsberg's well-publicized difficulties with the U.S. Customs. It is perhaps James Wright's famous "Autumn Begins in Martins Ferry, Ohio" that epitomizes the implicit violence and inwardness of the national mood as expressed in its policies and pastimes in recent years, a self-destructiveness reflected in our art as well (one thinks of Plath, Berryman, and Sexton), whether the poet is participant or onlooker:

> Therefore,
> Their sons grow suicidally beautiful
> At the beginning of October,
> And gallop terribly against each other's bodies.[2]

The season of decline, the futile energies, the expendable beauty, all aspects of our culture, have been indelibly captured here—along with the appropriate image of male-organized gamesmanship, mirror of the government and military. This national climate is necessarily affected by the global one; what has become a new and terrible burden for contemporary American poets in particular and for Western poets in general is the news brought by mass media of worldwide suffering, for some of which the United States bears direct responsibility. Living in the nuclear age—confronting each day the enforced compatibility of our lives with a technology and its potential, nearly unimaginable effects—has made poetry in some ways harder to write. Much of recent history imposes silence. Compelling, unforgettable images of reality comprise a forbidding knowledge to poets living in a privileged, isolated society largely intent on material gain. Knowing how illusory the economic wealth, how fragile the rights and privileges we enjoy, the poet may feel the

*Reprinted with permission from *CEA Critic* 48 (Spring 1986), 58–67.

need to compensate, atone, perhaps. Misfortune, too, is the result of arbitrary forces in their indifferent operation—and yet to simply accept this seems cold, inhuman, and ultimately unworthy of the poet and person in our time. This dilemma is reinforced by at least two of the possibilities of expression open to poets: (1) if one uses the images of a cheap, insensitive culture—even to grotesquely exaggerate them, condemn them—one nonetheless reproduces those images and perpetuates them; and (2) if one attempts to empathize with others or imagine possible catastrophes with the hope of alleviating or preventing suffering, one violates another's experience or sensationalizes one's own predicament and, without meaning to, provides a form of self-congratulation, evidence of one's sensitivity. In both possibilities, the potential to flatten or polemicize poetic language is great. And there is also the knowledge that the same media that bring the burden of increased awareness have trivialized the written word, poetry in particular. It is not that, for example, a poem could never equal a documentary image—an unfair equation—but rather that even the most heartfelt protest is unlikely to move policymakers. All of these forces combine to suppress the voice of social conscience, and fortunately for us they do not entirely succeed.

It is instructive to note by way of contrast how modern poets from oppressive, war-torn societies more easily integrate political statement into their art, thus—for our purposes—making the American poet's predicament more plain. Poets who have themselves lived through periods of violent social upheaval naturally address political events in the context of personal experience and their authority, the weight of their words, compels attention. No American poet, I think, could write the concentrated, luminous, unsettling works that are the Hungarian poet János Pilinszky's poems, with their hard insights into the nature of pain and selflessness, nor the unflinching acknowledgments of responsibility, at once deeply personal and declamatory, in the German poet Marie Luise Kaschnitz's poems. One's work, one's life can seem very trivial when set against such uncompromising poetry.

And yet, it is an East European poet, Czeslaw Milosz, who suggests how American poets might confront the historical moment without inferiority:

> The poetic act changes with the amount of background reality embraced by the poet's consciousness. In our century that background is, in my opinion, related to the fragility of those things we call civilization or culture. What surrounds us, here and now, is not guaranteed. It could just as well not exist—and so man constructs poetry out of the remnants found in ruins.[3]

This knowledge is shared, no nation's exclusive property; a poet of any country may honestly and fully incorporate consciousness of the arbitrary (and hence changeable) nature of civilization and its politics into his or her work as long as the fundamental commitment is to the expression of reality, the respect for truth expressible in words. A poet's first loyalty is to language—to his or her art—and it is the deepest sense of expressible reality in its conjunction with words in their finest music and texture that necessitates poems, brings them into being. Yet another poet personally familiar with some of this century's tragedies, the Russian poet Marina Tsvetaeva, concludes her magnificent essay "Art in the Light of Conscience" by saying, first of Mayakovsky and then of poets in general:

> He lived a human being and he died a poet.
>
> To be a human being is more important, because more needed. The doctor and the priest are more needed than the poet because they are at the deathbed, while we are not. Doctor and priest are humanly more important, all the rest are socially more important. (Whether the social is itself important is another question, which I shall have the right to answer only from an island.) Except for parasites, in all their various forms,—everyone is more important than we are.
>
> And knowing this, having put my signature to this while of sound mind and in full possession of my faculties, I assert, no less in possession of my faculties and sound mind, that I would not exchange my work for any other. Knowing the greater, I do the lesser, this is why there is no forgiveness for me. Only such as I will be held responsible at the Judgment Day of Conscience. But if there is a Judgment Day of the Word, at that I am innocent.[4]

Of course, Tsvetaeva wrote poems with political themes, yet her commitment to her art is total and unambiguous. In the recent American tradition, one can think of "At the Bomb-Testing Site" (1957) by William Stafford and "The Armadillo" (1965) by Elizabeth Bishop as examples of poems edged by a sharpened awareness of political and historical forces by poets whose work is largely reflective and personal in nature. If a poet's gift dictates a kind of poetry that is not dominated by political themes, that does not preclude an awareness of politics or the possibility of exercising social responsibility in other spheres. Other poets, however, more explicitly and consistently integrate this awareness and sense of responsibility into poetic language. Denise Levertov is among them:

> We are to ask, then, of the political poem (which in our time means relatively brief, and therefore, ostensibly lyric, poems that deal nevertheless with social observations and even opinions, such as the lyric used not typically to deal with) that it affect our senses and engage our aesthetic response just as much as one with whose content—spring, love, death, a rainbow—we can have no argument. . . .
>
> What those of us whose lives are permeated by a sense of unremitting political emergency, and who are at the same time writers of poetry, most desire in our work, I think, is to attain to such osmosis of the personal and the public, of assertion and song, that no one would be able to divide our poems into categories. That is, at any rate, my own probably unattainable goal. . . .[5]

In Levertov's work, and quite recently, in Carolyn Forché's, we see a very powerful acknowledgment of this aim, a lyrical coming-to-terms with this mandate; their work will serve here to exemplify some of the effects on technique in contemporary American poetry made by the urgent, and in their case, open, recognition of the political dimension.

Over the years, Levertov has created a political poetry, most recently in the section "Age of Terror" in *Candles in Babylon* (1982) and the section "Prisoners" in *Oblique Prayers* (1984).[6] It may be significant that she thus groups her poems expressing political protest and moral outrage, suggesting that they spring from a single impulse distinct from that inspiring poems on religion, nature, love, that they require such segregation (hence "my perhaps unattainable goal . . ."). Indeed, in "Age of Terror," it is the theme of schism, of the human alienation from self and nature, that underlies the section; the first poem, "The Split Mind," speaks of an imaginary governor signing a bill for development of a nuclear plant, oblivious to the potential danger to the granddaughter sitting near him:

> How deep, how deep
> does the split go, the fault line
> under the planned facility,
> into his mind? (73)

The theme of schism has its counterpart in the creative process, a visible split between what is imagined and what has been experienced, for in the same group of poems Levertov conspicuously creates characters and projects scenes rather than draw on personal day-to-day observations. This use of the imaginative faculty is, of course, poetic license, but in context it suggests that in her view it is no longer enough for poets to draw on their standard stock of images, to look within the self, the soul. In a revealing image from the poem "Desolate Light," she would draw back from a well, potential image of the collective soul, because it is dark, no longer useful, perhaps poisoned:

> we gaze, and see gleaming,
> deep in the black broth at the bottom,
> chains of hope by which our forebears
> hoisted themselves
> hand over hand towards light. (77)

For us, the black broth, uranium-contaminated, at best promises oblivion; we cannot go back to times of facile hope. We cannot delve into subterranean depths of self because these cannot show us how to survive. Thus she calls upon the imagination, that which would project us out of the self. This technique applies to her own imagined experience; the poem "Vron Woods" pictures a forest, names its trees, celebrates the poet's presence—"I was there wholly"—only to conclude: "These were the Vron Woods, / felled / seven years before I was born, / levelled / to feed a war" (75). In "Age of Terror," Levertov imagines the aftermath of a nuclear war, an unknowable "Afterwards" (98), in which, spiritually, she rejoins members of her family. And in the nearly hopeful "Re-Rooting," the poet describes the process of persistently re-anchoring trees to earth as the difficulty and indispensable task that is poetry, only to destroy the metaphor, reveal it as illusion: "And I wake, / as if from dream, but discover / even this digging, better than nothing, / has not yet begun" (102). Just as words are not themselves what they would have us picture, the imagination cannot save us, cannot re-route us—and it seems to me that in this poem, Levertov arrives at the conclusion that the technique of projecting the self into imaginary situations—the Vron Woods before her birth, the post-nuclear Afterwards, the eternally post-lapsarian garden, the mansion of the morally blinded governor—cannot heal the schism but only confirm it, itself a symptom of a reality too harsh, too horrible to confront in its totality. That Levertov does not write such poems in *Oblique Prayers* but rather refers to events that have happened, to works that exist, suggests that she has chosen to re-root her poetry in the present moment in its historical dimension.

Yet in both books Levertov calls into question more than the imaginative faculty when dealing with the theme of social injustice and violence and the lack of reverence for life; she asks, courageously, whether poetic language is any longer enough. In *Candles in Babylon*, she includes "A Speech: For Antidraft Rally, D.C., March 22, 1980" (92–96), presented on the page as a poem, yet with the note: "Written for an antidraft rally (which was attended by 35,000) this piece really *is* a speech, and not properly classifiable as a poem" (117). In *Oblique Prayers*, in a work called "Perhaps No Poem But All I Can Say and I Cannot Be Silent," she says, thinking of the massacre in Beirut: "My father—my mother— / I have longed for you. / Now I see / it is well you are dead, / dead and / gone from Time" (36), clearly eschewing the technique of projection used in "Age of Terror," where she imagines rejoining her parents after a nuclear war. "The Cry," also in *Oblique Prayers*, opens: "No pulsations / of passionate rhetoric / suffice / in this time / in this time / this time / we stammer in / stammering dread / or parched, utter / silence" (44). Can poetic language, with all its inherent power and richness—but also its tendency to draw attention to its own immediate resonances, its inherited resources—be the instrument of rectification, of human correction? Is the poet, having gained an audience, obligated to sacrifice, if necessary, art with its source in contemplation to efficacy, to social action?

Each poet has to find an utterly personal and authentic answer to that question. For Levertov, perhaps two tendencies in these books suggest a new response: (1) her use of the collective pronoun "we," in itself rare, which states conviction in solidarity, in identification with others, as an effort to heal that schism between private and public selves suggested in "The Split Mind"; and (2) her return to traditional religious imagery and language in poems such as "Mass for the Day of St. Thomas Didymus" where she asks:

> is it implied that *we*
> must protect this perversely weak
> animal, whose muzzle's nudgings
> suppose there is milk to be found in us?
> Must hold to our icy hearts
> a shivering God? (*Candles in Babylon*, 114)

This is not a reactionary movement—Levertov has always drawn on Judaeo-Christian imagery and Biblical language—but rather a redefinition of the self's relation to a reality it cannot understand, an unconditional affirmation of life in which the beseeching dog is mirror image of a God seeking warmth and sustenance from humankind. In the poem "The Task," significantly not in the section of *Oblique Prayers* reserved for nominally political poems, Levertov finds a synthesis in poetic language for conscience, artistry, and personal belief:

> God is absorbed in work, and hears
> the spacious hum of bees, not the din,
> and hears far-off
> our screams. Perhaps
> listens for prayers in that wild solitude.
> And hurries on with the weaving:
> till it's done, the great garment woven,
> our voices, clear under the familiar
>   blocked-out clamor of the task,
> can't stop their
>   terrible beseeching. God
> imagines it sifting through, at last, to music
> in the astounded quietness, the loom idle,
> the weaver at rest. (78)

The same questions of the schism between truth and falsehood, self and others; of the need, creatively, to reflect that profound alienation without compromising the self; and of the recognition of the limitation of poetic language mark also the work of the younger poet Carolyn Forché in her book *The Country Between Us,* the Lamont Poetry Selection in 1981.[7] Forché went to El Salvador in response to an invitation from friends of the poet Claribel Alegría, whose work she was translating; while reporting on civil rights abuses, she witnessed incidents of violence and oppression that are the basis for many of the poems in this, her second book, which Levertov herself praised as having "no seam between personal and political, lyrical and engaged" (back cover of paperback edition). Because Forché draws directly on personal experience as witness—the witness of an observer, as opposed to the witness of a protester—her way of meeting the same challenges to her poetry differs from Levertov's, as it must, providing another mode of expressing political awareness and responsibility.

Whereas Levertov presents, then, the dulling of human sensitivity in the person of a fictional governor, Forché, in "The Colonel," recalls a real colonel who, after dinner with the poet and a mutual acquaintance, returned to the table "with a sack used to bring groceries home. He spilled many human ears on the table. They were like dried peach halves. There is no other way to say this" (16). The dailiness, the domestication of horror—also Levertov's theme—and the oddness of poetic language as expressed by the simile throw into relief the surreality of the poetic process confronted with a reality far more terrible than anything it could invent, the appalling spectacle of ears deaf and made deaf to its music, more powerful than its truth. This prose poem was reproduced in the exhibit of photographs from El Salvador shown last year at the Everson Museum of Art in Syracuse, representing the *juxtaposition* of poetry to documented reality that appears to be Forché's way of defining her art, of presenting her witness (and perhaps a viable response to that problem photography and film impose on the writer who can respond only with words). Her poetry would not compete with that documentation, but complement it, act as a lens allowing readers to focus on something beyond itself. That attitude respectful of limits extends to languages; in "The Island," Alegría says: "Deya? A cluster of the teeth, / the bones of the world, greener / than Corsica. In English / you have no word for this. I can't / help you" (12). And of course the cultural differences between North America and Latin America are underlined, accepted, and explored:

> Although José Martí has said
> we have lived our lives in the heart
> of the beast, I have never heard
> it pounding. When I have seen
> an animal, I have never reached
> for a knife. It is like
> Americans to say it is only a bear
> looking for something to eat
> in the garbage.
> But we are not unalike. (10–11)

Forché draws attention to the reality and stubbornness of human, cultural, and historical differences, draws these into her poems, assimilates them, if only through the persistence of memory, an after-image—again, always to be compared to the event—in contradistinction to Levertov's use of projection to present situations otherwise too horrible, overwhelming, to contemplate. Where Levertov uses the imagination to get around realities that otherwise defeat and block logic and language, Forché relies on perception, expressed in a low-key, matter-of-fact style, to produce a similar effect of surprise and horror, to galvanize us with the recognition of the absurdity and cruelty, the arbitrary nature of political and social injustice. Memory can humanize, if allied with empathy, even as, without it, it exposes inhumanity—as in the poem "The Visitor":

> In Spanish he whispers there is no time left.
> It is the sound of scythes arcing in wheat,
> the ache of some field song in Salvador.
> The wind along the prison, cautious
> as Francisco's hands on the inside, touching
> the walls as he walks, it is his wife's breath
> slipping into his cell each night while he
> imagines his hand to be hers. It is a small country.
>
> There is nothing one man will not do to another. (15)

As the visitor—the prisoner's wife imagined, the imminent reaper Death, the poet briefly inside prison walls—this is how Forché sees her vocation: sometimes guest, sometimes inspector, always witness. Her poetry is the writing on the prison walls of North American isolation: a friend tells her:

> Your problem is not your life as it is
> in America, not that your hands, as you
> tell me, are tied to do something. It is
> that you were born to an island of greed
> and grace where you have this sense
> of yourself as apart from others. It is
> not your right to feel powerless. Better
> people than you were powerless.
> You have not returned to your country,
> but to a life you never left. ("Return," 20)

As the situation of the poem implies, conversation—communication—is possible, but it can never erase historical accident, unwanted truths, willful blindness, the deafening and deafness. Poetic language—Forché uses repetition as emphasis to dramatize its usefulness—must awaken us to the reality of the present moment, must speak to us, Forché's North American audience, in our situation, must show us that our reality, itself juxtaposed to that of the Salvadorans, is equally arbitrary, unreal, falsely safe:

> There is a cyclone fence between
> ourselves and the slaughter and behind it
> we hover in a calm protected world like
> netted fish, exactly like netted fish.
> It is either the beginning or the end
> of the world, and the choice is ourselves
> or nothing. ("Ourselves or Nothing," 59)

The poet chooses ourselves—plural, North American, speakers of English, hearers of her words. Poetry cannot change the world, cannot alter realities—but it can move hearts, waken individuals. Its tragedy and its privilege, its limits and its possibilities, are voiced in Alegría's question ending the poem "The Island": "Carolina, do you know how long it takes / any one voice to reach another?" (12)

Both Forché and Levertov, their voices grounded in moral outrage and personal involvement in the issues none of us can afford to ignore, unmask poetic rhetoric in favor of the realities they would witness, transcend artificial boundaries between poetry and prose or poetry and public address in creating speech responsive to political and social problems. Levertov's affirmation of life and its dignity extends to all forms of life—plants and animals, human beings and the mysterious Other beyond; Forché's emphasizes an expanded awareness of cultures, a North American, or rather, a United States citizen's consciousness of the limitations of her country's spiritual and geographic borders. Levertov speaks as a leader, conscious of her authority and influence, rallying others to causes she espouses wholeheartedly; Forché speaks in conversation with fellow writers and acquaintances, learning from them, the testimony of her memories challenged and deepened by different, complementary experiences.

It has been said that, with the war in Vietnam, America entered history—became self-conscious in the historical sense, looking backward as inevitably do declining powers. How true this conjecture is is open to question, the fate of the Indians, the treatment of blacks, the discrimination against various ethnic groups, and the Civil War being proof enough that we were never as innocent as we would care to believe. Yet there has been a definite shift in poets' sense of the nation—of its relativity in a world of many nations, all subject to the same universal laws—that make the "democratic vistas" open to, and in a sense opened by, Whitman in his poetry, something now to search for, work for, stand for. The works of Levertov and Forché suggest a number of conclusions about American poetry in relation to this challenge: that there is a necessary tension—a certain anger and even despair—in poetry that would consolidate personal and artistic integrity, inscribing them as one in the social sphere; that this tension—a kind of redistribution of gravity in the moral and artistic sense—is reflected in the breaking down of barriers between genres (prose and poetry, non-fiction and works of the imagination) conspicuous in the work of these poets; that this breaking down of barriers extends to an international awareness (cf. Levertov on Hikmet and Solzhenitsyn, her translations of Guillevic; Forché's translations of Alegría); that women poets, precisely because they need not identify with the conventions and points of view of a predominantly male tradition, may have greater freedom in their poetry to forge an identification with the oppressed; and that, while other modes of reflecting political and social consciousness are possible in lyric poetry, the works of Levertov and Forché represent a significant current in contemporary American poetry, integrating the forceful use of colloquial American speech with a demonstrable commitment of social justice that transcends national boundaries. That we have such poets who will not let us forget the value of compassion, free speech, and openmindedness is our good fortune; that such human voices, humane voices, can still be heard in our American wilderness should let us take heart, for we need, and can accept, nothing less than these.

Notes

1. Anne Bradstreet, "The Prologue" in George McMichael, ed., *Anthology of American Literature*, 2d ed. (New York: Macmillan, 1980), I: 94.

2. James Wright, *Collected Poems* (Middletown, Conn.: Wesleyan University Press, 1972), 113.

3. Czeslaw Milosz, *The Witness of Poetry* (Cambrige, Mass.: Harvard University Press, 1983), 97.

4. Marina Tsvetaeva, "Art in the Light of Conscience" in Carl R. Proffer, ed., *Modern Russian Poets on Poetry* (Ann Arbor, Mich.: Ardis, 1976), 184.

5. Denise Levertov, "On the Edge of Darkness: What Is Political Poetry," *Light Up the Cave* (New York: New Directions, 1981), 126–28.

6. Levertov, *Candles in Babylon* (New York: New Directions, 1982) and *Oblique Prayers* (New York: New Directions, 1984). Page numbers in the text refer to these editions.

7. Carolyn Forché, *The Country Between Us* (New York: Harper & Row, 1981). Page numbers in the text refer to this edition.

Mythopoeia, the Moon, and Contemporary Women's Poetry

Dianne T. Sadoff*

I

Mythology and archetype, male-imagined fables of identity, mythopoeic approaches to literature, all force feminist critics to confront, accommodate, or transform an exaggerated gender-based description of culture. Jung's apparently innocent definition of archetypes as "formal factors responsible for the organization of unconscious psychic processes,"[1] however, leads directly to exaggerated notions of masculine and feminine; to that problematic archetype, the anima, and its more problematic counterpart, the animus; and to passionate academic arguments about androgyny. In his article, "Androgyny: The Sexist Myth in Disguise," Daniel A. Harris concludes the entire concept of androgyny, which is based on anima-animus readjustments, has "no positive value" in liberating the study of literature from stereotypes, since the anima is itself a gender-based stereotype.[2] Harris quotes many of Jung's objectionable passages about the anima from *The Archetypes and the Collective Unconscious,* including the famous ones in which Jung implies the anima is man's bitch and burden: "She is the serpent. . . . She intensifies, exaggerates, falsifies, and mythologizes all emotional relations with [a man's] work and with other people of both sexes. . . . She is full of snares and traps, in order that man should fall, should reach the earth, entangle himself there, and stay caught, so that life should be lived."[3] Harris then quotes passages from "Woman in Europe" which delineate the crux of the anima-animus problem: the anima affects the male positively by making him intuitional, integrative, less aggressive, and negatively—if the conscious life is unbalanced—by making him "touchy, irritable, . . . jealous, vain, and unadjusted";[4] the animus apparently affects the female solely by "stop[ping] up the approaches to her

*Reprinted, in part, with permission from *Massachusetts Review* 19 (Spring 1978), 93–102, 109–10.

own feeling. She may even become frigid."[5] The masculine intellectual, rational, and judgmental animus, then, resides in the female unconscious; but since these are the very aspects of the intellect our society values, Jung immediately implies that women are all soft-headed by nature, that intellectual women are animus dominated and overly masculine, and that non-aggressive men are somehow unpleasantly effeminate.

Although I am tempted to agree in part with Harris' responses to the concept of androgyny and to his analysis of the animus problem, we cannot ignore the fact that men and women are to each other "the opposite sex." Harris also fails to recognize that Jung and his followers try valiantly to deal with the thorny anima-animus problem. In his last published volume, Jung becomes aware he has slighted women's consciousness in the bulk of his writings; he attempts to soften the implication that all intellectual women are "masculine" by referring to a feminine archetype, the moon. "Luna is primarily a reflection of a man's unconscious femininity, but she is also the principle of the feminine psyche, in the sense that Sol is the principle of a man's. . . . If, then, Luna characterizes the feminine psyche and Sol the masculine, consciousness would be an exclusively masculine affair, which is obviously not the case since woman possesses consciousness too." Jung solves this problem by deciding that woman's "consciousness has a lunar rather than a solar character. Its light is the 'mild' light of the moon, which merges things together rather than separates them. It does not show up objects in all their pitiless discreteness and separateness, but . . . blends in a deceptive shimmer the near and the far . . . into an unsuspected unity."[6] Jung now allows women intelligence, but the equivocal rhetoric of this passage demonstrates Jung's deep belief the female consciousness is somehow more mysterious and less verifiable than is male, and must therefore fail to make adequate judgments and distinctions.

Other Jungians have made perhaps more satisfying accommodations with the animus problem; Emma Jung, for example, both apologizes for and clarifies her father's thinking. "Confronted with . . . the animus," she writes, "the woman's task is to create a place for it in her life and personality, and to initiate some undertaking with the energy belonging to it. . . . Only when this masculine entity becomes an integrated part of the soul and carries on its proper function there is it possible for a woman to be truly a woman in the higher sense, and, at the same time, also being herself, to fulfill her individual human destiny."[7] Unfortunately, however, Emma Jung, like her father, asserts that women's intellect and creativity are basically different from those of men: feminine mentality has an "undeveloped, childlike, or primitive character; instead of the thirst for knowledge, curiosity; instead of judgment, prejudice; instead of thinking, imagination of dreaming; instead of will, wishing." And on creativity, Emma Jung's ideas deny women genius: "There are many women who have developed their powers of thinking, discrimination, and criticism to a high degree, but there are very few who are mentally creative in the way a man is. . . . The creativity of women finds its expression in the sphere of living, not only in her biological functions as mother but in the shaping of life generally. . . . The development of relationships is of primary importance in the shaping of life, and this is the real field of feminine creative power."[8] Despite Barbara Charlesworth Gelpi's response to Emma Jung, "The Androgyne," in which she argues that Jung attempts to "overcome the universal denigration of the feminine,"[9] Jung's article appears saturated with a now-familiar female fear of the intellect, of ambition, of discipline, and of rigor.

The female Jungian, Irene Claremont de Castillejo, deals most successfully with the animus problem. Although she believes women experience stronger ties to "undifferentiated thinking" than do rationalistic men, de Castillejo refuses to accept Jung's anima-animus equation, and admits the "notion that [women] were only intelligent people by virtue of an animus had grated uneasily" on her. De Castillejo solves the problem ingeniously; by following Erich Neumann and refusing to use the term "soul" interchangeably with "anima," as Jung does, she decides that the "ego is masculine in women as well as in men, [and] that the soul appears as a feminine figure not only in men but also in women."[10] Although she seems only to have inverted the troublesome categories of masculine and feminine, de Castillejo's theories finally allow women to be intelligent rather than either unconscious or animus-ridden.

Like female psychologists, female literary critics must also confront masculine definitions of feminity. The landscape of our mythology reflects masculine activity and female passivity: the land, with its hills, rills, chasms, and wooden caverns is female; the sea, source of all life, the symbol of womb toward which we journey in regression, the fluid of undifferentiated being, unconsciousness, and pre-separation bliss is female. The impregnating sky is masculine, and the male hero moves over the landscape, questing after his identity and immersing himself in the unconscious sea. Woman becomes passive nature, man its active and heroic inhabitant. Ellen Moers helps us deal with the ways women writers inhabit this mythological landscape; rather than reject female landscape because of its masculine tradition, Moers discovers that women writers adopt the landscape for their own works, and explore female identity by transforming the perspective from which we view female landscape.[11] In this way, women writers appropriate a male tradition, yet make it reflect feminine issues and concerns.

In addition, women writers will now remind the literary community of the ways mythology stereotypes women. Adrienne Rich, in response to Galway Kinnell's plea for a return to mythopoetic perceptions, believes that masculine imaginations of woman as "eternal mystery" reveal male fear of the female, and result in patterns of extreme idealization as well as "objectification and domination" of women by men. Rich asks the male poet to reject his "handed-down myths," and calls for a "new bisexuality in poetry written by men"; her example of the bisexual poet is Walt Whitman, whose acceptance of both masculine and feminine imaginations allowed him to experience the being in himself capable of "tenderness, vulnerability, [and] mutuality."[12] Rich's article demands just what women writers and feminist critics now exhort from the culture: a wholesale revaluation, a transformation, even a rejection of traditionally masculine archetype and mythopoeia.

II

As Jung knew when he attempted to modify his thinking about female consciousness, man has for centuries associated the moon with all aspects of woman and her sexuality. In patriarchal cultures, the incestuous moon goddess, wife of the sun, gives birth to a son who dies and is born again and who then becomes her lover; she is the archetypal Great Mother. In matriarchal cultures, the Great Mother can also be a Virgin, an unmarried goddess who is not related to a god as wife or counterpart, but is singularly herself, and her own mistress. This moon goddess, however, can also be a prostitute, and can demand ritual prostitution of her female virgin attendants in order to liberate them from individual, egoistic sexuality.[13] Whether wife, Great Mother, sacred prostitute, or virgin, then, sexuality is central to the moon goddess's identity and to worship of her.

The moon's most important earthly influence, fertility, relates directly to her sexual function. She presides over agricultural planting, growth, and harvesting; in some cultures she presides over pregnancy and childbirth—in the Maori tribe, the male opens the vaginal canal, but the moonbeam fertilizes the ovum (Harding, pp. 21–24). But the fertility-bringing moon, because of her phases, becomes dualistic, or sometimes triune: she brings life during her crescent, but death and destruction during her waning phase. In Greek mythology, the goddess of love, Aphrodite, represents the bright moon, while Hecate, goddess of sorcery and witchcraft, represents the dark moon.

The moon's phases also account for man's association of the moon with femininity. Like the moon, women have monthly cycles, and in all branches of the Indogermanic family of languages we find cognates for "month" and "moon." Male fear of and bafflement about female menstrual cycles undoubtedly caused this association in primitive times; the Maori called menstruation *mata marama*, or moon sickness. The Babylonians associated the full moon with Ishtar's menstrual period; this time was *sabattu*, or evil day of Ishtar, hence our *sabbath*, which is now observed at each of the moon's phases rather than only during her full moon (Harding, pp. 56–62). By extension from phases and their relation to the menstrual cycle, man associates the moon with fickleness, lunacy, and inspiration: "In these unaccountable qualities of the moon['s phases], man has seen a symbol of woman's nature which to him appears erratic, changeable, fickle, not to be relied on" (Harding, p. 65). Because the waning moon presides over storms and other natural disturbances, she brings lunacy, insanity, but also vision; unlike the sun, which reliably rules the day, the changeable moon rules the night, and becomes associated with the unconscious, with genius and abnormality, with inspiration and religious ecstasy, with madness and lunacy (Harding, p. 114). In Greek mythology, for example, Cybele blasted her son Attis with ecstasy which drove him mad.

What, we might then ask, does all this moon mythology mean? What cultural fantasies about the female does it reveal, or what needs fulfill? If, like Jung and Harding, we assume all primitive myth is projection of the unconscious onto the natural world, we must interpret moon mythologies as man's protection from his fear of woman, the other; menstruation, pregnancy, motherhood, and the complexity of human sexuality all separate women's experience from men's and often complicate relations between the sexes. Each aspect of the moon goddess's qualities also protects man from the feminine within himself and allows him to project that quality onto woman and her goddess, the moon. Most moon legends also reflect the culturally dualistic portrayal of woman: the virgin and the whore, the source of inspiration and madness, the life-giver and -destroyer.[14] When a woman writer encounters these mythologies, she must reinvent, revise, and transform them to fit her own female body, her female identity, her unique female experience. Contemporary women poets correct dualistic moon myths by reexamining both aspects of the moon goddess, the virgin and the prostitute; but now the virgin goddess embodies female self-doubt and fear of sexual involvement rather than the male-imagined chaste, cold, fickle moon, and the prostitute goddess embodies the transforming power of female sexual desire rather than the male-imagined Great Mother. Myth and archetype are reimagined female.

III

Denise Levertov, for example, uses the moon's cycles and phases as emblem of natural growth and change in *O Taste and See* and in *Relearning the Alphabet*.[15] Levertov's poetry celebrates process: the recurring cycles of nature, the natural unity of birth and death, the reciprocities of imagination. In "Another Spring," for example, Levertov deals with the natural dialectic which unites opposition and repetition through process; she imagines "In the gold mouth of a flower / the black smell of spring earth" (ll. 1–2): mouths golden, full of opening and desire, speaking of birth and renewal, bite through and into an earth made from death. Human beings, existing in this repeating cycle of death and rebirth, recapitulate Adam and so "Death in us goes on / testing the wild / chance of living" just as "Adam chanced it" (ll. 9–12). The moon and the sky mirror the earth's cycles and repeat its paradoxical golden and black colors, as Calavera unites gold ore in a black earth with seasonal renewal: "Golden-mouthed, the tilted smile / of the moon westering / is at the black window, / Calavera of Spring" (ll. 13–16). The poem, then, creates dualism—birth and death, winter and spring, new moon and old moon, Adam and we moderns—then gathers duality into ever expanding cycles, moon phases, and unifying patterns. The poem closes with a celebration of process-as-unifier of human and natural time: "I am speaking of living, / of moving from one moment into / the next, and into the one after" (ll. 18–21); death is "in the spring air" and air "means / music to sing to" (ll. 22–24). The westering moon, its cycles as unifier of oppositions, becomes an emblem of natural wholeness.

The moon also participates in Levertov's poems about the process of the imagination, which resembles the process of nature: it appears in opposite guises which can be seen dialectically as one; it creates continuity amidst discontinuity; it unifies the subjective poet with the objective world. But the imagination is also wholly different from nature; it is inspired, it is lunatic, it is the dark side of the moon. The poem "In Mind" juxtaposes apparently opposite women; one an innocent, natural woman, "smelling of / apples or grass" who is "kind," "very clean," and "without ostentation" yet has "no imagination" (ll. 3–10); the other a "turbulent moon-ridden girl" who is either girl, "old woman," or "both," who dresses in paradoxical "opals and rags, feathers / and torn taffeta," and who "knows strange songs" and is "not kind" (ll. 12–17). One woman is nature, the other the imagination; the poem structures a paradox within a dualism. Yet the wholesome woman and the moon-ridden lunatic both live "in mind"; old and young, riches and rags, the imagination and nature, couplets as well as solitary, fractured lines—all are contained in the complex, paradoxical imagination of the woman poet who creates herself.

In the opening poem of *O Taste and See,* "Song for Ishtar," Levertov invokes the Babylonian moon goddess as emblem for the female imagination; the poet is a "pig," the moon goddess a "sow," and the poet becomes one with the world by having sexual intercourse with the moon. But this intercourse is not simple; the masculine "pig" poet lives in an implicitly female landscape, a "hollow" filled with mud—and later in the book, in "Hypocrite Women," Levertov calls the female genitals, "caves of the Moon." And the moon's shining penetrates the poet's hollow, as the moon assumes a masculine sexual identity regardless of her femininity. Ishtar, oldest of moon goddesses is, however, androgynous; her worshipers invoke her as "Oh my God and my Goddess" (Harding, p. 94). This sacred sexual act mirrors the union of opposites throughout the poem: the muddy hollow "gleams / and breaks in silver bubbles"; desire is "black" with the moon's "great shining." And the moon's duality—her aspects of life-giver and -destroyer—become one through desire: "When she opens her white / lips to devour me I bite back / and laughter rocks the moon" (ll. 8–10); at the end of the poem, both participants lose their separate characteristics as pigs, and moonbeams get all mixed up and the lovers "rock and grunt, grunt and / shine" (ll. 12–13). The final, one-word line, "shine," reaffirms the joy of becoming one with Ishtar, as well as the peace and tranquillity of closure and of orgasm. The process of the imagination is sexual, as the poet interacts with nature and the imagination makes him one with it; and this imaginative process, like Ishtar, is androgynous, and affirms the multiple sexuality of the poet, who, both male and female, sexualizes experience and makes it joyful.

Levertov's *Relearning the Alphabet* emphasizes duality and the struggle to change, rather than the achieved unity of the earlier *O Taste and See;* the book moves from "Elegies" to "Relearning the Alphabet," with "Wanting the Moon" as middle transformational section. Death and dualism imply frustration and loss, and the section named for the moon longs for—hungers after— eventual unification of opposites: moon and not-moon, man and woman, vision and barrenness. Again, imagination is desire; sexual intercourse creates unity. An implicit Leda poem imagines Zeus's rape of the swan as poetic transformation; the poet "rise[s] up / with changed vision, / a singing in [her] ears" ("Wings of a God," ll. 22–24). The woman poet longs for the moon, and "not the moon"; for a "flower on the other side of the water," and "not a flower," for a "young man," a "jester" whose face, like lanterns and the moon, "is awake with its own light," and whose loving joy when united with the woman poet's imagination would create wholeness ("Wanting the Moon, I"). But rape is not love, and longing is not cured; the poet goes on "Waiting," "Wanting the Moon, II" "Craving" with "A Hunger," wanting to "seize / the gaiety of change from within" by becoming a cloud, wanting to cure change by lying down "in the dreams / of a young man." The woman poet craves man; the swan craves immortality through sexual intercourse with the god.

Toward the end of this moon section, a final moon-poem completes our equation: moon equals desire. In "Adam's Complaint," we moderns once more recapitulate the first man because desire never fulfills itself, either in individual lives or throughout human history. "Some people, / no matter what you give them, / still want the moon"; give them bread, salt, and meat, they are "still hungry"; give them the marriage bed and a cradle, "still empty arms"; give them land, "still they take to the roads"; "dig them the deepest well, / still it's not deep enough / to drink the moon from" (ll. 1–16). The paradox of human desire demands continual and escalating fulfillment; the poet relates this lesson cynically, yet with a certain sad humility, since the poet too wants the moon, can never get enough fulfillment, can never drink deeply enough of the moon's desire.

Yet this very hungry, devouring desire transforms "Elegies" into "The Singer," then into "A Tree Telling of Orpheus," and, finally, into "Relearning the Alphabet." In "The Singer," three adjacent moon poems sum up the emerging transformational model: in "Equilibrium," a woman hungers for sexual fulfillment, hating "the single ocean, / the one moon" (ll. 27–28). In "Secret Festival; September Moon," the moon presides over the beginnings of fulfillment and harmony: a "pandemonium of owls" sings an "antiphonal" song with fox "obligato"; the owls "raise / the roof of the dark," and "ferocious [is] / their joy in the extreme silver / the moon has floated out from itself" (ll. 1–17). In "Moon Tiger," the personified animal moon prowls around a dark bedroom with twin beds; the passive, frightened speaker whispers to her companion, "I'm coming in with you" (l. 18), and sexual unity appears possible. This section of the book emphasizes singing and art, and works toward the section which is the sole poem, "A Tree Telling of Orpheus"; the transformational tree is often home for the changeable moon in mythology, and both here work toward the liberation of imagination through desire as well as toward the making of art.

In the final "Relearning the Alphabet," the poet creates a microcosm of the book's entire transformational structure. The search for joyful, spontaneous imaginative expression, for desire fulfilled, culminates in the acceptance of process and "the grace of transformed / continuance" (G). Searching for " 'Imagination's holy forest,' " the woman-poet once more envisions the jester, "someone dreamed / on the far bank," or "seen / in epiphany" (I, J). And the moon, desire, is again the transformational agent, its chaste fire the burning away to vision: the woman poet "wanted / the moon and went / out to sea to touch / the moon" (M), hoping to be *burned by the cold moon to cinder*" (N). The moon's cold burn transforms absence and the desire for permanence into acceptance of process, of "transformation, continuance," faith, and "acts of magic" (R). The poem, built on a transformational model, discovers transformation as the center of human experience; continual change, like the moon's phases, becomes the goal of both life and art. In microcosm, then, and in macrocosm, *Relearning the Alphabet* finds joy through acceptance of human process and imagination; the woman poet touches the moon, is changed by it, and experiences the joy of both time and sexuality by doing so. . . .

These three contemporary women poets, then, recreate moon as image and mythology from a female perspective, and reimagine all aspects of the goddess's character: her inspiration, her lunacy, her duality, and most important, her sexuality and her cyclic nature. Precisely because the moon presages change, because her phases imitate the rhythms of feminine time, Denise Levertov, Nancy Willard, and Diane Wakoski create an aesthetics of change in which the moon becomes transformational agent; whether the moon is image, as in Willard and Levertov, or mythological goddess, as in Wakoski, she participates in a poetics which desires female change, growth, and rebirth. Female poets, then, reappropriate older patterns of transformation, which, according to Erich Neumann, were in primitive cultures the domain of the female: "In this matriarchal world, the spirit world of the moon, corresponding to the basic symbolism of the Archetypal Feminine, appears as a birth—and indeed as rebirth. Wherever we encounter the symbol of rebirth, we have to do with a matriarchal transformation mystery, and this is true even when its symbolism or interpretation bears a patriarchal disguise."[16] Moon goddess and female create spiritual transformation.

Levertov's poetry celebrates this alteration in the female experience; her poems imagine the moon's transforming fire creating joyful change, acceptance of natural process, and the partnership of men and women who love one another. The power of female sexuality, which is imaginative energy, recreates woman and joins her with a man and with the world. Like Levertov, Willard celebrates the powers of the imagination, but unlike Levertov, she emphasizes the contrasexual aspect of the creative process in which the marriage of masculine and feminine produces wholeness, or spiritual union. The poet and his wife both participate in poetry-making, and their marriage in effect recreates the universe: together they harness the powers of the imagination and rename the cosmos; they imitate, re-imagine, and assume the moon's inspiration, transforming her inflexible phases into the shining material of the imaginative process.

Unlike both Willard and Levertov, Wakoski writes a document of female failure to change; her persona, Diane, attempts to imitate the fertile, moist aspect of the dual moon goddess, but fearing her own femininity, ends up the bitch goddess or negative female, the chaste Diana, fearing the male she inevitably loves, punishing him for his sexual approach, and eventually finding herself abandoned by him. The failure of the female persona informs us as fully about women's experience as does the success of Levertov's and Willard's transformational poetics; the moon's cycles, the goddess's duality, allow sexual and imaginative failure as well as transformation and rebirth. While Levertov and Willard solve the anima-animus problem by uniting the female with the male in sexual or contrasexual union, Wakoski falls into the animus trap; her persona, afraid of her sexuality, represses the feminine and causes energy to flow destructively into the masculine aspects of her psyche. Diane's self-doubt makes her hate men without fully realizing it is herself she truly hates.

Regardless, then, of female success or failure in a poetics of transformation, moon mythology and imagery no longer portray women from a masculine perspective. Levertov, Willard, and Wakoski transform the female experience into poetry; they imagine sexuality and change from a female point of view, and with the fully feminine voice.

Notes

1. C. G. Jung, "Synchronicity: An Acausal Connecting Principle," in *The Structure and Dynamics of the Psyche*, from *The Collected Works of C. G. Jung*, VIII (New York: Pantheon Books, Bollingen Series XX, 1960), 436. See also C. G. Jung, "Archetypes of the Collective Unconscious," in *The Archetypes and the Collective Unconscious*, from *The Collected Works of C. G. Jung*, IX, i (New York: Pantheon Books, Bollingen Series XX, 1969), 5–6.

2. *Women's Studies* 2 (1974), 171. This entire issue debates the concept of androgyny from feminist perspectives.

3. Jung, *The Archetypes*, 28, 70, 26; Daniel A. Harris, "Androgyny: The Sexist Myth in Disguise," *Women's Studies* 2, no. 2 (1974):179.

4. Jung, *The Archetypes*, 70.

5. C. G. Jung, "Woman in Europe," in *Civilization in Transition*, from *The Collected Works of C. G. Jung*, X (New York: Pantheon Books, Bollingen Series XX, 1964), 119; Harris, 180.

6. C. G. Jung, "The Personification of the Opposites," in *Mysterium Coniunctionis*, from *The Collected Works of C. G. Jung*, XX (New York: Pantheon Books, Bollingen Series XX, 1963), 179.

7. Emma Jung, "On the Nature of the Animus," in *Women and Analysis*, ed. Jean Strouse (New York, 1974), 257, 260.

8. Ibid., 241–42.

9. In *Women and Analysis*, 262.

10. *Knowing Woman: A Feminine Psychology* (New York, 1973), 170. See also Ann Belford Ulanov, *The Feminine in Jungian Psychology and Christian Theology* (Evanston, Ill.: Northwestern University Press, 1971), 269: "The highest phase of confrontation and individuation in both sexes is initiated by the feminine: for the man, through the anima, which leads to the self; for the woman through the feminine self, not through any contrasexual elements. . . . It is the feminine which completes the individuation of *each* sex."

11. *Literary Women: The Great Writers* (New York, 1976), ch. 11, "Metaphors: A Postlude."

12. "Poetry, Personality, and Wholeness: A Response to Galway Kinnell," *Field*, no. 7 (Fall 1972), 13, 17–18.

13. M. Esther Harding, *Woman's Mysteries, Ancient and Modern* (New York, 1955), 88–97, 103–4, 144–53. I am much indebted to Harding's survey of moon mythologies; further references to specific passages in her book will appear parenthetically in my text.

14. Wendy Martin, "Seduced and Abandoned in the New World: The Image of Woman in American Fiction," in *Woman in Sexist Society: Studies in Power and Powerlessness*, eds. Vivian Gornick and Barbara K. Moran (New York, 1972), 329–46, bases her well-known article on man's need to define woman as dualistic.

15. (New York, 1964) and (New York, 1970). All references in my text are to these New Directions editions.

16. *The Great Mother: An Analysis of the Archetype* (New York, 1955), 58–59. See also ch. 15, "Spiritual Transformation," and Ulanov, Pt. III, "The Psychology of the Feminine."

Denise Levertov:
Her Illustrious Ancestry
Virginia M. Kouidis*

One of the most rewarding directions of inquiry suggested by the question of Denise Levertov's significance among contemporary poets is the mapping out of the particular cultural ancestry she perpetuates. If, as has been frequently noted, Levertov is unusual among contemporaries for the richness of her familial and literary legacy, she is even more exceptional for the loving and graceful assimilation of that legacy into a poetics of connection. Love expresses itself in her generous and fearless exploration of the resources of the past; grace in her seamless transformation of the past's moral and aesthetic lessons into present relevance. Among poets often unreflectively eager to follow Ezra Pound's advice to "make it new," Levertov's version of the American literary lineage that runs, erratically, from Ralph

*Reprinted with permission from *North Dakota Quarterly* 55 (Fall 1987), 103–22.

Waldo Emerson to William Carlos Williams continues to offer our poetry and culture "the long stem of connection" it so badly needs. Requiring ever fresh attention—attention revealed in poetic form itself—the tradition becomes irrelevant only as a poet is content with a superficial reading of the world.

I

Levertov indicates in the early poem "Illustrious Ancestors" (OI)[1] that her foremost (as in priority-in-time and regard) ancestors are familial. The poem pays tribute to two Russian-Jewish and Welsh ancestors from the late 1700s and early 1800s, the "Rav / of Northern White Russia" and "Angel Jones of Mold," a tailor, for their bequest of Albert Schweitzer's "Reverence for Life" ("Origins of a Poem," PW 53). Reverence begins in attention to the physical world and moves to awe before its mystery.

> Well, I would like to make,
> thinking some line still taut between me and them,
> poems direct as what the birds said,
> hard as a floor, sound as a bench,
> mysterious as the silence when the tailor
> would pause with his needle in the air.

This visionary heritage was passed to Levertov by her Welsh mother in an incident that serves as the prototype of all future acts of attention. In "The Instant" (OI) mother and daughter have gone before breakfast to gather mushrooms in the Welsh countryside. Suddenly the mother points ecstatically to a rare view of Mt. Snowdon fifty miles away. The incipient poet experiences a moment of mystic enlightenment: "Light / graces the mountainhead / for a lifetime's look, before the mist / draws in again."

Mt. Snowdon is the most prominent feature of the cherished childhood landscape where Levertov learned to attend to nature's large and small splendors. Other features of the treasured topography are remembered in the poem "A Map of the Western Part of the County of Essex in England" (JL).

> I am Essex-born:
> Cranbrook Wash called me into its dark tunnel,
> the little streams of Valentines heard my resolves,
> Roding held my head above water when I thought it was
> drowning me. . . .

This landscape echoes with immediate family history and a fabled ancestral past. It has marked the poet's comings to consciousness and continues to offer a sustaining connection to all new landscapes:

> an old map
> made long before I was born shows ancient
> rights of way where I walked when I was ten burning with desire

for the world's great splendors, a child who traced voyages
indelibly all over the atlas, who now in a far country
remembers the first river, the first
field, bricks and lumber dumped in it ready for building,
the new smell, and remembers
the walls of the garden, the first light.

The spiritual rooting this landscape provides is the subject of many later poems. In "Chekhov on the West Heath" (*LF*) London's Hampstead Heath and Chekhov become one—"A place of origin / gives and gives, as we return to it, / bringing our needs." On the Heath, in 1941, she read Chekhov to a sick friend and learned an essential lesson: "it has to do / not with failure, defeat, frustration, / Moscows never set out for, / but with love." In the essay "My Prelude" (*LC*) Levertov remembers Burnham Beeches, near the ballet school of her evacuation from London during the Battle of Britain, where she came into assurance of her poetic vocation. And in "Living Alone (I)" (*FD*) she cherishes an experience of adult solitude for the childhood serenity it recalls. Walking silently home of a spring evening, she feels that "surely no note is changed, / sung in Valentines Park or on steep streets in the map of my mind / in the hush of suppertime, everyone gone indoors. / Solitude within multitude seduced me early."

A series of poems Levertov wrote upon the death of her mother at ninety-three, in Mexico, insist upon the mother's significance as caretaker of the first garden, or landscape, as guardian of the first light. In "Death in Mexico" (*LF*) the mother's too-slow death is measured against the rapid dissolution of her beloved garden, and in "The 90th Year" (*LF*) the poet remembers that in her mother's (English) gardens she receives first instruction in world-transforming attention.

It was she
who taught me to look;
to name the flowers when I was still close to the ground,
my face level with theirs;
or to watch the sublime metamorphoses
unfold and unfold
over the walled back gardens of our street . . .

Significantly, the dying mother is also remembered by the passages she has marked in her beloved books, for it was she who seems to have initiated her daughter into the literary heritage. The mother (and father) along with the BBC School Programs educated Levertov at home. In addition to whatever structure there was to this education, the family read aloud to each other from nineteenth-century novels; and Hasidic lore came to Levertov and her sister through their scholarly Anglican Jewish father. An anecdote in "An Interim" (*RA*) suggests how the natural-mystic and literary legacies were joined in the mother. Levertov recounts being taken at fourteen, by her mother, to Beachy Head to recuperate from the measles. She is grouchy and her mother entertained her by reading aloud from George Eliot. In a troubled adulthood, the poet remembers the peace she felt there on the seashore with her mother and their books: "Peace could be / / that grandeur, that dwelling in majestic presence, attuned / to the great pulse."

Levertov recalls in "The Untaught Teacher" that when she assumed the unfamiliar role of teacher at American universities and colleges in the mid-1960s she wanted, following Rainer Maria Rilke's advice to the Young Poet, through the example of her childhood's "erratic and fortuitous" reading to enable her students to discover "correspondences, equivalents" in their own early lives. She hoped that by "searching out clues to their own impulses to write, they might find unexpected sources of strength" (*PW* 160).

The literary "childhood" that bore such fruit was happily eclectic. The syllabus Levertov gave her first students began with "fairy tales [including Beatrix Potter] and English poets, especially the thirties' poets who were my first introduction to contemporary writing; then Williams, Pound, Stevens, and on to Duncan and Creeley and to poets younger than myself about whose work I was excited *that* year . . ." (*PW* 159). She adds other names to this Master reading list, among them Keats and Tennyson, Yeats, Eliot, Rilke—on the role of the poet, but also his poems—Chekhov, Emerson, Thoreau and, through Robert Duncan, Hilda Doolittle of the *Trilogy*. T. S. Eliot she rejects as an enduring influence, but she acknowledges the encouragement she received from him, at twelve, and later, at sixteen, from Herbert Read, both of whom responded at length, in writing, to poems she had sent them.

Levertov's very most illustrious ancestor in this fortuitous literary lineage is William Carlos Williams. For Levertov Williams' "historical importance is, above all, that more than anyone else he made available to us the whole range of the language, he showed us the rhythms of speech *as* poetry—the rhythms and idioms not only of what we say aloud but of what we say in our thoughts" ("William Carlos Williams, 1883–1963," *PW* 254). Williams, of course, also reformulated her family lessons in close observation. His dictum "No ideas but in things," joined to E. M. Forster's admonition "Only connect," forms a craft, aesthetic and moral statement that reverberates "through the poet's life, through *my* life . . . ("The Poet in the World," *PW* 116). She summarizes her debt to Williams in the late poem "Williams: An Essay" (*CB*) for his gift of "the long stem of connection."

Williams' poetry first of all helped Levertov to reassess the English Neo-Romanticism to which she had apprenticed herself in the 1940s. Since *Here and Now* (1957), her second volume of poems and her first American volume, she has taken as her own Williams' experiments with the (American) idiom and field composition, and his use of an unpoetic subject matter. However, she has given to this poetics her own cosmopolitan female voice, refined organic forms and personalized imagery, effortless sonorities, and a female and political subject matter. A dreamy cadence and vision are much more hers than his, as is her mystical and religious bent; she is also more inclined to abstract meditation than Williams.

A passage from "Scenes from the Life of the Peppertrees" (*OI*) exemplifies Levertov's early mastery of a characteristic Williams' mode that enables the development of a distinct, personal poetics of immediacy and connection. The poem's "tipping buttons of light" are one instance of her substitution of fresh perception for cliched image. Such re-visions accomplish the illumination of the commonplace missing in the poetry of many self-styled descendants of Williams. For Levertov these poets' gray transcriptions of their unexperienced lives reflect what Rilke describes as the " 'unlived, disdained, lost life, of which one can die' " ("Line-Breaks, Stanza-Spaces, and the Inner Voice," *PW* n 20).

> The yellow moon dreamily
> tipping buttons of light
> down among the leaves. Marimba,
> marimba—from beyond the
> black street.
>   Somebody dancing,
> somebody
>   getting the hell
> outta here. Shadows of cats
> weave round the tree trunks,
> the exposed knotty roots.

By the various dionysian rhythms of the dreaming moon, jingling Mexican marimbas, hurried human departure, and the stealthily weaving cats we are reminded of Williams' passionate dances with the dark center of his own locality. Levertov generalizes no meaning; rather, the disjunctive rhythms are first subdued by the languor of "dreamily," and then drawn together along the tension between the illusions of moonlight and the reality-gripping "exposed knotty roots" that tip the moonlight earthwards. Implicit is the definition of a poetry as this dance of the moonlight with the street's scenes and sounds, and the tree roots.

The reality-defining illusionistic moonlight of the "Peppertrees" also constitutes part of Wallace Stevens' more elusive influence on Levertov's poetry. She prefers Stevens' short early poems to the later philosophical ones, and she quotes from his essays on the nature of art and the responsibility of the poet. In a 1964 interview with Walter Sutton she says that Stevens' poetry gave her "a sense of magic, the same almost surrealist magic that Garcia Lorca has—a reminder of how, at a certain pitch of awareness of language, one can make marvelous leaps. . . . [Stevens' images] aren't illusory, because they reveal reality."[2] In addition to the kind of lunar distortion employed in the "Peppertrees," Stevens' magic may influence her verbalizations of nature's ever-surprising and delightful metamorphoses. "Tomatlan (Variations)" (*HN*), recalling his love of exotic place names, mates the sea wind to "The green palmettos of the / blue jungle." The wind "touches them / lightly, and strokes them, and / screws them, until they / are blue flames, / green smoke, and / screws them again." The recent "Sundown Sentences" (*OP*) is Levertov's re-vision of the last section of Stevens' "Sunday Morning." The poet remembers that for much of her life she too has found that nature's (ambiguously) self-sufficient beauty would suffice. She retains some of Stevens' (and Keats') images, and she moves from one to another with her predecessors' sonorous ease. However, the visual attentuation of her form and the precise brevity of her images produce a leaner landscape, one whose unvarying repetitions are haunted by Stevens' snow-man (and in the context of the entire volume, threatened by man-made ruin).

> Redwings repeat with unslaked thirst
> their one sweet song.

> The rain's cleared off and the cats are dreamily
> watching the lucid world, perched on the fence-rail,
> striving for nothing; their shadows grow long.

> Delicately,
> two hilltop deer
> nibble the sky.

Ezra Pound's ancestral legacy is likewise his early poems, not the *Cantos*. Pound's significance is suggested by Levertov's rereadings of the *ABC of Reading*, a source for many of his major statements on rejuvenation of poetic language ("Dichten = condensare!"). She may also have found in Pound a model of the poet-pedagogue, and in the *ABC* an inspiration for her two volumes of essays on poetry and the poet. In these, she like Pound offers up exemplary ancestors and a wealth of practical advice on the poetic craft.

Finally, among the great American modernists there is H. D. In the essay "H. D.: An Appreciation" Levertov recalls that she came to this poet relatively late but found in her much to admire and use. In terms of craft, H. D. offered instruction in precision, the musical sound of experience, and "the possibility of the disappearance, in the crucible, of *manner*" (*PW* 248). Both poets see their lives in mythic terms, H. D. seeking specific mythic parallels while Levertov uses the informing mythic pattern of life as a pilgrimage "from one state of being to another" ("The Sense of Pilgrimage," *PW* 63). Both poets are dreamers and visionaries, and Levertov credits H. D. with helping her find a way to penetrate the darkness—the mystery of self-abnegation required for shedding the self's chrysalis. As James Breslin notes, Levertov's "magical realism," her ability to imbue precise detail with visionary import, is indebted to the "spiritual realism" of the *Trilogy*.[3] There we also find a precedent for Levertov's growing awareness of a Word behind words, and for such images of self-transformation as the earth worm and butterfly.

Levertov transforms the heritage of Williams, Stevens, Pound, and H. D. into a life-affirming poetry of seldom equalled imagistic brilliance, colloquial eloquence, and verbal precision. Through visually expressive organic forms she connects language to felt life in transparent images that illuminate experience long dulled to triteness or overwhelmed by its own elusiveness. Such are the wineglasses of "The Year One" (*TSA*). Situated in the poet's ecstatically painful rebirth at mid-career into deepened political commitment, the wineglasses are aesthetically and politically revelatory. They are charged with the emotional security and complacency of social ritual and civilized pleasure that must be shattered in the moral and political parturition:

> the clamor
>
> of unquenched desire's
> radiant decibels shattering
>
> the patient wineglasses
> set out by private history's ignorant
>
> quiet hands. . . .

Levertov salutes her modernist lineage in "September 1961" (*OTS*). The poem originates in the sorrow of anticipated silence, the approaching loss of Williams, Pound, and H. D.

> This is the year the old ones,
> the old great ones
> leave us alone on the road.
>
> The road leads to the sea.
> We have the words in our pockets,
> obscure directions.

Death announces itself as the failure of language that leaves "the horizon / ringed with confused urban light-haze." (Does Levertov allude here to a line she remembers elsewhere from Emerson: " 'The health of the eye demands a horizon' " ["Some Notes on Organic Form," *PW* 12]?) Their descendants inherit an awareness of continuity, a sense of direction—toward the sea of release and extinction, and the understanding that the sea is reached through diversion "into deep woods." Shouldering their duds, so to speak, the next generations

> count the
> words in our pockets, we wonder
>
> how it will be without them, we don't
> stop walking, we know
> there is far to go, sometimes
>
> we think the night wind carries
> a smell of the sea . . .

These ancestors hand over the eternal questions about love, death, separation and loss, old age, and the elusive mystery that glimmers through natural and domestic fact. They offer an articulate consciousness of political impingements on quotidian complacency; a preference for the natural to the urban landscape; and a commitment to language as the map by which one becomes cognizant of, if not reconciled to, the sea. The literary heritage, intertwined with the familial and firmly rooted in the maternal natural world, yields the poetics that is also Levertov's metaphysics, epistemology, politics and pedagogy. With its teachings she first broke into song and, during the last twenty years, has met numerous personal and political crises.

II

Among contemporary critics the issue of how to live with one's literary ancestors has led to the formulation of evaluative criteria which tend to ignore or minimize a poet like Denise Levertov. Her affirmation of ancestors sets her apart from mappers of the anxiety of influence and analysts of the Freudian family romance. Similarly, her commitment to the humanistic search for truth and her only slightly shaken faith in the expressive power of language do not attract critics who see an unbridgeable gap between experience and language. In contrast to their challenges to Western culture's humanistic faith, she cherishes Ibsen's advice that, "The task of the poet is to make clear to himself, and thereby to others, the temporal and eternal questions which are astir in the age and community to which he belongs" ("The Poet in the World," *PW* 111).

Among critics who link merit to ancestry, some seem myopically preoccupied with purity of lineage. They seek to grant priority to one kind of poetry by establishing a clear line of descent from a particular paternal forebear. These critics line up post–World War II poets as descendants of Stevens *or* Pound/Williams; as out-dated modernists or explorers of some avant-garde postmodernism. Levertov has probably fared least well among advocates of the Stevens paternity who ignore her.[4] From their perspective she must seem a perpetrator of the apostases of Williams' counterpoetic. Others, including some Pound/Williams sympathizers, find Levertov's mystical impulse to coherence and joy outdated, her poetry too attuned to the themes and forms of the tightly structured and autonomous Romantic lyric.[5]

In their eagerness to divide the contemporary poetry scene into predetermined families these critics overlook the totality of Levertov's poetry and the diverse possibilities inherent in her poetics of connection. Unshackled by any longing for clear distinctions, she herself creates a lineage, as we have seen, that includes Williams, Pound, *and* Stevens. She had gradually adapted this heritage to her personal need for a poetry of immediacy permeated by glimmers of transcendent value. With admirable frequency she has attained the objective of her tribute to Robert Duncan: "One does not emulate such a master, except by being more oneself" ("For Robert Duncan's Early Poems," *PW* 243).

Feminist critics who, like Black aestheticians, feel their group's experiences and expression have been devalued and repressed by the dominant white male literary culture are uneasy with Levertov's largely male tradition, even though it is the liberating tradition of Williams whose benefits they all reap. Her subjects, themes, and tone do not consistently heel to a feminist poetics that Elaine Showalter has labeled "gynocritics."[6] It asks that women writers be primarily concerned with expressing and evaluating their experiences as women in society and as women artists. Unable to ignore Levertov's achievements and her frequently parallel course, many feminist critics have followed the lead of Suzanne Juhasz in offering a qualified appreciation. In *Naked and Fiery Forms,* a study of the emergence of feminist poetry, Juhasz condescends to Levertov as a "transitional and significant" "feminine" poet who writes about women but who has not evolved to the exemplary awareness attained by Adrienne Rich.[7]

Feminists generally make too easy a distinction between these two most illustrious contemporary poets whose poetry testifies to their shared first priority—the language. They prefer Rich's rage and isolation to Levertov's celebration and solitude; Rich's feminist to Levertov's broader social consciousness. In fact, in matters of literary ancestry and patronage neither poet has been the thwarted female poet Cress of Williams' *Paterson.* Both have studied widely and perceptively in the modernist annals of their guild, although the masters are not quite the same: there is more Yeats, Stevens, Robert Frost, and W. H. Auden in Rich's ancestry. Both have moved to a poetry of experience that seeks to cancel the distance between the poet and her subject.[8] As a young poet Rich received the endorsement of academic poets like Auden, while Levertov was promoted by Kenneth Rexroth and then the Black Mountain poets. It is interesting to speculate on the role the particular composition of Rich's ancestry played in her early dissatisfactions and later feminist rebellion; in any case, whereas Levertov felt enabled by her sense of the past, Rich's ancestry, in the early poem "Merely to Know" (*Snapshots of a Daughter-in-Law,* 1959), has threatened her with suffocation: "Wedged in by earth works / thrown up by snouters before me, / I kick and snuffle, breathing in / cobwebs of beatle-cuirass: . . . . / My predecessors blind me. . . ."

Among their significant similarities, Levertov and Rich share the compulsion to connection, an admirable characteristic of many feminine writers. Alice Walker, Black novelist and poet, speaks in "Saving the Life That Is Your Own" for such contemporary artists who wish to leave literature squarely centered in life.

> What is always needed in the appreciation of art, or life, is the larger perspective. Connections made, or at least attempted, where none existed before, the straining to encompass in one's glance at the varied world the

common thread, the unifying theme through immense diversity, a fearlessness of growth, of search, of looking, that enlarges the private and the public world. And yet, in our particular society, it is the narrowed and narrowing view of life that often wins.[9]

Walker's search for ancestral connection is resolved in neglected Black women writers and illiterate cultivators of gardens; Rich's in a female lineage, literary as well as more broadly cultural; Levertov's in an eclectic, largely male ancestry. Only when these lines of connection become intolerant of each other, obscuring new connections and genuine artistic merit, do they endanger the poetic enterprise.

III

The specific English landscape of childhood enables Denise Levertov to generalize a poetic landscape—of trees and forests, mountains, gardens and houses, rivers and the sea—through which to ask the "temporal and eternal questions" Ibsen and her modernist ancestors require of the poet. This geographic and psychic topography is sustained by the well, or spring, a repository of values elsewhere attached to cherished ancestors. The well symbolizes the poet's essential center, its waters connecting her to the mystery of origins and to the final surety of the sea. The well moves us more deeply into the ancestral lessons, partly through the allusions it allows us to make to other epistemological and metaphysical critiques of the well.

Two companion poems from *The Jacob's Ladder*, "The Well" and "The Illustration," mythologize the nature-mother-daughter/poet relationship that is Levertov's well of origin. The well is located in the dream-remembered lake of Valentines Park of childhood: "mistaken directions, forgotten signs / all bringing the soul's travels to a place / of origin, a well / under the lake where the Muse moves." The image of the Muse was presaged in an illustration out of childhood, " 'The Light of Truth'—frontispiece / to 'Parables from Nature,' 1894"; she also has a source in Annie Sullivan, Helen Keller's teacher; and Levertov associates her with a fairy tale character, "the young/ old grandmother, demonic yet benevolent ("The Sense of Pilgrimage," *PW* 74). However, other poems indicate that the Muse is most significantly the mother, the first reader of nature who opened "the doors of the world." Dreamed by the poet who stands on a bridge, the Muse "wades into deep water" to fill her pitcher from the lake's spring and then spills/spells the word *water* into the poet's hand. This gesture, prototype of the connection Levertov seeks to effect between world and word, she elsewhere remembers as Wordsworth's statement, "Language is not the dress but the incarnation of thought" ("An Admonition," *PW* 58).

The well feeds the lake, tributary of the Roding River whose own movement is toward the sea. It is both part of the process of life and resistance to it, Levertov's most significant figuration of her preferred geometry-of-the-self as radiating metamorphoses from a center of being. As in "The Lagoon" (*OI*) wells and quiet well-like depths are the breeding waters of the imagination.

> This lagoon with its glass shadows
> and naked golden shallows
> and mangrove island, home of white herons,
> . . . .
> draws the mind
> down to its own depths
>
> where the imagination swims,
> shining dark-scaled fish,
> swims and waits, flashes, waits and
> wavers, shining of its own light.

The well as source of Muse and self is allegorized in "A Pilgrim Dreaming" (*LF*), and the well of "Slowly" (*LF*) feeds cherished solitude. "To Kevin O'Leary, Wherever He Is" (*FP*) images the well as giver of selfhood in the form of the Hebrew (ancestral) version of her name. A variation of the well—a deep pit or hole—is used to image the source of the passion essential to poetry. Learning from Russian artists, in the poem "Conversation in Moscow" (*FD*), their preference for Dostoyevsky's "darknesses and illuminations" to Turgenev's social awareness, Levertov is led to their shared artist's knowledge that the artist must not "lose touch with the source, / pretend it's not there, cover over / the mineshaft of passion" from whose depths tolls the bell of despair and "wildest joy." These versions of the well are crucial to the well image of *To Stay Alive*. In the midst of her political/spiritual crisis Levertov is advised by a friend to plumb her own well: "Get down in your well, / / it's your well / / go deep into it / / into your own depths as into a poem."

"February Evening in Boston, 1971" (*FP*), from the same period, defines those well waters as the Emersonian tradition of visionary connection and socially responsible poetry. In a setting that Levertov several times uses, she, like Emerson before her, is crossing a common and is lured to celebration by the evening's beauty.

> The trees' black hair electric
> brushed out,
>   fierce haloes.
>
> And westward
> veils of geranium hold their own,
> even yet. Transparent.

The impulse to joy, however, is subdued to plaintive nostalgia by the threat of the "obscene silence," consequence of the impending global annihilation that will leave no one to hear her song or continue the tradition that calls upon the poet to celebrate the world's splendors. It is not logic but spiritual

longing, perhaps, that permits her wistful affirmation of the ancestral covenant: "It was the custom of my tribe / to speak and sing; / not only to share
the present, breath and sight, / but to the unborn. / Still, even now, we reach
out / toward survivors. It is a covenant / of desire."

While Levertov's impulse is Emersonian, her method has strong affinities with Henry David Thoreau, in *Walden* American literature's foremost
meditator on wells.[10] For both writers a well is usually a free-flowing supplier
of a lake or pond, itself a large well for self-immersion. Thoreau calls Walden
"my well ready dug," but he allows that a domestic version can also serve. In
"Where I Lived, and What I Lived for," he puns on "well[-being]" to emphasize a well's benefits: "It is well to have some water in your neighborhood, to
give buoyancy to and float the earth. One value even of the smallest well is,
that when you look into it you see that earth is not continent but insular. This
is as important as that it keeps butter cool."

In her later poetry Levertov becomes increasingly concerned with what
Thoreau calls earth's insularity, but her earlier satisfaction is the divinity
immanent in the watery (and earthly) particulars. The influential literary
texts here are Thoreau's notebooks. He and the natural paradise he records
are among her "Great Possessions." They are part of " 'that reality,' " she
quotes Marcel Proust, " 'from which we become more and more separated as
the formal knowledge which we substitute for it grows in thickness and
imperviousness—that reality which there is grave danger we might die without having known and yet which is simply our life.' " And from the notebooks: " 'Thurs. Dec. 10 1840. I discover a strange track in the snow, and
learn that some migrating otter has made across from the river to the
wood . . .' " ("Great Possessions," *PW* 100).

Levertov chooses as an epigraph for the poem "Joy" (*SD*) a quotation
from Thoreau that might serve as epigraph to the body of her work: " 'You
must love the crust of the earth on which you dwell.' " (Is it fortuitous that
"dwell" contains "well"?) This crust is valuable in itself and for the mystic
and, later, religious transformations it permits. Her objective is the sort of
metamorphosis Thoreau worked upon Walden and its surrounding woods. In
"Artist to Intellectual (Poet to Explainer)" (*LF*) the movement from the "obvious" to self-expanding cosmic knowledge—the identification of eyes, wells,
and skies—finds Levertov reaching back to Thoreau and out among contemporary poets to George Oppen, especially to "the obvious / Like a fire of
straws / Aflame in the world . . ." of Oppen's "From a Phrase of Simone
Weil's and Some Words of Hegel's" (*Seascape: Needle's Eye*, 1972).[11]

> "The lovely *obvious!* The feet
> supporting the body's tree and its crown
> of leafy flames, of fiery
> knowledge roaming
> into the eyes,
> that are lakes, wells, open
> skies!"

In turning from Thoreau to Emily Dickinson and Robert Frost we come to eminent meditators on wells who, with the exception of brief allusions to Dickinson, Levertov omits from her literary genealogy. The omission of Dickinson is the more puzzling. Among twentieth-century American poets it has been de rigueur to admire Dickinson's innovations in form and language, her attention to natural and domestic detail, her ability to draw the reader into the persona's terrors and ecstasies, her inquisition of the cosmos from the confines of an Amherst bedroom. Given Levertov's eager student's eye and embrace of diversity, it is unlikely that she too has not found much to admire in Dickinson. Still, she is not included in the syllabus.

What affinity Levertov has with Dickinson rests in the latter's grounding in a beloved (childhood) landscape, "Emily's / New England fields" ("Lucy," *FP*), and her use of nature, as in "Emily's black birds," in "A Dark Summer Day" (*RA*), to image states of extreme emotion. There are, however, significant and fairly obvious differences of temperament and tone. Dickinson was a recluse, while Levertov has quite literally stormed the barricades of her historical moment; and the parental religious heritage that provides much of the drama of Dickinson's poetry offers Levertov sustaining assurance as to human purpose. Both poets are readers of nature. But for Dickinson the natural world often serves as compensation for grander disappointments, or it refuses to reveal the truth she seeks. Hers is commonly a poetry of deprivation—"I had been hungry, all the Years." Levertov is not without moments of felt separation from nature and its revelation, but usually nature opens to her possibilities of radiating metamorphoses. Her poetry characteristically rings with plenitude.

Dickinson's well poems exemplify her uneasy relationship to nature's otherness. Unlike Thoreau and Levertov, who plumb the mysterious water depths and submit the self to purifying self-immersion, Dickinson stands awe-stricken before and apart from a well's opaque waters. In "What mystery pervades a Well!" she approaches the well in childish delight; but before her admiration it glasses over in "an abyss's face." "I Know where Wells grow—Droughtless Wells—" describes her stratagem for avoiding such deception. The poet's thirst has caused her to imagine a child's pretty and harmless well, where "Pepple—safely plays—"

> It's made of Fathoms—and a Belt—
> A Belt of jagged Stone—
> Inlaid with Emerald—half way down—
> And Diamonds—jumbled on—

A charming fantasy, but the child-poet cannot afford a bucket and so remains thirsty, being too high up to drink directly. In her poverty, of imagination or courage, she remembers other, droughtless wells with ready buckets, read of "in an Old fashioned Book" where "People 'thirst no more.' " She can only conjecture what these buckets meant; they and their text are but a memory.

She must prefer her own imaginary well, even though it costs her "dearly" in relinquishment.

> Shall We remember Parching—then?
> Those Waters sound so grand—
> I think a little Well—like Mine—
> Dearer to understand—

Robert Frost's similar separation from nature, often through allegory, and his inversion of the transcendental certainties must in large part account for his exclusion from Levertov's syllabus. (Interestingly enough, however, the surface of Levertov's geographic/psychic landscape resembles no other poet's as much as it does his.) Frost's famous well poem "For Once, Then, Something" points to key differences. Like Dickinson's well his is walled: "Others taunt me with having knelt at well-curbs / Always wrong to the light. . . ." Addressed, it seems, a question of cosmic dimension, the well returns only the poet's preposterous laureled self-image; until, "once," he discerns "a something white, uncertain, / Something more of the depths— and then I lost it." The whiteness may have been "Truth? A pebble of quartz?"

Levertov characteristically fixes her attention on the pebble and finds that the natural world leads her to a vision of truth inaccessible to the rustic deductive processes of Frost's philosopher. Thoreau reinforced her mother's early teaching in this tactic, but William Carlos Williams is the most exemplary ancestral naturalist. His "The Bitter World of Spring," to all appearances a retort to Frost, contains no well as such, but its waters are certainly those from which Levertov and Thoreau dip. Like Levertov in "The Well," Williams stands on a bridge, in the "bridge- / / keeper's cubicle," observer and caretaker of the stream below, untempted to the leap into the Passaic he made in "The Wanderer." His observation of the jumbled emergence of spring leads him to think of "the fight as to the nature of poetry" and to the question "Shall the philosophers capture it?—" Like Frost he looks into the water and distinguishes a whiteness, but Williams' inductive vision discovers a vivid and complex natural system that resists allegorical Truth:

> Casting an eye
>
> down into the water, there, announced
> by the silence of a white
> bush in flower, close
> under the bridge, the shad ascend,
>
> midway between the surface and the mud,
> and you can see their bodies
> red-finned in the dark
> water headed, unrelenting, upstream.[12]

In "Williams and the Duende" Levertov cites the image of the shade ascending as illustration of Williams' "theme of defiance" (*PW* 260–62) of resistance to the sea's pull. Crucial to the poetry of Williams and Levertov is the fact that this resistance is expressed in form as well as theme. Williams' meticulously patterned stanzas, whose line divisions single out the particulate beauties of the water, call attention to the act of observation as distinct from the process observed. The aim, as Levertov says of organic form, is to combine the inwardness of the thing observed with the experience of observation. In contrast to this kind of interpenetration, which is not self-negation, Frost, and to some extent Dickinson, erect skillfully jagged walls of traditional poetic forms that reflect the self's dis-ease in the natural world.

This selective charting of literary wells suggested by Levertov's teaching syllabus comes at last to the dry wells and polluted rivers of T. S. Eliot. The dry hearts and rock wall of Levertov's "The Fountain" (*JL*) allude to Eliot's poems of the 1920s, while the poem's drought in spring images her early and continuing opposition to his parched landscape: "Don't say, don't say there is no water. / That fountain is there among its scalloped / green and gray stones, / / it is still there and always there / with its quiet song and strange power / to spring in and / up and out through the rock." However, Levertov's poetic autobiography records that after nearly two decades of public and private challenge to her ancestral faith, she is brought near to Eliot's sense that the values of the past serve only to mark present degradation. Her despair results from the exceptional, and unexceptional, social evil of our historical moment—racial injustice, the war in Vietnam, irreversible environmental destruction, nuclear energy and the threat of nuclear war, U.S. involvement in Latin America. The old certainties have also been blurred by personal crises and the mirror's testament to her own mortality. As a result of such challenges, the ancestral well of the fairly recent "Desolate Light," in *Candles in Babylon*, becomes a pit of past struggle whose wisdom does not supply the present. The poet gazes "Into the open / well of centuries," and fears that the "chains of hope by which our forebears / hoisted themselves / hand over hand toward the light" do not address her needs. Levertov will carry the struggle against this despair into *Oblique Prayers*, although she is able to conclude *Candles in Babylon* with the affirmation of "The Many Mansions," a poem reaching back to the Thoreau-like waters of "The Lagoon" and to parental Christianity. She chides herself for forgetting the world of the white herons whose particulate beauties now emanate a single radiance: "the vision / was given me: to know and share, / / passing from hand to hand, although / its clarity dwindles in our confusion, / / the amulet of mercy."

IV

The sum of the many well-like bodies in Denise Levertov's poetry has been the birthright knowledge that *origins* and *originality* share the Latin root *oriri*, "to rise." Connection to the past has sustained poetic innovation.

Oblique Prayers (1984), however, presents two challenges to this fruitful continuity. The first, evident in all volumes since *The Sorrow Dance* (1967), is the difficulty her poetics has in reconciling public evil with nature's beauty and the human impulse to affirmation. She has worked distinguished lyric transformations on personal sorrow, but with the exception of the Olga poems (*SD*) and the journal sequence *To Stay Alive* she has not often written political poetry that meets the high standards she sets for it in her essay "On the Edge of Darkness: What Is Political Poetry?" (*LC*, 115–129). Unable to assimilate the fragmentations of civic disharmony into her poetics of immanence, of connection, she turns for wholeness to parental Christianity, or at least an embryonic version of it.[13] Without relinquishing nature's gods, she addresses, as in the poem "Of Rivers," the "God of the gods, whom the gods / themselves have not imagined." Certainly her major literary ancestors have faced in their later lives a similar need to find a larger context for their love of the earth's crust. One thinks of Williams' and Stevens' late celebrations of the poetic imagination, and of H. D.'s mystic and mythic explanations of her life's quest. But in *Oblique Prayers*, admittedly an early stage of her religious awakening, Levertov has yet to secure her rediscovered faith against generalized despair and affirmation. In this volume, her political and religious poems are usually her weakest; they are often didactic and cliched, lacking the imaginative illumination, the verbal precision and freshness of image characteristic of her best poetry. This is not to say, however, that there are not some fine poems in the volume.

Within the religious context, "oblique" of the title has multiple implications. In one sense, the poems are unconventional prayers addressed to the reader's social conscience and to God's mercy. "Oblique" may refer to the poet's uncertainty as to the possibility of prayer. It also images her misalignment with the plumb line of her existence; and it hints at her skewed relation to the direct line of descent of her family tree. She has lacked her parents' faith as well as her literary ancestors' artistic alternatives to despair. Finally, like the word *decipherings*, title of the first section and its opening poem, "oblique" points to a mystery.

In a prefatory note Levertov calls attention to the thematic division of the volume into four sections and to the thematic arrangement of poems within each section. This concern for structural coherence is related to the thematic search for wholeness. The volume opens with the mystery suggested by "Decipherings" and progresses to the religious vision of the final section, "Of God and of the Gods." The first section prepares for the religious turning of the last by working complete elaborations of the opening poem's cryptic images, and the third section's fourteen translations from the French poet Jean Jourbet shares Levertov's thematic and formal concerns. However, the political poems of the second section, "Prisoners," appropriately resist assimilation into the volume's larger pattern except as instance of intractable political evil.

The poem "Decipherings" gives essential direction to the rest of the

volume, taking up such familiar Levertov subjects as personal metamorphosis, artistic transformation (of which the Jourbet translations are an example),
and nature's repetitious, and thereby ultimately unsatisfying, metamorphoses. In it the poet asserts her need for a stable moral center. The well
which has often imaged this center is now renamed, as in several earlier
poems, a "center / of gravity." The poem's short lines and clipped, almost
elliptical syntax reflect the fragmentation and dispersal that prompts the
search for wholeness. The abbreviated images are cyphers, tesserae to be
brought together in a loose design. The opening segment reaffirms the ancient wisdom that the self's flight is possible only through attachment to the
earth.

> When I lose my center
> of gravity
> I can't fly:
>
> levitation's
> a stone
> cast straight as a lark
>
> to fall plumb
> and rebound.

The obstacle to flight is fractured experience that requires imaginative
transformation. Thus, "half a wheel," "half a loaf," and a baby severed from
its mother's body become the rising sun, "leavened / transubstantiation," and
a floating "thistledown engine." The "felt life" of each of these transubstantia-
tions "forms and / reforms cloudy / links with / the next / / and the next" much
like a sequence of chimes and gongs that "resound" to rhyme with and restate
the earlier "rebound." The poem concludes in a synesthesia of sound into
color and back to sound of "blue or / perhaps vermilion" tesserae: "what one
aches for / is the mosaic music / makes in one's ears / / transformed."

"Man Wearing Bird" elaborates what is probably the key cypher of
"Decipherings," the lark or bird. The poem extrapolates upon a newspaper
account of a mental patient who stopped traffic along a roadway by standing
with two large wings flapping above his head. In a surrealistic re-vision of
this account the poet imagines herself as the patient. The bird, representative of the abused natural world of "Prisoners" and ancient symbol of the
Holy Spirit, is dead and awaits resurrection through the poet's prophecy: "It
died / for me to find, / to lift like the Host / / and place aloft. . . ." Long a
baker of bread, the poet will find her mission in transubstantiation of the
abandoned divinity. She will imbue the unvarying repetitions of Stevens'
redwings in "Sundown Sentences" with religious significance.

The section's final poem, "Another Revenant," offers a "long-dead"
ghostly ancestor as guide on the spiritual journey. The visitor may be a
specific ancestor, or possibly the embodiment of collective ancestral wisdom.

Significantly for this journey beyond the maternal natural world into the father's paternalistic Hebraism and Anglicanism the visitor is given the masculine pronoun. Through his memories the poet and two friends account for the "gray unresonant / gaps and rifts" in their lives. His memories are "visible threads / woven amongst us, gleaming / a fabric / one with our listening."

Weaving becomes the volume's primary image of transformation. It is introduced in the first section's "Grey Sweaters" as "an oriole's nest, / woven of silvery milkweed silk" and her publisher James Laughlin's "old grey sweater," "the knit and purl of the poem's row / re-raveled." The image is completed in the final section's "The Task" where God weaves the "great garment." If God hears the beseechings of humanity, he "imagines it sifting through, at last, to music / in the astounded quietness, the loom idle, / the weaver at rest." God's imagining of lamentation into music of course recalls the synesthesia of "Decipherings" and resolves the mystery of worldly fragmentation. But Levertov achieves a unity of vision beyond this particular volume in the final poem, "Passage," whose long lines are redolent with the rhythm of benediction. The weaving of the artist/God is modified in the sewing of her tailor ancestor Angel Jones of Mold, one of the "Illustrious Ancestors" from the early volume *Overland to the Islands* (1958). His meditations "were sewn into coats and britches"; and now the poet feels the assurance that the spirit who walked the waters and grasses of the past, "moves burnishing / / over and again upon mountain pastures / a day of spring, a needle's eye / space and time are passing through like a swathe of silk." The challenge in future poems will be to connect the rediscovery of this familial religious legacy to realism of the late twentieth century. To accomplish this should assure Denise Levertov a place in the canon of contemporary American poetry.

Notes

1. Unless the title or date of one of Levertov's volumes is relevant to the discussion, volume titles will be abbreviated and placed in parentheses in the text. Titles and page numbers will be given for references to her prose writing. With the exception of Levertov's first three volumes, New Directions in New York has published all of her work, including *Collected Earlier Poems 1940–1960*: copyright © 1979 by Denise Levertov; and *Poems 1960–1974*: copyright © 1976 by Denise Levertov. The following chronological list of individual volumes includes abbreviations for works cited in the text: *The Double Image* (London: Cresset Press, 1946); *Here and Now* (San Francisco: City Lights Books, 1957)—*HN*; *Overland to the Islands* (Highlands, N.C.: Jargon Society, 1958)—*OI*; *With Eyes at the Back of Our Heads* (1960); *The Jacob's Ladder* (1961)—*JL*; *O Taste and See* (1964)—*OTS*; *The Sorrow Dance* (1967)—*SD*; *Relearning the Alphabet* (1970)—*RA*; *To Stay Alive* (1971)—*TSA*; *Footprints* (1972)—*FP*; *The Poet in the World* (prose)—*PW*: copyright © 1973 by Denise Levertov Goodman; *The Freeing of the Dust*—*FD*: copyright © 1975 by Denise Levertov; *Life in the Forest*—*LF*: copyright © 1978 by Denise Levertov; *Light Up the Cave* (prose)—*LC*: copyright © 1981 by Denise Levertov; *Candles in Babylon*—*CB*: copyright © 1982 by Denise Levertov; *Oblique Prayers*—*OP*: copyright © 1984 by Denise Levertov. All quotes used by permission of New Directions Publishing Corp.

2. Quoted in excerpts from Sutton's "Conversation with Denise Levertov" from the *Minnesota Review*, in *Denise Levertov: In Her Own Province*, ed. Linda W. Wagner (New York: New Directions, 1979), 37.

3. *From Modern to Contemporary: American Poetry, 1945–1965* (Chicago: University of Chicago Press, 1984), 143–75. Breslin's chapter on Levertov's poetry through *O Taste and See* (1964) is probably the best recent overview of her early poetry, and it is useful in situating her within the reaction to New Critical formalism.

4. Most notable of the advocates of the Stevens paternity is Helen Vendler, who omits Levertov from her anthology *The Harvard Book of Contemporary American Poetry* (Cambridge: The Belknap Press of Harvard University Press, 1985).

5. Charles Altieri, *Enlarging the Temple: New Directions in American Poetry during the 1960s* (Lewisburg, Penn.: Bucknell University Press, 1979) 225–44, challenges the adequacy of Levertov's "aesthetics of presence" for the political critique she has undertaken; Bonnie Costello, " 'Flooded with Otherness,' " *Parnassus* 8, no. 1 (1979–1980), 198–212, discusses the romantic symmetries that make Levertov's poems seem "posed and inauthentic."

6. "Feminist Criticism in the Wilderness," in *The New Feminist Criticism: Essays on Women, Literature, and Theory*, ed. Elaine Showalter (New York: Pantheon, 1985), 243–70.

7. *Naked and Fiery Forms: Modern American Poetry by Women, A New Tradition* (New York: Harper & Row, 1976), 57–84. Tess Gallagher offers an on-the-mark rebuttal to Juhasz's similar condescension to Marianne Moore, in "Throwing the Scarecrows from the Garden," *Parnassus* 12, no. 2; 13, no. 1 (1985), 45–60.

8. Rich, "Poetry and Experience" in *Adrienne Rich's Poetry*, ed. Barbara Charlesworth Gelpi and Albert Gelpi (New York: Norton, 1975), 89.

9. *In Search of Our Mothers' Gardens* (New York: Harcourt Brace Jovanovich, 1983), 5.

10. Levertov's connection to Thoreau via the well image has also been noted by Rudolph L. Nelson, "Edge of the Transcendent: The Poetry of Levertov and Duncan," *Southwest Review* 54, no. 2 (1969), 201.

11. *The Collected Poems of George Oppen* (New York: New Directions, 1957), 205. Copyright © 1975 by George Oppen. Quoted by permission of New Directions Publishing Corp.

12. *The Collected Later Poems of William Carlos Williams* (New York: New Directions, 1963), 75. Copyright © 1948 by William Carlos Williams. Quoted by permission of New Directions Publishing Corp.

13. Levertov's political poetry has provoked the most interesting recent criticism of her work. In addition to Altieri's chapter on Levertov in *Enlarging the Temple*, the best of this criticism includes: Sandra Gilbert, "Revolutionary Love: Denise Levertov and the Poetics of Politics," *Parnassus* 12, no. 2; 13, no. 1 (1985), 335–51; Paul A. Lacey, "The Poetry of Political Anguish," *Sagetreib* 4; no. 1 (1985), 61–71; and especially Lorrie Smith, "Songs of Experience: Denise Levertov's Political Poetry," *Contemporary Literature* 27, no. 2 (1986), 213–32.

INDEX